Will Baker

Culture and Identity through English as a Lin

Developments in English as a Lingua Franca

Editors
Jennifer Jenkins
Will Baker

Volume 8

Will Baker

Culture and Identity through English as a Lingua Franca

Rethinking Concepts and Goals
in Intercultural Communication

DE GRUYTER
MOUTON

ISBN 978-1-5015-1588-0
e-ISBN (PDF) 978-1-5015-0214-9
e-ISBN (EPUB) 978-1-5015-0216-3
ISSN 2192-8177

LLibrary of Congress Cataloging-in-Publication Data
A CIP catalog record for this book has been applied for at the Library of Congress.

Bibliographic information published by the Deutsche Nationalbibliothek
The Deutsche Nationalbibliothek lists this publication in the Deutsche Nationalbibliografie;
detailed bibliographic data are available on the Internet at http://dnb.dnb.de.

© 2015 Walter de Gruyter, Inc., Berlin/Boston
This volume is text- and page-identical with the hardback published in 2015.
Typesetting: Asco Typesetters, Hong Kong
Printing and binding: CPI books GmbH, Leck

♾ Printed on acid-free paper
Printed in Germany

www.degruyter.com

To Jeed, Ben and Katy

Acknowledgements

Firstly, I would like to thank all at DeGruyter Mouton for their support with publishing this book especially Lara Wysong, Emily Farrell and for encouragement in the early stages Birgit Sievert.

I owe a particular debt of gratitude to the series editor Jennifer Jenkins whose guidance from proposal to final manuscript has been invaluable. Furthermore, in her role as Director of the Centre for Global Englishes at the University of Southampton, and as an advisor and colleague throughout my time at the Centre, she has been very influential in the thinking and evolution of my ideas.

Indeed, the members of the Centre for Global Englishes have been crucial in shaping the ideas presented in this book, especially through the lively and entertaining seminar series at lunchtimes and afternoons (and often into the pub afterwards). In particular, I would like to thank Robert Baird and Mariko Kitazawa whose shared interest in complexity and English as a lingua franca (ELF) resulted in a joint publication on the subject (Baird, Baker and Kitazawa 2014) which has been drawn on liberally, with kind permission, in this book. I also need to thank Haibo Liu for her data on the National English Curriculum in China and Chittima Sangiamchit and Yusop Boonsuk for their additional data on English use and policy in Thailand. Furthermore, I am indebted to other colleagues at the University of Southampton for their help and support, especially Julia Hüttner for listening to my half-formed (possibly half-baked) ideas and offering sound advice and Rosamond Mitchell who as my PhD supervisor and first head of department encouraged and supported my interest in the subjects presented here.

I am indebted to the British Council whose ELT Research Award scheme (2010–2011) funded and made possible the research reported in chapter seven. I would also like to thank the anonymous reviewer of the manuscript for such encouraging and constructive feedback. I am also very grateful to Zhu Hua for permission to reproduce:

> Figure 4.1 Alignment and misalignment between self-orientated and ascribed identities (Zhu 2014: 217).

And also for kindly sharing an early draft of an article on ELF and intercultural communication (Zhu Hua 2015) which has been very useful in writing this book.

I am very grateful to Michael Byram for permission to reproduce:

> Figure 5.1 Byram's (1997: 73) model of intercultural communicative competence.

Finally, I would like to thank the many researchers, too numerous to mention, at the annual International ELF conferences who have helped form the thinking in this book and also to the research participants who gave up their time and constitute so much of the content of this book.

Table of contents

Chapter 1
Introduction

"Did the mind discover likeness in the unlike in order to clarify
the world, or to obscure the impossibility of such clarification?
He didn't know the answer. But it was one hell of a question."
– Salman Rushdie, Shalimar the Clown (2006: 180)

There is currently no shortage of books addressing intercultural communication, culture and identity. This should not be a surprise, as the quotation from Salman Rushdie's character Max Ophuls underscores, questions about 'likeness', 'the unlike', or 'the other' to use a term from sociology and sociolinguistics, provide seemingly endless scope for discussion. These are certainly not new questions but the increasing contact with difference, the unlike and the other brought about through the acceleration of globalisation and associated communicative technologies in recent decades have raised awareness of these issues. Questions concerning our understanding of others and the cultures they are part of have been of interest to anthropologists, ethnographers, linguists and intercultural communication scholars, to name a few, for centuries. More recently, our ideas and construction of difference and the other have come under increasing scrutiny. Through investigating these topics are we trying to "clarify the world, or to obscure the impossibility of such clarification"? Is the other really as different or as similar as we think or are our comparisons simply an artefact of our preconceptions? Should we even be investigating the other, by undertaking such investigation are we not constructing and reifying the distinctions and differences we are trying to overcome? Should we be trying to 'overcome' the differences, is there a danger that in doing so we homogenise and restrict diversity?

Given the already extensive literature on these issues why add further to it? Firstly, as Rushdie's Max Ophuls notes, it is "one hell of a question" and worthy of continued investigation. As societies and cultures change and develop so the answer, or rather answers, to questions of difference, likeness and the other are likely to change too. Secondly, and of central relevance to this monograph, issues of language are often marginalised and simplified in such discussions. While applied linguists are becoming increasingly interested in matters concerning intercultural communication, culture and identity, this is a relatively new development. Of course questions about the relationship between language and culture are not new. Indeed writings by Humboldt, Boas, Sapir and Whorf on this subject have been foundational for many branches of linguistics. However, these writings were typically concerned with intracultural communication, in other words communication within social or cultural groups.

Much less attention has been given to communication across or between cultural groupings. Since World War Two research into intercultural communication, or cross-cultural communication as it was typically termed, has grown considerably particularly through the influential work of Edward T Hall and Geert Hofstede. However, language does not form a central part of this research and when it is investigated it is often approached unproblematically with simplistic language, nation and culture correlations assumed. With the interest in intercultural communication in applied linguistics this is changing and the linguistic aspects of intercultural communication are now receiving considerably more attention. Yet, here too there are still major shortcomings in many of the approaches taken. In particular, there seems to be little awareness of, or interest in, the actual language through which much of this intercultural communication takes place, namely English. English is frequently approached as if it were a neutral choice as the medium of intercultural communication or in a reified and simplistic manner. Where the role of English is investigated, there is still little awareness of how it functions as a lingua franca in the majority of interactions and the implications this has for understanding intercultural communication.

It is these shortcomings or areas of neglect that form the rationale for this book. I will investigate these issues though a consideration of points of convergence and divergence between intercultural communication research and English as a lingua franca (ELF) research. In particular I will argue that ELF research has some major implications for our conception of the relationships between communication, language, identity and culture. This is not because there is something unique about communication through ELF, although the scale of ELF use is unprecedented in the history of lingua francas, but rather because the growing field of ELF research provides a substantial body of knowledge documenting how cultures and identities are constructed and enacted in intercultural communication. Thus, while intercultural communication is now a well-established field, although relatively new compared to many, and ELF a newly emerged but already substantial research domain (there is an annual conference, journal and book series devoted to the subject alongside numerous articles and monographs), there has been little attempt to synergise findings from the two fields. This has very recently begun to change. The first AILA Research Network on ELF in 2012 addressed this theme in part, the sixth annual international ELF conference in 2013 was entitled 'Intercultural Communication: New perspectives from ELF', an edited volume on this subject is in production (Dervin and Holmes, forthcoming) and a special edition of the Journal of English as a Lingua franca also addresses this subject (2015, 4/1). This monograph, thus, aims to join this newly emerging area of interest in exploring how ELF and intercultural communication research can inform each other and further add to our understanding of culture and identity in intercultural communication through ELF.

In this book I will argue that one of the main challenges that ELF gives rise to in our understanding of language, communication, culture and identity is to test the traditional assumptions concerning the purposed 'inexorable' link between a language and a culture and in turn identity. Due to the multitude of users and contexts of ELF communication the supposed language, culture and identity correlation, often conceived at the national level, appears simplistic and naïve. However, it is equally naïve to assume that ELF is a culturally and identity neutral form of communication. All communication involves participants, purposes, contexts and histories, none of which are 'neutral'. Thus, we need new approaches to understanding the relationship between language, culture and identity which are able to account for the multifarious and dynamic nature of ELF communication. Such alternative approaches will have important consequences not only for ELF research but for how we characterise intercultural communication in general. Alongside this reconsideration of the links between languages, cultures and identities in intercultural communication there needs to be a proper exploration of the implications for practice, especially for teaching and learning.

Connected to teaching and learning, a central concern within both intercultural communication research and applied linguistics has been how we characterise the competences needed for successful intercultural communication. In particular new ways of looking at intercultural communicative competence are necessary that go beyond an understanding of 'a language' and its links to 'a specific culture'. To understand how users of ELF communicate successfully we need a framework for conceptualising the knowledge, attitudes and skills they employ in relation to the diverse contexts of intercultural communication. This reconceptualization of culture in intercultural communication will in turn have wide-ranging ramifications for how we approach English language teaching (ELT) and teaching intercultural communication. The role of culture and intercultural communication in language teaching has gained in prominence, in theory at least, over previous decades. However, ELF studies suggest on the one hand that knowledge, skills and attitudes related to intercultural communication should be a more prominent part of ELT, while on the other, that the often simplistic notions of other cultures and languages envisaged in ELT materials should be questioned. An alternative, less essentialist, approach to ELT and intercultural communication pedagogy is needed. These concerns can be summarised in four questions presented below.

1. What are points of convergence and divergence between ELF and intercultural communication research?

2. What influence (if anything) do studies of intercultural communication through ELF have on our understanding of the relationship between culture, identity and language?
3. What are the implications of ELF research for conceptualising intercultural communicative competence?
4. What are the consequences (if any) of ELF and intercultural awareness (ICA) research for teaching English (ELT)?

These questions are used to guide and focus the discussion in this book and are explicitly addressed as the arguments develop. To accomplish this the book is roughly divided into two sections. In the first section theories and research related to intercultural communication, culture, identity and ELF are explored. In the second section implications for practice and particularly notions of intercultural communicative competence, intercultural awareness and English language teaching are considered. In writing this book I have been equally interested in both theory and practice and felt that it was important to include a proper in-depth exploration of the implications of current research and theory on intercultural communication and ELF for pedagogy. Too often research based monographs leave discussions of implications (which in applied linguistics are typically related to pedagogy) to the final chapter or a short section in the conclusion. While this may be perfectly justifiable given the research led aims of many texts, this relegation of pedagogy to a final afterthought often fails to adequately address the complexity of different pedagogic approaches, classrooms, learners, and teachers. Brief attempts to discuss pedagogy also frequently fail to offer enough detail in their pedagogic recommendations to be meaningful to those involved in teaching or teacher training and education. This book of course makes no claims to be relevant to all teachers or teaching settings but pedagogic concerns are given equal weighting to theoretical concerns. In dividing the book in this way the first section addresses the initial two questions outlined above, related to key theoretical concepts in intercultural communication, and the second section addresses the final two questions, related to more practical issues in intercultural education and ELT.

However, it is important that this is not interpreted as reifying distinctions between theory, research and practice. Indeed, constructing theory and conducting research are clearly forms of practice just as teaching is (Kramsch 2009). Likewise, in answering questions about intercultural communicative competence and awareness and related teaching approaches, research and theory will be drawn on. Furthermore, as the term 'applied' indicates in applied linguistics the relationship between theory and practice is closely interconnected. Widdowson (1980) in the first issue of the journal 'Applied Linguistics' makes a distinction between linguistics applied i.e. the application of linguistic theory to language issues or problems and applied linguistics which involves mediation between theory and practice with practice driving theory as much as vice-versa (see also Widdowson 2000). This point is reinforced by the most commonly cited definition of applied linguistics as "the theoretical and empirical investigation of real world problems in which language is a central issue" (Brumfit 1995: 27). Brumfit's definition takes a similar perspective to Widdowson in positioning 'real world problems' related to language as central and *then* investigating how theory and empirical investigation can inform or be informed by these problems. Hence this monograph can be viewed as very much in the tradition of applied linguistics in investigating real world problems; how we understand culture and identity in complex and diverse intercultural communication scenarios through ELF and how we teach to prepare learners to use English as a lingua franca for intercultural communication. In attempting to address these problems the relationships between current theory and practice are explored in a holistic manner that eschews proposing or reinforcing distinctions between them.

1.1 English as a lingua franca (ELF)

Before proceeding further it is important to briefly outline what is meant by the term ELF in research. Other key terms in the title and questions above, 'intercultural communication', 'culture' and 'identity', are all dealt with in separate chapters, and discussions of the nature of ELF communication and research in relation to each of these are provided there. Thus, given the likely audience for this book and the already extensive recent writing on the nature of ELF (e.g. Jenkins, Cogo and Dewey 2011; Seidlhofer 2011; Mauranen 2012), an entire chapter devoted to a general discussion of ELF as a phenomenon and field of research did not seem necessary. Nonetheless, for those who are less familiar with ELF research a short overview of ELF and related terminology, as it is understood in this monograph, is given. Furthermore, this should also help to clarify the later discussions and avoid misinterpretation in understanding what is referred to when considering ELF studies and communication.

   Firstly, one of the major factors for the increasing interest in ELF is the now well-documented growth in English language use in recent decades. The number of native speakers of English is estimated to be around 328 million, making it the third largest language in terms of L1 speakers, slightly behind Spanish (329 million), but a long way behind Chinese (over 1 billion) (www.ethnologue.com). However, where English becomes different to other languages is in terms of L2 or non-native users[1]. Although exact figures are difficult to produce, Crystal's (2008) estimate of 2 billion is widely cited as a reliable 'conservative' estimate. The fact that L2 users of English now greatly outnumber L1 users of English has major implications for the way we view English as a language and as a medium for intercultural communication. In particular, scholars have been suggesting for several decades now that given the extensive use by L2 users, 'ownership' of English and the 'norms' of communication through English will no longer be the solely under the authority or influence of those users from its Anglophone origins (Widdowson 1994; Brumfit 2001). The use of English as an official L2, particularly in post-colonial settings, has been studied and documented extensively in World Englishes (WE) research, leading to the establishment and general acceptance of many 'new' varieties of English such as Indian, Singaporean and Nigerian English (e.g. Kachru 1990; 2005; Schneider 2007; Kirkpatrick 2012). However, the most extensive use of English as an L2 (or rather as an additional language since it may be an L3, L4 etc ...) is not as an officially recognised and codified variety, but rather as a lingua franca by the majority of users who do not speak any established 'variety' of the language. ELF research is thus very different from the varieties approach taken in World Englishes, a point returned to later.

ELF has been defined by Seidlhofer as "*any use of English among speakers of different first languages for whom English is the communicative medium of choice, and often only option*" (2011: 7, italics in original). This is a commonly cited definition that clearly captures the function that English performs as lingua franca for intercultural communication. It is functional in the sense that the focus is on the *use* or *function* of *English* as a lingua franca. Importantly, it includes native speakers of English (NES), unlike some earlier definitions (e.g. Firth 1996; House 1999), since NES also engage in intercultural communication through English and it is important that we do not exclude a potentially interesting area of intercultural communication from research. Furthermore, to exclude NES from our definition of ELF would be to assume that intercultural communication involving NES is fundamentally different to that involving non-native speakers of English. This is problematic in that it makes assumptions about the communication before investigation and reifies the native/non-native distinction. A further functional definition of ELF which is of relevance to this book is provided by Jenkins who states that, "ELF refers to English when it is used as a contact language across linguacultures" (2006: 159). This definition explicitly recognises the intercultural

---

1 Of course English is not the only global language and Spanish, for example, has a large numbers of L2 speakers (Mar-Molinero 2004). Chinese is also increasing in use and is now only slightly behind English in terms of internet use (http://www.internetworldstats.com/stats7.htm).

aspects of ELF communication in referring to different linguacultures (a term that will be discussed in detail in chapter three). Lastly, from a research perspective Baird, Baker and Kitazawa define ELF "as a field that enquires into various aspects of the use of English among speakers who do not share a first language" (2014: 191). This definition draws on and shares much with the previous two definitions but shifts the focus from the functions of English to an open research agenda.

One of the most comprehensive characterisations of ELF as a field of research that adds detail to the short definitions above is provided by Mauranen (2012). To summarise and somewhat simplify Mauranen's argument, she distinguishes between three perspectives on ELF: the macrosocial, the cognitive and the microsocial, which provide a backdrop or framework for analysing ELF interactions (2012: 15). The macrosocial perspective is concerned with the wider speech community and language change. In relation to ELF this includes issues of globalisation, communities of ELF speakers, and how we might conceive of them, and the influences ELF may have on language changes in English. The cognitive perspective concerns the individual and in particular the relationship between language and the mind. Mauranen draws extensively on usage based theories of language (e.g. Tomasello 2003; Bybee 2006) and this will be explored in detail in chapter three where it is suggested that English used in ELF communication is best approached as a complex adaptive system (e.g. Larsen-Feeman 2011). The microsocial perspective is concerned with interaction and the speech event. It is at the microsocial level that all of the three perspectives come together. As Mauranen explain it "The different 'levels' at which language takes place, our different perspectives, are thus angles on one phenomenon, language in use" (2012: 55). This microsocial perspective is the level that research typically centres on since this is the only directly observable phenomena and the one from which the other perspectives can be indirectly accessed. ELF research has thus been mostly concentrated at the level of speech event. These distinctions between three different scales or levels of language are important in that they help to clarify what is being discussed or examined when conducting research. Following this, similar distinctions will be made use of later in chapter three when examining the relationships between language and culture and outlining how both concepts might be approached in ELF research.

A crucial feature that all these definitions and characterisations share is that ELF is not treated as a variety of English in investigations; rather ELF research is concerned with the variable use of English in intercultural communication. This is perhaps an obvious point to those familiar with ELF research but it is one of the most common misinterpretations of how ELF is conceptualised in research and one that continues to be repeated (e.g. Pennycook 2010: 49, see also the discussion in chapter two). This misinterpretation may in part be due to earlier research where it was suggested that there were 'core' features of ELF in terms of phonology, lexis and syntax (Jenkins 2000; Seidlhofer 2004). However, these were proposed tentatively and while subsequent research (e.g. Kirkpatrick 2010) has generally confirmed the frequency of earlier identified features, a great deal of variation has also been documented. Thus, while aspects of phonology, lexis and syntax are still of interest to ELF researchers, there is a consensus that there is too much variation in ELF communication for any variety to emerge (Baker and Jenkins 2015). Furthermore, ELF researchers have also increasingly questioned the notion of language variety itself (e.g. Seidlhofer 2011; Mortenson 2013; Baird, Baker and Kitazawa 2014), a theme returned to in chapter three.

It should also be acknowledged that there is a degree of fuzziness to the above definitions of ELF since it is important that enquiry into intercultural communication through ELF remains open to the diversity of participants and settings in which communication is likely to occur. Thus, for example, in later chapters instances of speakers of the same first language communicating in English as a second language (L2) will sometimes be investigated. This is justified as other speakers in the setting may not share a first language. In educational settings, for instance, the teacher may have a different L1 but the class students share an L1 or the purpose of the class may be to prepare learners for communication through ELF. Therefore, while it is important to define or characterise a field of study in order to provide a shared understanding of goals and knowledge, examples such as those given previously, underline the need to approach definitions with flexibility so as to not prematurely cut off potentially productive lines of research.

Closely connected to ELF not being a variety of English is the point that ELF researchers are not suggesting that ELF communication is unique compared to other kinds of intercultural communication. A number of scholars have recently made clear in their research that their findings, whether related to pragmatic and communication strategies, variability or conceptions of language, do not position ELF as *sui generis* (see Ehrenreich 2011; Björkman 2013; Mortenson 2013; Baird, Baker and Kitazawa 2014). Similar findings have been documented in intercultural communication research through languages other than English (Kramsch 2009). Moreover, in the multilingual scenarios in which English is used as a lingua franca other languages may be used in a similarly fluid manner. Nonetheless, ELF research is important due to the scale at which ELF use is occurring. Although there is nothing new about lingua francas, as outlined at the beginning of this section the extent of ELF use is unprecedented in the history of lingua francas. To emphasise the point again; this is not necessarily to suggest that English as a language is any different to other languages used for intercultural communication. It may be that any language used on such a large scale for intercultural communication would begin to display the characteristics we have seen of English used as a lingua franca. However, the scope of English use as a lingua franca is unique in the history of lingua francas. As such this makes it an important field of study and places ELF research in a position that is especially likely to produce new insights concerning the global uses of languages for intercultural communication.

Some of the subjects and domains that ELF researchers have been concerned with over the last few decades have included corpus studies, pragmatics, language attitudes and ideology, intercultural communication, identity and culture, English language policy and pedagogy, business English and academic English. Corpora related to ELF include: VOICE (Vienna Oxford International Corpus of English) consisting of 1 million word corpus of spoken ELF from European settings (http://www.univie.ac.at/voice/page/index.php); the ELFA (English as a lingua franca in academic setting) corpus which is a 1 million word corpus of spoken ELF in academic settings (http://www.helsinki.fi/englanti/elfa/elfacorpus); and the ACE (Asian Corpus of English) corpus which is also a 1 million corpus of spoken ELF interactions from Asia (http://corpus.ied.edu.hk/ace/). Issues explored within pragmatics have included accommodation, code-switching and other multilingual communication strategies and will be discuss in chapter two and chapter five. Attitudes and ideology have been an extensive part of ELF research since the beginning, particularly in relation to conceptions of 'standard' English and the prestige or otherwise of Anglophone Englishes, other varieties of English and ELF (e.g. Jenkins 2007; 2014). Intercultural communication research linked to ELF obviously has many overlaps with pragmatics but also involves issues of identity, community and culture, all of which have been concerns of ELF researchers, as will be documented in chapters two, three and four. While there have been discussions of English language policy and pedagogy for some time in ELF research (e.g. Jenkins 2000), this has become especially important as the implications of the extensive use of ELF for intercultural communication becomes more apparent within ELT. Overviews of research in these areas will be presented in chapters six and seven and involves issues such as teaching models and content choices. Finally, two domains that have received particular attention in research have been English as a lingua franca in business (BELF) (e.g. Ehrenreich 2009; Louhiala-Salminen and Kankaanranta 2011; Bjørge 2012) and English as a lingua franca in academia (ELFA) (e.g. Mauranen 2012; Björkman 2013; Jenkins 2014) due to the extensive use of ELF in these areas. Fuller overviews of all these research subjects and domains can be found in Jenkins, Cogo and Dewey (2011), Seidlhofer (2011), Mauranen (2012), Jenkins (2015) and Galloway and Rose (2015).

That ELF research is not about documenting and studying varieties of English makes it fundamentally different to World Englishes (WE) research. While

WE research is similarly concerned with diversity in uses of Englishes and securing linguistic rights and status for English speakers outside of Anglophone 'inner circle' settings (e.g. Kachru 2005), it still adopts an essentially modernist perspective on language in which discrete varieties of language, in this case Englishes, are associated with nations and geographically situated communities. Additionally WE research has focused on post-colonial or Kachru's outer circle contexts. ELF research, in contrast, is concerned with more fluid and dynamic uses of English in which there may be no fixed physical communities with which language can be associated. While this was previously typically connected with Kachru's expanding circle settings, more recently research has cut across the three circles and indeed questioned the relevance of the three circle model (e.g. Jenkins 2014; 2015). As such ELF research is more closely aligned with postmodernist perspectives on language in which language is viewed as a social practice rather than a definable discrete system with clear boundaries between languages and varieties of language. Furthermore, rather than use the term inner circle, with its connotations of superiority and centrality, the term Anglophone will be more often employed in this book. While it is roughly analogous to the inner circle, it does not carry the same baggage and is more focused on the ideological construct of the Anglophone English speaking countries in the discourses around English. However, it must of course be recognised that Anglophone settings are far from homogeneous and contain a great deal of diversity. Multilingualism is also a feature of many Anglophone countries as well, even if it is not recognised in much of the discourse on English, especially in ELT.

ELF research also needs to be distinguished from EIL (English as an international language) research. EIL has in the past been associated with claims that an international variety of English might emerge which is not based on any one national variety (see Jenkins 2007 and Seidlhofer 2011 for critiques of this). However, more recent writing on EIL has moved on from this, explicitly rejecting the possibility of such a supranational variety (Matsuda and Friedrich 2012: 19). Nonetheless, EIL scholars still approach English from a varieties perspective as the following quotation illustrates "once it is (tacitly) decided that English is used, more than one *variety* of English is often represented in such situations because *each speaker brings a variety* that he or she is most familiar with" (Matsuda and Friedrich 2012: 18, emphasis mine). This suggests a very different approach to English, and language in general, than that currently taken in ELF research. In its concern with varieties of language EIL can be viewed as more closely aligned with WE research than ELF (see also McKay and Bokhorst-Heng 2008; Sharifian 2009; Alsagoff et al. 2012; Matsuda 2012). However, it should be noted that some scholars use the term EIL in a similar way to the characterisations of ELF given here (e.g. Pahn 2009). Nonetheless, given that the majority of research into English used for intercultural communication drawn on in this book uses the term ELF, and the relevance of characterisations of ELF presented above, the term ELF will be used here.

Although there are clearly major differences in the focus of study in ELF, EIL and WE, as well as fundamental differences in the perspectives on language taken, all three fields share a desire to expand research and understanding of Englishes beyond the narrow confines of 'native speaker' Anglophone settings. As such, all three fields offer an alternative to the current orthodoxy in English language teaching (ELT) and Second Language Acquisition (SLA) research. Additionally, all three fields are often concerned with similar subject matters such as language attitudes and ideology, language policy and pedagogy, pragmatics, identity, culture and language. The term Global Englishes is made use of in this monograph to capture this shared set of interests. Global Englishes is defined as "the linguistic and sociocultural dimensions of global uses and users of English" (http://www.southampton.ac.uk/cge/about/). Thus, Global Englishes provides a useful general umbrella term that covers all three fields and their concerns with diverse characterisations of Englishes worldwide.

Many of these characterisations of English use and users contain references to native and non-native speakers. However, the concept of a native speakers and the distinction between native and non-native speakers has long been problematized in applied linguistics (e.g. Rampton 1990; Cook 1999; Davis 2003; Llurda 2006; Pennycook 2012) and ELF research has added to this critique. Of course L1 or mother tongue speakers of a language may self-identify or be identified as native speakers of that language and these are important ideological and social categories. However, linguistic or functional distinctions between native and non-native speakers are notoriously difficult to agree on and there is a growing consensus in applied linguistics, at least in more socially orientated research, that the distinction is unhelpful and more likely to obscure rather than aid enquiry. This is especially relevant to intercultural communication through ELF (or any kind of intercultural communication) where communication may proceed in a manner that is different to intracultural communication between speakers who share English as a first language (although it is important not to oversimplify L1 communication where speakers may not always share communicative expectations). In this sense it could be argued that English is no one's native language in ELF communication since all participants will need to adapt and adjust their language and other communicative practices to ensure successful communication. Nonetheless, given the prevalence of the terms native and non-native speaker in the literature it is impossible to avoid reference to them. Therefore, these terms are used with the caveats explained here and although for ease of reading 'scare quotes' have not been used, the terms should be read as if they are in scare quotes.

1.2 Overview of the book

Chapter two begins by outlining what is meant by intercultural communication in this monograph and how this influences the framing of the discussions of culture and identity. Due to the focus on intercultural communication through ELF, an examination of points of convergence and divergence between the two fields is offered. Communication through ELF is by its nature a process of intercultural communication and hence of great relevance to intercultural communication research and similarly intercultural communication studies deal with many issues of concern to ELF scholars. However, I will argue that ELF research has frequently been marginalised or misunderstood in intercultural communication literature to date. Nonetheless, there is the potential for much productive cross-over between the two fields, particularly given the growing empirical and theoretical base of ELF studies providing data and discussions on matters of direct relevance to intercultural communication including notions of culture, identity and successful communication. It is these issues which will then form the subjects of the following three chapters.

Chapter three forms one of the core theoretical discussions for this book. Here the relationships between language, communication and culture are explored in intercultural communication through ELF. Influential theories of culture will be presented including structuralist and post structuralist approaches with a particular focus on culture as discourse, practice and ideology. This will also include considerations of how culture is understood in contemporary societies and the effects globalisation has had on our understanding of this. I will suggest that due to the multiple scales at which culture can be characterised and its dynamic nature, complexity theory can be used as an effective metaphor or meta-theory for thinking about culture. To support this argument, key aspects of complexity theory and emergentism will be outlined. Following this complexity theory will be used as a lens through which to consider the relationships between languages and cultures combined with the concept of linguacultures. This theoretical discussion will be supported and illustrated through the use of data from ELF studies that have investigated the cultural dimension to communication. Finally, I will argue that such studies force us to reconsider how we conceptualise the categories of culture and language in intercultural communication and advocate the need for critical approaches to these categories.

Chapter four comprises the second core theoretical discussion for this book. In this chapter the relationships between culture, identity and intercultural communication through ELF are considered. As with chapter two critical approaches to these concepts will be adopted and the notions of complexity, fluidity and emergence in relation to cultural identities will be explored. Key theories of identity will be outlined with a characterisation of cultural identity given. The central role of language and discourse in the construction and negotiation of identities will be emphasised. Alongside this the role of difference and othering in identity construction and ascription in intercultural communication will be considered as well as tension between local, national, and global identifications. I will argue that the concept of interculturality provides a useful heuristic for interpreting the complexity of cultural identities in intercultural communication. Again, similarly to chapter two, the theoretical discussion will be supplemented with data from empirical ELF studies illustrating the relevance of cultural identity and interculturality to the analysis of intercultural communication through ELF.

Chapter five provides a transition between the more theoretical concerns of the first part of this monograph and the more practice orientated and pedagogic concerns of the second half. This chapter contains a critical review of previous concepts of communicative competence and intercultural communicative competence (ICC) and puts forward the notion of intercultural awareness. Communicative competence has been foundational in our understanding of the elements of successful communication in applied linguistics, intercultural communication and language teaching. However, it has come under increasing criticism for being too narrowly conceptualised for L2 use and intercultural communication, particularly in ELF research. Alternatives to communicative competence will be discussed with a focus on the notion of ICC and contemporary developments of it in relation to language pedagogy. However, I will argue that many of these approaches still retain at their core a concept of language and culture in which language is associated with a fixed geographically located cultural group, typically at the national level. Much thinking has still not adequately accounted for the complexity and fluidity of intercultural communication through ELF where no such stable relationships can be assumed. I will outline the concept of intercultural awareness (ICA) as an alternative or development of ICC that accounts for the knowledge, skills and attitudes needed to manage the diversity of cultural practices, references and identifications documented in intercultural communication and ELF research. Empirical data from my own research which demonstrates aspects of ICA in practice and in development will be presented.

Chapter six explores the implications of ELF research and ICA for language teaching and particularly for approaches to culture and the intercultural in ELT. This involves an examination and critique of current approaches in ELT which typically simplify and essentialise the intercultural and cultural dimensions to second language use as well as marginalising or ignoring ELF findings. Alternative approaches to ELT are considered including intercultural, Global Englishes and ELF perspectives. These alternatives underscore the importance of locally relevant and adaptable, post-methods approaches to teaching. In parallel a post-normative approach to language, communication and culture will also be explicated. I will then offer my own recommendations for integrating ICA into classroom practice which incorporates many of the insights from intercultural education and ELF research. These recommendations consist of five broad themes for developing ICA in the classroom. However, they are not offered as prescriptive principles which are applicable in all settings but rather as issues of concern for pedagogic practice and examples of attempts to address these concerns through principles which are broad enough to be adaptable to different settings and needs.

Chapter seven continues the exploration of implications for pedagogy this time through an empirical study. I present a case study of a course in intercultural communication, intercultural awareness and Global Englishes offered to English language learners at a Thai university. The aims of the study were:

- to explore the feasibility of developing ELT materials which took a Global Englishes perspective as their baseline and that incorporated aspects of ICA into the approach;
- to investigate how such a course could be delivered;
- to consider the types of learning that took place and to document teachers' and students' evaluations of such a course.

The main findings from this research showed the relevance of more globally and intercultural orientated ELT materials and the positive attitudes of both students and teachers towards them. Of course the approach presented here and the findings are not applicable to all settings but it does provide an example of how these apparently complex themes and ideas can be translated into meaningful and effective pedagogy. In so doing the hope is that there are elements that will resonate in other contexts and lead to reflection on alternative means of presenting the diversity of Englishes and the intercultural in ELT classrooms. This challenges the current orthodoxy in ELT in which Global Englishes and interculturality are given a minor place and suggests they should occupy a more central role.

Chapter eight is the final chapter and offers a summary and conclusion. This is done through providing an overview of the answers to the four questions posed above. It also presents a number of suggestions for future research in relation to culture, identity and ELF communication alongside recommendations for pedagogy. In particular, I argue that given the growing body of empirical data in ELF research more wide-ranging investigations are now possible. This will enable further studies which explore in-depth the implications for both theory and practice in a number of different fields, but especially in intercultural communication and ELT.

Chapter 2
Intercultural communication and ELF

"What are we to make of this orientation to the study of culture? How should we respond to it in research on cultural difference and language? Does it perhaps make the study of "intercultural" relations and communication impossible, even reprehensible, because it fixes the notion of "cultural group" prematurely and in ways that do not reflect how cultural identity is nowadays lived and experienced?"
– Ylanne-McEwen and Coupland (2000: 208–209)

A young British English teacher from the UK is in his first teaching job in a private language school in Thailand. He enters his classroom to find 25 students waiting for him. This, he thinks, is a problem. The maximum class size is supposed to be 15 students and the students have had to bring in chairs and tables from other classrooms. However, they do not really all fit in the room and it is very cramped making classroom activities difficult. He teaches the class, but as soon as it is finished goes to see the manager of the school who is Thai. He explains the situation to the manager pointing out the supposed maximum number of students and the problems extra students are causing. Throughout this the manager listens with a smile on his face saying nothing. At the end of the teacher's explanation the manager grins, but says nothing, and walks away. The young teacher is now rather confused and upset. The manager appears not to be taking his problem seriously. He did not acknowledge his problem or make any offer to remedy it. In fact, the teacher thinks, his response was quite dismissive and the grin and smile on the manager's face reinforced this impression for him.

The next day the teacher returns to the class with some reluctance. However, on entering the class he is surprised to find 15 students there and the correct furniture arrangements. A new class has been started in the next room with the other 10 students. All of the teacher's concerns from the previous day have been addressed, leaving him rather perplexed. Later in the day he talks to an older, more experienced colleague about this. The colleague explains that in his experience a smile and a grin is a very normal response to a problem for Thai people, not a sign of condescension or dismissiveness. Furthermore, listening in silence is also an appropriate communicative response when someone is complaining. The English teacher has just learnt an important lesson in intercultural communication. If he is going to get along as an English teacher in Thailand, he is going to have to adjust his expectations of how communication proceeds and not presume the sort of responses he is familiar with from the UK[2].

In one sense this is a very clear example of miscommunication in intercultural communication. The participants have different expectations about how a particular interaction should proceed which leads to misunderstanding on the part of the English teacher. We could explain this by examining the different expectations in the UK and Thailand for complaining and the role of smiles and silence in communication in each of these cultures. And in this example we could probably go quite a long way with this kind of analysis. However, we also need to be cautious here, as the quotation from Ylanne-McEwen and Coupland (2000) at the start of this chapter underlines. In following such an analysis we have already made a number of assumptions. Firstly, that there is a cultural difference that gives rise to a problem to be solved. While there is clearly a difference in communicative expectations or practices here, the 'problem' should not overshadow the fact that the communication was actually reasonably successful. The teacher's concerns were clearly understood and addressed by the manager. Secondly, we have equated cultural difference with nationality, a British teacher and a Thai manager. Individuals identify with many different cultural, or other, groupings, with nationality being just one of them. In this example the participants' identities as employee and manager are surely just as relevant as being British or Thai. Closely related to identity are power relationships and the influence this has on communication. As a manager and employee what are the expectations in this scenario, how much does the manager need to address the problems of his employee? There are also linguistic issues here. The manager's proficiency in English is not particularly high and this may have influenced his responses. The employee has almost no ability to communicate in Thai. Linguistic choices are significant and cannot be ignored. The use of English added another dimension to the power relationships. Had the conversation proceeded in Thai it might have been very different. Lastly, and perhaps most importantly, we need to recognise that this is an intercultural interaction and both participants were aware of this. Therefore, as will be explored throughout this book, we would expect a degree of flexibility, adaptation and negotiation in the participants' communicative practices. People do not have fixed communicative practices and this is even more so in intercultural communication where we typically anticipate difference and potential for misunderstanding but also new or alternative communicative practices and cultural references.

---

2 This example is based on a real event, not an invented example for the purposes of this book. However, it is a personal recollection of the event rather than data collected for research and so is not presented as anything other than a personal anecdote.

In the rest of this chapter conceptions of intercultural communication will be explored in more detail. This is necessary as before addressing the two central theoretical themes of this book, culture and identity, it is important to delineate the scope of the discussion. Given the wide range of thinking concerning culture and identity some contextualisation of the issues addressed in this book are needed. Culture and identity are explored here in the context of intercultural communication and more specifically intercultural communication through English as a lingua franca (ELF). In this chapter I will thus investigate the points of convergence and conflict between intercultural communication research and ELF research. In order to achieve this it will be necessary to first begin with a characterisation of intercultural communication that is best suited to the concerns of this book. I will then proceed to an examination of what is shared and not shared between the fields of intercultural communication and ELF. Finally, consideration will be given to how research in both these areas can inform each other. This discussion is also intended as an introduction and framing of key issues related to culture and identity which will be developed in more depth in subsequent chapters.

2.1 Characterising intercultural communication

The choice of the word 'characterising' rather than 'defining' in the title above is not accidental. It would not be possible or desirable to present a fixed definition of intercultural communication here. Give the wide range of academic and professional fields that make use of the term intercultural communication one definition agreed upon by all would seem unlikely. These fields include (in no particular order) applied linguistics, which of course is the focus of this book, sociology, psychology, anthropology, communication studies, education, management, health care, human resources and marketing among others. The term intercultural communication has thus been put to work for an array of theoretical, empirical and professional concerns. While this could be seen as a weakness in the field and evidence of a lack of conceptual cohesion, it may also represent evidence of overlapping, although not identical, concerns in various aspects of contemporary social life which for one reason or another researchers and professionals have chosen to explore through the lens of intercultural communication. It must also be stressed that the approach taken in this book emphasises the necessity of recognising dynamic, complex and contradictory positions to phenomena in which we accept the partial and temporal nature of knowledge and theory (a point elaborated in more detail in chapter three in relation to complexity). We should, therefore, not expect to find a singular definition of intercultural communication applicable in all contexts and for all purposes. However, this does not mean we should not try to identify salient features of what it is we are investigating or delineate the scope of our investigations. Researchers and practitioners need working and workable characterisation or 'definitions'; yet, it is also crucial that we remember our definitions are always temporary and open to critique.

As might be expected from such a diverse and widespread field one of the key features of intercultural communication studies is its interdisciplinary nature. Indeed this book is very much part of this interdisciplinary tradition in attempting to combine insights from intercultural communication studies generally, and more specifically intercultural communication studies within applied linguistics, and insights from ELF studies. Examples of the many fields interested in intercultural communication were given above and overviews of the field typically contain articles written by scholars in different disciplines, often in collaboration with each other (c.f. Jackson, 2012). This multidisciplinary nature, while a strength, is not without problems. There can be a tension between the theoretical and practical aims of the field. This point is explicitly addressed by Lavanchy, Gajardo and Dervin who conclude that given the different aims of those interested in intercultural communication and the need for 'neat' formulas and answers in many practical fields, "[c]onsiderations of the dynamic dimensions of identities, cultures and belonging struggle to find an audience as broad as that of other, more simplistic and reductive interpretations that give the illusion of providing an ad hoc user's guide to social problems." (2011: 12). Nonetheless, this does not mean that dialogue between different fields, both theoretical and practical, should not be pursued. Within applied linguistics, studies have typically drawn on sociolinguistics, pragmatics, discourse analysis, and language acquisition as well as from more general fields of anthropology, ethnography, education, sociology and philosophy.

One approach to characterising intercultural communication as a field of study is to trace its historical development. There are many good overviews of this (c.f. Risager 2006; 2007; Piller 2011; Martin, Nakayama and Carbaugh 2012) and they will not be repeated here but some historical contextualisation is needed to gain a richer understanding of the use of the term. Piller states that "the discourses of culture, cultural difference and intercultural communication arose in the historical context of the nineteenth and twentieth century as part of the processes of colonialism." (2011: 18). Such discourse emphasised difference, otherness and cultural superiority and these themes are still present in much intercultural communication discourse today. Language education has also been a major part of the field of intercultural communication. Risager (2007) traces the development of the intercultural in language pedagogy and highlights the rise in national conceptions of language and culture, which also took place in the nineteenth and twentieth century, but notes that prior to this the nation was not necessarily the main focus in language pedagogy (2007: 4). It would be difficult to provide a history of the field, however brief, without referring to the work of Edward T Hall (1959; 1966; 1976) who Lavanchy, Gajardo and Dervin describe as "the "father" of intercultural communication in the United States and elsewhere" (2011: 3). As with the discourses of colonialism Hall's approach emphasised the differences between national cultures and foreign 'others' but this time in the context of the Cold War often in relation to military training. This has been re-placed more recently, according to Piller, with concern for the 'War on Terror' and cultural 'clashes' between 'the West' and 'Islam' (2011: 32). In the field of business and management Hofstede influential research took a similar approach in com-paring cultural difference at national levels in relation to business organisations (e.g. Hofstede 1984). Within politics intercultural communication has often be concerned with issues of multiculturalism; particularly communication between different cultural groups within nations and the extent to which different cultural groups should assimilate or maintain differences (e.g. Kumar 2003; Roberts and Campbell 2006; Bauman 2011). Many of these themes: otherness, cultural differ-ence, cultural comparisons and the role of the nation, continue to form a major part of contemporary discourse in intercultural communication; however, all of these notions have also become increasingly critiqued and problematized in the last few decades.

Turning to applied linguistics in more detail, alongside language education mentioned above, two particularly influential perspectives in the development of understanding intercultural communication have been intercultural pragmatics and discourse analysis. Again a detailed and comprehensive review is not the focus of this book (see Spencer-Oatey and Franklin 2009; Zhu 2011 and Jackson 2012 for good overviews) but a brief outline on a selection of important themes will aid in contextualising later discussions. Research in intercultural pragmat-ics has examined differences in pragmatic strategies and the related field of speech acts between groups from different cultures and how these differences are negotiated in intercultural communication (e.g. Blum-Kulka and Olshtain 1984; Wierzbicka 1985; Spencer-Oatey 2008). Politeness has been an area of particular interest within intercultural pragmatics with Brown and Levinson's (1987) work on the notion of face as a universal concept underlying all concep-tions of politeness probably being the most influential. Directly linked to this are Leech's politeness principles (1983) and more recently Leech's slightly less prescriptive politeness constraints (2005). However, the supposed universality of these notions has been questioned by researchers in non-Western settings (e.g. Matsumoto 1988). In addition, in attempting to apply 'universal' principles researchers may be simplifying and essentializing highly complex, variable and situationally dependent phenomena. Another key area within pragmatics has been accommodation theory which has involved investigations of how participants in intercultural communication adjust their speech to their interlocutors. Glies's (2009) communicative accommodation theory (CAT) has been central to such research and directly applied to intercultural communication (e.g. Giles, Bonilla and Speer 2012).

Discourse studies have utilised a range of techniques and approaches in analysis of examples of intercultural interactions. Scollon and Scollon's propose an interdiscourse approach (2001; 2012) which examines communication between different discourse communities, cultural or otherwise, and their related discourse systems (see also Kramsch 1998). The Scollon's ideas have been significant in applied linguistics and a number of key issues they raise will be returned to throughout this chapter. Conversation analysis has been employed in detailed microanalysis of the features of intercultural communication such as topic development, turn taking and repair and how these relate, or not, to relevant contextual features (see Seedhouse 2004 for a review in relation to applied linguistics). Gumperz's (1982; 1992; 2001) interactional sociolinguistics, which makes use of the techniques of conversation analysis to examine contextualisation cues, is the most well-known in this area. His research demonstrates how diverse interpretations of the contextual factors referred to in interactions (the contextualisation cues) can result in misunderstanding between different cultural groups. Other discourse orientated approaches include the ethnography of communication (Gumperz and Hymes 1986; Duff 2002; Saville-Troike 2003), language socialisation (Ochs 1996) and critical discourse analysis (Kramsch 1993; Norton 2000; Pennycook 2007). There is much overlap between the different fields described here, with an interdisciplinary orientation frequently followed, and studies have utilized features from both pragmatics and discourse analysis in research that links micro features of discourse to macro features of context and cultures.

So far we have seen that the term intercultural communication can be used to characterise a wide range of fields of research and professional practice. We have also examined, briefly, the historical development of the field that has given rise to a variety of concerns from military, to political, to educational and to economic. It can thus be seen that intercultural communication is a field typically characterised by its interdisciplinary nature. Within applied linguistics there has been a focus on how both micro features of discourse are employed in intercultural communication and the relation of this to macro level features of communities and cultures. However, more recently there has been a move away from describing and comparing cultures as bounded entities towards a more critical and dynamic approach that is interested in communication between people from distinct cultural groups *in interaction* with each other. Such an approach has of course been part of intercultural pragmatics and discourse studies for some time but, crucially, this has now been combined with a more critical perspective as to how we characterise these 'distinct cultural groups' which entails questioning the relevance and consequences of such characterisations. It is necessary to explicate in more detail what such critical approaches to understanding intercultural communication involve in order to arrive at a richer characterisation of intercultural communication.

2.2 Critical approaches to intercultural communication

2.2.1 Cross-cultural versus intercultural communication

At this point it is helpful to make a distinction between two terms which are sometimes used synonymously but which, following Scollon and Scollon (2001), will be differentiated here. Many of the historical approaches described in the previous section might best be characterised as cross-cultural communication studies in which distinct cultures are compared with each other. These supposedly distinct cultures are often treated as synonymous with national groups and the behaviour of each group, for example the Chinese and Australians, compared and contrasted (e.g. Hofstede, Hofstede and Minkov 2010). In contrast the term intercultural communication is used "to signal the study of distinct cultural or other groups *in interaction with each other.*" (Scollon and Scollon 2001: 539). This perspective marks an important change in the field as it puts the idea of cultural differences and similarities as changeable and negotiable at the centre of intercultural communication. In other words it recognises that people often behave in different ways in *inter*cultural communication to *intra*cultural communication (communication between people from the same culture). Figure 2.1, based on Scollon and Scollon (2001), provides an overview of the differences between the two approaches. The distinctions given below are, of course, a simplification and many studies do not fall neatly into one or the other of these categories. It should also be added that this is not to suggest that all cross-cultural communication studies are without merit. There are times when it may be useful to compare national level characterisations of intracultural communication and identify differences (see for example Spencer-Oatey and Franklin 2009; Guillot 2012). However, the figure serves to illustrate a more critical approach to intercultural

Cross-cultural communication studies	Intercultural communication studies
The study of the communicative practices of distinct cultural groups independent from interaction (e.g. Chinese communicative practices)	The study of the communicative practices of distinct cultural or other groups in interaction with each other. (e.g. Italians communicating with English)
Cultures are seen as separable entities	Cultures are not bounded entities with national borders, but fluid and dynamic with blurred boundaries
Cultures are viewed as relatively homogeneous	Cultures are heterogeneous, containing a great deal of variety among its members
Cultures are viewed at a national level	National cultures are one of many discourse communities which can be drawn upon in communication, others include gender, generation, profession, ethnicity etc.
A priori assumption about cultural groupings	No a priori assumptions about the discourse communities, cultural or otherwise, that will be drawn on in conversation
Experimental and quantitative research	Qualitative research using naturalistic recordings of instances of intercultural communication

Fig. 2.1: Cross-cultural communication versus intercultural communication (based on Scollon and Scollon 2001)

communication that has become increasingly influential. This more critical approach questions many of the tenets of early research such as cultural boundaries and a priori categorisations. As Scollon and Scollon stress in such approaches to intercultural communication "the analysis would not presuppose cultural membership but rather ask how does the concept of culture arise in these social actions. Who has introduced culture as a relevant category, for what purposes, and with what consequences?" (2001: 545). Crucially the previous quotation questions not just the manner in which culture is used in intercultural communication studies but also the use of the term culture itself. It is also important not to oversimplify the distinctions between intracultural and intercultural communication here. Cultural differences are only one category of difference. People who speak the same L1 but have very different experiences and identifications such as class, profession, education, gender, or region, to give just a few examples, may be as likely to experience differences in communicative expectations and practices. Similarly, cultural differences and different L1s may not be particularly salient in communication where much else is shared between participants, particularly if all participants are multilingual and experienced intercultural communicators. This is a point empahsised by Scollon and Scollon (2001) through the concept of interdiscourse communication outlined later in the chapter.

Similar critical question have been used by a number of recent scholars of intercultural communication within applied linguistics, for example Piller (2011) who uses these same questions to guide her discussion of intercultural communication. Zhu (2014) also warns of the risk of circularity and reification in the field if we assume differences in relation to cultural groupings *before* we begin analysis of instances of intercultural communication. However, she also notes in regard to the relationship between culture and communication in intercultural communication studies that "we also need to take care not to confuse the need to problematize the notion of culture at the conceptual level with the need for a working definition of culture for those disciplines and studies which investigate group variation." (Zhu 2014: 199). Thus, through critiquing the notions we make use of we are able to build more complex, sophisticated and deeper understandings of what happens in intercultural communication. Zhu goes on to offer a definition of intercultural communication, which like Scollon and Scollon's (2001) definition takes interaction and negotiation as central, but also adds the element of subjectivity in relating cultural and linguistic differences to the participants' perceptions, "the field of intercultural communication is primarily concerned with how individuals, in order to achieve their communication goals, negotiate cultural or linguistic differences which may be perceived relevant by at least one party in the interaction." (2014: 200).

To this we should also add that cultural and linguistic differences may also be perceived as relevant to the researcher too; however, with the caveat that there must be empirical or theoretical justifications for making use of such categories. In other words they cannot be presupposed. This is an important addition since we must take care not to conflate participant categories and categories of analysis employed by researchers. The two may coincide but they do not have to. Likewise, the researcher may choose to use participant derived categories, but this must be done knowingly. Brubaker and Cooper (2000), in relation to identity, make a useful distinction between 'categories of practice', which are similar to lay or folk theory, and 'categories of analysis' which researchers make use of. They also caution that we should not allow lay theories to dominate or overwhelm analysis; although we need to acknowledge the power of such lay theories in social realities. A similar position will be adopted here with notions of culture, identity and the intercultural explored from both participant and researcher perspectives. Such critical perspectives on intercultural communication have raised a number of important issues in the field as well as suggesting alternative approaches and conceptualisations which need to be outlined in further detail.

2.2.2 Critiques of terminology in intercultural communication

Firstly, the term intercultural itself has come under scrutiny. This involves consideration of both the 'inter' and the 'cultural'. Concepts of culture will be dealt with in detail in the next chapter so the focus here will be on the 'inter' of intercultural communication but this will inevitably involve some discussion of culture too. Perhaps surprisingly, less attention has been given to the term communication, at least explicitly, although much work in intercultural communication has been interested in what constitutes 'successful' communication and this will be discussed in more detail in chapter five in the context of intercultural communicative competence. The use of 'inter' suggests that intercultural communication is between cultures. However, this is problematic for a number of reasons in that it proposes that cultures have fixed borders and that intercultural communication takes place between these borders or boundaries but with the cultures remaining separate. Holliday (2011; 2013) is critical of what he terms the 'intercultural line' that is often posited in intercultural communication research, dividing one culture from another. This has led to the adoption of the term transcultural by a number of scholars (Welsch 1999; Pennycook 2007; Risager 2007) as 'trans' implies a less static view of cultures with transcultural communication occurring 'through' and 'across' rather than 'between' cultures. Other scholars have been critical of the term culture, in particular Scollon and Scollon (2001) and Scollon, Scollon and Jones (2012) put forward the term 'interdiscourse communication' as they believe that culture is too broad a concept. Different discourse communities such as gender, generation or profession are, they claim, more likely to be influential. Another significant term in current use is 'interculturality' (Young and Sercombe 2010; Dervin, Gajardo and Lavanchy 2011; Zhu 2014) which emphasises the dynamic, emergent and negotiated nature of intercultural communication.

All of these critiques raise important issues with the term intercultural which need to recognised; however, as Lavanchy, Gajardo and Dervin note, the debates on terminology often obscure more important issues in relation to the notion of cultures which are assumed by these terms, "debates about the merits of one of these words to the detriment of the others tend to overshadow the fact that all of them invoke the same basic assumption, that is, that different cultures exist." (2011: 5). How we might characterise culture and the implications of those characterisations has thus formed a central issue in intercultural communication studies and will be the subject of the next chapter. At this stage it will suffice to acknowledge that culture is an issue that cannot be avoided as Scollon, Scollon and Jones (2012) attempt by replacing it with another term, in their case discourse, since it is frequently invoked as an explanatory category by both participants and researchers in intercultural communication (and indeed it is frequently used by Scollon, Scollon and Jones (2012), despite their own recommendations). The approach envisaged by the use of term interculturality which "emphasises the emergent, discursive and inter- nature of interaction" (Zhu 2014: 209) is closest to the perspective taken in this book. However, in the interest of continuity with previous research this book will retain the use of the term intercultural communication and use it synonymously with interculturality.

2.2.3 Critiques of approaches in intercultural communication

Scholars who have taken a more critical approach to intercultural communication (e.g. Kramsch 2009; Holliday 2011; 2013; Piller 2011; Scollon, Scollon and Jones 2012; Zhu 2014) have often questioned what they perceive as a simplistic view of intercultural communication that dominates the field. As Piller explains, "some of the research that has come to centrally define the field is certainly cringe inducing in the ways in which it reproduces essentialist discourses of culture rather than questions them. Similarly disconcerting is the frequent misrecognition of material and social inequality as cultural difference." (2011: 172). This concern may be a little exaggerated given that the majority of contemporary writings, in applied linguistics at least, eschew essentialist explanations that correlate nations, languages, cultures and individuals. Nonetheless, it is a valid critique in relation to the more traditional cross-cultural studies discussed previously and a number of contemporary texts, even within applied linguistics, still adopt these essentialist positions (e.g. Hurn and Tomalin 2013). While culture, nation and language are all still relevant and important within intercultural communication research, perspectives which challenge simplistic correlations and question the use of these categories are necessary. In particular it is crucial that the ideological dimension and power structures in intercultural encounters are recognised. As Kramsch and Uryu (2012) point out, in voluntary intercultural communication cultural, linguistic and national categories and identifications may be negotiated by participants but in involuntary intercultural communication, for example immigration interviews, the more powerful group may impose their interpretations of these categories on participants often with detrimental consequence for the less powerful participants (see Blommaert 2010; Guido 2012).

Kramsch and Uryu go on to highlight four issues with what they term the 'structuralist approach to intercultural communication' (2012: 217) in applied linguistic in which language, culture and nation are seen as parts of an integrated whole. Of particular importance is the failure to adequately address how language and other symbolic systems create the cultures which are studied as part of intercultural communication; the failure to recognise the symbolic dimensions of discourse; the failure to conceive of intercultural communication as not only social and cultural but also political and ideological practice; and the failure to adequately connect micro analysis with the macro level sociohistorical context which results in a linear and simplified account of the role of power in intercultural communication. Instead they advocate a poststructuralist approach to intercultural communication that emphasises hybridity, third space and ecological perspectives, stressing "the relationality and non-linearity of cross-cultural [sic] entaglments and their links to historicity and subjectivity" (2012: 219). The notion of third space brought up here has been especially influential and will be returned to. Additionally the notions of subjectivity and identity have, alongside culture, been of primary concern in intercultural communication studies and will be considered in detail in chapter four.

Similar themes are taken up by Piller who also emphasises the ideologically and politically naïve position of much intercultural communication research.

> in interactions there are often simply different interests at stake and interactants may not actually want to understand each other. Intercultural communication research often creates the impression that if we just knew how to overcome our linguistic and cultural differences, we would get on just fine with each other and the world would be transformed into a paradise on earth (2011: 155)

Piller (2011) recommends that intercultural communication researchers pay more attention to social inequality and injustice rather than immediately resorting to essentialist references to presupposed cultural differences in examining intercultural encounters and difficulties. She also critiques the simplistic view of language adopted in much intercultural communication research which views language as an unproblematic, static entity. She suggests that intercultural communication researchers need to make more use of insights from sociolinguistics and multilingualism research into the variable nature of language, issues of language choice, linguistic proficiency and the relationships between language, power and ideology. Variability in language use and language ideology is another central concern in the approach to intercultural communication taken here and will be explored in detail in relation to insights from ELF research.

Alongside this, Piller highlights another key theme for the perspective adopted in this discussion; the notion of intercultural communication as a social practice or, as she put it, "social practice in motion" (2011: 173). A number of consequences are entailed by this move to viewing intercultural communication as a dynamic social practice. It is no longer possible to approach intercultural communication as a 'thing' which can be examined in a decontextualized manner and then generalisations drawn which would be applicable to all instances of intercultural communication, as in traditional cross-cultural research. Rather a more ethnographic perspective is needed in which instances of intercultural communication must be richly contextualised to achieve an understanding of any aspect of them. At the same time though, the diachronic nature of intercultural communication (or any other kind of communication) must be acknowledged (Blommaert 2010; Pennycook 2010). This means recognition not just of immediate context but also of the sociohistorical context of each instance of intercultural communication studied. It also entails an acknowledgment of the temporary nature of any characterisation of specific instances of intercultural communication and awareness that change is inevitable. This results in an irreducible tension between the dynamism or fluidity of any identified practices and the need for a degree of shared norms or 'fixity' in intercultural communication (Pennycook 2007: 8) both from the perspective of participants and researchers. Such an approach to intercultural communication, as a social practice rather than an object and of fluidity and change, rather than generalised rules, will also underpin the characterisations of culture and identity in subsequent chapters and the epistemological orientations this entails will be explicated in more depth through the discussion of complexity theory in chapter three.

A final concern that needs to be raised is the relationships between ideology, essentialism, and othering. Holliday (2011; 2013) has been critical of what he terms the 'neo-essentialist' approach (2011: 6) which is, he suggests, dominant in much contemporary intercultural communication research. Like Kramsch and Uyu (2012) he views neo-essentialist intercultural communication research as undergirded by a structuralist philosophy. Although there is now recognition of cultures as being complex and involving many different groupings, these are still seen as being contained within the default national paradigm and with deviations from this paradigm viewed as exceptions rather than the norm. This leads to a perspective in intercultural communication which makes a clear distinction between one's own cultural grouping (typically at a national level) and the foreign 'others' cultural group (see also Baker 2011b). Holliday terms this the 'intercultural line' which is "an indelible line between Self and Other" (2011: 164). The existence of such a divide results in the process of othering in which the foreign other is always separate from us and hence different and unknowable. Holliday (2011; 2013) illustrates how this results in the dominant ideology and discourse of intercultural communication research characterising 'the West' as the central, norm providing group and 'the non-West' as peripheral, marginal, deviant and 'other'. Issues of self and others are clearly related to identity and subjectivity and will be further explored in chapter four. For the present though it is necessary to note the manner in which intercultural communication research has often, perhaps inadvertently, contributed to othering and strengthening perceived divides between cultures.

In the previous section I adopted a broad characterisation of intercultural communication which focused on communication between interlocutors in which cultural differences were perceived to be of relevance to one or more of the participants and/or to the researcher. This section explored these ideas further through a critique of the terminology. That is, what 'inter' entails, how we understand 'cultural' and how this relates to 'communication'. Structuralist approaches that correlate nation, cultures, languages and individuals and make clear divides between cultures have been critiqued as simplified and essentialist. I have suggested that intercultural communication is best viewed as a 'social practice in motion' (Piller 2011) rather than a 'thing' that can be isolated and examined. This emphasises the importance of the relationships between the different elements in intercultural communication and a contextualised ethnographically based perspective to research. It also highlights the diachronic nature of intercultural communication in which social practices are related to sociohistorical contexts but also constantly in change. Thus, we need a holistic approach to language, communication, culture and identity combined with a reflexive perspective on concepts used where power relationships and ideologies are considered.

2.2.4 Alternative approaches to intercultural communication

A number of alternative (in the sense of being distinct from neo-essentialist, structuralist approaches) perspectives and metaphors related to intercultural communication have been adopted in contemporary theorisation and research. Three that will be made use of in this book are *third places* and the related concepts of hybridity and liminality, *transcultural flows* linked to notions of local and global, and *interculturality*. There are of course other important terms that are made use of in contemporary intercultural communication studies in applied linguistics and beyond. In particular the notion of critical cosmopolitanism (Holliday 2011; 2013) encompasses much of what is discussed here. However, many of the same themes are addressed by the three terms outlined here. Furthermore, Kumaravadivelu's (2008) notion of cultural realism is also of much use, particularly in relation to identity and education, and it will thus be dealt with in chapter four and six respectively.

Third places or spaces is a concept that is most associated with post-colonial theory (Bhabha 1994) but has had a large impact in applied linguistics and intercultural communication through the work of Kramsch (1993). Kramsch's (1993) discussion deals with the intercultural experiences of 'foreign' language learning. She views intercultural communication in language learning as taking place on a 'cultural faultline' (1993: 205) in which linguistic and cultural practices and products occupy a 'third space' (1993: 233) that is neither part of the language users' first language and culture (L1/C1) or the target second language and culture (L2/C2). In using language in this way previously established practices are questioned and new practices created. Such notions link in with ideas of hybridity in post-colonial studies (Bhabha 1994) where supposedly distinct cultures are adapted and mixed giving rise to new multicultural third spaces. The concept of 'liminality' and 'crossings', as proposed by Rampton (1995), shares many features with third places. Rampton's study of intercultural communication between different ethnic groups within the United Kingdom identified liminal moments or crossings (1995: 167) when language users who were not part of a given language community adopted that language for their own purposes and needs. This led to changes in the use and meaning of the language, or a 'code-alteration' (1995: 280) by minority or outside users. Rampton believes such crossings, where language is used in new and liminal ways in new communities, are common feature of L2 use. Brumfit (2006) adopts Rampton's concepts to propose that L2 learning and use is necessarily a liminal process that brings L2 users into new areas, in which languages and their cultural codes are unique to each individual and communicative encounter.

The idea of language being used to create liminal, hybrid or third spaces in intercultural communication will be drawn on throughout this book. However, we need to be cautious in our use of notions of hybridity and third spaces and retain as critical an attitude towards them as other concepts in intercultural communication. Holliday (2011) provides an insightful critique of third spaces which notes both the strengths and weakness of the concept. He suggests that "It cannot be denied that the possibility of 'crossing' a harder intercultural line and creating third spaces, in-between places, has massive potential for theorising cultural creativity" (2011: 165) but he also notes that "The concept of the intercultural line remains ... One does not have to be in-between. People have the power to be completely several things at once." (2011: 165). Third spaces, particularly as envisaged by Kramsch (1993), despite the emphasis on new communicative practices, still retains a reified sense of culture in intercultural communication in which language users are between delineated languages and cultures, the L1/C1 and the 'target' L2/C2. To be 'between' there must be a border. However, as Holliday suggests, we do not have to be between; we can be many things at the same time. Furthermore, in intercultural communication it is not always clear what languages and cultures we are between. In multilingual and multicultural environments it may not be possible to identify a clear L1-C1 relationship and even less a 'target' language and 'target' culture correlation. This, as we shall see later, is particularly true of intercultural communication through English as a lingua franca (Baker, 2011b). Indeed, Kramsch herself has recognised this in her more recent writings; critiquing her earlier conception of third place as too static for the more globally connected world we now live in, "Predicated on the existence of a first and a second place that are all too often reified in 'country of origin' and 'host country', third place can be easily romanticised as some hybrid position that contributes to the host country's ideology of cultural diversity" (2009: 200).

A commensurable notion which avoids some of the unnecessary baggage of hybridity and 'in-betweeness' is transcultural and transnational flows. As discussed previously the prefix 'trans' implies movement across and through rather than between and so can be seen as a more appropriate metaphor of movement for intercultural communication. The concepts of transnational and transcultural flows have their origin in sociology and anthropology in the theories of Appadurai (1996) and Hannez (1996). Both scholars offered theories that recognised the influence of the increasingly globally connected social worlds we live in on our understanding of culture and especially the erosion of national notions of culture. Their emphasis on cultural hybridity, complexity and change had obvious resonance with intercultural communication research.

Two researchers who have made extensive use of the concept are Risager (2006; 2007) and Pennycook (2007). Pennycook through an examination of the English used in hip-hop lyrics in a range of settings explores "the ways in which cultural forms move, change and are reused to fashion new identities in diverse contexts" (2007: 6). In Pennycook's examples cultural and linguistic practices related to hip-hop are in constant 'flow' moving from one context to another, while drawing on multiple sources of influence, and continually changing and adapting as they do so. Similarly, Risager (2006; 2007) discusses transnational flows of linguistic, discourse and cultural practices that cut across and through nationally conceived cultures and offers "a theoretically justified alternative to the national paradigm" (2007: 195). Drawing directly on Hannerz (1996), Risager (2006) suggests that languages and cultural forms should be seen as part of networks that spread around the globe mixing with other languages and cultural forms as they do so. She presents a vignette of the Tour de France used as a topic in a German language class in Denmark as an example of how complex global flows integrate in a particular local setting.

Lastly, Canagarajah (2005; 2007) in an examination of global uses of English outlines a view of languages and cultures as hybrid, diffuse and de-territorialized with constant movement between different local and global communities. More recently Canagarajah (2013b) has also adopted the trans prefix in theorising translingual practice and translocal spaces. Through translingual practice (2013b: 19) he emphasises the plurilingualism (or rather translingualism) present in much communicative practice and, like Pennycook and Risager, questions predefined and static distinctions and associations between particular languages and communities. In translocal spaces (2013b: 153) Canagarajah highlights, through data from skilled migrants in contact zones the expectations of linguistic and cultural difference and how norms of communication are open to change, negotiation and mediation. As Canagarajah explains, "the skill that is most valued in these spaces is the ability to shuttle across norms. The informants accommodate the different norms of English that people bring from different places to the translocal space." (2013b: 162). Thus, the concepts of translingual and transcultural flows in their emphasis on fluidity, adaptation and change are particularly important for the notions of the intercultural explored here. They also have much to offer theories of culture (and indeed this is their origins) and so will be returned to in the following chapter. However, we must also acknowledge that this does not remove more fixed and less negotiable norms in intercultural communication; neither does the transnational wholly replace the national. This leads to an inevitable and unavoidable tension between fluidity and fixity as Pennycook notes, "caught between fluidity and fixity, then, cultural and linguistic forms are always in a state of flux, always changing, always part of a process of the refashioning of identity" (2007: 8).

The final contemporary critical approach to intercultural communication that will be drawn on in this book is the concept of Interculturality. As already noted in characterising intercultural communication the perspective taken here is synonymous with that outlined in interculturality in emphasising the emergent, dynamic and interactional nature of culture and cultural difference in intercultural communication. Although there is some debate regarding the extent to which cultural norms can be related to pre-defined cultural groups in interculturality (Kecskes 2012), the predominant approach eschews a priori assumptions about culture norms and associations and instead focus on how, and if, they are negotiated and constructed in interaction (Sarangi 1994; Nishizaka 1995; Mori 2003; Higgins 2007; Young and Sercombe 2010; Zhu 2010; 2011; 2014). This is a reversal of the traditional approach in which cultural difference is assumed and then used to explain the interaction. Underlining this alternative orientation, Nishizaka states, "I want to treat this as a phenomenon to be investigated, instead of using interculturality – the fact that participants come from different cultures – as a given fact from which the argument should start" (1995: 302). Zhu notes that " 'being culturally different' is a socially constructed phenomenon ... a process rather than an end-product" (2011: 259); in other words, it is something that we *do* rather than something that we *have*. This theoretical and methodological approach to intercultural communication has, according to Zhu six main concerns:

1. Are cultural memberships always relevant to intercultural interactions?
2. What do participants do with cultural memberships?
3. How do participants do cultural identities?
4. What interactional resources are available for doing cultural identities?
5. Why do people bother with interculturality?
6. How far can participants go when doing interculturality? (2014: 209)

To address these questions interculturality researchers typically engage in detailed analysis of language and discourse in intercultural communication to explore the manner in which cultural norms, associations and identities are constructed and negotiated in interaction. For example, Nishizaka (1995) makes use of conversation analysis to examine an interview between a Japanese journalist and a foreign student in Japan discussing foreigners' views of Japan. The analysis highlights how the journalist distances himself from Japanese people through using 'they' to refer to the Japanese. Similarly the student refers to non-Japanese as 'foreigners' as if he were not part of this group. For both these participants their orientation to cultural groupings emerges from the interaction as ones unlikely to have been predicted by a priori ascription of each of them to specific cultural groups i.e. Japanese and foreigners. Zhu (2010) investigates intergenerational talk in diasporic families. Through an analysis of address terms and talk about social, cultural, and linguistic practice she illustrates the ways in which sociocultural practices and identities are made relevant to the interaction. Crucially from an interculturality orientation she also demonstrates the manner in which younger generations of diasporic communities bring about changes in the sociocultural values and develop new social and cultural identities.

Interculturality can thus been seen as embodying a number of principal concerns that will be dealt with throughout this book. Interculturality research has underscored the centrality of language and discourse in intercultural interactions and the construction of cultural difference. It has also emphasised the constructed, emergent, negotiated and, hence, dynamic and changeable nature of cultural practices, norms and identities. Interculturality is, therefore, something that we do, not something that we have. As Zhu proposes:

> "In sum, interculturality, as a new and emerging research paradigm, provides an analytical stance that focuses on the role of interactions and discursive practice in negotiating relevance of cultural identities. It examines whether and to what extent participants bring

about, align with each other, or resist cultural memberships oriented to by themselves or ascribed by others in interactions. It takes cultural identities as a process and outcome of negotiation, rather than something a priori. By doing so, it restores the central role of language practice in intercultural communication." (2014: 218)

2.3 Points of convergence and conflict between intercultural communication and ELF research

There is obviously the potential for much productive cross fertilization between intercultural communication research and research into ELF. Indeed, ELF communication is clearly a form of intercultural communication. Jenkins (2006a: 164) definition of ELF as communication in English between participants who have different "linguacultures" makes this point clear. While the more recent definition from Seidlhofer (as given in chapter one and repeated here for convenience) emphasises the linguistic dimensions of ELF communication, "*ELF as any use of English among speakers of different first languages for whom English is the communicative medium of choice, and often the only option.*" (2011: 7, italics in original), in the majority of instances this is likely to involve speakers from different cultures as well. This point is recognised by Mauranen when she states that "ELF speakers do not share a cultural background or a first language (2012: 5). Furthermore, a number of ELF scholars have explicitly related their research to the field of intercultural communication. Jenkins, in juxtaposing ELF approaches with EFL (English as a foreign language) approaches, claims that "ELF is about intercultural communication in the broadest sense, and this means mainly NNES-NNES interactions ... intercultural communication skills and strategies are paramount" (2014: 26). Likewise, Cogo and Dewey also assert that "the type of research we undertake is *intercultural* in nature (or maybe better still, *transcultural*), in that it concerns communication that takes place among speakers from various linguacultural backgrounds" (2012: 26, italics in original). Mauranen too observes that "[a]s ELF gains ground in international communication, the intercultural perspective comes increasingly to the fore" (2012: 243). In my own research I have also adopted an intercultural perspective viewing ELF as "the most common scenario for intercultural communication" (Baker 2015 In Press); most common in the sense that given the global spread of English, intercultural communication is more likely to occur through English being used as a lingua franca than in any other language used as a lingua franca or otherwise. However, to avoid misinterpretation, this is obviously not to suggest that intercultural communication through ELF occurs more frequently than all other forms of intercultural communication combined.

Yet, despite these statements on the part of ELF researches there has been surprisingly little cross-over between the two fields. While ELF scholars have recognised the relevance of their research for intercultural communication, this has typically not been the focus of research and so not explored in depth. This is beginning to change with a number of recent conferences, edited research collections and journal issues exploring productive points of convergence (for example Baker 2014; Pitzl and Ehrenreich forthcoming). However, such engagement is in a relatively embryonic stage at the time of writing this. There still remain many important areas in need of further consideration, as will be outlined in detail below, and a number of crucial points of divergence, as well as similarities, between ELF and intercultural communication research. Equally significantly there has been very little uptake of ELF research findings in the intercultural communication literature. ELF research seems largely to have been ignored or misrepresented. This is of serious concern given that, as stated previously; English is likely to be the most common language of intercultural communication and is most likely to function as a lingua franca in such scenarios.

2.3.1 Points of misunderstanding and divergence between intercultural communication and ELF research

A fundamental difference between intercultural communication research and ELF research is raised by Zhu (2015). She notes that intercultural communication studies begin from a perspective of *difference*; that is there is an assumption of cultural difference that is seen as important in understanding interaction. In contrast ELF studies start by looking at what is *shared*; primarily in terms of linguistic resources, but also communicative strategies, and investigate the influence of this on communication. The consequence of this focus on cultural difference for intercultural communication researchers has, as Piller (2011:) notes, led researchers to often only pay cursory attention to linguistic issues and a tendency to treat language as relatively unproblematic when its role is acknowledged. This may partly account for the lack of interest in ELF research, which has typically focused on linguistic issues, often investigating form and function simultaneously. The lack of awareness of linguistic issues in intercultural communication research represents a serious weakness in the field. For example, in Spencer-Oatey and Franklin's (2009) review of conceptual frameworks of intercultural competence and development (or intercultural interaction competence as they refer to it) from psychological and communication studies there is almost no reference to language. This is particularly concerning given the wide influence of frameworks such as Bennett's (1986) 'Development Model of Intercultural Sensitivity' and Gudykunst (2004) 'Intergroup effectiveness'. It is hard to envisage how one could be interculturally sensitive or effective without some awareness of the role of language, whether a first or other language, in communication.

Language issues have understandably been given a more central place in intercultural communication research within applied linguistics and especially within ELF. Most obviously there has been a concern with the influence of linguistic proficiency on participants' ability to effectively construct and interpret messages and information, as well as avoiding misunderstanding, in the language used for intercultural communication. This is an extensively researched area in both applied linguistics (e.g. Piller 2011; Jackson 2012; Zhu 2014 for overviews) and ELF studies (e.g. Jenkins, Cogo and Dewey 2011; Seidlhofer 2011 for overviews). Language choice and proficiency is also related to ideological and power issues in intercultural communication. Linguistic proficiency has a significant influence on participants' role in interaction, as Piller states "[w]ho we are in intercultural communication is to a large extent a function of our linguistic proficiency: you cannot 'be' an educational expert or a competent shopper if you do not sound like one." (2011: 146).

Within ELF studies Jenkins (2007), among others, has shown the crucial role of language ideology in construct of identities in English for non-native users of English. The choice of language may also give an advantage to some participants in intercultural communication. Those who are most proficient in the language may be better able to dominant the interaction. Deviation from preferred 'standards', e.g. standard British English, may disadvantage participants giving them lower status from the perspective of other participants (Milroy and Milroy 2012). What may be viewed as prestigious or appropriate in one setting may not be in another. For example using French for intercultural communication in Morocco may be viewed very differently from using French for intercultural communication in the US (see the negative reaction to the 2012 US presidential candidate Mitt Romney speaking French). Linguistic issues do not only apply to those speakers of additional languages. Native speakers of a language need to be just as aware of linguistic issues in intercultural communication. If native speakers fail to accommodate or adapt their language to the context of communication this may lead to misunderstanding and negative perceptions on the part of other participants. This may result in particularly negative impressions if the lack of accommodation is perceived as deliberate and an attempt to gain advantages of one kind or another in interaction. Studies such as Rogerson-Revell (2007) and Sweeney and Zhu (2010) have demonstrated the necessity of native speaker accommodation in ELF used in business settings (BELF). Björkman (2011; 2013) and Jenkins' (2014) come to a similar conclusion in academic settings.

However, while applied linguistics and ELF research agree in their interest in linguistic issues, which distinguishes them from much intercultural communication research, within applied linguistics ELF research has frequently been ignored. This lack of awareness of ELF research is problematic when investigating English used for intercultural communication given the predominance of ELF scenarios. For example, the Routledge Handbook of Language and Intercultural Communication (Jackson 2012) does not contain any references to ELF in over 600 pages. There are references to World Englishes (for example Sharifian 2012) but, as explained in chapter one, this is a very different paradigm that seeks to account for territorially based varieties of English rather than the inherent variation that is characteristic of ELF communication. While we would not expect intercultural communication research to only focus on English, it is of concern that where English is the explicit focus there is frequently no awareness of ELF research when addressing topics of relevance to the field. Piller (2011) is a clear example of this, providing no citations to ELF studies while offering frequent references to and examples from English to illustrate the commodification of languages, the ideology of status and exclusion underlying language choices and particularly the role accent and linguistic forms play in this and their relationship to identity, including 'native/non-native speaker' identity. That all these issues have been addressed extensively by ELF studies is not in itself a reason to critique overviews of intercultural communication that do not include them. However, of greater concern is that without including ELF research there is often a lack of understanding of how these issues play out in contexts with little direct connection to Anglophone or post-colonial settings. Such contexts are currently significant and influential settings in which we find English used.

Alongside a lack of awareness of ELF research has been a degree of misunderstanding in how ELF is characterised and what the implications for intercultural communication research might be. One critique has been that ELF research has been unaware of the political and ideological dimensions of intercultural communication (Holliday 2009; O'Regan 2014). Holliday believes that we must take seriously the claim that "the movement [ELF] is accused in some quarters of being a Centre plot to disenfranchise 'non-native speakers' by imposing an inferior linguistic model." (2009: 152). To this he adds that, in the case of culture, ELF research is still confined by 'the hegemony the Centre-West' (ibid) thinking. This ignores the fact that many ELF researchers are not from 'the Centre' as far as English is concerned. For example, two influential publications are Seidlhofer (2011) and Mauranen (2012) both written by scholars located in Kachru's 'expanding circle'. Other empirical ELF studies come from scholars who are neither from the 'Centre' nor the 'West' including those collected in Murata and Jenkins (2009) and Murata (2012) as well as more recent studies such as Wang (2013) and Xu and Dinh (2013) and there are a growing number of such studies. We might perhaps claim, as O'Regan (2014) does, that these scholars are suffering from a 'false consciousness' unknowingly adopting centre and western practices. However, ELF research has dealt explicitly with the ideological dimensions to intercultural communication through ELF (e.g. Jenkins 2007; 2014; Seidlhofer 2011), examining the power of 'standard English' ideologies, native speakerism and inner circle/centre discourses. Crucially the way such ideologies are framed within the ideology of ELF discourse itself is also recognised (Baird, Baker and Kitazawa 2014). Furthermore, to suggest that ELF research into intercultural communication, or any other type of research, is only valid if carried out by a pre-specified linguistic, geographical and cultural group (i.e. non-Centre/non-Western, non-native English speakers) is surely falling into the essentialist trap that these critiques are attempting to counter.

Another misconception or point of divergence is to suggest that ELF communication itself can be culturally neutral. Holliday, for instance, in reference to 'non-native' users of English in his research writes that "[t]hat all of my informants are remarkably articulate in English means that they are able to express their diverse cultural realities competently through English as a neutral medium" (2011: 147). While Holliday is correct in asserting that English can be used to express diverse cultural realities, it does not follow that English is a neutral medium. I have argued elsewhere (Baker 2011b), and in line with other intercultural communication scholars (Phipps and Guilherme 2004), that this represents a fundamental misunderstanding of communication. Communication, including intercultural communication and ELF, is never neutral; there are always participants, purposes, contexts and language choices, none of which are neutral and all of which involve negation and power relationships. Holliday's comment here may perhaps represent an example of intercultural communication research neglecting the linguistic dimensions of communication, but nonetheless the choice (or imposition) of English as the linguistic medium of communication is not a neutral one. However, this does not entail that English is necessarily tied to Anglophone or 'centre' cultures, and Holliday's claim regarding the variety of cultures English can be used to express and create is supported by ELF research as well (e.g. Baker 2009).

A related misconception is that ELF research has ignored or underrepresented the cultural dimension to ELF communication, in effect treating ELF communication as if it were culturally neutral. For instance, Canagarajah claims that ELF researchers have theorised "a value-free or neutral form of English" (2013b: 175) and similarly O'Regan believes "the ELF movement wishes to pretend that 'ELF' is ideology and culture free" (2014: 8). This is a topic that will be dealt with in detail in the following chapter; however, for the present it is enough to note that, while it has perhaps not always been of central concern, there are many studies that have explored the cultural aspects of ELF communication (e.g. Meierkord 2002; Pölzl and Seidlhofer 2006; Baker 2009; 2011a). Importantly, the majority of ELF researchers have recognised the significance of the relationship between culture and language, as the quotations at the beginning of this section demonstrate, and contrary to what Canagarajah (2013b) and O'Regan (2014) claim, eschewed culturally neutral or culture-free perspectives.

A persistent misunderstanding of ELF research is represented in Pennycook's (2010) and Canagarajah's (2013b) claims that ELF studies are too normative in attempting to account for homogeneous features of what are heterogeneous interactions and reifying distinctions between different linguistic and cultural groups such as native/non-native speakers and monolingual/multilingual communication. Pennycook argues, in a critique of both World Englishes and ELF, that "[n]either a defence of national languages and cultures, not a description of a core of English as a lingua franca, not even a focus on plural Englishes, adequately addresses questions of diversity under new conditions of globalization" (2010: 78). However, ELF research, as currently conceived, is no longer about establishing 'core' features or accounting for a plurality of regional varieties of Englishes. Such criticisms have been addressed in detail elsewhere (e.g. Seidlhofer 2006; Jenkins 2007; Jenkins, Cogo and Dewey 2011) and will not be repeated here. Canagarajah's (2013b: 62–68) comments are more nuanced in recognising that ELF research has changed and developed over time but again repeats the misinterpretation that 'form' is still central to research (2013b: 66). As will be argued throughout this book, ELF research is about much more than investigating linguistic forms. Although Canagarajah may be correct in highlighting a degree of tension in theorisation among ELF scholars concerning the roles of form, function and norms in communication, this is not a debate that is unique to ELF research. Furthermore, linguistic form, however we chose to theorise it, should still be of interest to us as linguists in our research, and not ignored. Finally, there seems to be an odd disjuncture between writers such as Pennycook's and Canagarajah's recognition of knowledge and theory as always partial, provisional and changing, and their reified critiques of ELF research as an unchanging and homogeneous field of enquiry. While early ELF research explored the possibility of 'core' features of ELF (Jenkins 2000; Seidlhofer 2004), this is no longer the case. Similarly, linguistic form was certainly a focus of such early 'core' research, but it was never the sole focus of ELF research (see Jenkins's (2000) extensive discussion of accommodation) and has become even less so more recently. Much more productive than a focus on whether ELF research is 'right' or 'wrong' and how the hypothetical position of ELF researchers differs from other researchers, is to examine in what ways ELF research, both empirical and theoretical, can contribute to our understanding of intercultural communication.

2.3.2 Points of convergence between intercultural communication and ELF research

Unsurprisingly, given that ELF communication is a form of intercultural communication, there is much in common between the two fields of research. It is also important to stress that while ELF research has emerged as a field of study in its own right, and has its own research traditions and aims, ELF is not a unique form of intercultural communication. For ELF researchers the use of *English* as a lingua franca in intercultural communication, as opposed to other languages as lingua francas in intercultural communication, is obviously the major area of interest. Yet, this does not entail ignoring the use of other languages used alongside English in plurilingual intercultural communication. Indeed code-switching and languaging have been major areas of interest for ELF researchers (e.g. Cogo 2012; Klimpfinger 2009). Moreover, this is not to claim that ELF is *sui generis* compared to other forms of intercultural communication as has been claimed by some (Firth 2009; House 2009). ELF is not a unique variety of English and the communication strategies, linguistic awareness and intercultural awareness observed in ELF communication are present in other forms of plurilingual and multicultural intercultural communication. Therefore, we might expect much productive cross-fertilisation between the two fields, and that indeed has been one of the major motivations for writing this book. Intercultural communication research has many decades of empirical studies and theoretical debate which ELF scholars can draw on and ELF research through investigating what is currently the most common form of intercultural communication is likely to produce findings of interest to all intercultural communication researchers.

Perhaps the most obvious first point of convergence is the similar perspective on communication; although, the two fields have taken rather different starting points. Intercultural communication research often assumes that misunderstanding or non-understanding is the norm in intercultural communication (Zhu 2015), whereas empirical findings from ELF research quickly established understanding as the norm (Firth 1996), despite the challenges of cultural and linguistic differences. Nonetheless, both fields have approached the communication they investigate as being plurilingual and multicultural in nature with a variety of linguistic and cultural backgrounds expected and hence a diversity of communicative practices. ELF research, in common with more contemporary approaches to intercultural communication, has focused on intercultural *interactions*. It has typically made use of naturally occurring data rather than simulated or elicited data with corpora such as the VOICE corpus and the ELFA corpus being the best known examples of this. Like much intercultural communication research in applied linguistics, ELF research has made extensive use of discourse and conversation analysis (e.g. Firth 1996; Cogo and Dewey 2012; Jenks 2013). Pragmatics has also been a major concern in ELF research and has drawn on intercultural and cross-cultural pragmatics literature (e.g. House 2002; Mauranen 2006; Kaur 2009; Cogo and Dewey 2012). ELF scholars have made use of similar metaphors and concepts to the more critical approaches to intercultural communication, described previously, viewing ELF communication as fluid, hybrid, dynamic and emergent (e.g. Dewey 2007; Baker 2009; Jenkins, Cogo and Dewey 2011; Baird, Baker and Kitazawa 2014). In keeping with this critical, poststructuralist approach, ELF research has also been concerned with questions of power and ideology, particularly around issues of standard language ideology and 'native speakerism' (e.g. Jenkins 2007; 2014; Seidlhofer 2011; Guido 2012; Baird, Baker and Kitazawa 2014).

Another clear point of convergence between intercultural communication and ELF research is an interest in what leads to successful communication. Although the different premises of the two fields has already been noted (misunderstanding as the norm versus understanding as the nom) both fields have been interested in identifying the elements of successful intercultural communication, whether it is to prevent the misunderstanding assumed in intercultural communication research, or to be better understand the success observed in ELF communication. Both fields have also conceived of successful communication as more than competence related to a defined set of linguistic features as envisaged in Chomsky's (1986) notion of linguistic competence. Within intercultural communication research this has involved various definitions and characterisations of intercultural competence and intercultural communicative competence typically involving a range of knowledge, skills and attitudes that are much wider than mastery of linguistic structures (see Spitzberg and Changnon 2009; Spencer-Oatey and Franklin 2009; Jackson 2012 for overviews). Although ELF research has not investigated the notion of competence in as much detail as in intercultural communication studies, there has been recognition from the beginning that the competence needed for ELF communication would go beyond linguistic structures. A central role for accommodation (Jenkins 2000) and other pragmatic strategies (House 2002) was quickly established in research and continues to the present (see Jenkins, Cogo and Dewey 2011 for an overview). Such is the importance of communication strategies that, as previously noted, many scholars have suggested that it is these, as opposed to linguistic forms, which should be central to ELF research (Firth 2009; Seidlhofer and Widdowson 2009).

Other contemporary research has attempted to relate the use of communicative and pragmatic strategies to a wider framework of attitudes towards and knowledge about intercultural communication through ELF (Baker 2009; 2011b). Most significantly though has been the attempt in ELF research to combine all of these different elements of knowledge, attitudes and skills to provide a holistic picture of intercultural communication through ELF. In particular, the attention paid to the variability of linguistic form and how this relates to other types of competences in ELF communication has added valuable insights into the type of linguistic competence needed for intercultural communication. Such research is still in its early stages though and conclusive accounts have not yet emerged. Nevertheless, notions of communicative or intercultural communicative competence are clearly a crucial area for both fields and the topic will be returned to in more detail in chapter five.

Linked to ideas of communicative strategies and especially accommodation, Zhu (2015) argues that negotiation is central to both intercultural communication and ELF research and practice. Similarly, in my own research into intercultural awareness in ELF and intercultural communication I have suggested that negotiation and mediation are key to successful communication (Baker 2011b: 203). Negotiation here is not just negotiation of linguistic forms and meaning but also negotiation in relation to social identities and cultural frames of references and practices. As Zhu explains it, "[n]egotiation is the very mechanism that enables participants in intercultural and lingua franca communication to employ, mobilise or manipulate diverse resources to achieve their goals of interaction." (2015: 2). Zhu links this to accommodation suggesting that the desire or need to accommodate is an essential part of creating understanding in situations where there are less shared recourses and mutual understanding cannot be assumed. Crucially in order to accommodate participants must be willing to negotiate meanings and references. However, as already highlighted, this does not just refer to meaning but also to identities and cultural frames of reference. Again, Zhu suggests that in order to accommodate to diverse socio-cultural expectations, positions, practices and references participants must be prepared to negotiate all of these aspects of interaction. However, she also cautions that negotiation may not always be offered in competitive situations where more powerful interacts can gain advantage by not accommodating.

One of the areas that Zhu focuses on in relation to negotiation is identity and this has been another shared theme between intercultural communication and ELF research. Much has been written in intercultural communication research, and even earlier in cross-cultural communication research, concerning the relationship between language and identity and the relevance of this to intercultural communication. While earlier research tended to correlate identity with nationality and an associated national culture (a subject that will be explored in more depth later), contemporary intercultural communication studies, in applied linguistics at least, take a more poststructuralist perspective. Identity, like other aspects of intercultural communication, is viewed as fluid, complex, constructed and negotiated. Identity is, therefore, not something we have but is something we do. Following this approach, intercultural communication research has examined the manner in which identities are enacted, constructed and negotiated in interactions and particularly the influence communicating in a second or other language has on this, as well as where cultural norms and references are not shared even when communicating in an L1. This has led to findings that reveal the way intercultural communication opens up spaces for new identities and identifications (e.g. Pennycook 2007; Kramsch 2009), the often highly negotiated (e.g. Zhu 2010; 2014) and possibly contradictory nature of this (e.g. Holliday 2010; 2011), as well as the manner in which unwanted identifications may be ascribed or resisted (e.g. Norton 2000; Duff 2002; Piller 2011). ELF researchers have also generally taken a similarly poststructuralist perspective investigating the way in which identities are constructed and negotiated in lingua franca communication. As with intercultural communication research, findings have shown how ELF is used in scenarios in which new, fluid identities are constructed alongside more stable L1 identities (Phan 2008; Baker 2011a). They have also demonstrated ELF users identifying with other plurilingual communicators in shared 'non-nativeness' (Hülmbauer 2009) as well as the use of their plurilingual resources, particularly code-switching, to signal different cultural identifications (Klimpfinger 2009; Cogo 2009). Researchers have also explored the way idioms and metaphors are used to reference particular cultural identities but are also co-constructed and negotiated in situ to ensure mutual understanding (Pitzl 2009; 2013; Seidlhofer and Widdowson 2009). Alongside this has been a concern with the ideological dimensions to ELF and identity and how perceptions of the status of different varieties of English influence identification through and with English (Jenkins 2007).

Closely related to issues of identity and identification are notions of culture. As discussed throughout this chapter, researchers in both ELF and intercultural communication have been interested in what and how cultural identities are enacted and constructed in interactions. Again ELF researchers have been more closely aligned with poststructuralist perspectives in intercultural communication through investigating the complexity of cultural identifications in interactions. This has typically involved examinations of cultural identifications as dynamic, multiple and emergent (Baker 2009; 2011a; 2011b). Culture has been investigated at a number of different levels in ELF studies and the tensions between identifications with different national conceptions of culture have been well documented in attitudes studies (e.g. Jenkins 2007; Wang 2013). Similarly tensions between local L1 associated cultural references, the immediate environment of the interaction and more globally recognised cultural references have also been investigated (Meierkord 2002; Pölzl and Seidlhofer 2006; Baker 2009). However, the majority of ELF studies have been concerned with more localised social groupings making use of the notion of communities of practice (Wegner 1998) to explain the types of dynamic and temporary communities in which ELF forms part of the shared resources of the community (Dewey 2007; Ehrenreich 2009; Seidlhofer 2007; 2011; Kalocsai 2014). While such an approach appears to be a productive one, a number of issues remain unaccounted for, particularly how these smaller communities relate to larger communities and cultures. It is also fair to say that the notions of culture and community have received far less attention than the related notion of identity in ELF research and certainly much less theorisation than in intercultural communication research. Indeed these concerns form one of the motivations for this book.

2.4 Conclusion

This chapter has presented an overview and characterisation of intercultural communication as a field of research emphasising those elements of interest to the discussions in this book. In particular the approach followed here will be a poststructuralist, critical one in which intercultural communication is viewed as complex, dynamic and fluid. This implies that any categories of analysis applied to intercultural research need to be approached as contingent and subjective. We need to ask, following Scollon and Scollon (2001), who introduces the concepts of culture, or the intercultural, with what purposes and with what consequences. It therefore follows that as researchers of intercultural communication we need to demonstrate the relevance of intercultural categorisations, often related to cultural and linguistic differences, to the participants in the interaction and/or to the analysis, while taking care not to conflate the two. Crucially intercultural differences cannot be assumed a priori to be relevant to all interactions we might chose to characterise as intercultural. Equally important is how language choices, social positions and cultural characterisations represent and create power structures and ideologies in intercultural communication.

The second aim of this chapter has been to demonstrate the links between intercultural communication research and ELF research. Most obviously this has involved a recognition that ELF is by definition intercultural in nature since ELF communication is typically defined as involving speakers from different lingua-cultures. While, it has been argued here, that ELF research has often been ignored or misunderstood in intercultural communication literature, there is the potential for much productive cross-over between the two fields. ELF research has taken a similar perspective to much contemporary intercultural communication research in viewing communication from a poststructuralist perspective where categories of language, identity, community and culture are seen as constructed, negotiable and contested. ELF researchers have also been interested in the ideological dimensions of communication and how power relations are enacted and contested through ELF communication. In particular three themes have emerged as potentially fruitful points of convergence where both research fields can inform each other. These, as outlined above, are notions of culture, identity and successful communication, or more precisely intercultural communicative competence, and each in turn will form the subject of the following three chapters.

Chapter 3
Understanding culture through ELF

"Culture is one of the two or three most complicated words in the English language"

– Williams (2014: 86)

"while culture is considered important to fathom, it is obscure and difficult to analyse. You can't see it; you can't count it in any obvious way"

– Ochs (2002: 115)

"It is hard to resist the conclusion that the word 'culture' is both too broad and too narrow to be greatly useful. Its anthropological meaning covers everything from hairstyles and drinking habits to how you address your husband's second cousin, while the aesthetic sense of the word includes Igor Stravinksy but not science fiction."

– Eagleton (2000: 32)

If intercultural communication has been characterised and put to use for a wide range of different disciplines and purposes, as was detailed in the previous chapter, we can make the same claims about culture but multiply them considerably. While intercultural communication as a term and idea is typically confined to specialist academic and professional fields, and not a frequent subject of public debate, the same is not true of culture. Culture, as we shall see, has been the subject of many academic fields but it is also an idea that is part of public consciousness. It is subject to debates and discussion as frequently in the media and politics as it is in the academy. Given such widespread use we might question, as Eagleton (2000) does in the above quote, whether culture has any meaning left as a concept or if it has become so diluted and overweening as to be analytically redundant. Indeed, Eagleton goes on to argue that culture needs putting back in its place and that "[t]he primary problems we confront in the new millennium – war, famine, poverty, disease, debt, drugs, environmental pollution, the displacement of peoples – are not especially 'cultural' at all." (2000: 130). Similar concerns in relation to intercultural communication are expressed by Scollon, Scollon and Jones who suggest that " 'culture' may not be a particularly useful word to use when talking about 'intercultural communication' " (2012: 3) as "culture is mostly too large a concept" (2012: 10). However, all of these scholars make extensive reference to the term or idea of culture and put it to productive use. What these critiques highlight then is not that we should necessarily abandon the use of culture in academic study, but that when drawing on the concept we need to be clear in what sense we are using it and for what reasons. To return to the questions raised by Scollon and Scollon (2001) in relation to intercultural communication we need to ask 'who has introduced the concept, for what purposes and with what consequences'. We also need to accept that, as Risager states, "there has been more or less a consensus that it is not possible to lay down an 'authorised' definition of culture" (2006: 42). In other words, our definitions of culture will always be partial and open to revision and change.

This chapter will present a characterisation of culture, as opposed to a definition, that is relevant to the concerns of this monograph. This entails examining how a number of different theories of culture, and especially culture in intercultural communication, can inform ELF research, but also how ELF research may inform our understanding of the role of culture in intercultural communication. In other words, to paraphrase the second question posed in the introduction, we will be asking what influence (if any) studies of ELF and intercultural communication have on our understanding of the relationship between culture, communication and language. To do this, particularly given the breath of scholarship on culture, it will be necessary to be clear about the perspectives on culture that will be adopted here and those that will not. A number of influential positions on culture which are of relevance to the present discussion will be explored including perspectives on culture as a product, as discourse, as practice and as ideology. This will be followed by a consideration of the relationship of culture to both nations and, of key importance to English as a global language, to globalisation. Given the multiple interpretations and scales at which culture can be understood it will be suggested that complexity theory offers a useful metaphor or meta-theory for thinking about culture, and significant features of complexity theory in relation to culture will be presented. The discussion will then turn to an exploration of the relationship between language and culture with a critical evaluation of linguistic relativity, a consideration of the notion of linguaculture and suggestions as to further insights that can be offered from complexity theory. Finally, approaches to conceptualising and researching culture in ELF communication will be explored with a particular focus on my own research. I will argue that culture, communication and language in ELF scenarios can be best understood through theories which highlight the complexity of the relationship, but also, crucially, that data from ELF studies forces us to reconsider how we conceptualise these categories (culture, communication and language) in intercultural communication.

3.1 Conceptions of culture

3.1.1 The development of the idea of culture

As with the characterisation of intercultural communication, the notion of culture in its current uses needs to be viewed in its historical context. Again, it is not the aim of this book to provide a detailed historical overview of the concept (see Eagleton 2000; Jenks 2005; Risager 2006; Bauman 2011; Williams 2014 for good introductions to this from a range of perspectives) but rather to outline which interpretations of culture will, and will not, be the focus of this discussion, to be aware of how such interpretations have come about and most importantly to show how they have led to the current concerns discussed here. However, this will inevitably be a selective process that will leave out many important theories and approaches to culture, for example neither cultural studies nor post-colonial theory are dealt with in detail, although ideas and writers from both fields are used. Therefore, no claims to comprehensiveness are made.

The most basic meaning of the word culture is as distinct from nature. In Latin *cultura* or *colere* refers to what is cultivated or grown as opposed to *nascere*, what is born or grows without aid. The debate about what is natural or innate and what is learnt in humans is of course a very old one, and given what we now know about genetics and evolution and the influence of learnt behaviour on innate features, not one that is likely to be resolved soon. This cultivation metaphor, according to Jenks, leads into the idea of culture as civilisation in the classical sense, and later in the enlightenment, as belonging to a society or "a collectivity that embodies certain qualities, albeit self-appointed, which distinguish it from the 'mass' or more lowly state of being" (2005: 8). In this sense culture becomes a goal and a hierarchical notion (Jenks 2005; Risager 2006). This can be applied to societies as a whole which are viewed as distinct and more or less civilised and cultured. Culture can then be proposed as a forward trajectory for society as it 'advances' towards becoming more cultured and civilised. This can also be related to individuals who through education and socialisation can be seen as developing culturally. The role of culture in 'developing' and 'improving' the individual and in turn society was most influentially articulated, in the English speaking world at least, through Arnold's (1869) 'Culture and Anarchy'. Bauman, summarises Arnold's argument as "[culture] seeks to do away with classes; to make the best that has been thought or known in the world current everywhere; to make all men live in an atmosphere of sweetness and light" (2011: 7)[3]. Such notions of culture

---

3 Bauman (2011) presents this as a direct quotation from Arnold, although it appears to be compilation of a number of phrases from Arnold's original text rather than a straight quotation.

also relate to the idea of 'high' and 'low' culture particularly in regard to the Arts and aesthetics with certain art forms (e.g. opera, classical music) and works of art (e.g. particular paintings, plays or novels) seen as superior, elitist and more 'cultured' than others. Although these hierarchical notions of culture will not be the subject of the discussion here, a number of important themes emerge which will be returned to. These include the relationships between culture and individuals and culture and society, the extent to which culture can be used to distinguish societies or groups and the relationship between culture and nation.

Another interpretation of culture that came to prominence in the nineteenth and twentieth century was the anthropological and sociological sense of the term referring to the whole way of life of a particular people. A well-known early example of this being Tylor's definition which states "Culture, or civilization, taken in its broad, ethnographic sense, is that complex whole which includes knowledge, belief, art, morals, law, custom, and any other capabilities and habits acquired by man as a member of society." (1871: 1). This early ethnographic account, while containing elements that are recognisable in many contemporary definitions of culture, is still linked to the hierarchical understanding of culture in that Tylor's aim was to compare 'lower' and 'higher' cultures. Following this ethnographic perspective in the early twentieth century Boas (1911) made use of anthropological approaches to studying the cultures of indigenous Americans. However, he was highly critical of hierarchical perspectives as ethnocentric and racist. Instead he adopted a cultural-relativist position in which cultures were explored in their own terms and with no connotations of superiority and inferiority. Boas also placed language at the centre of his studies proposing that "the form of the language will be moulded by the state of the culture" (1911, reprinted in Valdes, 1986: 7) thus, highlighting the close relationship between language and culture. However, he was also clear that language and culture are not synonymous and that new thoughts are possible without yet being encoded in languages, and that languages are capable of changing and adapting in response to changes in culture. This insight distinguishes his ideas from strong versions of linguistic relativity (discussed in more detail later) which Boas is often associated with (e.g. Valdes 1986). Cultural relativism and the close relationship between culture and language have been two highly influential approaches to the study of culture in anthropology and ethnography but also in intercultural communication and most recently applied linguistics.

Boas can also be seen as part of, or at least influencing, the semiotic understanding of culture in ethnography and anthropology where culture is seen as symbolic meaning making. Lévi-Strauss (1966), among others, has been very influential in this approach following Durkheim's (1964) structuralist perspective to culture; although, there are important differences between Durkheim's and

Lévi-Strauss's theories of culture which are beyond the scope of this discussion. For Lévi-Strauss language, along with a number of other symbolic systems, represent and express aspects of the physical and social reality that make up culture "men communicate by means of symbols and signs; for anthropology, which is a conversation of man with man, everything is symbol and sign" (1966; 114). Furthermore, the dialectical relationships between physical and social reality and the symbolic systems also form the structure of culture. Thus, culture and society are viewed as parts of a related whole; a system or a structure which can be described and delineated. It is, therefore, possible to explain an individual's behaviour in reference to, or rather as a function of, the social structure. The influence of such structuralist perspectives can be seen, according to Holliday (2011), in essentialist understandings of culture, such as Hofstede's (1991), that explain individuals' communicative behaviour as a function of the social structures that are embedded in nationality conceived cultures.

Geertz is perhaps the most influential anthropologist to take a semiotic approach to culture stating that "it [culture] denotes an historically transmitted pattern of meanings embodied in symbols, a system of inherited conceptions expressed in symbolic forms by means of which men communicate, perpetuate, and develop their knowledge about and attitudes toward life." (1973: 89). However, despite sharing this semiotic perspective, Geertz differs substantially from structuralist approaches in that he does not see culture as a structure to be described and delineated in terms of rules and relationships but rather "the analysis of it to be therefore not an experimental science in search of law but an interpretive one in search of meaning." (1973: 5). This interpretative ethnographic perspective to researching cultures in which 'thick descriptions' of aspects of particular cultures are offered in place of universal laws continues to be very influential in current research not just in anthropology but also in intercultural communication and applied linguistics and he is still much quoted. While it is not clear to what extent Geertz would agree with much contemporary post-modernist thinking about culture, in important ways his ideas foreshadow some of our current concerns. This is especially true in his view of culture and thought as something that is an interactional practice rather than a static thing that people have, "human thought is basically both social and public – that its natural habitat is the house yard, the market place, and the town square" (Geertz 1973: 45).

Along with the shared view of culture as semiotic, and hence the central role of language, both structuralist accounts of culture, such as Lévi-Strauss, and interpretive perspectives, such as Geertz, also share an interest in what is universal and particular in cultures. The universal concerns what is shared by all humans that enables them to create culture and what it is about culture that distinguishes humans from other animals. This is a search for universal features or constructs of cultures that all cultures or conceptions of culture share. Alongside this, though, is an interest in the particular details of specific cultures that distinguishes one culture from another; whether it is the rules and relationships of social structures in different nationally defined cultures under structuralist accounts or the thick descriptions of particular cultural practices and interpretative orientations to cultures. Geertz sums up these two concerns when he writes:

> If we want to discover what man amounts to we can only find it in what men are: and what men are above all other things, is various ... And the cultural pattern involved are not general but specific – not just marriage but a particular set of notions about what men and women are like, how spouses should treat one another, or who should properly marry whom (1973: 52).

From this rather selective account of the development of the idea of culture a number of key concerns and approaches are raised which will be explored in detail throughout the rest of this chapter. Cleary the anthropological and sociological account of culture as 'a way of life', rather than the civilizational hierarchy or high art perspective, is the conception that has been drawn on in intercultural communication and ELF research and is most relevant to the concerns of this book. Most significantly is the notion of culture as semiotic and symbolic. Related to this is the central role of language in interpreting culture. But also some tensions have appeared, in particular the relationship between the universal and specific in culture, the extent to which culture is a deterministic structure or a localised interactive practice, and the relationships between the individual, culture, society and nation. These last relationships are particularly complex in intercultural and lingua franca encounters where the cultural contexts and cultural identifications are likely to be highly fluid and resist a priori categorisation and generalisations.

3.1.2 Culture as product

Perspectives of culture as a product, that is a thing which is shared by groups of people, have been one of the most common approaches to understanding culture in intercultural communication. This is how culture has been traditionally conceived (although Risager (2006: 49) cautions that it would be a gross oversimplification to see all traditional or classical accounts of culture in this way) and is probably closest to the dictionary definition of culture. Thus, the Oxford dictionary defines culture in this sense as "the ideas, customs, and social behaviour of a particular people or society" (http://www.oxforddictionaries.com). Jandt (2010: 15), in a well-known intercultural communication text, defines culture in a similar manner as "the totality of that group's thoughts, experiences, and patterns of behaviour and its concepts, values, and assumptions about life that guide behaviour and how those evolve with contact with other cultures". Jandt follows this definition with reference to Hofstede's (1991) four categories of culture: values, rituals, heroes, and symbols, which are expressed through his influential onion metaphor of culture. Hall's (1976) cultural iceberg is another prominent metaphor in which the external, observable part of culture, behaviour and beliefs, forms the tip of the iceberg above the water. However, the majority of the iceberg, and hence culture, is unobservable and out of people's awareness. This includes many beliefs, values and thought patterns. In all of these metaphors, and the conceptions of culture associated with them, the idea of culture is a 'thing' that people 'have' which can be described, delineated and distinguished between different groups of people. As already discussed in relation to intercultural communication, such characterisation of cultures can easily result in essentialist and deterministic depictions of others which hinder rather than help understanding in intercultural communication.

While it is relatively easy to critique dictionary definitions of culture and the rather simplistic characterisations given above, the notion of culture as a thing or a system that can be described has been pervasive in its influence. Along with research such as Hofstede's and text books such as Jandt's, other more complex characterisations of culture also follow a similar conception of a container or thing with a clear structure that can be delineated and distinguished. The most evident example being the structuralist accounts of culture in anthropology, described previously, such as Durkheim (1964) and Lévi-Strauss (1966). However, more interpretative anthropological accounts of culture, including Geertz, also view culture as a system. Geertz writes that "it [culture] denotes an historically transmitted pattern of meanings embodied in symbols, a system of inherited concepts express in symbolic forms" (1973: 89). If we contrast this with Geertz's most famous quotation on culture we see a dilemma or a contradiction, "Believing, with Max Weber, that man is an animal suspended in webs of significance he himself has spun, I take culture to be those webs, and the analysis of it to be therefore not an experimental science in search of law but an interpretive one in search of meaning" (Geertz 1973: 5). On the one hand we have the desire, certainly on the part of researchers but also many others interested in culture, to account for 'something', to be able to delineate what it is that is shared or 'transmitted', but on the other hand we have the recognition, at least in more interpretative ethnographic approaches, that culture is not likely to be a system in the sense of physical systems with laws. While Geertz does not draw any conclusions on this matter, the extent to which it may or may not be productive to view culture as a system is a key question which will be returned to throughout the discussion in this chapter.

One important development in the idea of culture which was not dealt with in the characterisations presented previously is cognitive perspectives on culture. Cognitive accounts of culture are presented here as they can be seen as part of the product approach to culture. In locating culture as a thing in the mind, usually as patterns or schemata which are drawn on by the individual, the view of culture is very differently to the more practice oriented semiotic approaches that see culture as public and co-constructed in social action. One of the main early representatives of this tradition, Goodenough was heavily influenced by structural linguistics and attempted to uncover the 'cultural grammar' of systems and rules through methods of analysis analogous to those utilized in structural linguistics (Risager 2006: 45). He offered the following definition of culture from a cognitive perspective:

> A society's culture consists of whatever it is one has to know or believe in order to operate in a manner acceptable to its members ... Culture, being what people have to learn as distinct from their biological heritage, must consist of the end product of learning: knowledge ... By this definition, we should note that culture is not a material phenomenon; it does not consist of things, people, behaviour, or emotions. It is rather an organisation of these things that people have in mind, their models for perceiving, relating and otherwise interpreting them. (Goodenough 1964: 36)

Thus, while culture, in this account, is not a material thing, it is still a thing in the mind, the central part of which is knowledge shared by the individuals who are part of the same cultural group. More recent cognitive conceptions of culture still retain this basic tenet of culture as knowledge (Strauss and Quinn 1997; Wierzbicka 2006; Riley 2007; Sharifian 2011); what individuals in a culture need to "know in order to act as they do, make the things they make, and interpret their experiences in the distinctive way they do" (Holland and Quinn 1987: 4). Using concepts from schema theory, culture is described as internal mental organisations or schemata and metaphors for interpreting the world and deciding how to behave. By experiencing similar socially mediated experiences, such as schooling, people will develop shared 'cultural schemata' which enable members of the same culture to make broadly similar interpretations of social interaction. Again the primary means for transmitting and understanding these schemata is language. For example, Quinn (1987) uses the example of US metaphors for marriage, such as marriage is enduring, marriage is difficult, which express shared beliefs in American culture about marriage and give 'clues' as to the underlying cultural model at work. Wierzbicka (1997; 2006) makes use of the analogous idea of 'cultural scripts' to explain the manner in which we think and communicate in specific situations in ways that are considered culturally appropriate. Significantly, she also claims that this is embedded in particular language structures, so for example there are cultural scripts of English that reflect an Anglo-centric way of communicating and thinking. This is clearly a controversial idea and closely related to linguistic relativity which will be explored in more detail later.

Cognitive theories have been criticized for focussing too narrowly on internal mental processes, and in particular by proponents of semiotic views of culture, most significantly by Geertz (1973), for the idea that there can be any kind of internal meaning separate from external interaction. However, more recent cognitive theories have taken greater account of the relationship between internal mental processes and meanings, and external shared social meanings. Riley, while maintaining that culture is a 'social knowledge system', also emphasis the intersubjective nature of it, "the distribution and acquisition of knowledge takes places during dyadic or group interactions in which the participants establish *intersubjectivity*, a state of shared meaning" (2007: 33, italics in original). Additional criticism has come from critical cultural theories which reject the static, 'unproblematic' portrayal of culture in cognitive theories. Again more recent cognitive theories have been more aware of this issue. Sharifian (2011) outlines a cognitive theory of culture that views schemata, or cultural conceptualisations to use his terminology, as complex emergent systems which are not static but are constantly negotiated and renegotiated. Additionally, both Riley and Sharifian are concerned with the ideological and power issues of different knowledge structures in communication; an area that was absent from many earlier theories. Gee (2008) also provides an example of thinking on culture that combines cognitive cultural models, with discourse and ideology with an explicit focus on power relationships. However, genuine differences still exist between theories of culture in the extent to which culture is seen as internal and intrapersonal or external and interpersonal, and as with structuralist accounts, if culture should be approached as systematic and structured or as a situated practice. Nonetheless, it seems likely that any theory of culture will need to take account of internal cognitive processes, whether or not we find it productive to refer to them as culture.

In sum, viewing culture as a product, a thing, a container or a structure is problematic. It can easily result in overly-deterministic and essentialist portrayals of culture and cultural difference. It overlooks much of the negotiated, contested, changeable and situated nature of culture. However, outside of academia it is often the most common understanding and use of the idea of culture where cultures are typically associated with defined national groupings who share a set of common characteristics (Piller 2011: 14) and culture is almost treated like a material entity that can be measured and divided. Significantly it is the product approach, frequently alongside national correlations, that is most prominent in L2 language teaching. A product characterisation of culture is especially problematic for intercultural communication and ELF research as cultures and cultural identifications are not easily or clearly delineated in such communicative scenarios. However, important issues have been raised in this discussion as to the extent to which we can view culture as a system, both in the generic sense and in the particular sense related to specific cultures (national or otherwise). Issues have also arisen concerning the location of culture, internally as cognitive conceptualisations or externally as social practice. Given the dynamic nature of intercultural communication and ELF, as outlined in the previous chapters, it is likely that less static and more fluid approaches to culture will be most productive in addressing these issues. It is to such poststructuralist understandings of culture that we now turn.

3.1.3 Culture as discourse

Just as discourse has been influential in intercultural communication and applied linguistics more generally so too has a view of culture as constructed in and through discourse. It must be noted that in many ways discourse is as large, complex and diffuse a term as culture with many different interpretations and uses. However, it is not the aim of this chapter to provide a detailed account of discourse. For the purposes of this discussion, and similar to Scollon, Scollon and Jones' (2012: 8) interdiscourse approach, discourse will be viewed from the perspective of 'Discourse with a capital D' (Gee 2008). Following this, discourse is given a broad interpretation in which we can discuss the discourse of particular domains such as the 'discourse of education', the 'discourse of globalisation' or the 'discourse of ELF'. It is important to state at the beginning that discourse is not the same as language. We can express the same discourse in different languages, for example the discourse of environmentalism has spread globally and occurs in a range of languages. Nonetheless, while language, discourse and culture are not synonymous, the links between them are close.

A leading proponent of this approach in applied linguistics is Kramsch (1993; 1998; 2009) who defines culture as "1 Membership in a discourse community that shares a common social space and history, and a common system of standards for perceiving, believing, evaluating, and acting. 2 The discourse community itself. 3 The system of standards itself." (1998: 127). A discourse community is, according to Kramsch, made of members of a social group who not only share a languages but "also the topics they chose to talk about, the way they present information, the style with which they interact" (ibid: 7). To this she adds a second dimension which is the historical perspective. Any cultural practices which can currently be identified have come about through the socially sedimented memories of those who are part of the culture, "the culture of everyday practices draws on the culture of shared history and traditions." (ibid). These two dimensions of culture, the social (synchronic) and the historical (diachronic) respectively, are similar in many ways to the earlier structuralist accounts of culture (and indeed make use of the same Saussurian terms on which they were based). However, Kramsch adds a third dimension, that of common imaginings. The cultural imagination is, argues Kramsch, crucial to the way in which we shape and view our cultural reality. In addition, the discourse communities themselves and their shared histories are to a large extent imagined communities. Furthermore, and also unlike structuralist accounts, Kramsch emphasises the critical dimension to culture, "culture, as a process that both includes and excludes, always entails the exercise of power and control" (ibid: 8). Thus, what are accepted as the 'common' values and beliefs, what history is remembered and what imaginings are deemed worthy are issues of struggle and conflict. Linked to this, cultural discourses are also used to distinguish between insiders and outsiders, those who are considered part of the culture and those who are not. Therefore, the contested nature of culture results in an understanding of culture as "fundamentally heterogeneous and changing" (ibid: 10) again marking a departure from structuralist accounts of culture.

Scollon, Scollon and Jones (2012) are another group of influential researchers who take a discourse approach to understanding culture. As noted at the beginning of this chapter, Scollon, Scollon and Jones (2012) question whether the notion of culture is too broad and diffuse to be of use to researchers of intercultural communication. While they do not reject the term culture and acknowledge that it may be a useful heuristic (2012: 3), given the multiple interpretations of the term and the dangers of reification, they suggest instead the term discourse system. A discourse system is defined as "a 'cultural toolkit' consisting of four main kinds of things: ideas and beliefs about the world, conventional ways of treating other people, ways of communicating various kinds of texts, media and 'languages', and methods of learning how to use these other tools" (2012: 8). Examples of such discourse systems include: systems related to small localised groups such as families; larger discourse systems related to gender, sexuality, generation, and profession; and more overtly ideological discourse systems such as Utilitarian discourse systems, associated with capitalism, and Confucian discourse systems. They make an important distinction between discourse communities and communities of practice and discourse systems. While the former refer to bounded groups of people the later refers to the "broader systems of communication in which members of communities participate" (Scollon, Scollon and Jones 2012: 9).

Thus, instead of analysing intercultural communication as communication across cultures they advocate an *interdiscourse* approach in which the analysis focuses on participants' use of different discourse systems. This, the authors claim, allows for a more flexible approach in which people are not reduced to their membership of particular countries or ethnicities as in structuralist approaches. Instead the complexity of intercultural, or interdiscourse, communication is recognised with people simultaneously participating in many different discourse systems and with discourse systems cutting across the traditional boundaries of cultural analysis. Just as importantly people are not controlled by discourse systems which distinguishes them from structuralist accounts which view individuals as controlled by cultural structures. Discourse systems provide a set of tools used in communication and while to a certain extent they put limits on what can and cannot be communicated they can also be appropriated and adapted for different purposes. Given this extra level of flexibility in discourse approaches to culture this is a perspective that is likely to be better suited to understanding culture through ELF than structuralist accounts.

3.1.4 Culture as practice

Closely related to the notion of culture as discourse, is the idea of culture as practice. Again there is a large literature on practice which will not all be explored in detail here. Put in its simplest terms this perspective on culture views culture as something we 'do' rather than something we 'have'. This has been most memorably expressed through Street's (1993) notion of 'culture as a verb' which shifts the focus from the static view of culture associated with a noun to the more active and process orientated view associated with a verb. Risager (2006) outlines how practice approaches have positioned themselves in opposition to structuralist perspectives and culture as a system. Rather than using analogies from structuralist linguistics to describe culture, according to Risager (2006: 48), influences were drawn from practice-orientated linguistic philosophy such as Wittgenstein. Thus, seeing culture as practice focuses not on the systematic nature of culture but on how "the symbols are created and recreated in 'the negotiation' between people in interaction" (Risager 2006: 49). Culture is here viewed as constructed and subjective. It is also not reducible to individuals, since it is inherently intersubjective. In other words, the construction of cultural practices can only take place through interaction. Such a process orientated view of culture leads to characterisations that are complex, multiple, partial, contradictory and dynamic. Cultures can also be approached from this perspective at many different levels or scales as we are able to examine the construction of national cultures, ethic cultures, regional cultures, work cultures, family cultures and so forth, without contradiction.

Holliday (2011; 2013) proposes a theory of culture related to applied linguistics that views culture as a constructed social practice. Holliday makes use of social action theory in which culture is a 'negotiated process' and a 'trajectory of action' (2011: 58–59). While Holliday does not deny the influence of social structure and dominant discourses in the formation of culture, he also emphasises the importance of personal trajectories in which culture is more expressive and negotiated. In contrast to structuralist notions of culture there is 'messy complexity' and 'indefinite movement' between more established and more personal constructions of culture (2011: 59). For Holliday then culture is both product/created and production/creating. A key part of Holliday's understanding of culture is the notion of small cultures (1999; 2011; 2013). Small cultures are defined as "cultural environments which are located in proximity to the people concerned. There are thus small social groupings or activities wherever there is cohesive behaviour, such as families, leisure and work groups, where people form rules for how to behave which will bind them together." (2013: 3). Holliday believes that the creation of small cultures is a universal cultural process that we all continuously engage in and that, furthermore, it is from small cultures that all other cultural groupings (e.g. nations) develop. Part of the construction of small cultures involves the 'routinisation' (Holliday 2013: 49), or, in terms more commonly used in practice theories, social sedimentation, of particular repeated social practices which become the cultural practices of a cultural grouping. For Holliday cultural practices are defined "as ways of doing something which relate to particular cultural environments" (Holliday 2013: 6). These include much of our everyday behaviour such as eating, washing and communicating, and they are the central part of cultural identity; although, we may not always be consciously aware of them. Equally crucial for Holliday is that it is cultural practices that are used to distinguish between cultures, "they are often the things we think of when describing 'a culture' as being different from another" (Holliday 2013: 6).

Somewhat surprisingly, and in contrast to many theories of practice, Holliday locates cultural practices in the artefact and product domain of his 'grammar of culture' (Holliday 2013: 6). This association with product would suggest a more static view of cultural practices to that outlined at the beginning of this section. However, Holliday (2011; 2013) while recognising that we are to an extent constrained by existing social structure which restricts the cultural practices we can engage in, also allows for negotiation and dialogue with dominant structures. Through social action theory, Holliday claims, we can see how personal trajectories generate this dialogue, and also conflict with dominant cultural structures, as "individuals construct and struggle with culture" (2013: 165). Holliday thus highlights an important tension in viewing culture as practice. The tension between the amount of freedom individuals have to negotiate and construct cultural practices and the limitations imposed by already sedimented or routinized cultural practices. This tension also underscores the importance of the sociohistoric dimension from which current practices emerge, as mentioned in earlier discourse approaches, in our understanding of cultural practices and how they are constructed.

There is clearly a large degree of overlap in the characterisation of culture as practice with the notion of culture as discourse to the extent that Pennycook (2010) asks if practice can be seen 'as the new discourse'. However, neither Pennycook nor Holliday see them as synonymous and Holliday makes a number of distinctions between them. For Holliday discourses are a cultural 'product' like practices but they are not actions themselves; rather they are ways of using language to think about and organise ideas about culture (2013: 101). Discourse "can draw people into adopting and conforming to cultural practices. This can result in a loss of agency, hiding and cutting off other practices, or encouraging the adoption of beneficial practices" (2013: 124). Therefore, what we think about culture in general, and particular cultures, depends on the different discourses of culture we are part of. This would suggest that discourse and practice are to some extent at different 'levels' and this is the position that Pennycook (2010) adopts. For Pennycook practice can be seen as "the meditating level, the middle ground, the meso-political, between broad social categories and micro events" (2010: 127). These broad social categories are equated with the 'Big D' discourses, discussed earlier, and would include discourses of culture. Pennycook further claims that viewing language as a local practice "gives us a more useful way of thinking about culture" (2010: 108) that allows us to see language practices as closely tied to cultural practice, but not synonymous. In other words, cultural practice does not have to be linguistic practice, and vice-versa, and importantly we are not tied to essentialist nation, culture, language correlations. Similar distinctions between language, discourse and culture are also drawn by Risager (2006) and this topic will be returned to in the discussion of language and culture.

3.1.5 Culture as ideology

Part of both discourse and practice approaches have been critical perspectives on culture in which culture's multiple and contested nature is recognised. In particular the notion of cultural as ideology is often drawn on, for example Piller states that "Culture is an ideological construct called into play by social actors to produce and reproduce social categories and boundaries, and it must be the central research aim of a critical approach to intercultural communication to understand the reasons, forms and consequences of calling cultural difference into play." (2011: 16). Similarly, Gee writes that

> Cultural models are not all wrong or all right. In fact, like all models, they are simplifi-cations of reality. They are the ideology through which we all see our worlds. In that sense, we are all both "beneficiaries" and "victims" of ideology, thanks to the fact that we speak a language and live in culture. But we can – or at times are morally obligated to – interrogate our cultural models and replace them with others, sometimes even with explicit and well developed theories. Ultimately, these new theories are models too, but, we hope, better ones. (2008: 29).

For both Piller and Gee then it is crucial that any cultural construction or model we use is questioned and interrogated. However, as Gee (2008) makes clear, this is not to suggest that some cultural characterisations are ideological and others not. All understanding of culture whether, for example, everyday folk theories, structuralist or poststructuralist are ideological. What is important is that as researchers interested in culture one must be explicit about the ideology that underlies the particular construction of culture that is being used.

Seeing culture as ideology also brings up interesting questions about whether different conceptions of culture are superior to others, returning us to the earlier concerns of hierarchical notions of culture. This is not simply a matter of devel-oping ever more powerful theories of culture for research but concerns questions of the superiority, or otherwise, of certain values and ways of understanding the world. The quotation from Gee clearly suggests that there are 'better ones' to be developed and he is not alone in interpreting ideology and culture in this way. Bauman, in a critique of current political interpretations of multicultural-ism in Europe, argues that the cultural relativism of multiculturalism entrenches otherness and erects barriers between communities in which the status and levels of privilege of different groups are explained "as a condition which should not be interfered with, in deference to its venerable cultural values" (2010: 48). This, Bauman argues, provides a convenient culturalist (and racist) excuse for the dominance of particular groups over others. Instead of a relativist position on culture in which there is a right to all beliefs, Bauman advocates a right to dialogue "in the course of which the merits and defects of the differences under consideration can be discussed and (with any luck) an agreement on their recog-nition can be reached." (2010: 95). Such a viewpoint, he believes, offers an alter-native to both "oppressive homogenisation – and on the other, the high-handed and soulless indifference of non-engagement." (2010: 95). However, dialogue in-volving potentially homogenising cultural ideologies is not without difficulties of the most extreme kind. Eagleton, recognising Said's insight that "culture can even be a battleground on which causes expose themselves to the light of day and contend with one another" (1985: xiv), argues that current conceptualisations of culture have become a political issue in which "culture as sign, image, meaning, value, identity, solidarity and self-expression is the very currency of political combat ... In Bosnia or Belfast, culture is not just what you put on the cassette player; it is what you kill for" (Eagleton 2000: 38).

A less dramatic, but equally important point, in relation to intercultural communication is made by Piller (2011). Although Piller does not focus on problems of moral and ethical relativism or fundamentalism, as in Bauman's and Eagleton's arguments, she raises similar concerns about the manner in which culture is used to suppress certain groups and how "In some contexts, racism disguised as objective assessments of cultural competence or linguistic proficiency serves to justify social exclusion, particularly unfair access to desirable employment." (2011: 142). She goes on to argue that it is crucial that any attempt to investigate cultural difference does so from the perspective of social justice rather than using culture as a convenient and 'lazy' explanation for observed differences (2011: 172). This entails recognises cultural differences as a manifestation of inequality and material differences. For Piller, linguistic differences are a central part of such inequalities

> In thrall to a cultural worldview, we see culture where linguistic proficiency and communicative competence (or their lack), and inequality and injustice would explain much more (...) It is only by insisting on shining the spotlight on the material-linguistic basis of communication that we can maintain the intellectual and moral integrity of exposing 'culture' as a pretext for exclusion and injustice. (2011: 173).

This obviously links back to the earlier discussion in chapter two concerning the dangers of essentialism and simplistic, stereotyped views of others in intercultural communication. In particular the correlation between nation and culture is especially problematic. A critical approach to our understanding of culture involves uncovering the ideology that underlies attempts to construct a coherent narrative of national culture, a consideration of which groups' interests are served by such ideologies and a recognition of alternative groups and ideologies that are excluded. It is important though that we do not simplify the notion of ideology and present it in an overly deterministic and structuralist manner. Ideology is not just imposed by powerful groups on passive powerless groups and neither is it fixed and unnegotiable. Both Holliday (2011; 2013) and Piller (2011) illustrate how essentialist and othering discourses and ideologies are adopted by those being othered. For example, Piller (2011: 120–125) examined Filipino 'mail-order bride' websites in which Filipino women presented themselves in a manner that reinforced the stereotypes of Asian and particularly Filipino women. Piller believes that such examples show how material and gender inequalities are shifted into discourses of essentialised cultural difference.

However, this perspective does not only apply to national conceptions of culture. Again in chapter two we saw how Holliday's (2011; 2013) and Kramsch's more recent writing (2009; 2010) have been critical of the reification of hybridity and third place cultures without proper consideration of the ideologies that lie behind them. This is clearly expressed in the following quotation from Kumarava-divelu drawing on his own experiences of living in India and the US.

> Proponents of cultural hybridity would expect me to create a 'third culture', or a 'third space', without allowing either my inherited Indian culture or my learned American culture to fully determine my values and beliefs (...) I do not believe I am dangling in cultural limbo. Instead I believe I live in several cultural domains at the same time – jumping in and out of them, sometimes with ease and sometimes with unease (2008: 5)

Kumaravadivelu goes on to note that such cultural complexity is part of all of our lives. If culture is no longer solely associated with nationalist ideologies, then we are all members of multiple cultures and continually engaged in 'jumping in and out' of different cultural domains.

3.2 Culture, nation and globalisation

3.2.1 Characterisations of nation

As should now be apparent, one of the major ideologies underlying much discourse on culture revolves around national ideologies that construct a powerful link between nation states and national cultures, which is also frequented correlated to a national language. This has already been discussed in relation to stereotyping and essentialism in intercultural communication and also in in reference to product approaches to culture that view culture as a thing possessed by nations. Anderson's (2006) theory of 'imagined communities' has been very influential in conceptualising the link between culture and nation. For example, this was referred to earlier in Kramsch's (1998) definition of culture as partly an imagined community with shared creative and historical imaginings. Anderson explains the imagined nature of nation in the following manner, "It is *imagined* because members of even the smallest nation will never know most of their follow-members, meet them, or even hear of them, yet in the minds of each lives the image of their communion." (2006: 6). Of course, that nations are imagined into being does not diminish their power but it does enable us to examine the underlying mythology or ideology of particular constructions of nation and culture. As Anderson goes on to explain, "by proposing the concept of 'imagined community' *IC* juxtaposed paradoxically a kind of *gemeinschaft* attractive to all nationalists with something unsettling, neither 'imaginary' as in 'unicorn', nor matter-of-factly 'real' as in 'TV set'." (2006: 225). Anderson argues that the development of national ideologies was closely tied to language and in particular the standardisation of language through the printing press. However, Anderson has been critiqued for taking a simplistic and essentialist view of language in failing to adequately account for the equally ideological construction of standard languages (Joseph 2004). This is a critique that is of relevance to the discussion here as intercultural communication research, such as Hofstede (1991), repeatedly conflates nation, culture and language with the latter category in particular frequently ignored or treated unproblematically. Therefore, it is essential that we treat notions of language (returned to in section 3.4 on language and culture) in the same critical manner as culture and nation. Nonetheless, Anderson's notion of imagined community has proved powerful in considering how nations and cultures are constructed. Furthermore, as Joseph (2004: 125) concludes, Anderson is right to highlight the importance of language alongside political and economic factors in this process.

Building on Anderson's theory of imagined communities, Billing's (1995) 'banal nationalism' has been equally influential. Billing defines banal nationalism as "the ideological means by which nation-states are reproduced" (1995: 6). Here the focus is not so much on the construction of nations but on how they are maintained and reproduced in our everyday lives. Billing draws attention to the way in which nationalism and the nation is an unnoticed, and hence banal, part of our daily social practices and landscape. Examples include the presence of national flags on buildings, national images on coins and bank notes, weather forecasts which are confined to national borders, and of course the maps that delineate those national borders. All of this seeks to normalise the nation and hide its constructed and temporary nature, "an ideological pattern in which 'our' nationalism ... is forgotten: it cease to appear as nationalism, disappearing into the 'natural environment of 'societies'" (Billing 1995: 38). As Piller notes, while the discourses of nationalism usually originate from the political institutions that constitute the state, including education, they "are then taken up by non-state actors and become enmeshed with a range of discourses that at first glance have nothing to do with nationalism at all, such as the jokes and intercultural communication advice" (2011: 60). As with Anderson's imagined communities, national language is an important element of banal nationalism both in uniting all those who 'share' the national language and in distinguishing those who share a different language. Again we can see how through banal nationalism the nation, language and culture become unconsciously conflated. This is a conflation that becomes reproduced in concepts of culture in intercultural communication and, to return to Piller's earlier point, results in "intercultural communication advice as another instance of banal nationalism, a discourse that reinforces readers' sense of national belonging rather than one that leads them to genuinely engage with difference and diversity." (2011: 65).

Risager draws a useful distinction between political and ethnic conceptions of the national (2007: 14). She categories imagined communities and banal nationalism as political understandings of nation in which "the building of a nation consisted in creating a common citizenship, based on a common political, legal and economic (state) system, a common culture (including a 'myth-symbol complex'), a common religion and a common language, beginning with a common standard written language." (2007: 15). This is the model typically followed in Western Europe but also spread around the world e.g. India. In contrast the ethnic concept of nation does not begin with the political institution of the state but is based on the idea of "a collective name, a common myth of descent, a shared history, a distinctive shared culture, an association with a specific territory, a sense of solidarity" (Smith 1986: 22, cited in Risager 2007: 22). Central and Eastern European countries previously ruled by dynasties such as the Habsburgs are given as examples of such nations. While imagining a shared culture is a powerful aspect of the ideology of both national systems, Risager believes the ethnic system is particularly pervasive in furthering the ideology of an inseparable national language and (ethnic) culture. This distinction between ethnic and political concepts of nation is particularly important in relation to current understandings of globalisation and the transnational, as while political conceptions of nation are territorially bound, ethnic cultural communities are not.

3.2.2 Characterisations of globalisation

Globalisation is often presented as undermining the place of nations in social systems and hence the role of nations in cultural characterisations. Although there is no agreed upon definition of globalisation, and I do not intend to attempt one here, it is important to provide an outline of what is envisioned by making use of the term. Firstly, it should be stated that globalisation is not anything in itself rather it is a useful umbrella term to refer to a number of interrelated processes. Those processes have been defined in different ways according to various theoretical and practical orientations. Scholte (2008) offers a characterisation of globalisation that encompasses a range of relevant perspectives while simultaneously underscoring what globalisation as a term adds to our understanding of social relations. He characterises globalisation as "the spread of transplanetary

– and in recent times also more particularly supraterritorial – connections between people. From this perspective, globalisation involves reductions in barriers to transworld social contacts. People become more able – physically, legally, linguistically, culturally and psychologically – to engage with each other wherever on earth they might be." (2008: 1478). The central aspect of this, and what prevents globalisation from becoming a hollow concept, is a qualitative and quantitative change in the nature of social space. This, Scholte argues, distinguishes globalisation from terms such as internationalisation, liberalisation, universalisation and westernisation, all of which are descriptions of processes which have been long established and do not require any new thinking in regard to social space or relations. In contrast supraterritorial connections, which are described as "transworld simultaneity (that is, they extend anywhere across the planet at the same time) and transworld instantaneity (that is, they move anywhere on the planet in no time)" (2008: 1480), cannot be mapped on to traditional territorial spaces. Thus, "globalisation has constituted more than an extension of the compression of time relative to territorial space that has unfolded over a number of past centuries." (2008: 1480). The instant movement around the globe of currencies such as the US dollar or Euro, a call centre in India processing data for a customer in the US, or global sports events watched simultaneously around the globe are all given as examples of supraterritorial connections.

However, Scholte adds some important caveats to this. While he argues that the scale and scope of supraterritorial connections are a particular feature of the present time and a break from previous more territorially defined social spaces, he acknowledges that territory itself is a concept that rose to prominence over the last two or three centuries, culminating during the nineteenth century period of colonialism. Furthermore, he is not suggesting that territorial spaces have become irrelevant, as we shall examine further in relation to nationalism and globalisation, but their role has changed. Additionally, the transplanetary connections, as opposed to supraterritorial connections, that are also a major part of globalisation have a longer tradition and so represent less of a paradigm changing phenomena. Importantly, and as stated at the start of this discussion of globalisation, Scholte cautions against reification of the global noting that "While globality is a discrete concept, it is not a discrete concrete condition." (2008: 1493). There is not a physical global domain by itself, rather the global involves the interconnections between various local, regional and national domains. How these different domains come together is not discussed by Scholte but it will later be suggested that the notion of global flows can aid in envisaging this.

Scholte's notion of the supraterritorial can be viewed as analogous to Blommaert's (2010) concept of *geocultural* globalisation. Geocultural globalisation refers to "the emergence of new communication technologies, increasing and intensified global capitalist processes of accumulation and division of labour, and increased and intensified global inequalities resulting in new migration flows" (2010: 13–14). These are distinct from *geopolitical* globalisation which is an older and deeper process, according to Blommaert, involving a capitalist expansion which took hold in the nineteenth century and "affects the deep social, political and economic fabric of societies" (2010: 13). Blommaert's perspective agrees with that of Scholte in characterising geocultural globalisation as taking place at a different scope, speed and intensity to geopolitical globalisation, and as affecting social structures. However, Blommaert argues that geocultural changes are not fundamentally different from the longer geopolitical changes and that they should be regard as a phase in the more long term geopolitical processes of globalisation. Block (2012), adopting a similar perspective to Blommaert, is critical of applied linguistics more generally in focusing on cultural approaches to globalisation (or the geocultural to use Blommaert's term) at the cost of the material, political and economic aspects and so only producing a partial picture.

There are clearly genuine differences in these approaches as to the extent to which we are currently experiencing a paradigm shift in social structures and relationships and this is a question that only hindsight will resolve. However, the differences are also, to an extent, related to questions of emphasis and focus. Block (2012) may be right to question what he sees as the exclusive concern with culture and to suggest that applied linguistics might benefit from further study of the political, economic, and class issues related to globalisation. Yet, in a field as interdisciplinary as applied linguistics there is a danger of elevating one theoretical perspective above all others. Following Widdowson's (1980: 2000) notion of *applied* linguistics, rather than linguistics applied, we need to adopt and adapt different theoretical perspectives depending on the issues investigated. Thus, researchers should eschew imposing particular theoretical frameworks, linguistic or otherwise, a priori on all issues of language and communication. Given the concerns of this book clearly the cultural dimensions to globalisation are of primacy. This does not have to be ahistorical though, as Blommaert and Block believe, neither does it entail ignoring material inequalities or concerns with social justice as scholars such as Piller (2011) and Holliday (2011; 2013) have shown.

3.2.3 Global flows

As already suggested in chapter two the notion of transnational and transcultural flows is particularly productive when examining the cultural dimensions to globalisation and in turn the influence globalisation has had on conceptions of culture. To summarise what was presented in chapter two, the concepts of transnational and transcultural flows have their origin in sociology and anthropology in the theories of Appadurai (1996) and Hannez (1996). Hannez through the concept of the *global ecumene* attempts to analyse "the interconnected of the world, by way of interactions, exchanges and related developments, affecting not least the organization of culture" (1996: 7). To do this he makes use of four frameworks of cultural flow: *forms of life*, consisting of everyday social practices which are decentred and disorganised; *the state*, referring to the more deliberate and asymmetrical flow from the state to its subjects; *the market* related to commodified culture from buyer to seller, again organised; and *the movement* related to social and cultural movements such as environmentalism or religious movements which are typically organised and centrifugal (1996: 69–70). Appadurai identifies five *flow scapes: ethnoscapes* or flows of people; *technoscapes* or flows technology; *financescapes* or flows of money; *mediascapes* or flows of information; and *ideoscapes* or flows of ideas (1996: 32–33). Both scholars emphasise the interconnectedness and networks of social relations that characterise contemporary societies and the resultant complexity of cultural systems and practices. However, neither suggests that the nation state will disappear as a cultural focus to be replaced by a transnational culture. Instead they document the changing role of the nation as just one aspect of cultural identity among a multitude of others. Appadurai writes that "What I would like to propose is that we begin to think of the configuration of cultural forms in today's world as fundamentally fractal, that is, as possessing no Euclidean boundaries, structures, or regularities." (1996: 46). Interestingly he goes on to suggest that chaos theory may offer a way of understanding this new conception of culture. Although he does not elaborate on this point, the potential for complexity and chaos theory to deepen our understanding of culture will be the focus of the next section.

In applied linguistics the metaphor of global cultural flows has been most extensively explored by Risager (2006; 2007) and Pennycook (2007), as previously noted. Risager (2006; 2007) believes that we need to move from a national to a transnational paradigm in thinking about language and culture. From a global perspective we can view languages as spreading across cultures and cultures as spreading across languages in networks of linguistic and cultural flows (2006: 2). These notions will be returned to in the exploration of the link between language and culture and particularly in relation to linguaculture and the language-culture nexus and so will not be elaborated on in more detail here. Pennycook also utilises the metaphor of flows to explore Global Englishes and hip-hop, writing that "Transcultural flows therefore refer not merely to the spread of particular forms of culture across boundaries, or the existence of supercultural commonalities (cultural forms that transcend locality), but rather to the processes of borrowing, blending, remaking and returning, to processes of alternative cultural production." (2007: 6). For Pennycook, then, globalisation does not replace the local, or national, but rather results in the need to examine the way the local is connected in complex ways with global flows of cultural forms. Pennycook argues that metaphors of flow, movement and spatial frames of 'trans' theories, and of particular relevance to this discussion, transculturality, move us beyond the unhelpful dichotomies of local/global, national/transnational. This enables us to explore alternative spaces of cultural production, or existing spaces that have been ignored, and "allows us to get beyond the question of uniformization or particularization, and opens up an understanding of cultural movement" (2007: 47). The idea of culture as movement and change is a crucial one and will be brought up again in relation to complexity theory.

While the notion of global cultural flows, the transnational, transcultural and supraterritorial are all productive ways of imagining culture on a global scale, we need a degree of caution in our interpretation of the implications. I would not, therefore, agree with Piller that "They [globalisation and transnationalism] demonstrate quite clearly that nation-based ways of approaching intercultural communication have become obsolete." (2011: 72) and neither would many of the authors cited here. Nation states have not disappeared and, as Holliday (2011; 2013) demonstrates vividly, they still exercise a powerful pull on cultural identifications "it is a fact that people everywhere really do use, talk about, explain things in terms of, and present themselves with national cultural profiles, despite their lack of scientific basis means (sic). These profiles are therefore *real* in their minds and have to be taken seriously." (2013: 164). Nonetheless, the increased interconnectedness brought about by the processes of globalisation, whether we see this as a new phase in an old process or a paradigm change in social structures, means we need to recognise that national cultures, however we might chose to characterise them, are just one scale or level in the complex multitude of cultural characterisations or systems we take a part in.

3.3 Culture and complexity

It is hardly surprising given the multiple accounts of culture presented so far that many writers on the subject come to the conclusion that culture is complex. Firstly, in the general sense of the term this is typically taken to mean that culture is multiple, on many levels or scales, contested, and fluid. This was a perspective that united characterisations of culture as discourse, practice and ideology and distinguished them from previous structuralist accounts of culture and it was also a theme that ran through examinations of culture and globalisation. Secondly, there is a more technical use of the term complex associated with the concept of complex adaptive systems, chaos and emergence. This second use of the term complex provides an especially powerful heuristic for thinking about culture. In particular it offers an approach to culture that reconciles the tensions between post-modernist and poststructuralist (or whatever other term is chosen from the plethora in current use) accounts of cultures and the more systematic and structured accounts of culture. From post-modernist perspective culture is always fragmented and partial, often to such an extent that culture is no longer discussed but is replaced by discourse, ideology and identification. In contrast more systematic accounts of culture view it as a product, practice and process, which is shared, recognisable and hence describable. Complexity theory, I suggest, offers not a middle way between these two approaches, but a view of culture in which it can be both these things at the same time.

Before providing a brief characterisation of complexity theory a number of important caveats are needed. Complexity and chaos theory were developed in the physical sciences and mathematics rather than in relation to the social sciences. Clearly there are significant differences between physical systems such as in physics, chemistry and biology and social systems. While, from a relativist position, it may be possible to argue over the degree to which physical systems are dependent on human actions and perceptions of them, it seems unlikely that anyone would argue that social systems are independent from human perceptions or actions. We therefore need to be mindful when taking notions and metaphors from one field and applying it to another least we misrepresent and restrict our investigations. As Seargeant cautions when discussing the multidisciplinary nature of linguistics more generally,

> To become an object of scientific investigation it is necessary that that object be delimited and have boundaries imposed upon it, but with such regulation comes the danger of partialism, of ignoring the holistic picture (albeit out of practical necessity) in favour of something more manageable. The result is an object of study refracted by different disciplines, each of which attempts to animate an isolated feature while (temporarily) numbing the rest of the organism. (2010: 1)

Furthermore, complexity theory is not presented here as a means of modelling culture mathematically, or otherwise, as has been the case with other social systems (for example Miller and Page 2007). Models are of course useful abstractions and simplifications for researchers but culture, as characterised so far, would seem too large, complex and diffuse to be susceptible to useful abstractions in the form of models. However, as a metaphor, lens or heuristic the central features of complexity theory, as outlined below, provide a productive way of thinking about culture. As long as we do not confuse our metaphors with reality, as Baird, Baker and Kitazawa argue, "Metaphors provide valuable conceptual tools in focusing and organising theoretical and empirical research" (2014: 179). Thus complexity theory can be seen as a meta-theory for how we might approach theories of culture. The use of complexity theory, metaphorically, does not entail strictly following the principles of complex adaptive systems or chaos theory, but rather, following Blommaert, "I use complexity as a perspective, not as a compulsory vocabulary or theoretical template. It offers me a freedom to imagine, not an obligation to submit." (2013: 10).

Complexity theory has been defined in a number of different ways depending on the field of enquiry to which it has been applied but for the purposes of this discussion the following characterisation from Miller and Page offers an illuminating introduction to the ideas.

> At the most basic level the field of complex systems challenges the notion that by perfectly understanding the behaviour of each component part of a system we will then understand the system as a whole. One and one may well make two, but to really understand two we must know both about the nature of "one" and the meaning of "and". (2007: 3)

Here Miller and Page succinctly sum up a number of key features of complex systems. Firstly, that we need to approach complex systems holistically; individual components do not explain and are not synonymous with the whole system. Secondly, relationships between parts of the system are integral to the system; the 'and' is as important as the 'one'. Another fundamental feature of complexity theory is that the components and the relationships between them are constantly in change. As Cilliers explains we must pay attention to "the relationary nature of complexity, and especially to the continuous shifting of those relationships. Any acknowledgement of complexity will have to incorporate these shifts and changes, not as epiphenomena, but as constitutive of complex systems." (1998: 112). Thus, complex systems are dynamic systems that are continuously undergoing change and adaptation. In addition to this, small changes in parts of the system can lead to large changes in the overall system.

This notion of nonlinearity, in which the relationship between parts of the system change the system overall, is neatly summed up in Gleick's now famous quotation that "nonlinearity means that the act of playing the game has a way of changing the rules" (1988: 24). Nonlinearity also means that complex systems are never complete due to this constant variation and adaptation. Moreover, "For complex systems to maintain themselves, they must remain open to their environment and change when conditions require it." (Taylor 2001: 156). Taylor here emphasises that just as the relationships between the components within systems are a fundamental part of systems, so the relationships between systems are also crucial to the characteristics of complex systems and result in continuous adaption and change. Thus, complex systems can be viewed as systems within systems in which there is constant interaction and transformation blurring the boundaries between systems and meaning that no two interactions are ever the same as each system will have changed, either marginally or greatly, as the result of previous interactions. Gleick provides another succinct summary of this when in relation to chaos he writes, "to some physicists chaos is a science of process rather than state, of becoming rather than being." (1988: 5).

Closely related to the dynamic and constantly changing nature of complex systems is the other fundamental aspect of complexity theory, emergence. Again Miller and Page offer a useful basic characterisation, "emergence is a phenomenon whereby well-formulated aggregate behaviour arises from localised, individual behaviour" (2007: 45). This is connected to the idea, explained above, that we cannot explain a phenomenon by reducing it to its constituent parts. In other words, "emergence ... occurs only when the activities of the parts do not simply sum to give the activity of the whole" (Holland 1998: 147). This makes reductionist accounts impossible since explanations of each of the individual parts is not the same as an explanation of the system. Furthermore, simple elements and relationships in combination can give rise to complex systems. Both Miller and Page (2007) and Gell-Mann (1994) point out that many different disciplines in modern science rely on the notion of emergence. As Gell-Mann explains it, "One of the great challenges of contemporary science is to trace the mix of simplicity and complexity, regularity and randomness, order and disorder up the ladder from elementary particle physics and cosmology to the realm of complex adaptive systems" (1994: 119–120). However, it is important that we do not confuse these levels on the ladder, as Gell-Mann terms it, with reductionism. Gell-Mann is clear that while higher level complex systems such as culture are dependent on more fundamental systems such as psychology, biology and chemistry, they are not reducible to them. Each level emerges from the previous but at the level of complex adaptive systems there are features that are lost if it is explained in terms related to lower level systems. Therefore, while we can accept that biology offers constraints on human cultures, nobody would expect a full explanation of culture from biology.

It is equally important to note that emergence here does not suggest a final state that *emerges* fully formed from individual components and their relationships. The dynamic nature of complex systems means that they are always in a state of *emerging* but never reaching a final end point. Nonetheless, while nothing is permanently fixed in complex systems, patterns and stabilities do *emerge* from this constant change. Significantly, this order emerges spontaneously from self-organisation rather than external organisation; although, as already discussed, it may be in response to or adaption to other external systems. Such emergent systems are regularly seen in nature in, for example, the behaviour of a flock of birds or the structure of an ant colony. It is these stabilities that allow us to call them systems and study them as such. Larsen-Freeman summarises this range of features of complex systems as follows: "complexity theory seeks to explain complex dynamic, open, adaptive, self-organising, non-linear systems. It focuses on the close interplay between the emergence of structure on one hand and the process of change on the other." (2011: 52).

The parallels between complexity theory and practice and process under-standings of culture seem obvious here, particularly in their focus on dynamism, emergence, openness and non-linearity. Following these earlier approaches and complexity theory, as outlined here, we can conceptualise culture as a complex social system, as opposed to natural system, that emerges through individuals' joint participation in the world giving rise to sets of shared knowledge, beliefs, values, attitudes and practices. This sharedness comes about through the social sedimentation of particular sets or systems of knowledge, beliefs, values, atti-tudes and practices in which repeated usage gives rise to the emergence of norms and patterns. These cultural systems are necessarily intrasubjective and inter-subjective. In other words cultural systems exist in relationship to each other and through interactions between individual components of the system. Relation-ships are thus a crucial part of the system with culture emerging from 'networks' of individual interactions (Taylor 2001), but not being reducible to any one indi-vidual, and also in response and adaptation to other cultural systems. Equally importantly, given the high degree of individual variation, cultures are constantly in change with new knowledge, beliefs, values, attitudes and practices becoming socially sedimented while older ones fall out of use. At the same time this social sedimentation provides a degree of stability. A two way relationship is thus main-tained in which individuals are influenced by the emergent norms and perceived systematicity of culture, while at the same time their individual behaviour results in changes in the overall system. These constant changes or movements that are part of the system mean a full account is never possible and the system is in a constantly emerging state with no fixed end point or clear boundary. Finally, at the risk of repetition, it must be remember that this is not to suggest that culture is a physical system that can be measured; instead, viewing culture as a complex social system provides a useful heuristic for researchers who are interested in culture for whatever purpose.

3.3.1 Culture and complexity in the social sciences and applied linguistics

Despite the revolutionary influence of complexity theory in many fields its impact has not been extensive in the social sciences. As Blommaert writes, "Those ideas are decades old by now, and many of them have become common sense. But not, I observe with regret, in sociolinguistics and many other branches of the human and social sciences" (2013: 10). It may be that much of this is not new in social sciences, as Widdowson notes, "[i]t needs no chaos or complexity theory to tell us that natural phenomena, including human behaviour, are unpredictable, elusive of conceptual control. And yet control them we must ..." (2012: 7). It may also be, in part, due to a reluctance to adopt the discourse of other fields and particularly the natural sciences with their tinge of positivism and reductionism. Yet, as Gleick (1988) argues, chaos and complexity theory make clear the importance of interdisciplinary research in which no scientific field, or system described within it, can be seen in isolation from other systems. Furthermore, complexity theory offers a meta-theory of systems that is much closer to post-modernist and post-structuralist understandings of social phenomena than pervious deterministic structuralist accounts. Taylor explains that "systems and structures – be they biological, social, or cultural – are more diverse and complex than deconstructive critics realize. Emergent self-organizing systems do act as a whole, yet do not totalize. Furthermore, emergence involves an irreducible unpredictability that creates the opportunity for aleatory events." (2001: 155). Similar points are made by Cilliers who argues for the "fruitfulness of combining complexity theory with post-structuralism" (1998: 136) in scientific enquiry. In both quotations the authors underline that in approaching social systems, such as culture, as complex systems we are able view them as complex, multidimensional, dynamic, and irreducible but nonetheless *conceptually control them*, to use Widdowson's terminology, as a recognisable 'whole', even if it is a constantly changing and contested whole. We are thus able to incorporate insights from both post-structuralism and structuralist accounts of culture, while avoiding an overly deterministic explanations of the influence of culture on social structure and action. At the same time we are able to evade the idiosyncratic characterisations, in which 'anything goes', of which post-structuralism and relativism has sometimes been accused.

Although complexity theory has not been explored in as much detail as might be expected in social sciences, and more specifically applied linguistics, it has not been completely ignored. In particular Larsen-Freeman has made extensive use of chaos and complexity theory to explain second language use and learning (e.g. Larsen-Freeman 2002; 2011; Larsen-Freeman and Cameron 2008). However, her perspective is different from one the one taken here in that she goes further than a metaphorical use of complexity and her focus is on language rather than culture. Nonetheless, her research on complexity and language has proved fruitful and she has also explored the links between ELF and language as a complex system (Larsen-Freeman 2014). Within ELF research a number of writers have suggested that language might best be approached as a complex system (Seidlhofer 2011;

Mauranen 2012; Hülmbauer 2013) but with the exception of Baird, Baker and Kitazawa (2014) none have explored the idea in detail and again the focus has been on language rather than culture. Emergentism has been somewhat more influential in applied linguistics and linguistics (e.g. Hopper 1987; 1998; Tomasello 2003, 2008; Bybee 2006; Ellis and Larsen-Freeman 2006; 2009); although, again the emphasis has been generally been on language rather than culture. However, all of these accounts view language from a holistic perspective in which "language cannot be usefully segregated from its ecology" (Larsen-Freeman and Cameron 2008: 79) which would presumably include culture. Indeed, within linguistic anthropology, Tomasello (2008) and more recently Everett (2012) have explored the links between language and culture in detail from an emergentist position and their ideas will be returned to in the discussion of language and culture.

In specific relation to culture, at this time complexity theory and emergence has had very little influence in applied linguistics or intercultural communication research. Two exceptions to this are Sealy and Carter (2004) and Sharifian (2011). Sealy and Carter (2004) adopt a position that is commensurable with much of the discussion here, stating that, "we believe the concepts of emergence and complexity are crucial to explaining social action" (2004: 77). Thus, for Sealy and Carter culture and language are explained as emerging from human interaction in the world but are not reducible to that interaction. They view culture as a system of *propositions* concerning knowledge, beliefs and norms which are distinguished from the *practices* in which people engage (2004: 133). When people act they are able to draw on the cultural systems but they are free to ignore those norms or they may follow the norms but reject the beliefs, i.e. they are acting against their beliefs or concealing their 'true' beliefs. Sealy and Carter also propose that social structures should also be separated from the cultural system as social structures are not necessarily shared or accept by all who may identify with a particular cultural system and neither are the social structures necessarily synonymous with the beliefs and norms of the cultural system. Therefore, "we can distinguish between the members of any given 'culture' and the relationships between: these people as contemporary human actors; the propositions, 'rules', and knowledge that make up the cultural system; and the enduring social relations which structure the context within which the people act" (2004: 137). Each of these systems and sets of rules are seen from a complexity perspective as emergent and open-ended and, of particular relevance to the discussion here, "the inherent complexity and multidimensionality of any proposed account of intercultural communication" is underscored.

However, there are a number of differences between Sealy and Carter's approach to culture, complexity and emergence and the position I wish to outline here. While it is not explicitly stated, Sealy and Carter explore the notions of complexity and emergence in a metaphorical sense but, despite their call for greater theorisation in applied linguistics, do not explore either notion in much depth. Furthermore, their rejection of culture as practice and as individual cognition, combined with their commitment to culture as emergent and intersubjective, leaves them in the rather awkward position of locating culture in a similar manner to Popper's (1992) notion of World 3, in which cultures exist in a separate reality from individuals and the material world (Sealy and Carter 2004: 80–84). However, in the discussion here culture is not seen as separable from the characterisations made by those who use it, whether researchers or everyday folk theories; although, with the crucial caveat that neither is culture reducible to those individual interpretations. Sealy and Carter also appear to conceive of practice in a manner that is synonymous with social action. This is a more limited sense than that described earlier and thus misses an opportunity to further explore the relationship between the micro level of individual actions and macro level of cultural systems, as Pennycook's (2010) notion of practice as the mediating meso-political level does. This also omits one of the key insights of complexity and chaos theory, noted above, concerning the interaction between micro levels and macro levels and the manner in which events at the micro level, which appear random and unordered lead to the emergence of regularities at the macro level. As Gleick explains "Energy in natural systems exists on two levels: the macroscales, where everyday objects can be counted and measured, and the microscales, where countless atoms swim in random motion, unmeasurable … chaotic and near chaotic systems bridged the gap between the macroscales and microscales." (1998: 260). This example clearly refers to the natural sciences and some caution, as already stressed, is needed in transferring these ideas to other fields. For instance, we are not measuring or counting culture. Nevertheless, the resonance with emergentist and complex accounts of language and culture seems clear, with individual interactions appearing random but when aggregated giving rise to enough regularity that we can meaningfully study linguistic or culture 'systems'.

Sharifian (2011) applies complexity theory in a more detailed manner in his cultural cognition and conceptualisations theory of culture. Sharifian's theory of culture is based on cognitive approaches to culture but in adopting a complexity theory position he is able to avoid some of the earlier problems such as an overly static, product orientated perspective and the failure to acknowledge the shared and interactional nature of culture (see section 3.1.2). For Sharifian "Culture groups are formed not just by the physical proximity of individuals but also by relative participation of individuals in each other's' conceptual world." (2011: 4). It is this sharing of a conceptual world that determines membership of a culture. This conceptual world is made up of what Sharifian terms cultural conceptualisations; cultural schemas and categories that comprise a cultural worldview (2011: 5). While his account is clearly cognitive up to this point, he makes an important move away from earlier accounts. He claims that such cultural conceptualisations are distributed and emergent and hence not reducible to any one individual. Individuals may share more or less of the cultural conceptualisations that constitute a cultural system but no individual shares all of the same conceptualisations. This allows individuals to identify to differing degrees with particular cultural systems and of course to identify with multiple cultural systems. Furthermore, these cultural conceptualisations are not static but are constantly changing. Sharifian summarises the difference between his approach and earlier cognitive theories of culture as the follows

> I argue that the cultural conceptualisations ... may best be described in terms of 'distributed representations' across a cultural group. Many accounts of cultural schemas in the literature have treated these conceptualisations as static knowledge that is equally shared by the members of a cultural group. The reality of cultural conceptualisations, however, does not lend itself to such reductionist accounts. Members of a cultural group usually possess various degrees of knowledge/awareness of their cultural conceptualisations (2011: 11)

Sharifian goes on to outline how these emergent cultural conceptualisations can be approached as complex systems through listing a set of parallel properties of complex adaptive systems and culture (2012: 23–24). Firstly, culture, like a complex system, is a whole that is more than the sum of its parts; the distributed cultural conceptualisation of a cultural group is not the property of any individual member of the group. Secondly, culture is part of a system of nested systems, systems within systems, in which the components of a cultural system are themselves complex systems; in Sharifian's example the individuals that make up a cultural group. Thirdly, culture is an open system where boundaries are hard to delineate and usually depend more on "the observer's needs and prejudices than any intrinsic property of the system itself" (2011: 24). The boundaries between one cultural group and another, thus, become difficult to discern. Lastly, the relationship between the system and the components, cultural conceptualisations and the individual, is two way and circular. Individuals' actions are influenced by the cultural cognition of the group but at the same time individuals' actions and cognition influence the cultural cognition of the group.

There is much in Sharifian's theory that is commensurable with the characterisations of culture offered so far, particularly in relation to complexity. However, there are also some significant differences. While Sharifian recognises that culture is distributed across groups of people and includes "their physical environment, artefacts, tools, rituals, paintings, dance, etc ..." (2011: 21), the practice aspect of culture is not developed in any detail. The accounts of culture presented so far have underscored that culture is both cognition and interaction in social practice. Just as individuals' cognition gives rise to the emergent cultural system, so too do individuals' actions and participation in social practices. Sharifian, as with previous cognitive accounts of culture, would appear to overemphasise the cognitive aspect of culture, although not in this case as something within individual minds. However, as researchers of culture it is not only people's cognition that we are interested in, which can be very difficult to access anyway, but also how people do or perform culture in practice.

Like the majority of accounts of culture, Sharifian's shares a perspective on culture in which language is the main medium for the creation and transmission of cultural systems. However, his conceptualisation of the relationship between language and culture proposes that cultural metaphors, categories and schemas are 'inherent' in each system of language (Sharifian 2011: 29). So, for example, there are cultural metaphors and categories that are embedded in the English language. This is highly problematic and renders his theory, in its current form, of limited relevance to the discussions in this book. As will be outlined in detail in relation to linguistic relativity, it is difficult to see how this applies to global languages such as English which are used by a huge range of speakers who would identify themselves, or be identified with, a vast variety of cultures or cultural systems. Indeed, having now outlined various approaches to characterising culture in which it is seen as, above all, a complex (in a number of senses of the term), multiple and dynamic social system, it is now necessary to consider this relationship between culture and language from such a perspective in further depth.

3.4 Culture and language

3.4.1 Linguistic relativity

One of the most widespread conceptions of the relationship between language and culture is linguistic relativity. This is the notion that we experience the world as we do due to the language we speak. According to linguistics relativity our language divides up and categorises the world in particular ways and hence controls the way in which we view the world. Thus, if we see culture in the anthropological sense as a worldview, then culture and language become inseparable since our culture is constructed through language. If this were true this would entail that groups of people who speak different languages have different ways of seeing the world. This idea can be traced back to the Romantic Movement with writers such as Herder and Humboldt proposing an inexorable link between languages and cultures. Similar notions were also developed by Boas (1911) and most prominently by Sapir and Whorf (1939) in what has come to be known as the Sapir-Whorf hypothesis. The Sapir-Whorf hypothesis states that "the "real world" is to a large extent unconsciously built up on the language habits of the group. No two languages are ever sufficiently similar to be considered as representing the same social reality" (Sapir cited in Whorf 1939). There are two interpretations of this hypothesis, the strong form and the weak form. The strong form, also known as linguistic determinism, proposes that our language controls and constrains our worldview. This interpretation has been largely discredited and is clearly wrong. If the strong form was true, and we were only capable of thinking in one particular way due to our first language, then intercultural communication would be impossible as we would never be able to understand the meanings of anyone who had a different first language. It is also not clear how this would account for bilingualism and multilingualism. Indeed, it is not certain that Sapir or Whorf ever argued that this strong view was the case (Zhu 2014: 176).

Much more pervasive has been the weak form of linguistic relativity by which our language influences our thoughts and understanding of the world but does not control it. A great deal of research has been conducted investigating this (see overviews in Lucy 1992; Gumperz and Levinson 1996; Deutscher 2010) and there is a growing body of empirical evidence that different languages do result in different perceptions of aspects of the physical world as well as different ways of conceptualising the world. For example, in what Slobin (1996) refers to as the 'anticipatory effects of language' features of language, such as tense, pluralisation and different semantic categories, may cause a speaker to direct his/her attention to certain aspects of an experience, such as quantity or temporal sequence, in order to be able to linguistically code it later. However, crucially, these aspects of language are influences not constraints. It is possible to learn alternative ways of viewing and categorising the world which are different to those we are socialised into through our first language. So, taking the often used example of colours (Deutscher 2010), while there may be only one word for the colour 'blue' in English and two words in Thai 'see fah' and 'see nam nurghn' it is possible for an English speaker to learn to distinguish two types of blue in this way (indeed simply by adding the modifier 'light' or 'dark' to 'blue' in English a similar distinction is made).

This weak interpretation of linguistic relativity is perhaps not particularly profound; anyone familiar with more than one language or who has had to engage in translation will know the difficulty of translating particular ideas or meanings between different languages. Nonetheless, it reminds us of an important feature of intercultural communication that, as Piller puts it, "different people have different ways of doing things with words. This recognition of the relativity of our own linguistic and communicative practices is really quite liberating" (2011: 40). However, a number of interpretations of the implications of linguistic relativity are more controversial. Of particular relevance to this discussion is the idea that the different ways of categorising and thinking about the world are encoded within the linguistic forms of languages. This view was referred to earlier in relation to Sharifian's (2011) cultural conceptualisations theory and is summed up in the following quotation in relation to English used in intercultural communication "the English language ... carries with it values and beliefs which are hidden in linguistic codes but control from the depths the process of meaning making during human interactions" (Gu, 2009: 140). This interpretation is taken in the extensive work of Wierzbicka (e.g. Wierzbicka 1985; 1997; 2006) who has investigated the manner in which different languages contain particular 'cultural scripts' which are inherent to those languages. As Wierzbicka explains "cultural patterns can be studied in a verifiable and non-speculative way on the basis of linguistic semantics" (1997: 30)". Thus, for instance, through studying words such as 'reasonable' in English or *pošlyj* in Russian, Wierzbicka claims, we can gain an understanding of 'Anglo' (sic) or Russian culture respectively. She goes on to suggest that the implication of this is that there is "an internal cultural baggage" (2006: 312) to language so that "The English that ASEAN has used from the outset as its only language ... is, essentially, Anglo English, and it bears the imprint of the cultural history of the English language." (2006: 312).

Putting aside the research into English use in ASEAN (e.g. Kirkpatrick 2003; 2010a; Deterding and Kirkpatrick 2006) which demonstrates a much greater variety of English use then Wierzbicka seems aware of; there is a more fundamental misunderstanding here. This interpretation of the connection between language and culture seems to be both reifying linguistic forms and mistaking those forms as synonymous with cultural practices. It may well be that for those that are socialised into a particular language which is associated with a particular cultural group, e.g. the Russian language and Russian culture, then the links between the language and the cultural practices appear inseparable. However, as will be explained through the notion of linguaculture, this is an individual perception and link. There is nothing inherent in the linguistic forms of the language itself that 'carries cultural baggage' or cultural scripts. As research into Global Englishes, including both World Englishes and ELF, has shown there is a huge variety in the way English is used and the cultural scripts to which English linguistic forms are put to work. What is shared between users of the language that enables all of them to call it English is still far from established (Seidlhofer 2011; Widdowson 2012; Baird, Baker and Kitazawa 2014) but it seems unlikely that it is shared cultural schemata embedded in the language. This argument also relies on the already critiqued connection between a national language and a national cultural.

Culture and language operate on a number of scales with national being just one of them. The notion of cultural scripts, as used by Wierzbicka, represents a reification of language and culture and a reproduction of banal nationalism, and as such is more likely to be a hindrance to understanding the relationship between language and culture, particularly in the dynamic and negotiated instances of language use in intercultural communication.

Wierzbicka is not alone in drawing such essentialist conclusions about the relationship between language and culture. Both Edwards (2011) and Pennycook (2010) note that linguistic imperialism (Phillipson 1992) relies on similar ideas in assuming that there is something embedded in the English language that gives an advantage to those born in the Anglophone world. In other words, that speaking or writing English forces its users to attempt to think and act like an English native speaker. While few would deny that the use of English leads to a great deal of material and social inequality, this is not inherent in the semantics or syntax of the language. Rather it is a result of the practices and social structures that the language is used to created and represent. It should also be noted that World Englishes and ELF research has also illustrated how English is used to construct practices and social structures which are of benefit to groups other than Anglophone communities. There are also analogous problems in linguistic ecology (e.g. Mühlhäusler 1996), also raised by Pennycook (2010), which assumes that in losing a particular language we lose the cultural practices associated with that language and, just as problematic, that by preserving a language we will preserve the cultural practices. Language loss or death, especially due to domination of more powerful languages, is clearly a problem and there are many reasons we might wish to prevent it. Yet, as with linguistic imperialism, adopting simplistic arguments concerning the relationships between language and culture, such as those associated with more deterministic interpretations of linguistic relativity, are unlikely to provide meaningful engagement with the range of issues in linguistic and cultural loss and change.

3.4.2 Linguaculture and the language-culture nexus

One of the most extensive and detailed considerations of the relationship between language and culture, at least in applied linguistics, comes from the writings of Karen Risager (2006; 2007). Risager, as previously discussed, adopts a number of approaches commensurable with those taken in this book. Firstly, she is critical of simplistic approaches which unreflectively interpret the relationship between language and culture according to banal nationalism in which language, culture and nation are seen as inexorably intertwined. Secondly, Risager argues for a change in focus from the national to the transnational and emphasises the global flows of both language and culture in which they are viewed as connected through complex networks of global relations which are in constant movement. Thirdly, she underscores the complexity of the relationship, eschewing both simplistic nationalistic accounts and also culturally neutral perspectives on languages, while recognising the multiples levels and flows that converge in the relationship. Risager describes, what she terms, 'a cultural view of language' and interprets culture as meaning. She argues that this entails "language as *cultural practice*, as a carrier of various types of meaning, and the intention is to argue that language is never linguaculturally neutral." (2007: 170). Her explanation of this position and characterisation of language and culture is in itself complex and it is not possible to outline all of it here, so I will focus on the two areas of most relevance with some simplification necessary; linguaculture (or languaculture) and the language-culture nexus.

Before discussing these two areas several features of the conceptual framework Risager employs need further explanation. Risager makes an important distinction between a generic and a differential understanding of language and culture. In the generic sense referring to the universal phenomena of language and culture "language and culture are under all circumstances inseparable: human language is always embedded in culture" (2007: 12). The differential sense refers to the range of languages and cultures found in the world and "the question always has to be: What forms of culture actually go with the language in question? And this is an empirical question." (2007: 12). This is a significant move as it recognises that there is always a cultural dimension to language but at the same time allows us to distinguish between particular languages and their relationship to particular forms of culture. Following this argument, and in contrast to stronger interpretations of linguistic relativity, we can see that a particular language such as English is not necessarily linked to English (e.g. British) culture. It is 'an empirical question' what forms of culture 'go with' English.

Another important aspect of Risager's framework is the delineation of three interpretations or perspectives on language. These are:
- the sociological point of view: linguistic practice;
- the psychological point of view: linguistic resources;
- the system-orientated point of view: linguistic system. (Risager 2006: 86)

The first of these perspectives, the sociological point of view is very similar to practice as described earlier in this chapter in relation to culture; in other words, linguistic behaviour that can be observed. The psychological point of view relates to individuals' linguistic resources, which is similar to the idea of linguistic repertoires or even competence, although Risager rejects both these terms (2006:

80–81). Linguistic resources represent the idiolect that an individual develops over their lifetime. The relationship between the sociological and psychological perspective is close and the two often cannot be separated in research. As Risager explains:

> Linguistic practice and linguistic resources in the individual are thus the two necessary and mutually prerequisite forms of existence for language. Linguistic resources can only develop by virtue of linguistic practice, and linguistic practice cannot develop without the presence of linguistic resources in the participants. Linguistic practice represents the basic social function of language, and it is from here we get our empirical data about language. Linguistic resources are no less real but they are not accessible to observation, expect to a certain extent via introspection. (2006: 84)

The final perspective, the system-orientated view of language, is according to Risager a discursive construction and, in contrast to the previous two perspectives, is not a natural loci of language. Instead it is viewed as an ideological construct similar to the ideological constructions of culture given earlier. This three way distinction can be seen as similar, although not identical, to the three level distinction set out by Mauranen (2012) in relation to ELF. The sociological point of view is similar to Mauranen's microsocial perspective in that it relates to linguistic practice. The psychological point of view is similar to the cognitive perspective in its focus on the individual's internal representation and processing of language. However, how this can be characterised is discussed in rather different terms by each author. The system-orientated point of view shares features with Mauranen's macrosocial perspective; although, Risager is more focused on the ideological dimensions to this than Mauranen.

The three levels of analysis and understanding are then transferred by Risager to her interpretation of linguaculture. There is some potential for confusion between the two terms linguaculture and languaculture and Risager makes use of both Friedrich's (1989) notion of linguaculture and Agar's (1994) of languaculture in her formulation; although, she goes beyond these original conceptions in addressing the global roles of languages and cultures, especially as second languages. Additionally, she began by using the term languaculture (2006; 2007) but has more recently used linguaculture (2012), so I too will use linguaculture but treat it as synonymous with languaculture.

As already stated, Risager explores the relationship between language and culture from a position that views language as never culturally neutral but also allows cultures and languages to be separated. To do this Risager argues that "we need at least two different concepts in the interface between language and culture: linguaculture (associated with a particular language) and discourse (always expressed in language, but potentially moving across languages)." (2012: 106).

For Risager, when the links between language and culture are considered what is really being discussed is the link between language and linguaculture. This relationship can be distinguished at the generic and differential level. In the generic sense there is always a linguacultural dimension to language but of more interest is the relationship between particular languages and particular linguacultures. This relationship can be broken into three dimensions: the semantic-pragmatic, the poetic and the identity (2006: 115). These dimensions will not be discussed in detail but basically refer to the content side of language, the expressive aspect of language e.g. art, and language choice and social positioning respectively. Importantly, the distinctions should be seen as analytical and relational and may not be separable in instances of linguistic practice.

Again Risager adopts a sociological, psychological and system-orientated view of linguaculture, proposing that it should be understood as linguaculture in linguistic practice, linguaculture in linguistic resources and linguaculture in the linguistic system (2006: 119). This avoids an essentialist perspective in which the inseparability of language and culture is simply replaced by the inseparability of language and linguaculture. Risager also emphasises the importance of "the idiolectal nature of linguaculture as an aspect of the life history of an individual" (2006: 134). Therefore, the linguaculture that each individual expresses through language will be different and we can expect variation across the two natural loci of linguaculture, the sociological and psychological. At the same time in linguistic practice there will be a degree of structural constraint or normativity and closing down of variation and these enable us to think about the linguaculture associated with particular languages, such as the linguaculture of the English language or Newcastle English, (2006: 115). This is not the same as viewing linguaculture and language as the same though. Risager is clear that in the differential sense languages can be used with different linguacultures and that this is particularly the case when using a language that is not a first language (2006: 134). In such instances the language may be used with a mix or blend of L1 and target language linguacultures (2007: 173).

The next level in Risager's conception of language and culture is discourse, "The concept of discourse may be used as an intermediary concept between the concepts of language/linguaculture and the more general concept of culture". Here discourse is understood in a similar manner to the 'Big D' discourses, described previously, for example Gee (2008) and so will not be presented in detail here. It is associated with particular content areas, for example the discourse of Christianity or colonialism. Although discourse is primarily expressed through language, unlike linguaculture, it is not bound to any particular language or languages. This, Risager believes, leads to double view of intertextuality where "every communicative event may be seen as a confluence of two flows: a linguistic flow in a specific language, and a discursive flow within a specific topic area" (2007: 174). To illustrate this she gives the example of Danish immigrants in a bar in Barcelona discussing the Iraq war. In this instance we see a mix of the transnational flow of the Danish language and the transnational flow of the discourse on the war in Iraq.

The manner in which all these levels come together; language, languaculture, discourse and culture, is described by Risager as the language-culture nexus (2006; 2007) or more recently the language-culture interface (2012). Central to this understanding is that "the link between language and culture is created in every new communicative event" (2006: 185). This linking involves the coming together of a multitude of flows in complex and multidimensional layers. Most recently Risager (2012: 111) has proposed that these flows are: linguistic flows e.g. codes such as English, Danish, Swahili; linguacultural flows; discursive flows; and other cultural flows involving non-language meaning e.g. visual or musical behaviour. These flows can either come together in more convergent or divergent ways. So, for example, where there is a shared language and similar linguacultural background, as well as familiarity with the discourse, we might expect high convergence. If fewer of these aspects are shared, as may be the case in intercultural communication, we might expect more divergence. Risager goes on to state that the core of this language culture connection is the reference and meaning potential of language, "It is via its meaning and reference potential that language goes beyond itself and links up with (the rest of) physical, social and cultural reality" (2006: 186). In the generic sense this is a characteristic of all languages. However, crucially, in the differential sense "we have to look at the particular meaning and reference potential of the language involved" (2006: 186).

To summarise the argument, Risager sets out a convincing analytical framework by which we can understand how in a *generic* sense language and culture are always linked but, of significance for the focus of this book, in the *differential* sense the precise relationship between a specific language, e.g. English and particular cultural forms is an empirical question that can only be answered by investigating the connection, or interface, in an actual communicative event. A further important point is that there are two interpretations of the language culture relationship from a differential perspective. From a sociological point of view linguistic practices can spread across many cultural contexts and discourses and so separation between language and culture is easily observed. However, from a psychological point of view language and culture will always seem inexorably linked since the relationship between the two has developed over the life history of the individual and cannot be separated. Risager believes that one of the reasons for the pervasiveness of the notion of language and culture as inseparable has been an overgeneralisation from the psychological perspective to other levels. She further suggests that this perspective has been exploited for political reasons to construct an ideology in which a common cultural system expressed in a common linguistic system is presented as a property of the nation state (2007: 187).

Clearly, there is much in Risager's argument that is of relevance and use to conceptualising the relationship between language and culture in intercultural communication and ELF. The need to distinguish between different levels or scales of analysis when discussing and researching the relationship is crucial and a similar argument has been made by Mauranen (2012) as regards ELF (see chapter one). The notion of linguaculture as an approach to the language and culture connections for both individuals and communities will be used throughout this book. So too will the idea of the language-culture nexus in which we can examine the confluence of various linguistic, linguacultural, discursive and non-linguistic cultural flows.

Nonetheless, there are also a number of points of departure in my argument from Risager's approach, the most significant of which involves the interpretation of lingua franca communication. Risager, while recognising that lingua franca communication is no more neutral than any other types of communication adopts a simplified view of such communication.

> Language is never culturally neutral in the sense 'linguaculturally neutral'. When a language is used in a lingua franca situation, i.e. typically in a situation when it is used as a foreign language by all participants because they do not have any other common language, it is used with contributions from all these participants' own languacultures. This produces a considerable elasticity in the language's semantic and pragmatics but it also leads to a potentially lesser degree of precision. The conversational partners will probably adjust to each other and end up with some ad hoc compromise characterised by, among other things, power relations and levels of competence. In the lingua franca situation, it is therefore often the intersection of various linguacultures that are made use of so that few politeness markers, for example, are used as well as words with more situational-determined meaning. (2006: 123)

In this extract Risager appears to limit the cultural dimension to existing linguacultural connections. However, this neglects the potential for new cultural forms and references to be constructed and negotiated in interaction. As will be shown when discussing data from ELF research, it is not only the intersection of existing linguacultures that can be observed in interactions but also the creation of new relationships. This may be a question of emphasis, but nonetheless if gives an impression of lingua franca communication as an impoverished form of communication with, to paraphrase, 'less precision', 'ad hoc compromise' and 'fewer' features. This is a very different characterisation to that presented by ELF research which shows as much richness, diversity and creativity in lingua franca communication as any other form of communication (e.g. Seidlhofer 2011; Mauranen 2012; Pitzl 2012). Importantly, it is the fluidity and dynamism of ELF communication, along with many forms of intercultural communication, that produces much of the richness. Risager makes a similar point in highlighting the complexity of linguistic and cultural flows in other forms of intercultural communication, so it seems somewhat odd that this is not extended to lingua franca communication.

Throughout Risager's writing there is also a focus on the notion of target languages and target language communities. As an example, in relation to transnationalism, she writes that "The *target-language community* is not confined to a nationally defined language area but exists in a linguistic network with a potentially global range, mainly as a result of transnational migration and communication' (2007, p. 236, emphasis mine). However, for English used as a lingua franca there is not a clear target-language community that can be identified. It is not the Anglophone world or Anglophone English users who have migrated. While users may identify with an imagined international community of English speakers (e.g. Yashima 2009; Csizér and Kontra 2012), this is not a target-language community with an identifiable linguistic code or linguaculture. Similarly, the claim that such native speaker target-language communities should provide the default model for learners of English is equally difficult, "Some people seem to think that ongoing research projects on language (English) as a lingua franca will result in people beginning to teach English as a lingua franca ... In my opinion this is problematic ... the ultimate aim (the decisive model) for language learning must be a variety (or several) used by native speakers or near native speakers." (Risager 2007: 197). The applicability of such communities, their linguistic codes and the associated linguacultures would seem of dubious relevance to the majority of those learning English and this subject will be addressed in detail in the final chapters on pedagogy.

3.4.3 Language and culture as emergent complex systems

The final approach to understanding the relationship between language and culture to be outlined will be related to complexity theory and emergentism. This will be necessarily brief since an account of complexity theory and emergence has already been offered. It should also be stressed that this is presented as a supplement to the notion of linguaculture, as complexity theory provides, I believe, a perspective that enhances, rather than opposes, the detailed characterisation offered by Risager. As already discussed, just as culture can be understood as a complex system, so too can language. In many ways language is an ideal candidate to approach from this perspective since it meets many of the criteria for complex systems, displaying both systematicity, in the sense of apparent regularities, and also dynamism and fluidity as it continuously changes and adapts. Languages are also hard to delineate with the boundaries between one language and another impossible to categorically draw. This is particularly the case with a language like English that has a global spread and is present in many different settings and hence comes into frequent contact with other languages. Furthermore, language can be seen as emergent and not reducible to its individual components. That is, any description of language in a system sense is not synonymous with the individuals who use that language, as Risager characterisation made clear. We all have our own personal idiolects which differ from aggregated descriptions of language. Finally, language systems are clearly relational systems and this has been a foundation of linguistics since Saussure (although see Blommaert 2010; 2013 for a critique of Saussurian perspective on this relationship).

A full characterisation of the ontology of language would easily fill this book (see Harris 1981; Harris and Wolf 1998; Seargeant 2009; 2010; Mauranen 2012; Hall 2013 for contemporary examples relevant to this discussion) and even in relation to complexity theory and emergence goes beyond the remit of this discussion. However, a brief summary, following Baird, Baker and Kitazawa (2014), of some of the important issues for this discussion should suffice[4]. As noted in relation to culture, complexity theory has perhaps been most extensively used in the study of second language learning and use by Diane Larsen-Freeman (e.g. 2011 and Larsen-Freeman and Cameron 2008). From this perspective language is viewed "as a complex adaptive system, which emerges bottom-up from interaction of multiple agents in speech communities ... rather than a static system composed of top-down grammatical rules or principles" (Larsen-Freeman 2011: 49). Whilst there is debate over what constitutes the 'language' that would be a complex adaptive system, this emergentist view of language has its roots in emergent grammar (Hopper 1987, 1998). Hopper proposed that grammar is not made up of abstract principles but is the result of shared and repeated social interactions in which grammar emerges as a by-product of specific utterances, becoming 'sedimented' over time giving rise to identifiable patterns. As Hopper explains it, "[l]earning a language is not a question of acquiring grammatical structure but of expanding a repertoire of communicative contexts ... A language is not a circumscribed object but a loose confederation of available and overlapping social experiences" (1998: 171).

---

4 Sections of the discussion in this chapter have appeared previously in Baird, Baker and Kitazawa (2014).

Such a seemingly radical view, in which language essentially has no fixed grammatical basis, only repeated "combinations of such prefabricated parts" (Hopper 1987: 144), has extensive empirical support from research on usage-based theories (e.g. Bybee 2006; Ellis and Larsen-Freeman 2009) and anthropology (Tomasello 2003, 2008; Everett 2012), as well as some similarities with intergrational accounts of language, or rather communication, which also reject rule-based approaches (Harris and Wolf 1998). Tomasello (2003, 2008) outlines a theory of language and communication in which linguistic structures are seen as conventionalised patterns for interacting which are cultural practices constructed in the relevant discourse community. Thus, Tomasello writes that grammaticality "is just another case of the normativity of group behaviour, but with the added force of especially frequent habitual behaviour so violations sound strange" (Tomasello 2008: 292). This underlines the social nature of language in which "[l]anguage, or better linguistic communication, is thus not any kind of object, formal or otherwise; rather it is a form of social action constituted by social conventions for achieving social ends, premised on at least some shared understandings and shared purposes among users" (Tomasello 2008: 343). A similar position is taken by Everett who also adopts an emergentist perspective stating that "language is in the first instance a tool for thinking and communicating and, though it is based in human psychology, it is crucially shaped from human cultures. It is a cultural tool as well as a cognitive tool." (2012: 19–20). Both of these researchers are in agreement that language is not an innate abstract cognitive system (as Chomsky proposes) and instead place the link between language and culture as central. Therefore, from this perspective, language emerges from and adapts to, and with, wider cultural practices, as well as specific cognitive demands.

However, it should be noted, that neither Tomasello or Everett are concerned with intercultural communication and Everett in particular draws conclusions similar to more deterministic forms of linguistic relativity. There is also nothing inherent in complexity theory which necessitates a social view of language; although, complexity theory and emergentist views on language are commensurable with the practice perspectives, outlined earlier in relation to culture, in emphasising the importance of viewing language from multiple dimensions in which its contextual embodiment is crucial, and its isolation and compartmentalisation is problematic. This leads Larsen-Freeman and Cameron to state that "language cannot be usefully segregated from its ecology" (2008: 79). A position also adopted by Sealy and Carter, who, as discussed earlier, in arguing for a more socially grounded view of applied linguistics, propose that "linear, additive models and descriptions of people using language are unsatisfactory, especially in accounting for the complex ecology of the world … we believe the

concepts of emergence and complexity are crucial to explaining social action"
(2004: 76–77).

Again it needs to be stressed that, just as with culture, complexity theory
here is viewed as a productive heuristic or lens through which to view language.
It is not being suggested that it would be possible or desirable to construct a complex systems model of any particular language. However, by taking this perspective we can see how in evolutionary terms, language, in Risager's generic sense,
emerges from culture, again in the generic sense, but also how differential languages might emerge from differential cultural contexts. At the same time, while
recognising their close relationship, we can see that they are not synonymous.
Language is not reducible to culture or vice versa. Rather they can be seen as
nested systems, systems within systems, which mutually co-evolve with each influencing and adapting to the other and with the boundaries between them fuzzy
and blurred. Crucially, as with all complex systems, they are dynamic systems
which are constantly in change and hence no fixed description is ever possible
of them or the relationship between them. Just as crucially, and as repeatedly underscored, any attempt to offer an abstracted description of language and culture
and the relationships between them based on emergent patterns or regularities
cannot be read back into individual instances of linguistic practice or individual
psychological perceptions of linguacultures. As Risager has highlighted, in a position that seems completely commensurable with emergentism, the exact nature
of the relationship in each communicative event is always an empirical question.
There is also the question, central to the interests of this book, of the role of, and
relationships between, language and culture in ELF and to what extent it is fruitful, or not, to view them as complex systems in such communicative scenarios.
This question will be addressed in the following section that specifically focuses
on ideas of culture in ELF research.

3.5 Culture in ELF research

It is important to reiterate at the beginning of this discussion that presenting
ELF research in a separate section is not to suggest that communication through
ELF is unique in comparison to other types of intercultural communication. As
I have tried to show throughout this monograph the complexity and fluidity of
communication through ELF needs to be viewed in relation to the complexity and
fluidity of intercultural communication in general, not as separate from it. Nonetheless, given the scale of English use globally and the large amount of research
currently being undertaken in relation to this phenomenon, it seems likely that
new insights and understandings concerning the relationships between com-

munication, language and culture will appear here. However, it should also be recognised that while the intercultural nature of ELF communication has been accepted from the start, the cultural dimension to this has not received a great deal of attention. This does not constitute a critique of the field since given the relative newness of ELF research (less than 20 years at the time of writing) there are clearly areas that need further exploration and this has been one of the motives in writing this book. Furthermore, issues related to context and community have been of concern and this has also included some discussion of culture as the subsequent overview will illustrate. Moreover, the closely related concept of identity has received significantly more attention in the literature and this will be the subject of the following chapter.

To begin the discussion it is necessary to address a critique, brought up in the previous chapter, suggesting that ELF researchers have approached their subject as 'culture free' (e.g. Risager 2007: 166; Canagarajah 2013b: 175; O'Regan 2014: 541). It is telling that none of these critiques offer support for their claims with quotations from ELF researchers. However, there does appear to be a degree of conceptual ambiguity in understanding the relationship between culture and language among a small minority (although not majority) of ELF orientated research. For example, House (1999; 2003; 2012) has on a number of occasions presented ELF communication as, at some level, culture free. Most recently she has written that;

> ELF is a language for communication: a medium which can be given substance with different national, regional, local and individual cultural identities. ELF does not carry these identities; it is not a language in terms of which speakers define themselves (Hullen 1992; House 2003). When English is used as a language for communication, *it is in principle neutral* with regard to the different socio-cultural backgrounds of its users. (House 2014: 364, emphasis mine)

Yet, there are two different interpretations here. The choice of the word 'neutral' is perhaps unfortunate and, as already discussed in relation to intercultural communication, there is no such thing as neutral communication of any kind. This could lead to reading this passage as suggesting that ELF is a culturally neutral medium. However, it could also be read as suggesting that there is nothing inherent in the English language that links it to any particular 'socio-cultural background' and this is exactly the point made previously in the exploration of the relationship between language and culture more generally i.e. that particular linguistic codes are not inherently linked to particular cultures, or linguacultures. More problematic in this quotation is the idea that ELF is "not a language in terms of which speakers define themselves". As will be seen in the following chapter not only is this a conceptual misunderstanding of the nature of language and communication but there is also a great deal of empirical evidence from users of ELF that suggests the opposite is true.

The notion that culture and identity is something those involved in ELF communication can *add* or *take away* at will is perhaps a more prevalent misunderstanding in ELF research (although again it is a minority). Meierkord suggests that "lingua franca communication presents itself as being both a linguistic masala and *a language 'stripped bare' of its cultural roots*." (2002: 128–129, my emphasis). Similarly, Kirkpatrick proposes that ELF communication in international settings lies at the communication end of his "Identity–Communication Continuum" (2007: 173; 2010a: 139) implying that in some instances ELF communication avoids expressions of culture and identity. All of these approaches represent a misunderstanding of communication whether ELF, other kinds of intercultural communication and intracultural communication. To repeat a point already made in chapter two, communication, including intercultural communication and ELF, is never neutral; there are always participants, purposes, contexts and language choices, none of which are neutral. Even in the most apparently functional of social practices, such as buying a cup of coffee, there will be culturally influenced (although not controlled), expectations and schemata for the roles, relationship and other interactional patterns, such as how a customer and seller should behave in a cafe. Of course this is not to suggest that culture is always a relevant category of analysis or especially salient to participants. There will be many occasions where a focus on culture, at whatever scale, would tell us little of interest about the interaction. Furthermore, we need to guard against prior assumptions about how culture should be understood, as previously detailed; this is always an empirical question that can only be answered in relation to each communicative event. With these caveats in mind, the majority of ELF studies are in agreement that the data quite clearly demonstrates that ELF is not culture or identity neutral and neither is it restricted to native speaker, Anglo- linguacultural meanings and communicative practices (however they might be characterised). This offers a clear rebuttal to both the accusations that ELF researchers have ignored cultural and identity in communication and also more deterministic accounts of linguistic relativity or linguistic imperialism.

A study which makes use of earlier ELF research (e.g. House 1999: Meierkord 2002) but does not come to the conclusion that ELF is culturally neutral is offered by Pölzl (2003) and Pölzl and Seidlhofer (2006). Through what Pölzl and Seidlhofer term as the 'habitat factor' they investigate the manner in which ELF "is a global phenomenon, but locally realised" (2006: 172) and the role of culture in this. Habitat is defined as the "setting which interlocutors recognize as their own (their natural habitat)" (2006: 155), with setting in turn referring to the physical location of the communication which influences interaction behaviour. In the study of an interaction that takes place in Jordan between Jordanian Arabic L1 speakers and an Austrian German L1 speaker communicating in English, Pölzl and Seidlhofer illustrate the way in which the Jordanians make reference to aspect of their L1 linguaculture. They give as an example the use of *yǎni* by Arabic speakers which performs multiple functions in the discourse including as an extension marker, an inner negotiation marker (as in a pause), and as deictic centre marker to soften statements, similar to *I think*, as illustrated below.

Extract 3.1
1 S2: do you think it's uh difficult to study culture? (1)
2 S1: yeah i think (.) especially uh germany: i guess it's (1)
3 it's <6> hard </6>
4 S3: <6> yǎni </6> <7> it's hard </7> (Pölzl and Seidlhofer 2006: 162).

Pölzl and Seidlhofer conclude that "its occurrence can also be said to express an assertion of Arabic identity which the speakers feel is appropriate in this particular setting, where they are on home ground and talking about matters intrinsic to their own culture. In other words, the very occurrence of the Arabic expression might be interpreted as a habitat marker." (2006: 162). This offers an early attempt to characterise the relationship between language and culture through ELF that does not draw simplistic conclusions in which ELF communication is either seen as tied to Anglophone cultures or as culturally neutral. Here we see communication containing features of hybridity and fluidity. However, a rather static image of culture is presented in which it is treated as a thing that can be *transferred* between languages (2006: 172). The participants are also presented in an overly homogeneous manner in which they are assumed to share culturally based communicative practices, despite the very different characterisations they give of the cultures in the content of their discussion. Most importantly, the focus of this study is on a setting where there is a clearly identifiable L1 linguacultural connection and the authors, quite rightly, do not attempt to generalise from their findings to settings where this is not the case, as is likely in the majority of ELF communication.

Xu and Deng (2013) also examine the link between language and culture and local realisations but connect this with more multilingual and multicultural ELF communication. They explore how the meanings of certain English lexical items were defined by a range of English speakers from different cultures and how these meanings changed and varied. Xu and Deng employed a word association task related to a number of common English words such as noodle, tower and wedding. Their findings showed that "while the WE [World Englishes (sic)] informants largely share the categorization and denotative meanings of the stimulus lexical items, they also exhibit considerable variation in their interpretations of the lexical items" (Xu and Deng 2013: 372). Crucially, this variation included an awareness that the items have alternative meanings and denotations in both their own L1 and in other cultures and languages, and that this was likely to result in a degree of variation in ELF communication. This leads Xu and Deng to propose that "It can be understood that WE speakers are by nature English-knowing bilinguals or multilinguals, so they have multiple cultural perspectives in ELF communication" (2013: 375). These multiple perspectives also extend to the cultural schema associated with particular terms such as wedding. As one of the research participants from Burma explains,

> B's account: wedding is related to Buddhist rituals like we go to the pagoda, say prayers, and wish our long life and happiness together. So wedding in our culture is much associated with pagoda rather than church in Western country or just simply in the hotel or restaurant. Some people also hold wedding receptions at the monasteries not just to invite friends and relatives, but also to make some donations to the monks. (Xu and Deng 2013: 383)

This account of the range of meanings, denotations and schema that the participants report making use of, as well as the positions they adopt in which multiple cultural references and contexts, including local, 'other' and intercultural, are drawn on and constructed, fits well with the complex characterisation of culture and language given earlier. Importantly, unlike Pölzl and Seidlhofer (2006), this study is able to account for both the local and global at the same time, demonstrating the many scales that operate simultaneously in intercultural communication through ELF. Furthermore, and again commensurable with the claims in chapter two that ELF is not *sui generis*, Xu and Deng conclude that the variable use of English lexical items "provides further empirical evidence of the need to conceptualize ELF not as a linguistic entity but as a process of languaging that different users engage in" (2013: 384).

A prominent approach in ELF research to understanding the role of social groups in more fluid settings where multiple groupings, cultural references and identifications may be present has been to explore the concept of communities of practice (Wegner 1998) in ELF communication. Dewey, (2007), Seidlhofer (2007; 2011), Ehrenreich (2009: 2010), Smit (2009: 2010), Kaloscai (2014) and Vettorel (2014) all make use of the notion of communities of practice to explain the types of dynamic and temporary communities that ELF users may form and identify with but which share, to a greater or lesser degree, Wenger's three criteria of shared practices, jointly negotiated enterprise and shared repertories. However, they all add the caveat that communities of practice need to be treated as more fluid than originally envisaged and that they are perhaps better seen as "constellations of interconnected practice" (Wegner, 1998 cited in Ehrenreich, 2009: 134). Seidlhofer (2007) gives the examples of business communities, economic communities, and online communities such as chatrooms (see also Vettorel 2014). In these communities ELF forms part of the shared repertoire which enables shared practices and joint enterprise. While the majority of discussions are at the conceptual level, Ehrenreich (2009; 2010), Smit (2009: 2010), Kaloscai (2014) and Vettorel (2014) engage in detailed empirical studies which employ a community of practice framework. Smit's study is not concerned with issues of culture, as described here, and so will not be discussed further but Ehrenreich, Kaloscai and Vettorel all make reference to culture.

Ehrenreich' research focused on business managers in an international company in Germany and she illustrates how "the managers I studied can usefully be conceptualised as life-long learners, moving in and out of ELF-speaking CofPs [communities of practice] as well as adapting to and actively shaping their communities socially shared repertoires" (2009: 146). In specific relation to the language and culture link she again repeats the position that ELF communication is neither tied to Anglo-phone cultures or culture free but instead is culturally hybrid (2009: 141). She gives the example of address terms which are used according to the negotiated norms of the particular constellations of communities of practices the managers are part of, including national, regional and business cultures alongside the managers' positions and tasks within business communities. This resulted in a preference for "a multicultural mix of social deixis to a homogeneous approach, which might be imposed upon them in the name of a 'corporate culture'" (2009: 141).

Kalocsai's (2014) study focuses on a rather different group of participants, Erasmus exchange students in a central European setting. She examines the way her participants created a shared community, the 'Erasmus Family', in which the joint enterprise was the construction and maintenance of the community or family itself and the friendships. This was carried out through mutual engagement in parties and travel and with a shared repertoire of social practices relating to the parties, such as games and drinking, and travel, such as sightseeing and sleeping arrangements. Significantly the learning of and use of English as a lingua franca cut across all of these domains being a shared goal of the participants as well as part of their social practices and shared resources. The study does not address issues of culture in depth but does suggest that the Erasmus community of practice occupied a third space between the social networks of the participants' home countries and cultures and the local culture of the setting they were in (2014: 201).

Vettorel's (2014) study of blogging practices in which English is used as a lingua franca provides a more detailed examination of issues of culture and cultural identity in relation to communities of practice. The participants of Vettorel's study were Italians who wrote blogs in English primarily for a global, rather than local, audience. One feature she discusses in detail in relation to culture and communities of practice is code-switching. Vettorel's analysis of the blogs reveals two main uses of code-switching. Firstly, code-switching is used to signal local L1 cultural identities, primarily Italian and also more regional identities, such as Venetian, as well. Secondly, code-switching is used to signal affiliation to more globally connected communities and cultural affiliations. Vettorel gives the example of code-switching from English to Japanese among participants who were part of Anime communities and she suggests that such practices may be used to strengthen the cultural links and affiliations of such communities (2014: 155). She views these global communities through the lens of communities of practice but as with other ELF researchers prefers to see such communities as more fluid than traditionally conceived consisting of "constellations of interconnected practices" (Vettorel 2014: 157). Vettorel's study offers an interesting bridge between the local cultural references in ELF communication reported in research such as Pölzl and Seidlhofer (2006) and the more fluid globally orientated cultural references discussed in global Englishes studies such as Pennycook (2007). Importantly, as Vettorel makes clear in relation to code-switching, there is no conflict between these two orientations, the local and the global.

> The two strategies do not appear to be in contrast – i.e. privileging the local vs. the global, or vice-versa; on the contrary, they can rather be regarded as exemplifications of how English in its role of lingua franca can be fluidly employed alongside other languages to relate to aspects of linguacultural identity and broader cultural affiliations that are part of these multilingual ELF users' repertoires when addressing an international audience. (Vettorel 2014: 155)

Communities of practice has thus been a useful notion in understanding the construction of communities in ELF research, although often in a considerably modified and looser form to that originally conceived. However, as already noted, empirical research is still quite limited. Most significantly, with the possible exception of Vettorel (2014), there has been little in-depth consideration as to how these localised communities of practice relate to wider ideas of culture and the larger 'imagined' communities cultures are associated with. Furthermore, communities of practice is usually employed in a more instrumental manner than culture as there is typically a shared enterprise in communities of practice as opposed to more nebulous values of cultures. This instrumentality also makes communities of practice distinct even from Holliday's notion of small cultures which operate at a similar scale (Holliday 2013: 162).

Other approaches to social groupings in ELF research include the idea of imagined communities (Anderson 2006). Instead of being in the sense described earlier, in relation to nations, in ELF research it has been suggested that ELF users might identify with other ELF users due to their shared non-native or multilingual status (e.g. Hülmbauer 2009; Jenkins 2014: 37). Some evidence for this is found in studies which examine the extent to which learners of English orientate towards and are motivated by an imagined international community of ELF speakers (e.g. Yashmina 2009; Csizér and Kontra 2012). Other studies have examined how code-switching is used by ELF speakers to signal cultural identities (Klimpfinger 2009; Cogo 2010) and will be returned to in the discussion of identity. Finally, ELF has been closely tied to ideas of globalisation with its spread seen as both a result of and driving force behind globalisation. The global nature of ELF communication has been linked to cultural and linguistic flows, as described by Pennycook (2007), as well as the transformation perspective (Held et al. 2003) in which globalisation, from a cultural perspective, results in hybridity, fluidity and change rather than homogenisation. As Jenkins, Cogo and Dewey explain "This is especially relevant in light of ELF, since it is an archetypal setting in which communication transcends conventional linguacultural boundaries, with the result that cultural practices and language resources become interactionally transformed as they are performed. This represents a substantial challenge to the homogenization hypothesis." (2011: 304).

My own research has taken up the relationship between language and culture from a cultural and intercultural perspective, drawing particularly on the idea of linguistic and cultural flows, hybridity and third places, and represents possibly the most extensive body of writing within ELF research that has approached the subject from this standpoint (Baker 2009; 2011a; 2011b; 2012b; 2012c; 2014). Following Risager, a distinction is made regarding the relationship between language and culture in the generic and differential sense, suggesting that there is no *inexorable* link between the English language and Anglophone cultures. Drawing on data from two studies within a higher education setting in Thailand (although not confined to that setting), analysis of a number of different communicative events illustrated the way that various linguistic and cultural flows which are salient to the communication at hand converge. The data show ELF users drawing on multiple cultural frames of reference in the same conversation, and moving between and across local, national and global contexts in dynamic ways. Crucially, the data highlight new cultural products, practices and interpretations emerging from ELF communication. Two examples from Baker (2009) will be presented to illustrate these themes. The example below (extract 2) is taken from a recording of a conversation in a café in Bangkok. The two speakers, Nami (Thai L1 speaker) and Philippe (Belgian French L1 speaker), are discussing the game of petanque.

Extract 3.2[5]

```
1   PHILIPPE: no Marseilles is really nice really nice city south of France close you have
2   Nice Cannes it's really cool the food is amazing and they drink err Ricard
3   NAMI: Ricard
4   PHILIPPE: they play err petanque
5   NAMI: err
6   PHILIPPE: petanque
7   NAMI: petanque ahh petanque
8   PHILIPPE: yeah (?)
9   NAMI: there's some there's some people from my school that
10  PHILIPPE: you know that the French embassy they organise err a
11  championship every year in Thailand
12  NAMI: yeah
13  PHILIPPE: I've been there a few times
14  NAMI: do you play
15  PHILIPPE: ah
16  NAMI: do you play
17  PHILIPPE: no . I'm shit
18  NAMI: ((laughs)) you're really young ((laughs))
19  PHILIPPE: I know you have to be really old to play that game
20  NAMI: NO ((laughs))
21  PHILIPPE: maybe I'm not old enough
22  NAMI: no at school a lot of young students play petanque
23  PHILIPPE: maybe they think it's cool ... uhu
```
(Baker, 2009: 581–582)

Their discussion of petanque moves from national and regional associations (Southern France), to more transnational or global contexts (the French embassy in Bangkok), to other local associations (school students in Thailand). To use the terminology of transcultural flows, in this example we can see the *flow* of the cultural practice referred to by the participants as petanque. The cultural practices move between different localities and, significantly, are adapted and reshaped, rather than simply repeated, in each setting. This can be observed in the alternative characterisations and perceptions of the game, beginning with Philippe's assertion that you have to be old to play the game (line 19), to Nami's claim that it is also a game for the young in her experience (line 22) and to Philippe's acceptance that other interpretations of the game are possible (line 23). Importantly, no single characterisation or interpretation of the cultural practice that is referred to by the term petanque appears dominant, neither is it a hybrid charac-

---

5 Transcription conventions are given in appendix 1 for my own data. All other extracts follow the transcription conventions of the original publication.

terisation. Rather there are multiple cultural practices with both similarities and difference indexed by the word petanque and with the participants seemingly comfortable with these different associations (line 23). This example can also be seen as an instance of negotiation and adaptation in meaning that leads to the sort of wider awareness of multiple associations and meanings of cultural practices and their associated terms documented in Xu and Dinh's (2013) study of ELF users.

In the next example we see communicative practices negotiated in situ. Here Nami is joined by Oy (Thai L1 speaker) and Chas (Australian English L1 speaker) and they are having a discussion at Nami and Oy's university in Thailand. The researcher (Will) has just entered the room and the three speakers are deciding whether to end their conversation or not.

Extract 3.3

  1 OY: so carry on or drop it
  2 NAMI: I hate saying up to you because I'm not really conservative type girl ((laughs))
  3 don't like it
  4 OY: err I don't like it either
  5 CHAS: make a decision then ((gestures with hands to Nami and Oy))
  6 OY: yeah you make it you're older than me ((gestures with hand to Nami))
  7 CHAS: ((laughs))
  8 WILL: ((laughs))
  9 NAMI: [I think like . I think that's (?)]
10 OY: [a bit of respect] ((smiling and laughing))
11 NAMI: [thank you very much] ((places hand on Oy's shoulder smiling and laughing))
12 WILL: [that's very Thai] very conservative and Thai defer to the older person
13 NAMI: you used to be Thai ((places hand on Oy's shoulder laughs))
14 OY: ((laughs))
15 NAMI: actually no I don't think so actually I have a lot of things to do
16 CHAS: ok
17 OY: oh ok right (I'll go as well)
(Baker 2009: 577–578)

In this extract Nami, Chas and Oy can be observed openly negotiating who makes the decision on when to finish their interaction. Nami begins by suggesting she does not want to follow the 'traditional' Thai practice, as she understands it, of deferring to the male "I hate saying up to you because I'm not really conservative type girl" (line 2) and this is agreed by both Oy (line 4) and Chas (line 5). Oy then suggests following another 'traditional' Thai practice which is to defer to the older person (line 6). This seems to be taken as a joke by all the participants (line 7–11). When the researcher suggests that this could be interpreted as 'conservative' and 'Thai' as well (line 12), Nami makes an interesting response in reference to Oy, "you used to be Thai" (line 13). This indicates that there is a degree of negotiation in relation to performing a Thai cultural identity, which the participants, or at least Oy, are not strictly confined to. Presumably if Oy 'used to be Thai' she is able to take on a Thai cultural identity but is also able to be something else. Here we see communicative practices negotiated and emerging in the interaction. Previous practices and discourses are referred to and drawn on, particularly those associated with what the participants, and the researcher, regard as traditional Thai practices. However, there are also other overlapping practices and discourse systems related not just to Thai culture, but also gender and generation, illustrating the complexity of any cultural interpretation of a communicative event.

Both these examples (extract 2 and 3) highlight the emergent and negotiated relationship between language and culture in communicative events. In extract 2 we can observe negotiation of the meaning and interpretation of the word *petanque* and the associated cultural practices. We can also see the final outcome (in relation to this extract) in which there are multiple references: a game played by the old and by the young; a game played in the South of France, the French embassy and Thai universities; a game that is traditional and 'cool'. Thus, neither Nami nor Philippe's linguacultural connections with the word petanque are simply transferred to the interaction. They are adapted and possibly changed through the course of the exchange. In extract 3 we can see the negotiation of communicative practices for ending a conversation. There is open and playful discussion of established cultural practices, deferring to age and gender, but also the space to adapt and change individual practices. This could also be interpreted as the transfer of local linguacultural connections between local cultural practices and the Thai language into the English language. However, as with extract 2, if this is the case, it results in adaption and change of those cultural practices, not repetition. There is also the question of whether the participants would be more likely to follow established local cultural practice if the language was Thai. However, Nami's comment about not being conservative and agreement from Oy would suggest that there would be negotiation in Thai too; an interpretation supported by follow-up interviews (see Baker 2009: 579–580). There also appears to be discussion as to the extent to which individuals identify with a particular cultural system and associated practices, a theme that will be explored further in the following chapter. Extract 3 also underscores the complexity of the interaction in which multiple discourse systems and practices related to culture, gender and generation are all of relevance. Crucially, in both these examples it would not have been possible to state in advance how these linguistic, linguacultural and discursive flows would convergence and the meanings and practices that would emerge from the interactions.

3.6 Language and culture through ELF

An important aspect of the empirical examples of intercultural communication presented above is the use of English as a lingua franca to construct and represent links to a variety of cultures. Clearly English is in no way neutral in relation to culture or identity in any of these examples of communication. Viewing communication, identity and culture on some sort of continuum would also seem the wrong metaphor here since all of these aspects are equally likely to be relevant to the interaction. Yet, neither is Anglophone culture *embedded* or *inexorably linked* to the language. It is not possible, for example in either extract 3.2 or 3.3 to find cultural references, discourses or practices that could be interpreted as relating to Anglophone settings. It is also difficult to envisage how the communicative practices associated with particular Anglophone cultures are somehow constraining the interactions, as posited in weak versions of linguistic relativity (e.g. Wierzbicka 2006; Sharifian 2011). Instead, we see the links between language and culture emerging in situ as a result of adaptation and negotiation on the part of the participants. In relation to linguaculture we can see the influence of individual linguacultures as well as local linguacultures but here too the relationship is complex and adapted and changed throughout the course of the interactions.

The configuration of speakers in regard to their L1 needs some comment here as well. While extract 3.2 is a prototypical ELF scenario with speakers who have different linguistic and cultural backgrounds, extract 3.3 involves communication in English between two participants for who it is an L1 (Chas and Will) and two participants who shared Thai as an L1 and cultural background (Nami and Oy). In regard to the L1 English speakers, they can be seen as L1 speakers of their respective varieties of English, Australian English and British English, and so ELF could be viewed as an L2 for them too. Following established definitions of ELF though the communication between Nami and Oy would not be regarded as ELF communication due to what they share. It could of course be argued that the presence of Chas and Will makes it an ELF scenario. However, more significantly, I think, is that such communication questions the relevance of distinctions between linguistic codes and the associated notions of L1, L2 and lingua franca as a priori characterisations of all communicative events or practices. If we view the participants as ELF users in this extract, as has been done here, it is not clear to what extent English is an L1, L2 or lingua franca for them. All of the participants report using English in this manner on a daily basis and it is an established and prominent part of their communicative practices and linguistic repertoires (Baker 2009: 581). Of course for conceptual and analytical reasons it can be helpful to make distinctions between first languages, second languages, additional languages and lingua francas, yet we need to be aware that such categories are heuristics that may need reinterpretation, when appropriate, so as not to blind us to interesting phenomena, or close down new lines of investigation (Baird, Baker and Kitazawa 2014).

The discussion of language here also brings us back to the earlier issues of understanding the relationship between language and culture from a complexity perspective. It needs to be repeated that I am not suggesting that the relationship is different in ELF from other forms of intercultural communication (or any other type of communication). Neither am I suggesting that ELF is a particular linguistic code or that we need an understanding of the specific linguaculture of ELF. ELF is not a variety of English but rather a particular *use* of English, although, as illustrated, even this interpretation needs to be taken cautiously. Therefore, as explicated in Baird, Baker and Kitazawa:

> what is shared in ELF interactions that enables the participants to refer to the language as English is related to social experience rather than abstract rules. In many cases these shared experiences will be learning 'English' as a subject at school and then later engaging with wider communities which also make use of English. Thus, ELF users share overlapping repertoires of communicative practices and the associated conventionalised, but adaptable and variable, linguistic forms which form part of these practices. (2014: 182)

This leaves us with the question of what, if anything, in ELF communication that can be viewed as a complex system. The position taken here, following Baird, Baker and Kitazawa (2014), is that ELF itself is not a system, complex or otherwise. If ELF is not viewed as *sui generis*, in regard to either form or communicative strategies, it is not possible to posit a 'system' that can be associated with ELF. Rather we can view ELF as communication involving a number of interrelated complex systems that may include an individual's mental representations of language (Hall 2013), language as a social system (Sealy and Carter 2004), communicative strategies (Firth 2009) or even perhaps English itself (Larsen-Freeman 2011). These complex systems can be understood as interacting with and adapting to cultures as a complex systems in the multiple and emergent manner described earlier in this chapter (i.e. practices, discourses and ideologies). Of course viewing language and culture as the interaction of various separate (but related) complex systems is a convenient analytical move from a research perspective. For the participants in interactions linguistic forms, communicative practices and contextualised references may all be perceived and approached as part of a cultural 'whole' and sharp distinctions between any of them may appear artificial.

The implications for our understanding of English are explained by Baird, Baker and Kitazawa (2014: 183) in the following manner:

any "variety" of language such as English must be treated as a convenient heuristic to help identify regularities and patterns in language and present them as systems, or rather as complex adaptive systems, to avoid idiosyncratic accounts of language. This, of course, is a necessary part of research and enables us, for example, to suggest what facilitates communication between two speakers of the same language, e.g., "English." However, it is important to make clear that language users are not "drawing" on an English system and neither is their use of language synonymous with such a system. Such descriptions of particular languages, as suggested by emergentism, among others, are based on the aggregated behaviour of many individuals but not reducible to them. Furthermore, any such descriptions will necessarily be only partial since there are no clear or static boundaries between "varieties," "types," or "systems" of language.

This interpretation of language also links to Risager's (2006) previously explicated discussion of language systems (e.g. English) as "artificial," discursive, metalinguistic constructs which should be distinguished from the two "natural" loci of language, the social and the psychological. Mauranen (2012) similarly emphasises the importance of distinguishing between three levels in language analysis: the macrosocial, the cognitive, and the microsocial (as described in chapter one) and characterises English in ELF as a similect rather than a stable variety.

In acknowledging that ELF is not a variety of language we must recognise that descriptions of language and culture in ELF research are not attempts to describe unique linguistic and cultural systems. However, this in no way undermines the validity of ELF as a field of study or its relevance to understanding culture and language in intercultural communication. Given that ELF is the most common communicative scenario in which English occurs, and that English, however we define it, is currently the most prominent medium of intercultural communication, it is clearly in need of substantial research. Most importantly, the degree of variability and variation documented in ELF research to date compels us to question and reconsider many of the key concepts in intercultural communication such as language, culture and communication and the relationships between them.

3.7 Conclusion

"The world has not become a village, but rather a tremendously complex web of villages, towns, neighbourhoods, settlements connected by material and symbolic ties in often unpredictable ways. That complexity needs to be examined and understood." (Blommaert, 2010: 1). The image of the *complex web* of contemporary social life is one that has been adopted throughout this book. In this chapter I have tried to outline the role culture has in understanding this web. This has entailed a characterisation of culture that accounts for the influence it has both in research and outside of the academy (in folk theory) as a coherent but also complex phenomenon. The examination of the complexity of culture has critiqued static representations of culture in which it is regarded as a thing possessed by nations or individuals, but also recognised the influence of such perceptions particularly in relation to 'national cultures'. Alternative notions of culture as a process are more productive for the sort of investigations of interest to this book and ELF research in general. This has involved approaching culture as discourse, practice and ideology. It has also led to an understanding of culture operating on and across many scales from the local, to the national and the global. However, it is crucial to be aware that culture does not neatly fit within each scale; rather it involves movement across and between these scales. Indeed, the metaphors of movement and flow have emerged from the discussion in this chapter as central to understanding culture.

Also central to the understanding of culture offered in this chapter is the notion of complexity itself. Complexity theory has been outlined as a useful lens for exploring the complexity, fragmentations and fluidity of cultural characterisations *and* in accounting for how coherence and a degree of systematicity, of the complex dynamic kind, emerges from this fluidity. In other words complexity theory allows us to think about culture as both fluid but also as a whole, albeit a contested and constantly changing whole. Any characterisation of culture will necessarily be a 'snap shot' of a moving target, but this is an inevitable consequence of all attempts to describe and analyse. As Pennycook notes, to expect otherwise is "a bit like suggesting that the failing of photography is that it gives us a static image of the world" (2007: 126); however, we do, of course, need to be aware of what it is we are doing in our descriptions of culture and avoid reifying them, as has frequently been the case in intercultural communication research. In particular, as with the notions of the convergence of linguistic and cultural flows in the communicative event, and also Blommaert's emphasis on recognising that apparent synchrony is the collapsing of divergent histories in one instance of meaning making (2013: 118), we must recognise that interpretation of these moments is only possible because of this diachronic flow.

Given the interests of ELF research, and applied linguistics in general, the relationship between language and culture is clearly highly significant. Furthermore, the close relationship between language and culture made in many of the theories of culture discussed, and the importance of not taking language for granted, underscore the importance of taking an equally critical approach to language and its relationship to culture. This also goes back to the question raised at the beginning of this chapter, as to *what influence (if any) studies of ELF and intercultural communication have on our understanding of the relationship between culture, communication and language.* Again the metaphors of complexity and flow have proved productive in both characterising language and also its relationships to culture. It was stressed that ELF communication, or any other kind of communication, cannot be 'culturally neutral'. At the same time the strongest interpretations of linguistic relativity or determinism, in which a language contains a particular culture embedded in its syntax or lexis were also rejected. So there is no inexorable relationship between Anglophone cultures and the English language. An alternative is to view the relationship between language and culture as created in each instance of communication. The metaphor of flow was again employed to conceptualise the manner in which various linguistic, linguacultural, discourse and other cultural flows converge in a single communicative event to create the particular cultural practices and references in situ. This convergence is obviously influenced, and to a degree constricted, by previous connections, practices and references including individuals' linguacultural history and more macro-level discourses of culture. However, the exact connection between language and culture in interactions is, as Risager (2006) states, always an empirical question.

Finally, in specific relation to ELF studies it has been noted that culture has not been a major conceptual concern in research to date. A number of confusions in previous research were discussed, particularly that ELF is culturally neutral communication or the equally problematic metaphor of a continuum between communication, culture and identity. This seems to be based on a misunderstanding of the relationship between language, communication and culture and an assumption that culture in ELF would mean either Anglophone cultures or the participants 'home' culture. Nonetheless, it was suggested that findings from ELF studies offer valuable data that illustrates many of the themes discussed so far in relation to the complex and fluid relationships between language, communication and culture. Indeed, given the extensive use of English as a medium of intercultural communication and that this most frequently occurs in lingua franca scenarios, ELF studies have a central role to play in our understanding of culture, language and communication in contemporary social life. Furthermore, ELF research has also given rise to questions about the relevance of culture and language as categories of analysis and description for all communication. This is not necessarily to suggest that they are abandoned but we need to maintain a critical stance towards them and not allow them to restrict investigations. Thus, we may need to rethink their use in light of ELF orientated investigations. This is especially important in regards to notions of established first languages and cultures, and the links between them, as well as the more contemporary notions of hybridity and third places. It is not always clear what languages or cultures participants in ELF communication are 'in-between' or 'hybridising'. Data from

ELF studies, such as my own research (e.g. Baker 2009; 2011), illustrate participants regularly engaging in communicative practices that involve the use of different linguistic codes and a complex range of cultural references and practices. This links with contemporary research on plurilingualism in sociolinguistics (e.g. Pennycook 2007; 2010; Blommaert 2010: 2013; Canagarajah 2013b) which also questions the relevance of established boundaries between languages and cultures in multicultural, superdiverse communities. Thus, in addition to asking who introduces the concepts of culture, with what purposes and with what consequences, we need to expect that any answers will be complex, partial and transitory.

Chapter 4
Culture and identity through English as a lingua franca

> Who what am I? My answer: I am the sum total of everything that went before me, of all I have been seen done, of everything done-to-me. I am everyone everything whose being-in-the-world affected was affected by mine. I am anything that happens after I've gone which would not have happened if I had not come.
>
> – Salman Rushdie, Midnight's Children (1981: 535)

Identity is, as Bauman wryly observes, "the loudest talk in town, the burning issue on everybody's mind and tongue" (2004: 17). In many ways discussions of identity in social sciences are more prominent than discussions of culture. This may be due to the unpopularity of the previous structuralist and essentialist characterisations of culture and also the increasing size and complexity of the notion of culture, whereby scholars, such as the Scollon, Scollon and Jones (2012), question if culture has any analytical power left. It is perhaps easier and more productive to examine the manner in which individuals construct their identities and the different social groups they draw on, or are allocated to, in order to achieve this. Such an approach would certainly be commensurable with post-modernist and qualitative research in which the particular is of interest and generalisations are eschewed. However, a little reflection will reveal that identity is unlikely to be any simpler or easier to delineate than culture. Furthermore, we are left with the problem that in many instances the social groups that people identify with are described in terms of cultural groupings. We may wish to treat this as unreflective 'folk theory' but if we are to take subjective and emic perspectives seriously researchers will still have to deal with culture. Investigations of identity, then, do not replace investigations of culture; rather, there is likely to be much productive cross-over between the two notions and at times they may be closely related.

Identity, as with all the fields addressed in this book so far, is a wide and multiple field of enquiry and so, again, it is necessary to be clear about the focus of discussions of identity in this monograph. As the title of this chapter suggests there will be an examination of the relationship between culture and identity and particular interest in the close connections between the two concepts in what is sometimes referred to as *cultural identity*. This means that the discussion will not be primarily concerned with many other aspects of identity such as gender, ethnicity, class or generation. However, there is clearly much overlap between any categories of identity we might choose to distinguish and investigate, and so other aspects will not be ignored. The discussion will also, of course, centre on the relationship between language, culture and identity in intercultural communication and ELF. The relationship between language and identity, and more specifically, discourse and identity has been a major area of study in social theory and sociolinguistics in recent decades. It is therefore to be expected that identity has received a reasonable degree of attention in ELF research too, although, as already suggested, the cultural dimensions to identity have been rather less thoroughly explored.

Returning to the question that guided the previous chapter and will also guide this chapter, '*What influence (if anything) do studies of intercultural communication through ELF have on our understanding of the relationship between culture, identity and language?*', we are now in a position to consider the identity aspect of this. Much of the theoretical groundwork has already been done in the previous two chapters on intercultural communication and culture in relation to ELF. To briefly repeat, some of the major themes which came out of those discussions are; communication through ELF is viewed as a form of intercultural communication and as such ELF enquiry has adopted a similar position to critical intercultural communication literature in viewing communication from a poststructuralist perspective where categories of language, identity, and culture are seen as constructed, negotiable and contested. We thus need to ask, who introduces the concepts of culture, the intercultural, and now identity, with what purposes and with what consequences. Through an examination of the complexity of culture, static representations of culture, in which it is regarded as a thing possessed by nations or individuals, were critiqued, but also the influence of such perceptions particularly in relation to 'national cultures' was recognised. Alternatively culture can be investigated as a process, something we *do* and this has been especially prevalent in conceptions of culture as discourse, practice and ideology. Culture in ELF communication, and other forms of communication, operates on and across many scales from the local, to the national and the global. However, culture does not neatly fit within each scale; rather conceptions of culture, or cultural systems, involve movement across and between these scales with the boundaries blurred. Indeed, the metaphors of movement and flow have emerged from the discussion as fundamental to understanding culture. Equally crucial has been recognition of the complexity of culture. Complexity theory has been outlined as a useful meta-theory or conceptual lens for, on the one hand, exploring the complexity, fragmentations and fluidity of cultural characterisations and, on the other hand, in accounting for how coherence and a degree of systematicity emerges from this fluidity. Complexity theory, therefore, allows us to think of culture as a whole, but as a contested and constantly changing whole, and is thus very different to structuralist accounts of culture as a static deterministic system.

In this chapter I will explore the notions of complexity, fluidity, emergence and process in relation to cultural identities. This will begin with a brief sketch of the approach to identity taken here, stating what it is, and is not, and also why it is a relevant concept for understanding intercultural communication through ELF. The fundamental role of language and discourse in the construction of identity will be explicated. Due to its central place in much intercultural communication theory the notions of difference and othering in identity construction and ascription will be considered and critiqued. The discussion will then focus on cultural identities examining the different aspects of this as well as the relationships and tensions between local, national and global groupings in such identities. The notion of interculturality, outlined in chapter two, will be returned to as a useful framework for interpreting the multiplicity and complexity of cultural identities. The final part of this chapter will consider how identity has been approached in ELF research. A range of empirical studies will be drawn on providing evidence of the significance of identity in ELF communication (as in all communication) to both participants and researchers. Cultural identity and interculturality will also be shown to be productive concepts in the analysis of intercultural communication through ELF.

An important caveat is needed right at the beginning of the discussion, so as to avoid potential misinterpretation. While the focus of this chapter is on cultural identities, this is not to suggest the culture is reducible to individuals. As I have already argued, and based on emergentism, our descriptions and interpretations of culture emerge from the aggregated behaviour of individuals but are not reducible to any one individual. To assume that an individual is synonymous with particular cultural systems to which they may identify, or be identified with, is to essentialise the relationship between culture and identity. Individuals can identify with, or be identified with, particular cultural systems to a greater or lesser extent, but as made clear throughout this monograph, individuals are members of a great many social groups, including, potentially, multiple cultural systems. In other words, I may identify with some of the cultural practices, beliefs and values associated with English culture, but this does not determine my whole identity; it is only one aspect of it. Therefore, the relationship between culture and identity (and also language and identity) is likely to be as complex as any of the other phenomena discussed so far and it would be a mistake to conflate culture and an individual's identity, or their sense of a subjective self.

4.1 Characterising identity

4.1.1 Subjectivity and identity

Before outlining how identity is to be understood in this discussion an important distinction needs to be made between subjectivity and identity. Kramsch explain it in the following way,

> Identity refers to the identification with a social or cultural group, while subjectivity focuses on the ways in which the self is formed through the use of language and other symbolic systems, both intrapersonally and interpersonally. As individuals participate in multiple symbolic exchanges, themselves embedded in vast webs of social and power relations, subjectivity is conceptualised dynamically as a site of struggle and potential change. (2009: 25)

Identity can, from this perspective, be viewed as the network of social groups and social relations that we take part in and orientate towards, or, in other words, the web of social groups that we identify with. Subjectivity is the construction of the self, involving both the internal sense of self and the external projection of the self to others. The two notions are clearly closely related, we construct our sense of self based on the network of social groups that we identify with. Given this close relationship subjectivity and identity are frequently conflated in considerations of identity and some scholars (e.g. Joseph 2004) even reject the distinction. Nonetheless, for the present discussion, it is a helpful, if somewhat blurred, distinction since what is of most relevance to understanding intercultural communication through ELF is identity. That is, we are interested in the social groups which participants in ELF interactions orientate towards or are allocated to, and in particular we are interested in participants' identification with various cultural groupings. This is not to suggest that subjectivity is not important and writings such as Kramsch (2009) underscore the significance of understanding the subjective dimensions of multilingualism and second language learning, and indeed will be returned to in chapter six in relation to pedagogy.

4.1.2 The relevance of identity

Identity has become a preeminent concern in social theory and in turn in applied linguistics and intercultural communication; however, as Bauman (2004) notes, this has not always been true. In both the pre-modern and modern era, identity was relativity unproblematic. For the majority of people in the history of human societies social relations revolved around a local geographical region and the associated communities (although this is not to suggest this was true for all societies or groups within societies). There was, therefore, little choice available in social relations and groupings and subsequently change was relatively slow and social relations were reasonably stable. Nation states and national communities, as discussed in the previous chapter, added another level of complexity to social relations and the social groups which individuals could identify with and began the process of eroding the power of local communities. Nonetheless, Bauman argues, that the nation, while opening up the identity question also 'annexed' (2004: 19) the issue by positioning national identity as natural; an identity one is born into and that "would not recognise competition, let alone opposition" (2004: 22). In both pre-modern societies and modern nation states, questions of identity were not of high relevance to the majority of people, "After all, asking 'who you are' makes sense to you only once you believe that you can be someone other than you are; only if you have a choice, and only if it depends on you what you choose" (Bauman 2004: 19).

Whether we view globalisation as a relatively old process entering a new phase or as a recent fundamental change in social relations, Bauman makes a powerful case for recognising issues of identity as currently at the very centre of individuals' attention and 'life agendas' in a manner that was not previously the case. In what Bauman refers to as liquid modernity (2000; 2004; 2011), where the previous 'solid' social structures are increasingly 'liquefied' as they become ever less stable and more changeable, issues of identity have come to the fore. The traditional signposts of identity and sources of identification such as local communities and the state have become increasingly eroded. Instead, it is up to the individual to construct their own identities based on the apparent multitude of choices offered, as explained by Bauman, "We seek and construct and keep together the communal references of our identities while *on the move* – struggling to match the similarly mobile, fast moving groups we seek and construct and try to keep alive for a moment, but not much longer." (2004: 26). This description of identities and groups on the move resonates with the earlier discussions of global flows and transnational networks of communities and cultural resources. However, Bauman is not optimistic about this apparent dynamism and choice. According to Bauman by providing the appearance of choice and thus shifting the responsibility of identity construct to the individual, a contradiction or gap in contemporary liquid modern society results. In what Bauman terms the condition of individuality *de jure* and the desire to achieve individuality *de facto* (2000: 39; 2011: 69), individuals are given the responsibility and are expected to develop their own identities; however, the choices they are given do not match this desire and the constant change or liquidity of social structures makes the achievement of a secure identity and thus individuality an impossibility.

Bauman sums up this situation by stating that "In our world of rampant 'individualization' identities are mixed blessings. They vacillate between a dream and a nightmare, and there is no telling when one will turn into the other ... In a liquid modern setting, identities are perhaps the most common, most acute, most deeply felt and troublesome incarnations of *ambivalence*." (2004: 32)

In intercultural communication and the use of global languages such as English, which are deeply enmeshed in the processes of globalisation, the liquidity that Bauman emphasises will, as previously outlined, be a significant part of such communication and hence the links between language, culture and identity. Bauman is, I think, also right to highlight the contradictions and ambivalence that can arise from this, and we will examine instances of this later in the chapter. However, this liquidity also opens up new spaces and new forms of identity that would not have been previously possible and this too is a feature of cultural identities and identifications that will be explored in this chapter.

4.1.3 Identity and language

Having established the relevance and importance of identity in contemporary social theory and the fluidity, or liquidity, of the concept, paralleling the fluidity of culture, it is now necessary to focus specifically on approaches to identity in applied linguistics which have dealt with the relationship between identity and language. Firstly, and most obviously, identity is typically viewed as constructed, as opposed to given, with language and discourse assigned a central role in this (e.g.; Norton 2000; Joseph 2004; Pavlenko and Blackledge 2004; Block 2006; Riley 2007). Indeed, Joseph goes so far as to claim that language and identity are inseparable and that "the entire phenomenon of identity can be understood as a linguistic one" (2004: 12). While he is right to underscore the central, dominant role of language in the construction of identity, I think this is overstating the position as there are clearly non-linguistic aspects of identity. In particular appearance is for many an important feature of identity, although, of course, how appearance is interpreted or indexed is discursively constructed. Linked to identity as discursively constructed through language, poststructuralist perspectives have also been dominant in applied linguistics. Here the emphasis has been on the role of power relationships and the legitimisation of particular identities and the devaluing of others (e.g. Norton 2000; Pavlenko and Blackledge 2004; Block 2006). Poststructuralism typically draws on the work of Bourdieu (1991), in particular, in which the use of specific forms of language and linguistic practices are seen as sites of social struggle. Making use of Bourdieu's (1991) concept of linguistic capital, poststructuralist approaches have attempted to highlight how the use of language is always related to issues of identity and power with the use of 'non-standard' varieties of language and less prestigious languages both re-flecting and creating social stratification and inequality, "every time we speak, we are negotiating and renegotiating our sense of self in relation to the larger social world" (Norton 2010: 350). However, as the previous quote from Norton demon-strates, and as distinct from more deterministic readings of Bourdieu, there has also been an interest in how identities are negotiated and spaces for change and agency created in interaction (Joseph 2004: 75).

There has also been a focus on the multiple, fragmented and hybrid nature of identity in multilingual, multicultural and multiracial settings. Concepts dis-cussed earlier in relation to culture and hybridity, such as third spaces (Bhabha 1994), have been made use of to account for the spaces for identity construction multilingualism opens up. For example, Rampton's (1995) study of language use in urban multicultural communities makes use of the notion of *liminality*, which is in many ways synonymous with third spaces. He identified 'liminal moments' or 'crossings' when language users who are not part of a language community adopt and adapt the language for their own purposes or needs. This leads to a 'code-alteration' (ibid: 280) of the language by minority or outside users. This, Rampton claims, challenges absolutist notions of cultural, ethnic or linguistic identity and, while not rejecting the significance of such influences, suggests that they are dynamic and interactive rather than "a set of reified ethnic units" (ibid: 312). At the same time there has been recognition of the marginalisation of identities which do not fit the dominant discourse. Duff (2002) investigated the discourse of a multi-ethnic classroom in Canada in which English was an L2 for the majority of students. She concluded that the roles taken up by one group of L2 users were deliberately different to those offered by the dominant L1 norms of classroom participation and so this group were viewed as periphery partici-pants by the teacher. Duff suggests that L2 learners may adopt L2 identities and communication modes which neither conform to the norms of their L1 or the L2, which, like Rampton's participants, may serve their own interests but which are not recognised by those in more powerful positions.

However, as highlighted in chapter three in relation to culture, we need to guard against the reification of hybridity and account for the multiple and con-tradictory as well as the hybrid. We also need to recognise that negotiation and hybridity are not always possible. Pavlenko and Blackledge (2004: 21) propose three types of identity in regard to this: *imposed identities* (which are not nego-tiable), *assumed identities* (which are accepted and not negotiated), and *nego-tiable identities* (which can be contested by groups and individuals). They give the example of compulsory name changes imposed by local authorities on US immigrants as an instance of imposed identities. Immigrants may not have liked the name changes but they could do nothing about it. Assumed identities are identities that individuals have no interest in contesting. This often includes identities which are constructed as high status in dominant discourse, such as white, middle-class, male in the UK or US. Lastly, negotiable identities are those which can and are contested by groups and individuals. Examples of this were given above in relation to language choice in Rampton's (1995) study and learner identities in Duff's (2002) study. It seems likely that in ELF communication, given the multilingual nature of the communication, and that ELF is no one's first language, this final category of negotiable identities will be most relevant. However, this is not always the case and, as Piller (2011) highlights in relation to intercultural communication, issues of proficiency are significant. If we do not have sufficient proficiency or adequate linguistic resources we cannot perform the identities we may wish too, as Piller writes, "you cannot 'be' an educational expert or a competent shopper if you do not sound like one." (2011: 146). A final important issue to raise, and again similar to points made earlier in relation to culture, is that we need to guard against always assuming identity is relevant or important in analysis. If language choice/imposition is related to identity, then identity issues are always present in communication; however, in cases where identities are accepted by the participants and/or social relationships stable and uncontested they may not be particularly salient in understanding the interaction.

4.1.4 Identity, difference and others

A fundamental aspect of identity construction is that identity is always constructed in relation to others. As Riley expresses it, "In social terms, identity can, by definition, only be treated in reference with others, since others are its principal source. Discussing social identity as if it were an intrinsic property of one person makes about as much sense as discussing the sound of one hand clapping." (2007: 87). This is the case for both individual identity, or the self, and group identities, which are the focus of this discussion. This also results in a degree of tension or contradiction in our construction of identity. On the one hand we claim a shared identity or an 'identity-as-sameness' (Joseph 2004: 37) with the groups we identify with, for instance, our British or Chinese identity. On the other hand, we also define ourselves as unique and different from the rest of our group, claiming 'identity-as-uniqueness' (Joseph 2004: 37). This can partly be explained in relation to the earlier distinction between identity and subjectivity. Our sense of, and construction of, self is as a unique individual who is distinct from the imagined homogeneity of the groups we identify with. One way in which we do this is in identifying with many different groups, for example, ethnic, religious, professional, and regional, as well as national cultural identities. These constellations of different identities are what give our sense of self and identity its unique characteristics and also a dynamic aspect that provides for the accentuation of alternative group affiliations across contexts and times. As Joseph puts it, "these oppositions actually intertwine: identity-as-sameness is principally recognised through contact with what is different, while identity-as-uniqueness is established largely through the intersection of identity-as-sameness categories" (2004: 37).

This sense of difference and the other is equally applicable to groups as to individuals. Group identities are typically defined in terms that are as much about what they are not as what are shared characteristics. Tajfel's (1981) social identity theory was an early influential example of this in relation to the dichotomy between *in-group* and *out-group* in individual identity formation; however, Tajfel's focus on the individual and rather static views of groupings mean his theories will not be addressed further here. Postcolonial theory has been particularly powerful in this area and especially Said's (1985) notion of Orientalism in which a superior 'Western' self is constructed in dominant political and academic discourses and contrasted with an inferior 'Eastern' Other. The essentialism and othering of ethnic and cultural groups has been an important theme in postcolonial writing such as Hall (1995; 1997) and particularly in critiques of the racism latent in much superficial multiculturalism (see also Bauman's (2011) similar critique of this form of multiculturalism in chapter three). As Hall observes:

> Nobody would talk of racism but they were perfectly prepared to have 'International Evenings', when we would all come and cook our native dishes, sing our native songs, and appear in our native costume ... I have been deracinated for four hundred years. The last thing I am going to do is dress up in some native Jamaican costume and appear in the spectacle of multiculturalism (Hall 1991: 55–6, cited in Holliday 2011: 82).

Holliday proposes a sequence for the othering process through which social groups form a sense of coherence and identity.
1. Identify 'our' group by contrasting it with 'their' group.
2. Strengthen the contrasted images of Self and Other by emphasising and reifying respective proficient and deficient values, artefacts and behaviours.
3. Do this by manipulating selected cultural resources such as Protestantism or Confucianism.
4. Position Self and Other by constructing moral reasons to attack, colonize or help.
5. The Other culture becomes a definable commodity.
6. The imagined Other works with or resists imposed definitions. (2011: 70)

This process of othering occurs at all levels and, of significance for this discussion, at the cultural level in particular, with cultural groupings, whether they are regional, national or even global, always juxtaposed with other cultural groupings. In many cases the dominant discourse in constructing cultural groups also builds a superior positive image of 'our' culture in contrast to an inferior 'other' culture. Part of this process involves the construction of a line or barrier between cultural groups in which the characteristics of the members of one cultural group make them different and distinct from the members of another cultural group. As discussed in chapter two, this discourse of othering has been pervasive in much intercultural communication literature in which individuals are assumed to be different based on essentialised cultural identities.

4.2 Cultural identity

4.2.1 Cultural identity, ethnicity and race

While cultural identities, like all identities, are typically constructed from a diverse network of groupings and resources such as nationality, gender, generation, class and religion, as made clear in the previous section, ethnicity and race are two key elements of cultural identity. Zhu observes that, "Although cultural identity is *not only* about ethnicity and race, ethnicity and race *are central* to cultural identity to the extent that ethnic or racial identities are often conflated with cultural identity in practice" (2014: 204, emphasis mine). Zhu suggests this is related to the need to categorise others in interaction and that race and ethnicity, alongside sex, are categories that we initially draw on. To do this, she argues, we make use of audible, visible and readable cues which index pervious constructions of cultural identities for us. Importantly, this is a process that is as much about ascription by others as it is about self-selection (Zhu 2014: 208). This becomes most apparent when self-selection and ascription by others do not coincide. This is vividly described by Javier (2010) in her experience as a Canadian-Filipino English teacher in China. Her appearance, which for many students, Javier claims, was perceived as Chinese, would often be greeting by new classes or students with a mixture of surprise, disappointment and discomfort. She provides the following example to illustrate this:

> **Extract 4.1**
> New student: So, you're not Chinese?
> Me [Eljee Javier]: No, not at all!
> New student: Your family is Chinese?

Me: No, none of them are Chinese. Both my parents are from the Philippines.
New student: But your English is so good!
Me: Well, I'm a native speaker.
New student: Of course.

At this point I could tell that she wasn't convinced of my English credentials. I felt myself grow increasingly frustrated and I found myself defensively saying the following:

'I'm from Canada'

Suddenly the light seemed to go on. Her face lit up in a smile and she thanked me for my time before sitting down, obviously pleased with the news. (Javier 2010: 99)

Javier's experience is far from unusual in English language teaching in which there is a well-documented assumption on the part of many learners that an English native speaker is Caucasian. As Javier's example demonstrates self-selection as a Canadian native speaker of English contradicts the ascription by others, her students, as an Asian and hence non-native speaker of English. In Javier's case this identity was a negotiable identity, to use Pavlenko and Blackledge's (2004) categorisation, and so was negotiated to the apparent satisfaction of all the participants. However, in instances where identities are imposed and hence non-negotiable, for example in immigration and asylum cases, differences in self-selection and other-ascription of cultural identities can have more serious consequences (see Blommaert 2010 and Guido 2012).

4.2.2 Cultural identity and nationality

Alongside ethnicity and race another crucial aspect of cultural identity, as Javier's example illustrates, is nationality. Indeed for Javier it is her identification with a national grouping that convinces the student she is a legitimate teacher of English. However, as has been repeated throughout this monograph, the relationship between nation and culture is complex and this is equally true in the connections between cultural identity and nationality. Kumaravadivelu (2008) provides a framework for understanding cultural identity formation that incorporates national identities together with other 'realities', as he terms them. These four realities are global reality, national reality, social reality and individual reality (2008: 146). At the global level, Kumaravadivelu argues that economic and cultural flows are proceeding at an unprecedented rate but that it is cultural flows that are challenging national cultural identities. However, he goes on to note, in an analogous argument to that set out in global and transnational flows, that this is not necessarily resulting in cultural homogenisation, since cultural products and resources are adapted and used for local purposes "in a creative process of 'glocalization'" (2008: 147). He also points out that nations, societies and communities are in greater contact with each other than ever before and hence are more likely to influence each other, "Consequently, people in many parts of the world see unparalleled opportunities for cultural growth, and equally unparalleled threats to their cultural identity" (2008: 148). This results in pressures from both global realities and national realties. Kumaravadivelu is clear that the nation state still exerts a powerful influence, in the ways already described as an imagined community and through reinforcement in banal nationalism. He gives the rise in US patriotism post 9/11 as an example of the continued power of national cultural identities and of the desire for people to face some of the consequences of globalisation through national groupings. However, while recognising that nationalism remains a strong reality, Kumaravadivelu proposes that in addition to pressure from global realities, nationalism also faces pressure from social and individual realities. Social realities refers to the many communities we belong to such as ethnic, religious and linguistics groups, as well as communities of practice around specific interests or mutual engagement in a particular enterprise. Ethnic, religious and linguistics social realities pose a particular threat to national identities in their increasing challenges to the power of nation states through separatist movements such as Tamil speakers in northern Sri Lanka. Lastly, Kumaravadivelu's concept of individual reality concerns the subjective dimension of identity in which the individual brings together the other realties in differing and changing ways to construct the self.

To understanding cultural identity formation then we need to understand the dialectical relationship between all these different realities. However, crucially, Kumaravadivelu, goes beyond describing the formation of cultural identities and also suggests that to deal with the complexity of identity formation it is necessary to develop what he terms *cultural realism*.

> To start with a formal definition, cultural realism is the notion that any meaningful cultural growth in this globalized and globalizing world is possible only if individuals, communities, and nations adopt a pragmatic approach to identity formation that entails a true understanding of the competing forces of global, national, social and individual realities, and make a genuine attempt to translate that understanding into actionable plans. (2008: 157–158).

He goes on to state that "what the individual needs more than anything else to make sense of cultural realism and its impact on identity formation is global cultural consciousness" (2008: 164). This global cultural conscious requires continuous critical self-reflection and a deeper understanding of one's own cultural heritage and other cultures, themes that will be developed in the following chapter in relation to intercultural competence. For the present it is enough to note that while Kumaravadivelu recognises the many tensions in identities choices and the construct of a sense of self, in principle he suggests a way out of Bauman's (2004) *ambivalence* through a greater awareness of our cultural realities and the real and apparent choices they offer us in identity formation.

A scholar who has made extensive use of Kumaravadivelu (2008) notions of cultural realism and culture reality in writing about cultural identity and intercultural communication is Holliday (2010; 2011; 2013). Holliday also approaches identity as multiple and complex, but like Kumaravadivelu, does not dismiss the continued role of nations in cultural identifications. As Holliday writes, despite adopting a post-modernist, critical cosmopolitan stance in his research on cultural identity, the role of nation emerged from his data in unanticipated ways, "I was forced unexpectedly to appreciate the importance of nation, but not in ways I had predicted." (2010: 167). In later writing Holliday (2013) again emphasises the role of nation in his grammar of culture (see chapter 3) and individuals' interactions with national structures. However, for Holliday, nation is an external cultural reality which, although influential for many of his participants, also conflicted with personal cultural identities. He is also very strong in his rejection of nation as imposing a deterministic structure as in structuralist approaches to culture. Instead, and commensurable with the position taken in this monograph, he views individuals as having cultural agency and the space to engage in dialogue with social structures which "supports the notion of individually emergent and expressive cultural identities that defy established descriptions and allow for individual cultural trajectories" (2011: 66). He is also clear, again in agreement with the position adopted in this book, that this is not to suggest that there are individual cultures; rather, individuals construct different cultural identities based on the diverse range of cultural experiences, resources and groupings they have access to and experience of (2011: 66).

Holliday, then, sees cultural identity as constructed through multiple cultural realities from individual cultural trajectories, small culture formation (small social groups such as families and work places, see chapter 3), national social structures and global positioning and politics. Global positioning and politics is related to how we position ourselves and our social groups in relation to the rest of the world and introduces a global dimension to cultural identity (2013: 2). This may relate to 'international alignments' (2013: 23) e.g. identifying with social groupings on a global level such as international professional groups or class identifications across nations. Most significantly though, global positioning and politics is related to discourses of 'self' and 'other' and of difference. Holliday links this to the discourses of othering and Orientalism, described in the previous section, particularly as regards the construction of superior centre-West and an inferior peripheral non-Western 'other'. These discourses are, Holliday believes, often deeply held and difficult to either acknowledge or change and, while his data shows participants resistance to them, there is also evidence of their adoption by both those in the 'centre' and 'periphery' in their construction of cultural identity (2010; 2011; 2013). Holliday is especially critical of much contemporary intercultural communication research, which he terms as neo-essentialist, for its uncritical acceptance and use of these discourses (2011: 6). As an alternative to this top-down approach to researching cultural identities, in which such discourses and social structures are unthinkingly imposed on research participants, Holliday advocates a more emergent, bottom-up approach. This involves a critical examination of how discourses of self, other and difference are constructed alongside individuals 'dialogue' with social structures such as nations.

4.2.3 Cultural identity and globalisation

Two researchers who have focused on cultural identity at the global scale and in relation to the processes of globalisation are Pennycook (2007; 2010) and Canagarajah (2007; 2013b). In particular both researchers have explored the new spaces that globalisation has opened up for identity construction in multicultural and plurilingual settings. Pennycook (2007), as already discussed in chapter two, makes use of the notion of transcultural flows to explore how the global use of English gives rise to cultural forms and practices as well as new forms of identity. He uses transcultural flows "to address the ways in which cultural forms move, change and are reused to fashion new identities in diverse contexts. This is not, therefore, a question merely of cultural movement but of take-up, appropriation, change and refashioning." (2007: 6). Pennycook is especially interested in how cultural and linguistic practices are adapted in local settings as well as how this alters the local settings and, significantly, in turn the global flow of linguistic and cultural practices. This is, for Pennycook, a perspective that recognises global cultural flows as producing new forms of localisation and global identification (2007: 7). Pennycook (2010) further expands on this idea through characterising identity construction as the result of social practice (as explained in chapter three) and also in relation to performativity in Butler's (1999) sense. In other words cultural identities are performed through social practices. However, this is not simple repetition of existing practices; rather it is "fertile mimesis, of repetition that is never the same" (2010: 47). Identities, from this perspective, become the product of language practices, not a precursor to them; however, language practices in turn are "moulded by social, cultural, discursive and historical precedents and concurrent contexts" (2010: 125–126).

Pennycook also sees global flows not as flows from the centre to the periphery but as a more horizontal relocalization. Globalisation is therefore about the increasingly close relationships between different localities, or the web of villages, to use Blommaert's (2010) phrase. Transcultural flows, then, involve not the imposition of new cultural forms and practices in local settings but the adaptation and transformation of existing local practices through simultaneous flows between multiple localities (2010: 86). In terms of cultural identity this means that fixed relationships between languages, cultures and identities no longer hold. Pennycook refers to this as *metroethnicity* and *metrolingualism* and explains it in the following way, "As language learners move around the world in search of English or other desirable languages, or stay at home but tune in to new digital worlds through screens, mobiles and headphones the possibilities of being something not yet culturally imagined mobilizes new identity options. And in these popular transcultural flows, languages, cultures and identities are frequently mixed." (2010: 85).

Canagarajah (2007; 2013b) takes a similar perspective, as again explained in chapter two, to Pennycook in discussing the complex relationships between local and global communities and identifications in which "we are able to enjoy identities that transcend our native language, ethnicity, or place of birth." (2013b: 198). However, Canagarajah adds some important limitations to this position. Like Kumaravadivelu (2008) and Holliday (2010; 2011; 2013b), he highlights that there are social structures and dominant ideologies that mean we are not free to choose any identity we like and is particularly critical of the notion of metroethnicity (2013b: 199). In order to adopt these new 'freer' identities we need to negotiate identity within existing power structures and discourses and these may put limitations on the degree of choice we actually have. Canagarajah also notes that to members of minority communities, which are frequently part of the multilingual and multicultural settings envisaged in metroethnicity, postmodernist theory can be seen as a threat. In many cases their heritage languages and identities are already marginalised and post-modernist theory with its critiques of 'authentic' identities can be perceived as further eroding their claims to legitimacy. Canagarajah proposes that while we need to recognise the constructed and ideological nature of heritage languages, communities and identities, this does not necessarily undermine them, "ideologies are not always evil or limiting; they are also enabling. One can marshal a diverse collection of semiotic resources and "perform" one's identity and community through strategic practices" (2013: 200). He also suggests that through such an approach we can account for both the continuity and the developments, changes and adaptions to heritage languages, communities and identities. Canagarajah (2013b: 200–201) gives the example of the redefinition of Tamil ethnic identity for a younger generation in global diasporas which, while different to previous characterisations, can still claim to be continuing a vibrant ethnic identity and heritage language.

4.2.4 Cultural identity and interculturality

A final approach to understanding cultural identity which draws together many of the strands of the preceding discussion is the notion of interculturality. This too was introduced in chapter two in relation to intercultural communication and it is returned to here as a productive and highly relevant approach to conceptualising cultural identities in intercultural communication and hence in ELF research. To restate the points made in chapter two, the approach taken in interculturality studies is to investigate how cultural identities emerge from interactions through negotiation and construction *within* the interactions rather than a priori positioning and assumptions about cultural identities (Sarangi 1994; Nishizaka 1995; Mori 2003; Higgins 2007; Young and Sercombe 2010; Zhu 2010; 2011; 2014). In particular the framework offered by Zhu (2014) provides a useful heuristic for considering how intercultural identities are performed. It is therefore worth returning to, and exploring in more detail, the six questions presented in chapter two, which Zhu (2014: 209–215) sees as the main agenda and contributions of interculturality studies to understanding cultural identities.

- *Are cultural memberships always relevant to intercultural interactions?* This involves recognition of the multiple identities we have and that cultural memberships may not always be relevant to interactions. Even when they are relevant they may aid rather than hinder communication in intercultural communication.
- *What do participants do with cultural memberships?* This is related to which cultural memberships are made relevant by participants (for themselves and others). Similar to Pavlenko and Blackledge's (2004) earlier argument, cultural identities may be imposed, assumed or negotiable.
- *How do participants do cultural identities?* This is central to the construction of cultural identities and according to Zhu involves a number of different mechanisms. Firstly, membership categorisation is a prerequisite of having an identity and an individual is expected to meet the conventional assumptions of that category (although of course they also resist them). For example, the conventions of an Italian cultural identity may involve various ethnic conventions related to appearance, linguistic conventions (e.g. speaking Italian), and familiarity with associated cultural practices (e.g. greetings). Secondly,

cultural membership is made relevant in particular instances of interaction "through moments of identification by participants" (2014: 213). Given that participants belong to multiple categories that cannot all be performed simultaneously, particular categories will be made more salient at particular points in the interaction. Thirdly, while identifications are performed at particular moments, there is also a diachronic dimension in which the identity options available at that moment are based on participants' pervious knowledge of that membership category. Fourthly, to perform identities at particular moments, participants "rely on the combination of symbolic and indexical cues that evoke the relevance of particular category-bound features and activities associated with cultural identities" (Zhu 2014: 213). This is similar to Gumperz's (1982) notion of contextualisation cues.

- *What interactional resources are available for doing cultural identities?* This is related to the indexical and symbolic cues available to participants in interaction and includes topics of talk which may be related to cultural expertise, cultural references by names and address terms and use of language or code associated with a group.
- *Why do people bother with interculturality?* Zhu suggests that the key reason for doing this is in maintaining and developing social relationships as well as structuring participation in interaction.
- *How far can participants go when doing interculturality?* This is, according to Zhu, the most challenging aspect in interculturality studies since cultural identities are neither fixed nor completely free.

The fluidity of cultural identities and the relationship between them and the many other identities participants may perform in interaction have already been discussed. Alongside this though, it has also been seen that cultural identities are not completely free. As Bauman (2004) underscored there is a tension and ambivalence between freedom and belonging, and Kumaravadivelu (2008) and Holliday (2011; 2013) both expanded on this in relation to cultural identities. Thus, Zhu (2014) like Canagarajah (2013) is, quite rightly, critical of extreme perspectives (e.g. Pennycook 2010 and Dervin 2012) which view cultural identity as entirely decided by participants with a complete freedom of choice. As Pavlenko and Blackledge (2004) made clear identities are not always negotiable. Furthermore, Zhu goes on to outline what can be negotiated and how, "what can be negotiated by participants is the extent of alignment or misalignment between ascription-by-others and self-orientation and the relevance of cultural membership at a specific time in interactions" (Zhu 2014: 216). This is represented in figure 4.1 which illustrates how the differences between ascribed and self-orientated identities can lead to greater or lesser alignment of identities in interaction.

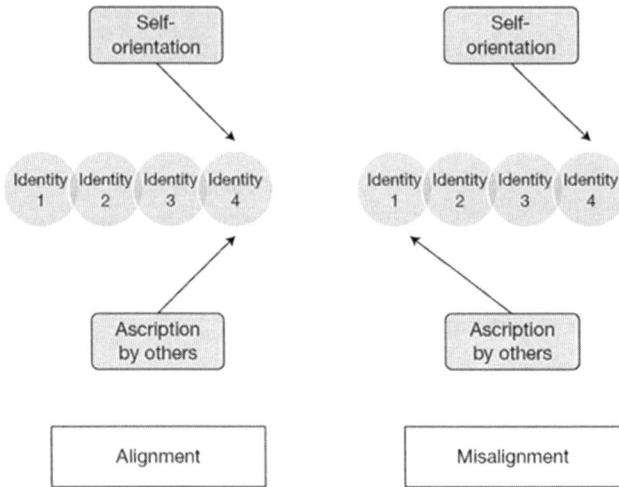

Fig. 4.1: Alignment and misalignment between self-orientated and ascribed identities (Zhu 2014: 217).

Interculturality then, as outlined by Zhu (2014), provides a way of conceptualising cultural identities that avoids essentialism and stereotyping and recognises the fluidity and complexity of cultural identities as one of multiple membership categories. It also accounts for the manner in which they are constructed in interaction on a moment by moment basis using a range of symbolic and indexical cues related primarily to linguistic, but also other, resources. At the same time though the perspective taken in interculturality also acknowledges that we are not free to choose any cultural identity we wish. At times particular cultural identities may be prescribed by others and non-negotiable (although less powerful participants may attempt, unsuccessfully, to resisted them), at other times cultural identities may be accepted and unproblematic and in such cases they may not always be salient to the interaction, and at other times still cultural identities may be negotiable. The degree of negotiation will involve the extent to which self-orientation and ascription-by-others are misaligned and the scope available for alignment. In the following section we will explore some of these themes in more detail through examples of identity construction from ELF research.

4.3 Identity in ELF research

As made clear throughout this chapter, language is viewed as a key part of identity construction, as Zhu explains "we have come to the view that language practices and identity are mutually dependent and interconnected. Language practices index and symbolise identities, which in turn impact on and feed back into language practices." (2014: 218). Given the central role of language in identity research and the correspondingly pivotal role of identity in socially orientated language research, it is to be expected that ELF researchers have been concerned with identity issues. However, as already noted in the previous two chapters, some ELF researchers have suggested that at times ELF might be culture and identity neutral (House 1999; 2003; 2012; Meierkord 2002; Kirkpatrick 2007). The previous outline of the relationship between language, communication and identity, and the earlier discussion of culture both underlined that identity issues are always present in social interaction; although, there may be times when they are accepted and unproblematic. In much of the discussions of 'neutral' ELF communication the claim seems to be focused on cultural identities associated with national conceptions of culture. In this sense the claim may be true in that there will almost certainly be instances where national cultural identities are not made relevant by the participants in ELF communication. However, this is to take a rather essentialist view of cultural identity in assuming that the only cultural identity those interacting through ELF can make relevant is national identities. As has been highlighted throughout this monograph, nation and culture associations and correspondingly national cultural identities are just one possible level or scale among many in interpreting culture and identity.

The majority of ELF researchers have adopted a more nuanced view of the relationship between language and identity and issues of cultural identity. Pölzl and Seidlhofer (2006), as explained in chapter three, provide empirical data demonstrating the manner in which local cultural identities are made salient in ELF communication. In their data ELF is used to make locally relevant linguacultural connections through which the participants constructed identities which demonstrated their membership of this local 'habitat' (Pölzl and Seidlhofer 2006: 162). Seidlhofer in later writings (2007; 2011) continues to explore the concept of identity in ELF related to less well defined or territorially bounded communities in which a great deal of ELF communication occurs. Again as discussed in chapter three, the notion of communities of practice has been considered in relation to the more transient, globally networked, virtual communities that many people now belong to and hence identify with. In such cases identity does not become an irrelevance but, as Seidlhofer (2011: 81–88) stresses, it means we need to move beyond traditional notions of identity associated with a local speech community in which there is regular physical contact. Ehrenreich (2009), Kalocsai (2014) and Vettorel (2014) offer empirical data illustrating the manner in which ELF is used to index and construct membership of both virtual networked communities of practice as well as more local communities of practice in which regular physical contact is a feature, but in which the communities are more transient then those traditionally described as speech communities in sociolinguistics.

One of the largest studies of identity in ELF research is Jenkins (2007) who conducted a worldwide survey of English teachers' attitudes towards English in relation to ELF and identity. In particular Jenkins focused on issues of identity related to an ideology prevalent in ELT in which the English language is associated with native English speakers from Anglophone countries. Her findings revealed a degree of ambivalence on the part of her participants in which they frequently wished to be identified with an imagined native speaker variety of English but also valued identities associated with their L1 and expressed through their English accent. As Jenkins explains it:

> NNS [non-native speaker] teachers may have very mixed feelings about expressing their membership of an international (ELF) community or even an L1 identity in their L2 English ... In most cases there was a strong sense that they desired a native-like English identity as signalled by a native like accent, especially in their role as teachers ... And yet most also expressed an attachment to their mother tongue and nationality, projected through their English accent, that they seemed reluctant to relinquish. (2007: 231)

Indeed, one participant in the study went as far as suggesting she was "linguistically schizophrenic" (2007: 214) which is not surprising given the divergent attitudes towards identity constructed through English described in the previous quotation. This though is not especially unique to ELF communication. Fracture and multiplicity, in which individuals index conflicting membership categories and identify with divergent communities, has been a recurrent theme in post-structuralist and post-modernist approaches to identity outlined so far. As such ELF research can be seen as contributing valuable empirical data to such approaches to understanding identity.

Furthermore, nativeness and its relationship to identity has been well dealt with in applied linguistics, and especially, in relation to English (e.g. Rampton 1990; Cook 1999; Davies 2003; Llurda 2006), with most discussions centring on the essentialised correlation between language, nation and culture. These arguments are familiar and will not be repeated here; although, the influence of this particular ideology on language teaching will be explored in more detail in the following chapters. However, some caution is needed in our interpretations of nativeness as a category of identification as well. What is indexed by nativeness as an identity, as with all identities, is contextually dependent. As Baird, Baker and Kitazawa (2014) argue, it is important not to reify the notions of nativeness and non-nativeness and to create false dichotomies in research. Thus, native like English, or rather English perceived as native like, may be used by participants in ELF communication for a range of purposes. For instance, in Jenkins' study

(2007) it was seen as a marker of professional identity as an English teacher. Kitazawa's (2013) research provides a clear example of the contextually dependent nature of indexing nativeness in ELF communication. In an interview one of her participants, an East Asian female business person, describes a German speaker of English as having 'good' English due to its native-like characteristics. However, as Kitazawa explains, this does not entail a desire to adopt a native speaker of English identity rather "what she evaluated highly was this 'achievement' accomplished by the German model, and not NS English itself. In this sense, it can be said that NS English may have its most powerful symbolic meaning when it is produced by NNSs." (2013: 196).

Jenks (2013) also recommends caution when applying identity terms such as native speaker, ELF speaker, EFL speaker or leaner. He employs membership categorisation analysis to "investigate what and how English language social categories are enacted in, and through, talk and interaction." (2013: 98). Importantly, this approach eschews a priori allocation of identities and instead investigates identities as they are constructed by participants, rather than interpreted by researchers, in the interaction. His study of chat room interactions, which would typically be considered ELF interactions, reveals that the category of ELF speaker is not one employed by the participants. Instead more relevant are social categories such as foreigner, language learner, and non-native. Nonetheless, as Jenks acknowledges, this does not render ELF irrelevant to discussions of identity. Rather it underscores the importance of explicit recognition of the theoretical and ethical issues raised in categorising and assigning identities for research participants. There may be sound theoretical and ethical reasons for discussing participant identities in relation to ELF. These may be related to raising awareness of the diversity of Englishes, challenging dominant native speaker ideologies or offering alternative forms of analysis to that typically used in ELT and SLA research. However, Jenks recommends that such positioning must be explicitly acknowledge and justified by researchers. This discussion also relates to the similar points made in chapter two as regards Brubaker and Cooper's (2000) warning not to conflate or confuse categories of practice employed by participants with categories of analysis used by researchers.

Other ELF research has also examined a range of different identities that are indexed and constructed through ELF interactions. Jenkins, Cogo and Dewey, drawing on the LINEE (Languages in a Network of European Excellence) project, report that in contrast to the native speaker orientations of English teachers, many younger users of English in Europe "identify with their own use of English rather than with a standard NS variety." (2011: 307). Jenkins, Cogo and Dewey state that for the majority of young Europeans English is used as a lingua franca (although as in Jenks' study (2013) they may not use the term) and that such uses of English are viewed positively as enhancing their interactions and place within a globalised world. Kalocsai (2009) in relation to the LINEE project, and in the study (2014) already outlined in chapter three, provides empirical evidence for this. She shows how from a community of practice perspective ELF serves as a key resource "in building and maintaining locally relevant identities." (2014: 212). She goes on to argue that due to the range of hybrid and new cultural resources that such communities of practice create and use, the corresponding "identities the members construct are multiple, fluid and dynamic" (2014: 212).

In addition, ELF studies have explored various features of language used to signal and construct identities in ELF interactions, including the use of idioms, metaphors and code-switching. Pitzl (2009; 2012) has investigated the relationship between creativity, idioms and metaphors in ELF communication. Based on data from the VOICE corpus she analysed multiple examples of creative language use, metaphors and idioms such as 'we should not wake up any dogs' and 'we have a lot of money in the sock'. Such language use draws on a range of references and may be based on adaptations and translations of participants' L1 idioms or metaphors, adaptations of English idioms or metaphors, or new creative idioms. According to Pitzl this creativity is intended to enhance communicative success at both a transactional and interactional level. In relation to cultural identity, idioms and metaphors can serve as intentional displays of a particular cultural identity (i.e. related to the L1 linguaculture), or as demonstrations of an awareness of other cultural identities (i.e. when making use of idioms from other linguacultures), but also in a more emergent manner they can "contribute to the interpersonal and interactional co-construction of local ELF intercultures" (2012: 47). Similar uses of language in communication through ELF have been reported in relation to code-switching in which it can be used as an explicit index of cultural identities and also of multilingual and multicultural identities (e.g. Klimpfinger 2009; Cogo 2010). Klimpfinger (2009), also making use of the VOICE corpus, illustrates a number of different ways this is done including tags such as *oui, oui* 'yes, yes', and specific cultural references which are linked to the interlocutor such as *Roma* rather than Rome. She also shows how interactants may orientate to more multilingual and multicultural identities by switching into the L1 of other participants (2009: 362).

Zhu (2015) applies the notion of interculturality to analyse of the way in which participants in communication through ELF orient to, assign or reject cultural identities. She also makes use of data from the VOICE corpus to present an example in which there was misalignment between self-oriented identity and that ascribed by others (extract 4.2). In this case an Argentinian participant (S3) rejects the ascription of Spanish identity from another participant (S2). Zhu then goes on to show how this was negotiated through the course of the conversation with S2 ascribing a Spanish identity based on language use but S3's continued resistance to this. S3 also gains support from other participants, for example S4 in line 25, who also resist identity memberships based on language alone. Furthermore, as Zhu points out, the distinctions between different varieties of Spanish are emphasised by the participants, for example S6 in line 16, so rejecting the notion of a shared Spanish speaking identity, which might at other times be made use of.

Extract 4.2
(S1: Spa-ES; S2, 4, 5 and 7: Ger-At; S3 and 6: Spa-AR; All participants are male except for S2 and7)

...

2 S2: yeah you're always speaking spanish so (.) <1> it </1> doesn't work @@@
3 S3: <1><L1spa> aun {but} </L1spa></1>
4 S3: <L1spa> ya que tenemos otra memoria y: {that we have another memory and} </L1spa> @@ (.)
5 S2: but maybe i'll change the subject and write in spanish or something like that (.)
6 S3: yeah but actually we're NOT SPANISH (2)
7 S2: hh (1) yeah but (.) you're <2> speaking </2>
8 S4: <L1ger><2> jetzt hast </2> ein <9> problem </9> {now you've got a problem} </L1ger><3> @@@ </3> @@ (.)
9 S3: <9><L1spa> ya aun {yes but} </L1spa></9>
10 S2: <3> no: </3>
11 S2: i don't know? (.) is it a problem? when i (.) when I say that you're spanish?
12 S5: yes it's =
13 S2: = but you're spa<4>nish-SPEAking </4>
14 S6: <4> yeah that's different </4>
15 S5: <4> yes it's exactly the same if </4> they say WE <5> have <un> xx </un></5>
16 S6: <5> it's a quite </5> different spanish =
17 S2: = yeah but we speak GERman. (.) <6> and you speak </6> spanish.<7> mhm okay </7>
18 S1: <6> you know even </6>
19 S1: <7> even for my </7>
20 S6: <7> it's different </7> it's a (prime) (.) <1><un> xxxx </un></1>
21 S5: <1> yeah but </1>
22 S4: <1> it's just </1>
23 S2: <1> ye- yeah </1> yeah <2> it's interesting i KNOW </2>
24 S6: <2> yeah </2>
25 S4: <2> think about it </2> when somebody tells us (.) well you're german i say no my GOD i'm austrian. (1)
26 S7: thanks god not @ =
27 S3: = no =
28 S2: = yeah but (.) but we are speaking german? (.)
29 S7: no
(Conversation between international students about language differences at a party. VOICE, LEcon352)
(Zhu 2015: 80–81)

This extract highlights the manner in which participants ascribe, resist and negotiate identities in this extract and particularly the way in which differences between national, ethnic, linguistic and cultural identities (in this case Argentinian Spanish speakers and Spanish speakers from Spain) which may not be obvious to others are emphasised. This leads Zhu (2015) to conclude that cultural identities should not be assumed *a priori* in intercultural communication through ELF. Negotiation between participants in relation to the degree of alignment between self-oriented and other ascribed identities is crucial.

Many of the studies cited above (Klimpfinger 2009; Pitzl 2009: 2012; Cogo 2010; Jenks 2013; Zhu 2015) have employed discourse analysis, of one kind or another, in their investigations of identity construction in ELF communication. This has proved a very productive approach and one that allows the researcher to uncover the way particular identities are made relevant by participants through the interaction itself, rather than making a priori assumptions. However, there is still a danger that this will produce a rather one sided understanding of identity that is based solely on the researchers' interpretations. In much qualitative research, and particularly in ethnography, insider, emic perspectives and participants own views are a crucial part of understanding social relations and structure, of which identity is a fundamental constituent. Studies, such as Kalocsai (2014), which include analysis of instances of discourse combined with a rich description of the context in which they occur and the participants' own interpretations of the interactions allow for a level of depth and complexity that would be hard to achieve otherwise. This is the approach I have followed in my own research examining issues of identity, and especially cultural identity, in communication through ELF (Baker 2009; 2011a).

Returning to an example presented in chapter three (extract 3.3) concerning the open negotiation of communicative practices, interviews with two of the participants in that conversation revealed a further level of complexity in their interpretation of the interaction and their identification with different groups. For example, one of the participants, Nami (female, Thai L1), makes the claim that "I'm not really conservative type girl" in the conversation which she explains in a follow up interview.

Extract 4.3
1. NAMI: oh that's the great up to you.... yes that's because Thai people if you observe I think you observe that girls like to say they don't like to make the decision ... everything is just man make a decision and girls aren't allowed to make a decision here in this society and I don't like it because I have my own right to do that too to do that too umm and so that's why I was like making it as a joke (?)

2. WILL: very interesting again so err do you think then when you do that you are going against Thai culture or doing something different to Thai culture

3. NAMI: umm it's against yes ((laughs)) but I think that it's new generation right now and all you need to do the culture will change due to many thing factors and so I think it's a time that umm Thai culture need to change too
(Baker 2009: 579)

Here Nami consciously identifies with, and also rejects, a number of different groups. Firstly, she rejects what she sees as the traditional female role of deferring to males in Thai society; however, in doing this she is also making her gender identity prominent. In line 3 she goes on to identify with a particular generation but also resists the suggestion that her behaviour is 'against' Thai culture, thus retaining her identification with this grouping. This example illustrates the fluid manner in which different identifications interact; national cultures, gender and generation and also a degree of agency on the part of the individual as well. As Nami says at the end of this extract, "Thai culture needs to change too" and she offers her behaviour as an example of more general generationally referenced cultural practices which are giving rise to this change.

At another point in the conversation in extract 3.3, Nami says to another participant, Oy (female, Thai L1), "you used to be Thai". This is followed by laughter on both their parts suggesting it was offered and taken as a joke. However, this indicates recognition, at least on Nami's part, that cultural identities are both self-selected and other-ascribed and that Oy has done something to suggest that others may not always interpret her behaviour as 'Thai'. Indeed, Oy spent a large amount of time with English speakers from the UK, claimed in interviews to speak English more often than Thai, and there was a feeling among other research participants in this group that Oy's identity was not 'authentically' Thai anymore. Oy appeared to be aware of this to a degree in her interview responses, as extract 4.4 shows, she identifies with a London accent in English which she is unwilling to change. Yet, extracts 4.5 and 4.6 highlight that she does not see this as necessarily in conflict with her identity as 'a Thai woman' or exclude her from orientating towards a Thai cultural identity when it suits here.

Extract 4.4
OY ... my friends ask me sometime they say can't you do it in Thai or in American accent and I say umm yeah but that would be funny to me and I don't really like it ... I got a bit of a London accent as well

Extract 4.5
OY: ... as I am a Thai woman or girl whatever you wanted to put it that way I still have to keep the culture with me

Extract 4.6
OY: yeah but I (don't know) in my life I still have to come back here [Thailand] and die here because it's my home
(Baker 2011a: 45)

These three extracts offer a good example of how an individual can identify with multiple groups which may, to others, appear contradictory. Yet, these apparently contradictory perspectives are not necessarily viewed as problematic by the participants. The research participants in this study (Baker 2009) also adopted identities in which they embraced an in-between role or position in which they were able to relate to more than one cultural grouping simultaneously. In the following extract Yim (female, Thai L1) explains why she believes she would make a good English teacher. She suggests that in teaching writing there are "spaces" between the expectations of foreign teachers (in this setting usually English native speakers) and Thai students. Sharing the same background as the student but also having experienced the process of learning to write in English and now being a successful writer in English, Yim feels she will be able to mediate between the two sets of expectations or as she puts it "delete the gaps". Thus, she appears to be putting herself forward in the role of a mediator *between* the two groups.

Extract 4.7
YIM: ... when there is a way for me to help Thai people with the English language and if there is a possibility to do that I will want to do that because like I like I told you earlier that about like the teaching writing you know there is some spaces between the foreign teachers and the students ... and yeah and I think as I have had some experience with those problems and I should be able to you know to delete the gaps between yeah and solve the problem some of them
(Baker 2011a: 45)

Participants also took on liminal identities which were not related to, or in-between, any particular cultural grouping but more fluid and dynamic. As Nami explains in extract 4.8 communicating through ELF (or with non-native English speakers as she terms it) 'opens people up' and moves them beyond their original cultural identities.

Extract 4.8
NAMI: it's different because in English you you can express yourself more you you you it's also because of the cultural thing when when you umm yeah when you speak with the native speaker right they are more open because of their culture as well but even if you speak with the other people who isn't who are non umm English speaker err English is a kind of message containing something that it will make other people more open I don't know maybe I'm wrong but that is what I observe people people speak more people tend to forget their own culture for a while and they become more open
(Baker 2009: 580)

In sum, through these interview extracts the participants express orientations to a range of identities in ELF communication. These include national cultural identities, but these also intersect with other identities such as gender and generation which are related in various ways to the participants' sense of cultural identity. The extracts here also show an awareness of cultural identities as adaptable and changeable. Furthermore, the use of English allows the participants to identify with various cultural groupings. In these extracts at least, orientating to multiple, possibly contradictory, cultural identities did not seem to be a problem for the participants. Indeed, a number of participants embraced both the role of being in-between and also the openness and liminality of cultural identities that intercultural communication through ELF enabled.

4.4 Conclusion

Throughout this chapter there has been an emphasis on identity and cultural identities as multiple, complex, fluid and always in process; as with culture, identity is something we do, and identity is performed. Language and discourse are seen as a core part of understanding identity and, again as with culture, the primary semiotic medium through which identities are constructed. The relationship between culture and identity is seen as significant in that cultural groups are one of the major groupings individuals identify with. However, it has also been made clear that identity and culture are not synonymous and culture cannot be replaced by discussions of identity alone. In particular, we need to be wary of essentialist correlations between self, identity and cultures. This was also linked to the danger of othering and essentialism that has been pervasive in much intercultural communication literature in which individuals are assumed to be different based on essentialised cultural identities. A number of different aspects of cultural identities were explicated including ethnic, racial, regional, national and global groupings. Thus, cultural identities are viewed as a complex network of interacting group identifications.

Of particular relevance to intercultural communication through ELF it was suggested that globalisation has led to the opening up of new spaces and resources for identity construction. However, it is also important that this does not lead to the assumption that individuals are free to choose and construct whatever identities they like. Identity construction takes places within existing social structures and these provide constraints on the choices available to individuals. The continued prominence of national groupings was highlighted as a particularly pervasive example of external restrictions on identity choices and constructions. Indeed, a recurrent theme in this chapter has been the need to be sensitive to issues of power and dominance in identity construction and awareness of the degree to which identities are self-selected or other ascribed, and correspondingly, to what extent identities are imposed, accepted or negotiated. Interculturality was put forward as a productive framework for investigating these diverse aspects of identity construction and especially for examining the manner in which different identities are made salient and negotiated in interaction which avoids a priori assumptions about participants' cultural identities.

The final section of this chapter examined empirical studies of intercultural communication through ELF. This research made it clear that identity was as relevant an issue in ELF as in any other form of communication. The growing number of studies in this area repeatedly demonstrates the different ways in which a range of identities are performed through ELF. While a minority of ELF scholars, particularly those that position ELF as culture and identity neutral, adopt a somewhat essentialist notion of identity which is correlated to nations, the majority of researchers in ELF have approached identity from a poststructuralist and post-modernist perspective. Thus, participants in ELF studies have reported and been observed using English to create and index multiple identities. Research has shown tensions between national cultural identities related to participants own L1 and the pull of 'native speaker ideologies', particularly in the discourse of ELT which associates the use of English with Anglophone nations and cultures. However, ELF research has also revealed participants constructing cultural identities which make the multilingual and multicultural nature of ELF communication prominent through references to both a plurality of cultures and in positioning the participants themselves as multilingual communicators. Alongside this, there is evidence of participants in intercultural communication through ELF embracing being 'in-between' cultures and adopting the role of mediators. At other times participants have reported the use of ELF as a medium through which they can construct identities that are not *between* any particular cultures or cultural identifications but something more fluid and liminal. Therefore, in answer to the question set at the beginning of the chapter, '*What influence (if anything) do studies of intercultural communication through ELF have on our understanding of the relationship between culture, identity and language?*', we can see that ELF studies provide valuable data illustrating the multiple ways in which culture, identity and language interact and the importance of approaching them in a holistic and situated manner in order to best understand intercultural communication through ELF. How participants in such communication make sense of and negotiate all this variation and complexity will be the subject of the next chapter.

Chapter 5
Re-examining intercultural communicative competence: intercultural awareness

> "although I do not suppose that either of us knows anything really beautiful and good, I am better off than he is – for he knows nothing, and thinks that he knows. I neither know nor think that I know."
> – Socrates in Plato's Apology (Translated by Benjamin Jowett, http://classics.mit.edu/Plato/apology.1b.txt)

Over the previous chapters we have explored the complexity of intercultural communication through English as a lingua franca. We have seen how language and culture come together in fluid and dynamic ways which change depending on participants, purposes and settings. An approach has been outlined in which categories of language, identity, community and culture are seen as constructed, negotiable and contested. This also involves a critical perspective whereby we question the relevance of each of these categories, as well as the how and why of such constructions, maintaining an awareness of the ideological positions and power structures that any particular construction involves. This brings us to the question of how participants in intercultural communication manage this fluidity and complexity. If, as suggested by ELF research, many intercultural interactions are successful, what knowledge, skills or competences do participants possess or make use of that enable meaningful and satisfactory intercultural communication. Within intercultural communication research these knowledge, skills and attitudes have typically been conceptualised through the notion of intercultural competence and intercultural communicative competence. However, in chapter two, much of the research on which traditional notions of intercultural competence are based was critiqued for a simplistic and essentialist treatment of culture, language and intercultural communication. Following a poststructuralist perspective, as adopted in much contemporary intercultural communication and ELF research, leads to the third question posed at the beginning of this monograph – *What are the implications of ELF research for conceptualising intercultural communicative competence?*

In order to answer this question a range of different notions of competence and intercultural communication will be explored. Firstly, communicative competence can be viewed as foundational to many of the subsequent discussions of intercultural competence and intercultural communicative competence in applied linguistics and so a critical evaluation of this will be presented, along-side more contemporary interpretations of it in relation to ELF. The discussion will then draw on the intercultural communication literature more widely with a brief overview of intercultural competence. This will lead into an exploration of intercultural communicative competence which combines aspects of both communicative competence and intercultural competence. There will be a focus on Byram's (1997) characterisation of intercultural communication competence (ICC) in relation to applied linguistics and language education, as well as more recent alternatives which have built on or been influenced by this. However, I will argue that all of these approaches have failed to adequately address the fluidity and complexity of intercultural communication through ELF, in which knowledge of particular target communities and associated communicative practices is insufficient as either a model of the competences of successful communicators or as a model of good practice in intercultural communication. Throughout the discussion many of the models and theories of communicative and intercultural communicative competence blend empirical and theoretical research with goals for training, teaching and learning. As such this chapter offers a transition from the research led concerns in the first part of this monograph to the pedagogic orientation of the second part.

5.1 Communicative competence

5.1.1 The foundations of communicative competence

It will be useful to begin with the notion of communicative competence to frame the discussion in this chapter. While writings on communicative competence are not as pervasive as the more interdisciplinary notions of culture and identity addressed so far in this monograph, the concept has received a great deal of attention within applied linguistics. Communicative competence in various forms has been foundational to many of the subsequent discussions of what successful communication entails and in the development of intercultural communicative competence. Although a detailed overview is not the purpose of this section, it is necessary to be clear what is meant by communicative competence, and also to examine the concept critically in the light of subsequent developments in understanding intercultural communication. In this respect ELF research, I will argue, has some particularly profound implications for how we might conceive of successful communication and the types of competence required for this.

The notion of competence used here is generally taken to refer initially to Chomsky's notion of formal linguistic competence as perfect knowledge of the language by "an ideal speaker-listener, in a completely homogeneous speech-community" (1965: 3). This is distinct from performance which is the use of the language in concrete situations by individuals. This competence/ performance distinction is often portrayed as mirroring Saussure's *Langue* and *Parole* distinction, with langue referring to the formal, abstract linguistic system and parole to its use. Competence here is clearly an idealised abstraction and one that has been extensively criticised in applied linguistics for its lack of relevance to understanding what happens in 'real-world' interactions. Of course, Chomsky's linguistic competence was not conceived in relation to 'real world problems' but it has been problematic and controversial when applied to real world language use, for example in SLA research. Such an abstract formalised view of language is also at odds with the emergentist and practice accounts of language offered in chapter three. Nonetheless, the notion of a competence that underlies any performance has been ubiquitous in conceptualisations of what is needed for successful communication.

In contrast to Chomsky's abstract notion of linguistic competence, Hymes' communicative competence, grounded in sociolinguistics, has been much more influential in applied linguistics. Hymes greatly expanded the scope of knowledge required to communicate successfully beyond formal linguistic properties to include a range of aspects related to knowledge of social context. This is formulated in four questions contained in the quotation below.

> I would suggest, then, that for language and other forms of communication (culture), four questions arise:
> 1. Whether (and to what degree) something is formally *possible*;
> 2. Whether (and to what degree) something is *feasible* in virtue of the means of implementation available:
> 3. Whether (and to what degree) something is *appropriate* (adequate, happy, successful) in relation to a context in which it is used and evaluated;
> 4. Whether (and to what degree) something is in fact done, actually *performed*, and what its doing entails.
> (Hymes 1972: 281)

Chomsky's original linguistic competence is covered by question one, but the following three questions are more concerned with actual use i.e. what is feasible (whether what is possible could actually be processed by interlocutors), what is appropriate (related to social context) and what is performed (what has previously been said or written). It is Hymes' communicative competence with its linking of linguistic knowledge, social knowledge and context that has informed the majority of subsequent writings on communicative competence and intercultural communicative competence.

However, there are a number of significant limitations to Hymes' notion, particularly in relation to intercultural communication through ELF. Hymes' communicative competence is still based around an idea of a native speaker operating within a defined speech community of which they have extensive knowledge. Hymes writes that, "There is an important sense in which a normal member of a community has knowledge with respect to all these aspects of the communicative systems available to him. He will interpret or assess the conduct of others and himself in ways that reflect a knowledge of each ..." (1972: 282). This is clearly problematic for intercultural communication and ELF in that it may be difficult or impossible to specify what 'a normal member of a community' is and hence the knowledge that they possess in common with other members of the community. Related to this point, it can be equally problematic establishing exactly what community participants in intercultural communication through ELF are part of and where the boundaries between knowledge associated with one particular 'defined' community or another start and finish. Even when communities can be established the transient nature of them makes identifying stable systems of knowledge of either what is consider appropriate or what has previously been performed difficult and of questionable relevance. It is also not clear how these features of competence relate to individuals communicating in a language which is not their first language, or in multilingual environments.

In addition, there have been various critiques of a number of other technical difficulties with Hymes' communicative competence (e.g. Widdowson 2003; Brumfit 2006), which do not need a full explanation here, but issues of relevance to this discussion are the isolation of different elements of communication with little consideration of the relationship between them and that the competence/ performance distinction has been retained. Some of these limitations are an inevitable part of any attempt to conceptualise, which necessarily involves a degree of categorisation, simplification and isolation. Yet, as made clear in complexity theory approaches to language, culture and communication relationships are an integral part of any system and cannot be ignored (a criticism also raised by Widdowson 2003; 2012).

Canale and Swain (1980) provide a characterisation of communicative competence which is based on Hymes' ideas but, unlike Hymes, directly addresses second language use and learning. In so doing the notion of communicative competence moved from a research heuristic to a model of communication and an associated set of pedagogic principles. Canale and Swain (1980) distinguished between three areas: grammatical competence, sociolinguistic competence and strategic competence. Canale (1983) later divided the original formulation of sociolinguistic competence into sociolinguistic and discourse competence. While the first two elements corresponded to Hymes' 'possible' and 'appropriate' respectively, the second two elements 'discourse competence' and 'strategic competence' were new. In particular, strategic competence, which involves strategies for overcoming communication breakdowns or difficulties, recognises interactional features of communication which are related to intercultural communication and second language use. This four element model of communicative competence has gone on to be hugely influential in approaches to communicative competence for second language users; in language policy, and particularly the Common European Framework of Reference for Languages (van Ek 1986; Council of Europe 2001); in language teaching, especially communicative language teaching (e.g. Nunan 1991; Celce-Murcia, Dörnyei and Thurrell 1995) and testing (e.g. Bachman 1990; McNamara 1995).

As with any influential and much discussed model or theory, communicative competence, as conceived by Canale and Swain (1980), has attracted a great deal of discussion and criticism. For example, placing grammatical competence as the first level of competence is controversial for a number of reasons and in particular it is not clear what the role of lexis or formulaic language is in this model and how this relates to grammatical competence, or even if they can be separated. Such concerns are not central to the purposes of this chapter and have been dealt with elsewhere (.e.g. Bachman 1990; Celce-Murcia, Dörnyei and Thurrell 1995); nonetheless, there are a number that are worth considering here. Firstly, in specific relation to this model, like Hymes' model, there is little representation of the relationship between the elements, indeed these four elements appear more as a list than a model. To repeat the criticism, if we view relationships as an essential part of any system of communication, language or culture this needs to be part of the model. Furthermore, both Brumfit (2001) and Widdowson (2012) argue that all of the models of communicative competence presented so far are overly static in their representations of language and communication. As Brumfit suggests, "there is a sense in which both Hymes, and Canale and Swain, seem to see the language user/learner as a passive victim of the inherited rule system of the past – there seems to be an almost Whorfian determinism in the discussion of apparently fixed rules waiting to be described" (2001: 52). There seems little space in these models for the negotiation, adaptation, variation and fluidity of language, communication and context that have already been noted as key features of intercultural communication.

Secondly, while Hymes specified 'a normal member of a community', Canale and Swain go a step further and suggest that the model for grammatical and sociolinguistic competence should be a native speaker. There are a number of examples that indicate they have a native speaker interlocutor in mind, for example they write about how important it is that, "second language learners' and teachers' expectations of tolerance to grammatical and sociocultural inaccuracies are to correspond to actual levels of tolerance shown by different groups of native speakers of the second language." (Canale and Swain 1980: 12). As already discussed, the concept of a native speaker is notoriously problematic and ill-defined and hence unlikely to be of much use as a model of successful communication (certainly not all native speakers of a language are good communicators). It is of even less relevance for ELF communication where native speakers of the language, English, are not present in the majority of cases and if they are the language is functioning as a lingua franca for them to. There is also an assumption, illustrated in the quotation above, that the burden of communicative success rests on the second language users and their attempts to communicate in a way that native speakers will 'tolerate'. The inclusion of strategic competence reinforces this perspective as again the burden is on the second language user to employ the necessary strategies to 'compensate' (Canale and Swain 1980: 30) for their lack of communicative competence. This is very much a deficit perspective in which second language users are viewed as inferior to native speakers of a language. However, this is a questionable assumption in multilingual intercultural communication where *all* participants need to accommodate to each other and adherence to one particular variety of language or set of socio-cultural norms is more likely to hinder than help communication (a point that will be developed further in later discussions of communicative and intercultural competence).

The assumption of the native speaker as the model of a competent communicator results in two further underlying theoretical difficulties with Canale and Swain's model and the subsequent influence it has had over language policy and practice. Firstly, there is a reification of language in which it is equated with a particular set of forms or a fixed code. This is clearly an idealisation of language since there is obviously a great deal of variety in native speaker language use, of whatever language. While some simplification is of course necessary in models, it can obstruct understanding if the simplifications become prescriptive and close off recognition of potentially appropriate language forms (what Widdowson (2003) refers to as the virtual language and explained below) that do not conform to this restricted norm. Secondly, there is a similar reification of social norms. Given the complexity of all communication, and especially intercultural communication, specifying what is, or is not, socially acceptable or appropriate is not possible in anything but the most general, obvious and tentative manner. The context or the communicative event itself is crucial to understanding what is considered appropriate amongst the participants and this can only be established in retrospect. Prescribing a set of rules of social norms is as likely to hinder successful communication as it is to aid it. This reification of language and communication is further exacerbated, as Leung (2005) notes, by the tendency, in

English language teaching at least, to interpret communicative competence and its components based on a narrow set of 'native speaker' norms derived from the intuitions of teacher trainers or material writers. In this sense, Leung claims, it serves the opposite purpose to Hymes' original concept of communicative competence which was to open up empirical, rather than intuitive, investigation as to what was appropriate in particular settings, as opposed to making unfounded generalisations.

Canale and Swain also retain the competence/performance distinction which it has already been suggested is problematic. While there is the technical issue of how you operationalise such a distinction (Celce-Murcia, Dörnyei and Thurrell 1995; McNamara 1995), there are also questions as to the validity of the distinction itself (see in particular Harris 1998). The competence/performance distinction is an important and wide-ranging debate, but of particular relevance to the argument here is that from an emergent perspective to language and communication, as outlined in chapter three, competence does not precede performance. So for emergentists such as Hopper "structure, or regularity, comes out of discourse and is shaped by discourse in an ongoing process. Grammar is, in this view, simply the name for certain categories of observed repetitions in discourse." (1998: 156). Similar points are made by Tomasello (2003; 2008) and Everett (2012) and were discussed in chapter three, so will not be repeated in detail here, other than to note that they also view communication and language as a cultural practice which does not require an underlying abstract grammatical competence which comes before performance is possible. Likewise, Harris notes that a rule-based model of communicative competence, whether based on linguistic, communicative or pragmatic rules is unlikely to account for the complexity of communication, "The plain fact is that no rule-based model of any kind so far proposed can come to terms with the real-life flexibility of communication situations and communicational processes." (1998: 44). Instead, Harris recommends dropping the term competence and instead replacing it with 'communicative proficiency' (1998: 44), which is in part dependent on past experiences but is equally dependent on the communicative situation at hand. Halliday too offers an early critique of the distinction, suggesting that we can "reject the distinction altogether on the grounds that we cannot operate with this degree and this kind of idealization" (1979: 38). He goes on to specifically critique Hymes in claiming that "Hymes is taking the intra-organism ticket to what is actually an inter-organism destination" (1979: 38). As Pennycook (2007: 60) notes, Halliday's positions represent a rejection of the distinction or at least an inversion of the relationship between performance and competence. From this perspective, as Pennycook argues, competence emerges in relation to "a wide array of social, cultural and discursive forces" (2007: 60) and does not reside as an internal abstract property of individuals. This more holistic view of communicative competence, or whatever we might chose to term it, in which distinctions with performance are rejected is an important development and an approach that will be returned to throughout the chapter.

5.1.2 Rethinking communicative competence

Pennycook's (2007) discussion of competence is particularly relevant as it is in direct response to the greater understanding we now have of the global uses of languages and the multilingual or plurilingual nature of intercultural communication. Indeed, the global role of many languages and the plurilingual nature of intercultural communication is a theme that has been addressed by an increasing number of scholars in relation to the linguistic dimension of communicative competence. Blommaert in recognition of the diverse range of registers, genres and contexts of language use argues that "no one knows all of a language" (2010: 103) and that 'partial competence' is the norm. He suggests that rather than focus on competences in specific languages it is better to conceive of competence in terms of repertories and resources which enable us to do particular things with a range of linguistic and pragmatic features. This echoes Hopper's earlier claim that "[l]earning a language is not a question of acquiring grammatical structure but of expanding a repertoire of communicative contexts" (1998: 171). However, while the notion of a 'multilingual repertoire' is attractive and underscores the importance of recognising the plurilingual nature of much intercultural communication, the idea is not expanded on in detail by Blommaert and the focus is still very much on linguistic features with little consideration of how this relates to other aspects of intercultural communication.

An earlier discussion of competence, which also recognised the significance of multi or plurilingual communication, is offered by Cook who has written extensively on the notion of multi-competence (e.g. 1991; 2002; 2005; 2012). Cook positions multilingualism at the core of investigations of competence and hence marks a significant break with the more monolingual approaches presented in the previous section. He defines multi-competence as, 'knowledge of more than one language in the same mind' (2002: 10). Furthermore, he is highly critical of the focus on monolingual native speakers in earlier discussions of competence, pointing out that monolinguals are the minority of language users in the world and arguing that multilinguals use language differently to monolinguals. Conceptions of competence then, for Cook, need to explain competence in languages not language. Cook suggests that, "With multi-competence the competence of a monolingual native speaker became in a sense irrelevant; it was the competence of the successful L2 user that mattered. Of course this begs the question of the difficulty of defining exactly what a successful L2 user might be, perhaps as chimerical as the native speaker ..." (2005). The notion of multi-competence and its focus on multilingual language users are clearly highly relevant to intercultural communication and ELF. Cook's main focus, though, is on the implications of this for SLA and so his model will not be dealt with further, but the notion of multilingualism as the baseline for competence will be drawn on.

A cognitive approach to competence is also adopted by Hall (2013) who argues for a plurilithic rethinking of Chomskyan I-language (individual internal representations of language), which in turn can inform understandings of English as a global language and lingua franca. He is, like Cook (2002) and Leung (2005), critical of monolingual assumptions of language knowledge and competence based on the intuitions of a small elite, "The theoretical accounts they develop are based on data from a subset of the set of closely overlapping actual I-languages used by a small group of educated speakers operating monolingually and monodialectally. Furthermore, the I-language data characterized have themselves been consciously or unconsciously filtered and fashioned by non-linguistic social conventions." (2013: 217). However, he argues that this does not invalidate the need for research on internal representations of language or the role of I-language in understanding communication. Simplifying the argument somewhat, he contends that a mental view of language can be equally plurilithic and does not need to be associated with discrete notions and ideologically based views of N-language (named languages e.g. English, French, and Chinese) and in fact I-languages do not recognise such boundaries, "In sum, a cognitive view, acknowledging that English resides in people's minds as (dynamic) I-languages, not as N- or P-languages, strongly reinforces, rather than denies, a plurilithic view of English." (2013: 223). As will be discussed at the end of this section, the extent to which communication involves competence in an internal linguistic system, such as that proposed by I-language, is debatable. However, Hall (2013) raises important issues about the role of cognitive processes in communication and many of his ideas are commensurable with emergentist and complex accounts of language in viewing language as dynamic and plurilithic and not dividing it along the ideological constructs of national languages.

Unsurprisingly, along with other researchers into plurilingualism, globalisation and language, ELF researchers have been critical of the role of an idealised native speaker's competence in conceptions of communicative competence. Seidlhofer (2011) argues that ELF research, which has questioned the concept of unitary discrete languages through demonstrating the variety of English use and forms, leads us to question the supposed self-evident native speaker competence. She writes that, "It may be accepted that a language is intrinsically variable, that its communities of speaker are far from homogeneous, but somehow the contradictory notion survives, and thrives, that is speakers nevertheless all have basically the same unitary competence." (2011: 89). Clearly in heterogeneous and plurilingual contexts, which are typically the contexts of communication through ELF, but also a daily reality in many communities, people will have different levels of competence in different languages and in different domains. Indeed, even speakers who share a first language and linguaculture will have different levels of competence in different domains and different levels of knowledge of the language. Whether it is the bingo hall, the football pitch, the lecture theatre or the doctors surgery, most people who 'share' a first language will have particular sets of linguistic resources or competences that are not shared by all who identify with that language group. As with Blommaert (2010), Seidlhofer concludes that, "competence will always be partial and incomplete" (2011: 80). This leads Seidlhofer to a critique of Hymes' (1972) notion of communicative competence, similar to one outlined earlier in this chapter (see also Jenkins 2000). However, she does not advocate abandoning the concept, but rather uncoupling notions such as feasibility, appropriateness and performance from native speaker communities and linking them to the sorts of communities that ELF interactions take place in. In such cases, Seidlhofer suggests, "quite different judgements are likely to be made about what is feasible, appropriate to context, and so on ... And indeed here one has to accept that it is likely to be appropriate in many, if not most contexts in which English is currently used, not to fully conform to native-speaker conventions." (2011: 91).

A similar position is adopted by Widdowson (2012) and Hülmbauer (2013) who both suggest alternative notions of linguistic competence in relation to intercultural communication through ELF. In particular, and like Seidlhofer, they make use of Widdowson's (2003) earlier idea of the virtual language to describe the kind of linguistic competence made use of ELF communication. Widdowson explain this notion in the following manner, "ELF users develop their own construct of the possible as a function of what is feasible and appropriate for their purposes, by exploiting the potential for meaning making inherent in the language, what I have called elsewhere the virtual language" (2012: 21). It is, according to Widdowson, a competence related to abstracted knowledge of their own experience of this virtual language that forms the competence of users of English in ELF communication. This will necessarily be different to native speakers since their experiences with the language are different to native speakers' primary socialisation in English. Indeed, Seidlhofer, Widdowson and Hülmbauer all claim that the underlying knowledge or competence in English in ELF must be different to native speaker competence. If participants in ELF communication were restricted to using pre-existing forms then communication would become much less efficient and successful since the language would not be adapted to the functions to which it is put. It is the *potential* for meaning making that is part of the virtual in all language that enables users to creatively adapt and change linguistic forms and communicative norms to fit the purposes they are needed for. In many ways this approach appears similar to Halliday's (1975; 1985) functional grammar and the oft quoted dictum that *form follows function*. However, Widdowson believes there is a crucial distinction between functional grammar and the virtual language as related to ELF "the construct of the possible in ELF represents the ongoing development of a genuinely functional grammar, where linguistic forms are pragmatically motivated by contextual function in contrast to Halliday's functional grammar, which is essentially the static semantic record of how functions in the past have become encoded in the standard language." (2012: 22).

The concept of a virtual English leads to a further question which Seidlhofer (2011) raises. Following from her characterisation of ELF as "not a variety of English but a variable way of using it: English that functions *as* a lingua franca. The absolutely crucial question, of course remains how that 'English' that functions as a lingua franca is conceptualised and how it functions" (2011: 77). For Widdowson this is an empirical question, "Descriptions of ELF already give some indication of the nature of this construct, and identifying its essential features is, I think, one of the major challenges of ELF research in the future." (2012: 21). However, descriptions of the English in ELF have been one of the major issues of controversy in ELF research. This is not the appropriate place to explore the arguments in detail (see for example Jenkins, Cogo and Dewey 2011; Seidlhofer 2011; Mauranen 2012; Hülmbauer 2013; Mortenson 2013; Baird, Baker and Kitazawa 2014) but while the majority of ELF researchers are in agreement that ELF is not a variety of language in the traditional sense, there is some disagreement as to the degree of stability and fluidity of language forms in ELF communication. So, for example, Seidlhofer explicitly rejects an emergentist approach to language and instead proposes that there is an "underlying abstract set of rules" (2011: 112) that forms the virtual English language that both ELF users and (ENL) English native language users make reference to when using English. While Widdowson (2012) makes no reference to underlying rules in his description of the virtual language, he too suggests that the notion of an underlying competence, as conceived by Chomsky, is a useful abstraction for understanding ELF and of course the competence/performance distinction is maintained. Hülmbauer makes use of the concept of the virtual language but writes that "ELF cannot be described by reference to a specific set of linguistic forms and rules." (2013: 68), suggesting a different interpretation to Seidlhofer (2011). She also makes reference to the notion of linguistic resources, similarly conceived to Blommaert (2010), inherent variation and plurilingualism. However, she writes that "the intercultural ecologies in which ELF exchanges happen do not only foster *the exploitation of virtuality beneath what is encoded in English,* but also take a plurilingual dimension." (2013: 68, emphasis mine), with the implication that there is an underlying structure that can be exploited.

This is a different interpretation of language to that offered in chapter three in relation to emergentism and complexity theory. To briefly summarise the argument, it was proposed that any system or structured account of language needed to be viewed as emergent from individual interactions but not reducible to them. Furthermore, the delineation of any particular language and features of that language are a convenient abstraction for researchers, policy makers and so forth, rather than a representation of a concrete entity. In this case there can be no 'underlying' system which language users are drawing on or exploiting. To expand on the quotation offered in chapter three:

> Interpretations of emergentism do not deny that with the need to communicate meaning (function) comes the knowledge of linguistic structures (forms). However, it does question the necessity of positing an underlying set of abstract rules to account for these structures. Emergentism suggests that any regular patterns of language use that can be described emerge from the aggregated or sedimented use of many individuals whose use of language is likely to be considerably more variable than these sedimented patterns. Furthermore, emergentism and complexity theory would also suggest that the patterns are learnt as part of communicative repertoires gained through repeated participation in contextualised communication, as opposed to drawing on abstract grammatical rules. Therefore, what is shared in ELF interactions that enables the participants to refer to the language as English is related to social experience rather than abstract rules.
> (Baird, Baker and Kitazawa 2014: 182)

Following this conception of language and communication the notion of grammatical competence, however it might be defined, is problematic. This is not, of course, to deny a role for linguistic competence in communicative competence, but it does suggest that it is not related to knowledge of a linguistic *system,* and certainly not a grammatical system, on the part of the individual communicator. Furthermore, as was made clear in the overview of research into intercultural communication, successful intercultural communication involves a lot more than mastery of linguistic forms. Additionally, practice and performance based accounts of language, discourse, communication, identity and culture, question the legitimacy of separating the study of linguistic forms from other aspects of communication. If we are to take this seriously any conception of communicative competence will need to address more than linguistic competence. This is not to suggest that ELF researchers have not been aware of this and, as will be explored later in this chapter, wider conceptions of communicative competence, particularly the notion of pragmatic competence, have been a significant strand of ELF research.

5.2 Intercultural competence

Within the wider field of intercultural communication research, in all its different orientations, the concept of intercultural competence has been as central as communicative competence has in applied linguistics. These conceptions of the competence needed for intercultural communication are useful in that they typically adopt a much wider perspective on communication than just linguistic competence, or the even narrower grammatical competence. However, as raised in chapter two, much research in intercultural communication has adopted a somewhat essentialist and overly structuralist perspective on the relationship between culture and communication and so there are considerable limitations to the relevance of these approaches. Additionally, the frequently unproblematic treatment of, or minimal concern with, language, which has already been shown to be central to understanding intercultural communication, represents another serious weakness and also limits their relevance for the discussions in this book. Nonetheless, a number of important themes emerge from these treatments of competence which will be drawn on later in discussions of intercultural communicative competence, cultural awareness and intercultural awareness. Therefore, a brief sketch of some of these key themes is needed; although, a comprehensive overview is not attempted and many important theories will no doubt be missing and generalisations and simplifications made (see, for example, Rathje 2007; Deardorff 2009; Spencer-Oatey and Franklin 2009 for overviews).

Intercultural competence has often been distinguished from cultural competence (e.g. Fantini 2012). Cultural competence is something we all possess and relates to our ability to interact successful in our first or 'own' culture. This is a competence that develops through primary socialisation into our own first language, culture and society and is very often not something individuals are aware of. This is distinct from intercultural competence which involves the ability to interact with people from other cultures, i.e. not our first culture. Intercultural competence, characterised in this way, is something that is developed later in life and often needs to be explicitly developed, as opposed to the 'natural' development of cultural competence, and not all adults manage this. Such notions of cultural competence and intercultural competence may have some use in distinguishing between intercultural and intracultural interactions; however, there are some fundamental difficulties with such a distinction. This distinction makes a clear language and culture correlation which results in a homogeneous view of culture and treats culture as a thing. For example Fantini writes "Cultural competence (CC) is something we all have – it is the ability that enables us to be members within our own society … Whereas all children *acquire the language (and culture)* that surrounds them not all adults do likewise entering a new society ... Yet intercultural contact (in positive contexts) affords the possibility of *entering a new language-culture.*" (2012: 270–271, emphasis mine). Yet culture and language are not synonymous, as was made clear in chapter three, and is apparent from any consideration of global languages such as English. There also appears to be an assumption here that cultures and societies are monolingual i.e. they share a common language. Moreover, culture is not a thing that can be 'acquired' or 'entered'. Culture is a process and a practice that we participate in rather than enter. This entails that clear distinctions between our own culture and other cultures are not possible, which in turn suggests that there is no clear distinction between cultural and intercultural competence. No member of a culture has full knowledge of a cultural system. Even in cultures or societies that we consider our own, as was discussed in relation to linguistic competence, there will always be areas that we have more or less competence in and this will vary between individuals. In other words, it would seem the divide between cultural and intercultural competence is hard to maintain. It may well be that we learn to communicate in particular cultural groups through a process of primary socialisation and with others through a process of secondary socialisation but this does not necessarily entail a different kind of competence.

Putting aside the difficulty of distinguishing between cultural and intercultural competence, there are nonetheless a range of aspects, features or elements of intercultural competence that have been identified across the many different characterisations. As Spencer-Oatey and Franklin (2009: 53) note, one of the shared goals of intercultural competence research has been establishing what is necessary for effective and appropriate intercultural communication. For instance Spitzberg and Changnon in a detailed overview of models of intercultural communication write that, "any competence conceptualizations are considered relevant that attempt to account for the process of managing interaction in ways that are likely to produce more *appropriate* and *effective* individual, relational, group, or institutional outcomes" (2009: 6, emphasis mine). Likewise, Fantini defines intercultural competence as "a complex of abilities needed to perform *effectively* and *appropriately* when interacting with others who are linguistically and culturally different from oneself." (2007: 9). In a general (non-technical) sense both these terms would seem useful in understanding the aims of intercultural competence. Appropriateness was of course also a criterion for communicative competence and highlights the importance of contextual factors in communication (i.e. what is appropriate in a particular context) and the subjective nature of successful intercultural communication (i.e. what is considered appropriate will depend on the judgements of participants in communication).

However, Spencer-Oatey and Franklin (2009: 54–55) also point out that there are some important limitations to the notion of appropriateness. Firstly, the focus has tended to be on cultural appropriateness as related to cultural generalisations. Yet, individuals do not necessarily conform to the cultural generalisations of cultural groups they may be associated with. Secondly, individuals in interactions are usually aware of the intercultural nature of the interaction and adapt their communication to this rather than maintaining fixed notions of appropriateness associated with a particular cultural group. This leads Spencer-Oatey and Franklin (2009: 54) to suggest that communicative appropriateness is a more relevant term, in which participants are concerned with appropriateness to the communicative situation they are part of. However, cultural frames of reference, expectations and identifications will still be part of this. Effectiveness as a goal has many of the same strengths and weakness as appropriateness; especially the need to understand it as situationally constructed by the participants in interaction. Finally, it is important to be aware that in communication participants may not always attempt to be appropriate or effective (at least in the sense of clearly conveying meaning). There may be occasions where participants in positions of power feel no need to communicate in a way that would be considered appropriate to all the other participants. On other occasions participants may not wish to be completely transparent in their communication. This does not necessarily imply a lack of intercultural competence; being inappropriate or ineffective may be done deliberately.

In addition to shared goals, models of intercultural competence have also typically shared sets of underlying characteristics. Spitzberg and Changnon (2009) in their review of major models of intercultural competence identify over 300 concepts and terms used. However, they also argue that there is a great deal of overlap and similarity between these supposedly different concepts, "The theories and models display both considerable similarity in their broad brushstrokes (e.g., motivation, knowledge, skills, context, outcomes) and yet extensive diversity at the level of specific conceptual subcomponents." (2009: 35). To the five broad components Spitzberg and Changnon (2009) identify as underlying most models (motivation, knowledge, skills, contexts and outcomes) they propose that developmental and diachronic dimensions should be added. In addition to the plethora of overlapping terms, Spizberg and Changnon (2009) also comment that the models are often not clear on the validity of either the distinctions between the different concepts, such as motivation and knowledge, or the relationships between them. They also suggest that the models are overly cognitive, rationale and conscious whereas intercultural experiences are also emotional and unconscious; features which have so far received little attention. Significantly, from the perspective of this discussion, Spizberg and Changnon (2009) believe that the models have not adequately dealt with the adaptable nature of intercultural competence and the role of adaptation as a core feature. This results in a focus on consistency at the expense of recognising variation. This is a theme that will be returned to later in discussions of ELF and intercultural awareness in which adaptation is key. Finally, they also note that the models have typically been developed in Western settings by Western scholars and so are likely to contain a degree of ethnocentrism in what they regard as successful communication. While the language is somewhat different, this reflects similar concerns to the notions of othering and orientalism discussed in chapter four.

Spencer-Oatey and Franklin (2009) undertake an overview intercultural competence from the diverse fields of psychology and communication studies, applied linguistics and foreign language education, international business and management studies. They too note the plethora of terminology and also the inconsistency by which it is applied. However, they also believe that there is a similar shared framework undergirding all of the models of what they term ICIC (intercultural interactional competence) (2009: 52). They reduce this framework to a distinction between just three components which they refer to as the ABC of ICIC (2009: 79). These are affective components (or attitudes), behavioural components (or skills) and cognitive components (or awareness). This affective, behavioural and cognitive framework has been very pervasive and provides a productive manner for considering the competences needed for intercultural communication, and will be returned to in the discussion of intercultural communicative competence. Spencer-Oatey and Franklin (2009) are nonetheless critical of many of the frameworks they review for their abstract nature and the lack of analysis of authentic intercultural communication used to support or illustrate the models. They believe that applied linguistics has much to offer intercultural competence studies in providing data from authentic instances of intercultural interaction (2009: 79).

5.3 Intercultural communicative competence

Intercultural communicative competence is at times used synonymously with intercultural competence (e.g. Jandt 2010; Fantini 2012). However, as Jackson (2014: 306) argues, outside of applied linguistics and foreign language education this has typically not involved a consideration of second language use in any depth, or indeed, as has already been noted, language at all. This represents a significant limitation to the field given the large number of intercultural interactions that involve the use of second languages (or third or fourth etc ...) and the pivotal role of language in communication. Unsurprisingly, within applied linguistics and foreign language education the linguistic dimension to intercultural communication has received a lot more attention and the concept of intercultural communicative competence has taken on an increasingly influential role over the last few decades. Intercultural communicative competence has been proposed as an extension of communicative competence but one that recognises the intercultural nature of second language use and so eschews the native speaker bias of earlier models of communicative competence. Communicative competence can be criticised for focusing too narrowly on linguistic competence underpinned by grammatical competence and intercultural competence for concentrating on wider communicative strategies while ignoring the linguistic dimension. Intercultural communicative competence combines the two approaches. The most detailed account of intercultural communicative competence in relation to foreign language education has been provided through the work of Michael Byram and colleagues on ICC (intercultural communicative competence) (e.g. Byram 1991; 1994; 1997; 2008; 2012a, 2012b; Byram and Buttjes 1991; Byram and Fleming, 1998; Byram, Nichols and Stevens 2001; Roberts et al. 2001; Byram and Grundy 2003; Alred and Byram 2006; Feng, Byram and Fleming 2009). Therefore, it will be Byram's research, and studies that have built on this, that will form the focus of this section.

Byram's (1997) model of ICC begins from the position that communicative competence and intercultural competence are different and that the two need to be combined for successful intercultural communication. He writes that, "The intercultural speaker needs intercultural communicative competence, i.e. both intercultural competence and linguistic/communicative competence, in any talk of mediation where two distinct linguacultures are present, and this is something different from and not comparable with the competence of the native speaker." (2012a: 89). As is also apparent from this quotation, he also rejects the notion of a native speaker as the model for competence and instead proposes the concept of the intercultural speaker who possesses ICC as the model for successful intercultural communication and foreign language education. As Byram explains "There are two kinds of reason for criticising the use of the native speaker as model ... It is the problem of creating an impossible target and consequently inevitable failure ... The second ground for criticism of the native speaker model is that, even were it possible, it would create the wrong kind of competence" (1997: 11); i.e. the second language learner would have to *become* a native speaker of the foreign language with the associated, undesirable, identity issues. Few learners of other languages want to become members of the 'target culture' of the language they are learning and this is of even less relevance for ELF where there are no fixed target cultures or groups. This entails a critique, although not a complete rejection, of earlier conceptions of communicative competence. Byram (1997) makes use of former conceptions of communicative competence, in particular van Ek (1986) and the notions of linguistic, sociolinguistic and discourse competence, but adds a detailed intercultural dimension to them to move away from the

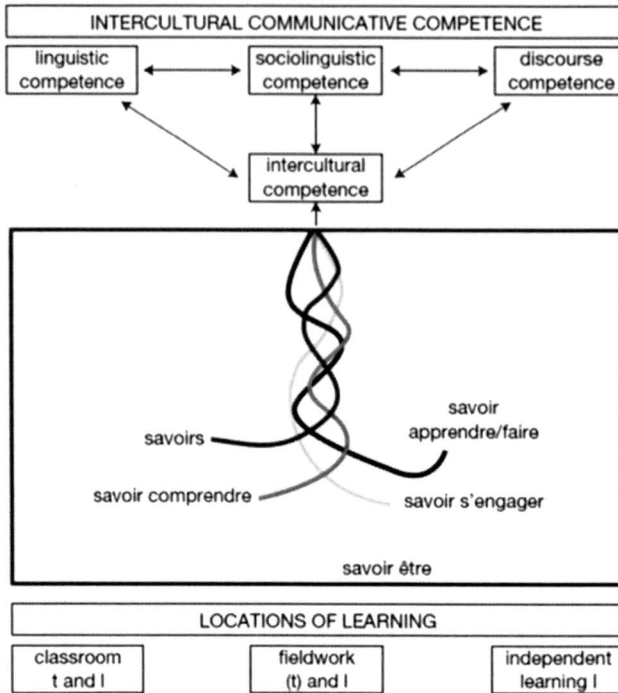

Fig. 5.1: Byram's (1997: 73) model of Intercultural communicative competence

native speaker model of communication and incorporate the knowledge, skills and attitudes necessary for intercultural communication. This is represented in Figure 5.1.

As can been seen from Figure 5.1 intercultural competence consists of five *savoirs* which are characterised by Byram in slightly different ways (1997: 34 and 50–54) but can be summarised as:

– **Attitudes (*savoir être*)** – Relativising the self, valuing others, curiosity and openness, readiness to suspend disbelief about other cultures and beliefs about one's own.
– **Knowledge (*savoirs*)** – Of self and other; of interaction: individual and societal, of social groups and their products and practices in one's own and in one's interlocutor's country, and of the general processes of societal and individual interaction.
– **Skills of interpreting and relating (*savoir comprendre*)** – Ability to interpret a document or event from another culture, to explain it and relate it to documents from one's own.

- **Skills of discovery and interaction (*savoir apprendre/faire*)** – Ability to acquire new knowledge of a culture and cultural practices and the ability to operate knowledge, attitudes and skills under the constraints of real-time communication and interaction.
- **Critical cultural awareness/Political education (*savoir s'engager*)** – An ability to evaluate critically and on the basis of explicit criteria perspectives, practices and products in one's own and other cultures and countries.

Byram's model also includes a learning dimension with 't' representing teachers and 'l' learners, in Figure 5.1, and the model is as much concerned with goals and approaches to pedagogy as it is in characterising the competences of successful intercultural communicators. The final savoir, critical cultural awareness, is central to this conception of intercultural competence as repeatedly stressed by Byram (1997; 2008: 162; 2009: 213; 2012b). It is critical cultural awareness that, Byram (1997: 53; 2008; 163) argues, enables the intercultural communicator to be aware of implicit values, perspectives and criteria in practices and products from their own and other cultures. Crucially it also enables the intercultural communicator to interact, mediate and negotiate in intercultural exchanges in a conscious manner drawing on the attitudes, knowledge and skills outlined in the rest of the ICC model.

Byram's conception of ICC fits very clearly into Spencer-Oatey and Franklin's (2009) ABC framework (see 5.2) with the model dividing up the components into attitudes, skills (behaviour) and knowledge (cognition). It is particularly useful for the detailed account it provides of what these components might be for both intercultural and communicative competence and crucially the relationship between them in ICC, shown in both the visual model (Figure 5.1) and the explanation that accompanies it. ICC also removes the problematic concept of native speaker competence and replaces it with the more appropriate notion of the intercultural speaker with a different range of competences. ICC emphasises the importance of interpretation, interaction, negotiation and mediation in intercultural interaction and communication and so in this sense there is a level of dynamism and flexibility to the model. Additionally, in focusing both on the learner's culture and different conceptions of it, and on foreign cultures, Byram highlights the need to understand the multi-voiced nature of culture which contains conflicting and contradictory views. Finally, the model also contains a pedagogic dimension and it has been within the field of foreign language education where it has had the most influence over the last few decades.

However, the strength of the model in relation to pedagogy also represents one of the major limitations of the model. While there is extensive empirical research as to the application of elements of the model to foreign language teaching (e.g. Byram and Fleming, 1998; Byram, Nichols and Stevens 2001; Roberts et al. 2001; Byram and Grundy 2003; Alred and Byram, 2006; Feng, Byram and Fleming 2009), there is very little empirical research demonstrating that successful intercultural communicators actually have or make use of the competences ICC delineates. In this sense ICC suffers from the same weakness as most other models of intercultural competence in its level of abstraction and lack of relationship to empirical data. Indeed, the original and most extensive discussion of the model (Byram 1997) offers no empirical data in support of either the overall concept of ICC or in relation to the components, the distinctions or the relationships between them. This is particularly problematic as the extent to which communicative competence and intercultural competence can be distinguished, as in ICC, is far from established. If we are to follow the more practice based approaches to understanding the relationships between language, languaculture, discourse and culture in which language and communication are seen as cultural practices, then they cannot meaningfully be separated like this. Of course it may be necessary to treat them as analytically distinct for the purposes of research, and even more importantly for the purposes of education (an issue returned to in the following chapters), but this needs to be done explicitly and the relevance of the model made clear as regards to theoretical discussions of intercultural communication, empirically based descriptions of intercultural communication, and education and training models. The title of the 1997 monograph 'Teaching and assessing Intercultural Communicative Competence' makes the purpose explicit, but the presentation within the text and the subsequent representations and interpretations by others are less clear about the goals and scope of the model.

Aside from these technical issues there are also underlying theoretical concerns with the model which limit its applicability to meaningfully interpreting actual instances of intercultural interaction (as opposed to providing pedagogic models), especially as regards intercultural communication through ELF. The most significant of these is that the model is focused on nationally and geographically bounded notions of culture. While culture is approached as multi-voiced it is still multiple voices *within* a national culture. The association between a culture, country and nation are apparent throughout the discussions of ICC and most tellingly appear in the central concept of critical cultural awareness defined as, "An ability to evaluate critically and on the basis of explicit criteria perspectives, practices and products in one's own and other *cultures and countries.*" (1997: 53, emphasis mine). This national baseline has remained a feature of ICC as seen in more recent discussions of critical cultural awareness which include the same associations between languages, communities and countries, "critical cultural awareness includes a critique of our own communities and societies as well as that of other countries. It does this because foreign language learning inevitably draws attention to other countries, where the language being learnt is spoken, and to the communities and society of those other countries." (2012b: 10). This national bias may be partly due to the model's focus on the use of, and teaching of, modern foreign languages in Europe where languages are typically taught in reference to particular national groups who speak the language, as opposed to languages used for lingua franca communication (Byram, personal communication). However, given the plurilingual and multicultural nature of many contemporary societies in Europe, and elsewhere, this assumption places an increasingly restrictive limitation on the model. In addition, individuals are members of groups and identify with communities which frequently transcend national boundaries for example, professional organisation, religious groups and fans of global sports. Furthermore, the applications of ICC in subsequent studies have moved beyond such contexts and in particular the model has been frequently applied to English language use and teaching (for example see the collection of studies in Byram and Fleming 1998; Byram, Nichols and Stevens 2001; Feng, Byram and Fleming 2009). Given that the predominant use of English in intercultural communication is as a lingua franca with no single fixed culture or country, the focus on nation and country is at odds with the actual use of the language and the communities in which it is used.

The emphasis on national conceptions of culture also results in another difficulty with ICC. In correlating culture and nation there is an acceptance and maintenance of a clear distinction between one culture and another since nations and countries do not overlap. This leads to the imposition of an intercultural line and a dichotomy between one's own culture and the culture of the 'other' (Holliday 2011). Holliday terms this a methodological nationalism (2011: 19) which results in a neo-essentialist approach to understanding intercultural communication, whereby national cultures are viewed as embodying particular mutually exclusive values and structures. However, intercultural communication research has clearly demonstrated that values and structures are not contained solely within national conceptions of cultures. ICC also assumes that successful intercultural communicators will need to mediate *between* cultures separated by the intercultural line. Yet, as explored in chapters three and four, people do not have to be in-between cultures, they can be part of many different groups simultaneously without being between anything. Furthermore, the approach to intercultural communication in ICC assumes that intercultural communication will involve difference and result in difficulties and that this can be explained in reference to culture. More critical scholars of intercultural communication have questioned both the assumption of difference and difficulties and the supposition of a cultural explanation when difficulties do arise (e.g. Baker 2011b; Piller 2011; Zhu 2014).

As Holliday writes in a critique of a priori assumptions of cultural differences in intercultural communication, "very similar differences or conflicts can be found *within* national settings." (2011: 20). Additionally, ELF research has highlighted that difficulties and differences are not necessarily the norm in intercultural communication and that much (although of course not all) intercultural communication through ELF is very successful (e.g. Jenkins, Cogo and Dewey 2011).

Indeed, as already suggested, the theorisation and empirical research related to this model of ICC demonstrates a limited awareness of current research into ELF and Englishes more generally. Byram's (1997: 113–115) initial recommendation for teaching English when its use will be as a lingua franca is still to focus the cultural content on British or American studies due to the dominance of these varieties of English. While Byram may be correct that ideologically these varieties are dominant, this does not do justice to the complex range of uses to which English is put in global settings or make any attempt to offer alternatives which challenge the status quo (a subject that will be returned to in more detail in the following chapters). Where ELF communication is discussed Byram seems to adopt a deficit position in which such communication is viewed as impoverished and simplified, as demonstrated through statements such as, "to use a lingua franca is reductive of their social identities, and diminishes them as human beings" (2008: 198). This repeats the naive position, discussed in earlier chapters, in which communication through ELF was proposed as culturally and identity neutral. A position which it is impossible to maintain since issues of culture and identity are part of all communication, whether a lingua franca or not; although, of course, they may not always be of relevance. Again this can be viewed as a consequence of positing national structures as the predominant frame of cultural reference and identity orientation and thus failing to account for other cultural groupings and identifications. Such an interpretation is confirmed in more recent writing by Byram in which he recognises that there is not a single linguaculture associated with English but then goes on to suggest that English is still related to "several countries – the UK, the USA, Australia and so on" (2012a: 93). This, Byram claims, makes misunderstanding more of a risk in ELF communication. Two deep misinterpretations of ELF and ELF research are highlighted here, firstly that misunderstanding is the norm and secondly that English can only be related to Anglophone settings. There seems to be no awareness of either World Englishes research or ELF research, or that there can be issues of culture and identity not related to national structures.

Recent developments of the concept of ICC have taken a more critical approach to intercultural communication and three of these have been particularly influential: Byram's (2008) notion of 'intercultural citizenship', Guilherme's (2002) 'critical citizens' and Risager's (2007) 'world citizens'. Nonetheless, they share many of the limitations of the original model of ICC in a focus on na-tional cultural structures and an unreflective assumption of the presence of an intercultural line. This in turn means that their applicability to understanding intercultural communication through ELF is restricted. Intercultural citizenship (e.g. Alred, Byram and Fleming 2006; Byram, 2008; 2012a), has been put forward as a possible educational aim and model in foreign language education, whereby successful intercultural communicators may take on an 'intercultural' identity, related to the experiences of language users communicating across less obviously defined cultural groupings. This involves a combination of intercultural com-petence and citizenship competences (see Byram 2008; 2012a) and in Byram's words opens the possibility of people working together "at a level that ignores the limitations of national frontiers" (2012a: 95). However, there is still an underlying assumption that people are between national cultures and national cultures still predominate; moreover, ELF continues to be treated simplistically.

Guilherme's (2002) 'critical citizens for an intercultural world' builds on Byram's model of ICC, particularly critical cultural awareness. She criticises much current language and culture pedagogy for approaching language and culture from a 'bounded' native speaker perspective. Guilherme recognises that cultures are regarded as always fragmented, contradictory and overlapping, but at the same time she believes it is possible to understand and teach them in a holistic way that explores the relationships between the general, particular and pluralistic. This leads Guilherme to advocate an interdisciplinary approach in-volving cultural studies, critical pedagogy and intercultural communication. There is also an overtly political stance in suggesting that human rights and citi-zenship training are crucial. Despite the greater prominence given to political and ideological aspects of intercultural communication and foreign language educa-tion, Guilherme's approach is still based on target communities of speakers and between 'native and foreign cultures' (2002: 219) and is situated in the foreign language tradition with the associated neo-essentialist ideology. Furthermore, there is no discussion of English as a lingua franca.

Risager's 'intercultural competence of the world citizen', while making use of Byram's earlier conception of ICC, explicitly rejects the 'national paradigm' of language and culture and instead adopts a 'transnational paradigm' (2007: 222) in which language learners are seen as part of a larger global community, in a similar manner to intercultural citizenship. Risager outlines ten competences of the world citizen with critical language and cultural awareness as key elements (2007: 227). Although there is much here that is potentially of relevance to ELF communication, the national is still given primacy (2007: 235–236) and the trans-national is typically used to refer to diasporas of target language communities rather than lingua franca communication. Indeed, as outlined in chapter three,

Risager shares many of the same misunderstanding of ELF communication as Byram and it is worth repeating her statement about the impossibility of ELF serving as a model for language use and hence intercultural communicative competence, "Some people seem to think that ongoing research projects on language (English) as a lingua franca will result in people beginning to teach English as a lingua franca. In my opinion this is problematic … the ultimate aim (the decisive model) for language learning must be a variety (or several) used by native speakers – or near native speakers." (2007: 197). In conclusion, although all three of these approaches represent an important move away from the dominance of the national culture and language correlation, they still maintain an intercultural line in which individuals are positioned either within or between national cultures and they all contain serious misrepresentations of ELF.

5.4 Alternatives to intercultural communicative competence

As has been shown in the previous section, while there is much potential value in ICC, at present the models have not adequately addressed intercultural communication through ELF and in particular there seems to be little understanding of intercultural communication where there is not a clear language culture correlation and no 'target' community or culture. A number of alternative conceptions of communicative competence which are relevant to intercultural communication through ELF were explored in section 5.2. These were helpful in moving away from the notion of the native speaker and a homogeneous speech community, with associated stable linguistic norms. While the types of linguistic competence described by Pennycook (2007), Blommaert (2010), Seidlhofer (2011), Widdowson (2012) and Hülmbauer (2013) form a crucial part of any conception of what is necessary for successful intercultural communication, the emphasis on linguistic competence at the expense of other competences means that they only partially describe the competences needed. What is equally important is a consideration of competences that adopts a similar transnational or intercultural approach but applies this to the knowledge, skills and attitudes associated with ICC. This section will consider a number of contemporary approaches that do just this; although, it will not attempt to cover all the notions of competence that are related to this. For example, interactional competence will not be considered (e.g. Young 2011) as, although important, many elements of it appear in other conceptions of competence discussed. Sharifian's (2011; 2012) competences associated with English as an international language (EIL) and pluralistic approaches to World Englishes are also not discussed. While they may at first appear relevant, the competences outlined are envisaged as related to particular cultural groupings that use varieties of English. As ELF is not conceived of as a variety and the lack of established communities has already been discussed, Sharifian's ideas are of limited relevance to this discussion. Instead the focus will be on performative competence (Canagarajah 2013b), symbolic competence (Kramsch 2009) and pragmatic and interactional competences as investigated in ELF research, all of which serve to illustrate the major themes that will form the rest of this chapter.

One approach to competence that both utilises Byram's notion of ICC and also addresses the needs of plurilingual communication that transcends national borders is Canagarajah's performative competence (2013b). As with earlier critiques of communicative competence, particularly Harris's (1998) communicational proficiency, Canagarajah rejects Chomskyan grammatically focused mental representations of competence in favour of a competence that relates to the *how* rather than *what* of communication and emphasises its practice based nature. In focusing on performance and procedural knowledge, performative competence is much closer to the attitudes, knowledge and skills of ICC outlined by Byram (1997; 2008), as Canagarajah acknowledges (201b3: 173). Like ICC, performative competence is quite broad in its scope moving from interactional strategies, related to micro-management of communicative events, to broader notions of language and social awareness, similar to language and cultural awareness, and also includes types of learning strategies. However, unlike ICC's focus on knowledge of distinct cultures and languages, performative competence explicitly explores translinguals "competence for plural language norms and mobile semiotic resources" (201b3: 173). Thus, rather than a competence related to specific languages, competence is conceptualised in relation to an integrated repertoire of language resources and the ability to employ these appropriately. Underpinning performative competence is *alignment* which Canagarajah defines as, "connecting semiotic resources, environmental factors, and human subjects in relation to one's own communicative needs and interests in order to achieve meaning … translinguals have the ability to align diverse semiotic resources to create meaning and achieve communicative success when words in isolation are inadequate and homogeneous norms are not available in contact zones." (2013b: 174).

Performative competence, then, moves away from the assumption of an intercultural line and communication that is between defined cultures, languages and communicative norms. Equally important is the emphasis on awareness of diversity and lack of pre-established norms in intercultural communication. Canagarajah (2013b: 178) also stresses the importance of cooperative dispositions which allows translinguals to develop performative competence. Performative competence thus brings together many of the strands of intercultural communication through ELF already raised as well as incorporating relevant elements from ICC. On the other hand, its applicability to ELF research is limited since Canagarajah, in common with many ICC scholars, also appears to misunderstand communication through ELF, or at least the majority of ELF research, in suggesting that it has been theorised as a value-free and neutral form of English (2013b: 175). Additionally, while performative competence is, according to Canagarajah, based on empirical data presented from his study, there is little evidence provided in support of the notion and in particular how the different elements of the model relate to each other is not explored in the same depth as earlier conceptions of ICC. Finally, many of the notions Canagarajah draws on, such as cooperation, linguistic and cultural (social) awareness have been explored in more depth in previous research, including in ELF, with more extensive empirical support (see Jenkins, Cogo and Dewey 2011 and Jackson 2012 for overviews).

Another alternative to ICC is offered by Kramsch's notion of symbolic competence (2009; 2010). Symbolic competence does not reject communicative or intercultural communicative competence, but instead seeks to incorporate a reflexive perspective that addresses the ideological, historic and aesthetic aspects of intercultural communication and language teaching (2009: 199; 2010: 1). Kramsch adopts a more critical view of culture to the nationally orientated perspectives in ICC and, further developing the discourse approach to culture presented in chapter three, characterises culture from a poststructuralist stance in which:

> Culture today is associated with ideologies, attitudes and beliefs, created and manipulated through the discourse of the media, the Internet, the marketing industry, Hollywood and other mind-shaping interest groups. It is seen less as a world of institutions and historical traditions, or even as identifiable communities of practice, than as a mental toolkit of subjective metaphors, affectivities, historical memories, entextualizations and transcontextualizations of experience, with which we make meaning of the world around us and share that meaning with others. (Kramsch 2010: 2)

Such a view of culture, for Kramsch, means that competence is about more than understanding a cultural other and one's own culture, it is also about understanding the fluidity of numerous 'discourse worlds' (2010: 3) in which change, multiple meanings and diverse interpretations are the norm. Kramsch also directly addresses the notion of multilingualism in language use and symbolic competence is a competence that is related to the use of multiple languages, the discourse worlds they create and embody and the changes to them that multilingual interaction may bring about. The ability of the multilingual subject to navigate this complexity is characterised as *symbolic competence* which involves:

- An ability to understand the symbolic value of symbolic forms and the different cultural memories evoked by different symbol systems.
- An ability to draw on the semiotic diversity afforded by multiple languages to reframe ways of seeing familiar events, create alternative realities, and find an appropriate subject position 'between languages', so to speak.
- An ability to look both *at* and *through* language and to understand the challenges to the autonomy and integrity of the subject that come from unitary ideologies and a totalizing networked culture.
(Kramsch 2009: 201)

There is clearly much in this definition, not all of which can be unpacked here, but crucially symbolic competence critiques the 'unitary ideologies' that result in reifying distinctions between learners' cultures/languages and other 'target' cultures/languages which are part of ICC and also Kramsch's own earlier notion of 'third places' (1993). Indeed, Kramsch (2009) herself has been very aware of the limitations of third places as a conceptual tool for thinking about intercultural communication and the risk of overly static interpretations of culture and language. Symbolic competence has come about as a response in which "the notion of third culture must be seen less as a PLACE than as a symbolic PROCESS of meaning-making that sees beyond the dualities of national languages (L1–L2) and national cultures (C1–C2)" (2010: 1). Thus, symbolic competence is described as a 'dynamic, flexible and locally contingent competence' (2009: 200). As the definition above outlines, there is also a reflexive aspect in which participants in intercultural communication are aware of the 'symbolic value' of language and can look 'at' language, recognising that people can be positioned unequally in and through discourse and language choices.

Symbolic competence, thus, moves beyond a competence associated with knowledge of the cultural and communicative practices of specific groups and into less static, more emergent terrain, in which competence involves a reflexive stance to the communication at hand, "embracing multiple, changing and conflicting discourse worlds" (Kramsch, 2010: 3). This is combined with a critical awareness of the symbolic systems being used to construct any representation of culture. Individual agency is also recognised with effective communication not only about "getting things done in the real world", but "redefining the symbolic reality of the real world". (Kramsch 2010: 5). All of these features suggest that symbolic competence would be well suited to ELF communication in which evaluations of successful communication are likely to be equally 'dynamic, flexible and locally contingent' and where negotiation and redefinition of 'symbolic value of symbolic forms' are to be expected. However, Kramsch does not address the issue of lingua franca communication or specifically ELF. While she recognises the blurring of boundaries between native and non-native speakers,

Kramsch's focus is on multilingual communication in communities in which native speakers are still present, or at least exert an influence, and particularly migrant communities or learners of foreign languages with identifiable, although complex and contested, target communities. This position is made clear in the following quotation:

> The symbolic power of language has been, of course, present in the training of teachers of English, French or German as second languages to immigrants, who are very aware of power inequalities between native speakers and non-native speakers and who learn the language in order to gain access to the world of the native speakers and become integrated into their culture. But in a globalized world symbolic power is more diffuse and less uni-directional. Non-native speakers transform the native speaker's culture in persistent and subtle ways … (Kramsch 2010: 12)

Although such a position may be appropriate for migrant communities or foreign languages such as French or German, the validity of this argument for English is much more debatable. The distinction between native and non-native in communication through ELF is often not of relevance. Of most significance though is the point emphasised throughout this book, that 'native speaker's culture' i.e. Anglophone cultures, are of questionable relevance when it comes to interpreting and understanding ELF. Therefore, there is no need to 'transform the native speaker's culture'. This does not, however, undermine the relevance of symbolic competence for understanding the competences needed for successful intercultural communication through ELF, but it is not a direction that Kramsch has explored herself.

Turning specifically to ELF research, many ELF scholars have argued that a reinterpretation of communicative competence is needed to understand the range of competences employed in intercultural communication through ELF. At the beginning of this chapter critiques of the linguistic dimensions to communicative competence from ELF researchers were outlined. ELF researchers have also examined a range of other competences which appear to be of relevance to understanding successful communication. Indeed, Seidlhofer and Widdowson suggest that rather than linguistic features "it may turn out that what is distinctive about ELF lies in the communicative strategies that its speakers use" (2009: 37). Although the caveat needs to be added that in the interpretation taken here, the communicative strategies used in ELF are not necessarily regarded as different to those used in any other type of multilingual intercultural communication. Nonetheless, competence in a range of communicative strategies has formed an increasingly important part of ELF research, often approached under investigations into pragmatics in ELF (e.g. Jenkins, Cogo and Dewey 2011). In contrast to communicative competence though, these communication strategies are associated with multilingual and multicultural communication and are not seen as 'compensating' for communicative deficiencies but rather as displays of pragmatic competence (Canagarajah 2007; Jenkins 2007; Seidlhofer 2011; Cogo and Dewey 2012).

One of the features of ELF communication that was noted from early studies, (Firth 1996; House 1999) and continues through to current research (House 2012), is that despite the expected difficulties and differences usually assumed in intercultural communication research, there appears to be a very low degree of misunderstanding and non-understanding in the ELF data studied so far. This has been attributed to the high-degree of mutual cooperation observed in interactions in which participants actively work together to ensure mutual understanding through flexibly and creatively employing a range of interactional strategies (Jenkins, Cogo and Dewy 2011). Canagarajah (2013b) makes a similar observation in performative competence when he discusses the importance of the cooperative disposition of translingual communicators. This is not to suggest that mutual cooperation is a feature of all communication through ELF. Jenks (2012) provides counter examples in which participants in internet chat-rooms are deliberately un-cooperative with certain participants. The high degree of cooperation seen may also be a feature of the type of data gathered so far in ELF research which has typically involved communication between elite or high status groups. More data from high stakes interactions in which there are clear power differences between participants may produce alternative findings. Guido's (2012) study of immigration encounters in Italy between immigration officers and migrants using ELF offers an instance of this. Nonetheless, cooperation has emerged as a persistent feature of empirical data concerning communication through ELF.

An important means by which this cooperation is achieved is through accommodation. Accommodation theory (e.g. Giles 2009; Giles, Bonilla and Speer 2012) has its origins in social psychology and its primary focus has been on identity and social relations; however, it also of relevance to understanding how speakers adjust their speech to facilitate understanding. It is this latter aspect of accommodation theory that has been adopted in ELF research and it has formed an important strand from the beginning (e.g. Jenkins 2000). Typically the focus has been on how participants modify and adjust their pronunciation and language to each other, following the convergent aspects of accommodation theory (rather than the divergent ones), in order to achieve understanding (Cogo and Dewey 2006; 2012; Cogo 2009; Hülmbauer 2009; Kaur 2009; Seidlhofer and Widdowson 2009). In particular, it has been shown that speakers in ELF communication frequently creatively adapt language to fit their own purposes with participants sharing the newly adapted word or phrase. For instance, Cogo and Dewey (2012: 106) provide an example of the use of the word 'plant' to describe someone who has suffered severe brain damage; what in 'standard' English is usually referred to as a 'vege-tative state'. This newly adapted word is introduced by one participant and then adopted and repeated by the other two participants in the conversation.

Another important strategy is the signalling of non-understanding in a manner that does not disrupt the conversational flow. This is especially through the 'let-it-pass' (Firth 1996) principle whereby non-understanding is typically ignored, at least initially, and only indicated when it is not resolved later through the development of the conversation and if it is still felt to be important to ensuring understanding (Pitzl 2005). Where non-understanding does occur, and it is felt to be important to the overall purpose of the interaction, strategies such as clarification, self-repair, repetition, reformulation and translation are typi-cally employed (Jenkins, Cogo and Dewey 2011; Seidlhofer 2011; Cogo and Dewey 2012). In addition to reacting to non-understanding after it occurs, research has also shown extensive use of pre-emptive strategies (Kaur 2009), whereby partic-ipants anticipate communicative difficulties and employ strategies to minimise the risk of non-understanding. Many of these strategies are similar to those used to rectify non-understanding. As Jenkins, Cogo and Dewey note, the use of these pre-emptive strategies gives an indication of why non-understanding is so rarely observed, since participants do not take understanding for granted, "but that speakers engage in a joint effort to monitor understanding at every stage of communication, even before non-understanding has taken place" (2011: 293). Other strategies used to build common ground and establish shared understand-ing include supportive turn-taking, simultaneous speech and utterance comple-tions (Pullin Stack 2009; Kaur 2011; Wolfartsberger 2011). Finally, code-switching and creative use of shared resources such as idioms have also been observed as a means of both signally cultural identities, as discussed in chapter four, but also in the construction of shared understanding (Hülmbauer 2009; Seidlhofer and Widdowson 2009; Seidlhofer 2011; Pitzl 2012).

In sum, ELF research has shown a high degree of pragmatic and, what has been termed, interactional competence (Kaur 2009; Young 2011) with successful intercultural communicators in ELF research demonstrating a range of strategies that go beyond linguistic competence alone. Much of this research has followed a conversation analysis approach (e.g. Cogo and Dewey 2012; Kaur 2009) and this has resulted in detailed examinations of how these different pragmatic and inter-actional competences are employed and evolve within interactions. However, as with all research methodologies, there are also limitations to this approach. In focusing solely on the interactions, a fundamental tenet of conversation analysis, this excludes the interpretative and ethnographically orientated research which featured in ICC and also performative and symbolic competence. It is only the interpretations of the researcher that are present under such an analysis and the participants own interpretations are absent. This is not necessarily a critique of these studies, since the focus of much of the research was not specifically on communicative competence and even less intercultural communicative competence. Nonetheless, together with this analysis of the micro features of successful intercultural communication, we need explorations of macro level elements related to identity and culture and a means of linking the two levels. In other words, we need an approach that connects the insights from ELF research with the earlier work on ICC and more recently performative and particularly symbolic competence. The following section will outline an attempt to do this through the concept of intercultural awareness (ICA).

5.5 Intercultural awareness (ICA)

ICA (Baker 2009b; 2011b; 2012b) builds on ICC's broad conception of the knowledge, skills and attitudes needed for successful intercultural communication. In particular in can be seen as a development of the central element of ICC, critical cultural awareness, which emphasises the need to reflect critically on cultural practices and their relationship to communication. However, whereas critical cultural awareness is focused on an awareness of 'one's own' and 'other' cultures, with the associated national conceptions of culture and language, ICA goes beyond this intercultural line and incorporates an understanding of the fluid, complex and emergent nature of the relationship between language and culture in intercultural communication through ELF. ICA is defined in the following manner:

> Intercultural awareness is a conscious understanding of the role culturally based forms, practices and frames of reference can have in intercultural communication, and an ability to put these conceptions into practice in a flexible and context specific manner in communication. (adapted from Baker 2011b: 202)

Awareness here is taken beyond its usual meaning and is used as a more loosely defined holistic term which includes knowledge, skills and behaviour. This avoids the problematic competence/performance distinction, at least in this general definition, and is frequently used in this manner in intercultural communication and education research (Risager 2004). Unlike cultural awareness, the reference to culture in the first part of the definition does not link culture to countries or nationalities, nor does it presuppose an 'our/their' culture distinction. The second part of this definition emphasises the need for flexibility in relation to emergent communicative practices and socio-cultural relations, which is again distinct

Level 1: basic cultural awareness

An awareness of:
1   culture as a set of shared behaviours, beliefs, and values;
2   the role culture and context play in any interpretation of meaning;
3   our own culturally based behaviour, values, and beliefs and the ability to articulate this;
4   others' culturally based behaviour, values, and beliefs and the ability to compare this with our own culturally based behaviour, values, and beliefs.

Level 2: advanced cultural awareness

An awareness of:
5   the relative nature of cultural norms;
6   cultural understanding as provisional and open to revision;
7   multiple voices or perspectives within any cultural grouping;
8   individuals as members of many social groupings including cultural ones;
9   common ground between specific cultures as well as an awareness of possibilities for mismatch and miscommunication between specific cultures.

Level 3: intercultural awareness

An awareness of:
10   culturally based frames of reference, forms, and communicative practices as being related both to specific cultures and also as emergent and hybrid in intercultural communication;
11   initial interaction in intercultural communication as possibly based on cultural stereotypes or generalizations but an ability to move beyond these through:
12   a capacity to negotiate and mediate between different emergent communicative practices and frames of reference based on the above understanding of culture in intercultural communication.

Fig. 5.2: The twelve components of intercultural awareness (adapted from Baker 2012b)

from critical cultural awareness. The reference to 'context specific' can be seen as similar to appropriate communication in Hymes' notion of communicative competence. However, these terms emphasize the situatedness of appropriacy and that it is a concept that is likely to vary between instances of communication. Lastly, *inter*cultural is used rather than cultural awareness since the focus is on awareness of intercultural communication rather awareness of particular cultures. In some ways transcultural awareness might be a better term, since, as explained in chapter two, trans is a more appropriate prefix and spatial metaphor than inter. Communication through ELF is not necessarily in-between anything. However, given the already extensive nomenclature of intercultural communication research the more conventional terms has been retained for simplicity and consistency.

This definition is, of course, rather general and abstract and further detail is needed as to what such intercultural awareness entails. ICA can be further characterised by the 12 elements and three levels shown in Figure 5.2. The 12 elements are presented in an order which builds from a basic understanding of cultural contexts in communication, particularly in relation to the L1 (Level 1: Basic CA,

Figure 5.2), to a more complex understanding of language and culture (Level 2: Advanced CA, Figure 5.2), and finally to the fluid, hybrid, and emergent understanding of cultures and languages in intercultural communication needed for English used in global settings (Level 3: ICA, Figure 5.2). Levels 1 and 2 are very similar to the savoirs outlined in Byram's (1997) model of ICC, and as already stated ICA can be seen as a development of this. Level 3 also contains some important aspects of critical cultural awareness, especially the role of negotiation and mediation. However, this is the level that goes beyond critical cultural awareness and ICC, since it directly addresses the fluid, complex and emergent nature of intercultural communication through ELF, where national cultures are only one of many orientations and resources that interacts may draw on and construct in communication.

To explain each level in more detail[6], level 1, basic cultural awareness (CA), shows awareness which is related to an understanding of cultures at a very general level with a focus on a generalised understanding of first culture (C1), rather than specifically orientated to intercultural communication; hence the title. To be more precise this involves a conscious understanding of the individual's own linguaculture and the manner in which it influences behaviour, beliefs, and values, and its importance in communication. This is then expanded to generalised statements about a C1, which may be characterised in a simplified and stereotypical manner. Reflection on, and the development of an understanding of, linguacultures and their relationship to cultural characterisations thus represents the starting point of this model. There is also awareness that others' linguacultures and cultural practices may be different, but this awareness may not include any specific systematic knowledge of this or indeed awareness of the concept of culture or linguaculture itself. This is combined with the development of an ability to articulate one's own cultural perspective and an ability to make general comparisons between one's own cultural interpretations and 'others'; although, again this may be at the level of broad generalisations or stereotypes and hence any understanding of culture may still be essentialist in perspective. Indeed, it is important to recognise that in attempting to model how language and culture may be perceived and used in intercultural communication essentialist positions may be adopted by those engaged in intercultural communication. Such positions, particularly related to national cultural characterisations, are a common part of folk knowledge and also much intercultural training. Any characterisation of intercultural communication and intercultural competence or awareness needs to account for them, even if we attempt to move beyond them.

---

6 An earlier version of this discussion appears in Baker (2011b).

These basic elements of CA lead to level 2 of CA involving more complex understandings of cultures and communication and moving away from essentialist positions. At this level there is an awareness of other linguacultures and cultures and a related awareness of the relativity of one's own linguaculture and cultural practices. Furthermore, cultures are seen as made up of many diverse groups, rather than homogeneous, and culture is also viewed as one of many social groupings individuals may identify with. This may be combined with specific knowledge of other linguacultures and cultural practices, although still perhaps at a national level. In relation to skills or abilities, at level 2 participants in intercultural communication should be able to make use of their cultural knowledge to make predictions for possible areas of misunderstanding and miscommunication. Intercultural communicators should also be able to compare and mediate between specific cultural practices and frames of reference at this level, although again this may be in relation to national or target communities. In this sense it is most closely related to earlier conceptions of cultural awareness and ICC. Nonetheless, like the more critical interpretations of ICC (e.g. Guilherme 2002; Risager 2007; Byram 2008), participants in intercultural communication should be able to move beyond generalisations in response to the specific instance of intercultural communication that they are engaged in.

The final level 3 moves from CA to ICA and incorporates the insights from poststructuralist understandings of culture, language and communication and the implications of this for understanding intercultural communication. ICA involves an awareness of the liminal and emergent nature of the relationships between language, culture and communication in much intercultural communication including through ELF. This goes beyond viewing cultures as bounded entities, however complex they may be, and recognises that cultural references and communicative practices in intercultural communication may or may not be related to specific cultures. Central to ICA is the ability to mediate and negotiate between different cultural frames of reference and communicative practices as they occur in specific examples of intercultural communication. This extends the role of mediation and negotiation in level 2, which were related to predefined cultural practices, to an awareness of the emergent nature of cultural forms, references and practices in intercultural communication. At this level understanding of culture and communication goes beyond the 'our culture', 'their culture' dichotomy inherent in much of ICC discourse. Instead ICA involves an awareness of cultures, languages and communication which are not correlated and tied to any single native speaker community or even group of communities. In specific relation to ELF there is recognition that English is used to express and enact cultural practices and forms that are related to a range of communities, moving between and across the local, national and global in dynamic ways that often result in emergent and novel practices and forms.

In terms of limitations, it should be noted that the elements of ICA presented in Figure 5.2 are, of course, an abstraction and that the distinctions between the different components are for analytical purposes. Equally importantly, while ICA is presented with three levels, and intercultural communicators may develop ICA through these steps there is no suggestion that this is necessarily the case. It may well be that some individuals learn to communicate in a way that is at level 3, ICA, from their earliest experiences, for example if he/she grows up in a plurilingual and multicultural environment. In contrast, as already discussed much intercultural communication in both practice and training does not progress beyond level 2. In other words ICA does not necessarily develop smoothly through the three levels. How ICA might be developed in education will be addressed in detail as the subject of the following two chapters. Finally, the twelve elements of ICA outlined in Figure 5.2 do not constitute a model of ICA since the relationships between the elements are not represented. Figure 5.3 addresses this through providing a model of ICA illustrating the relationships; however, this is inevitably at the expense of some of the clarity and simplicity of ICA outlined in 5.2.

In Figure 5.3 a distinction is made between conceptual ICA and practice orientated ICA which leads to the division of some of the original 12 elements between the two sides of the model resulting in 15 components in this model. While this distinction could be seen as sharing similarities with the competence/ performance distinction there are important differences. Firstly, conceptual ICA is as much about a conscious understanding of the role of cultures and languages in intercultural communication as it is about an underlying competence. This is represented by individuals' ability to talk about and explain the elements outlined in the model. Secondly, the double arrows and dotted line between the two sides of the model show that the relationship is a two-way one. While participants in intercultural communication may draw on previous knowledge and skills, these are constantly renewed and adapted through the interactions themselves and so the distinction between conceptual and practice orientated ICA is a fuzzy one. Thirdly, the particular knowledge, skills and practices that are necessary for successful intercultural communication will be situated and, to use Kramsch's (2009) terminology, locally contingent. This means that they cannot be fully specified in advance and hence the necessity of a two-way relationship between practice and knowledge and skills. The dotted lines between the three different levels and the double-headed arrows either side of the model also indicate that in terms of development individuals do not necessarily move in a linear manner through the three levels. Likewise in intercultural communication individuals may make use of different aspects of the model at different times and may 'revert' to lower levels

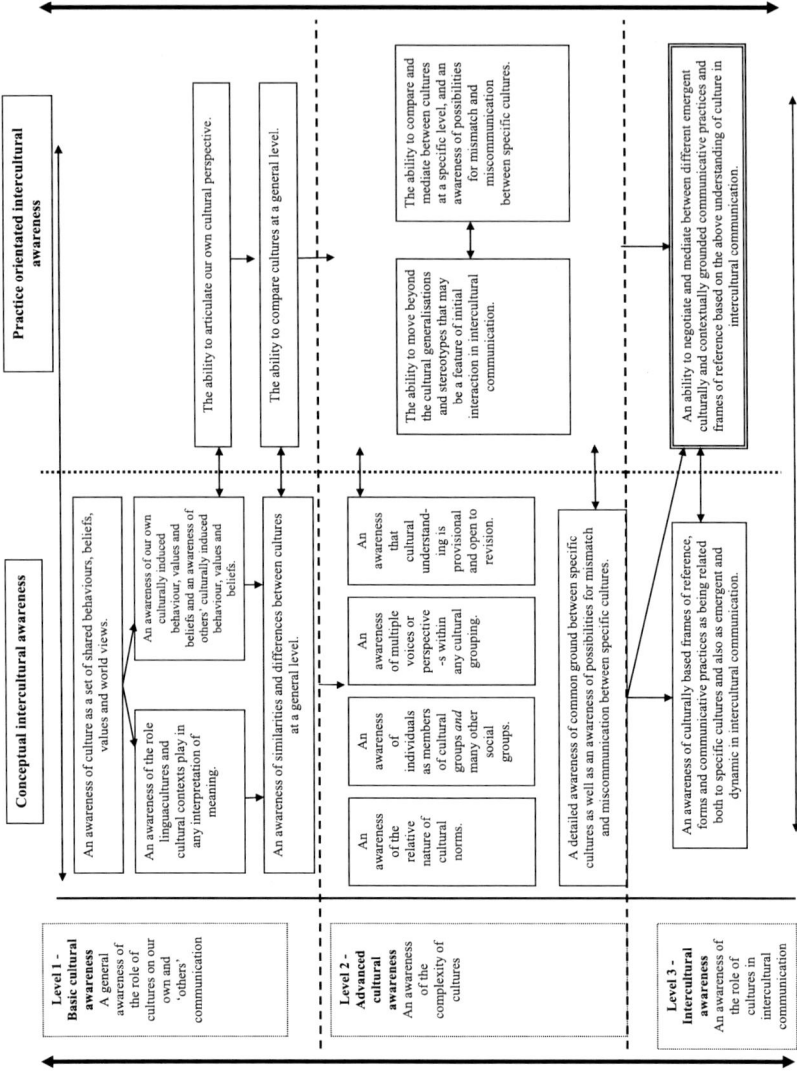

Fig. 5.3: A model of intercultural awareness

as well. Lastly, the arrows moving between the levels and across the conceptual and practice sections is an attempt to indicate (in as far as is possible in a static two-dimensional representation) the dynamic nature of the model in which the knowledge, skills and abilities of the individual are constantly in change.

At this stage the model of ICA is still at an abstract level and in order to avoid it remaining at this level it is necessary to explore how ICA relates to concrete examples of individuals engaged in intercultural communication through ELF and their interpretations of this. Although ICA is presented here in the framework of a theoretical discussion of intercultural competence, the model is based on a mixture of empirical and theoretical investigations and so it is not only an analytical construct. The examples here are taken from an ethnographic study of intercultural communication and ELF in Thailand (see Baker 2009; 2011b for more details). The extracts below come from interviews, focus groups and recordings of naturally occurring instances of intercultural communication. The participants are mainly Thai L1 speakers who are undergraduate students at a Thai university. The extracts were selected as they offered typical and/or particularly articulate examples of the key concepts and three levels in ICA.

Extract 5.1 Level 1: general comparisons between cultures
KAY: in Thailand everybody umm every children been taught that you have to work hard in school . so you have to get another maybe a high school the good high school and then when you are in high school you have to work hard to go to university ... because going to university is very important ... but umm I would like to know that English people what their opinion about going to university what is the important thing in the world if you cannot go you cannot pass to go to university ... I want to know that umm English people pay attention to the (that) stuff (Baker 2011b: 207)

In extract 5.1, Kay (Thai L1, female) is taking part in a focus group discussing cultural differences with other Thai participants and an English L1 speaker. In this extract she demonstrates a general awareness of a Thai cultural value she has experienced, the value of university and of the consequent belief and behaviour, the need to study hard, which she generalise to all other Thais "in Thailand everybody ...". She then also shows an awareness that this may not be a universal set of values and behaviours by asking whether "English people pay attention to the (that) stuff". This extract illustrates a number of features of the first level of ICA including an awareness of the effect of shared cultural values on behaviour, an ability to clearly articulate this, as well as an awareness of similarities and differences between cultures at a general level. However, this is still at a 'basic' level since there is no awareness shown in this extract of differences between values in Thai culture or of the position of either Kay or her interlocutor to speak for their respective cultures. At that same time it should also be realised that such 'stereotyped' discussions of cultures can serve as a starting point for more nuanced and complex characterisations as the interaction progresses.

Extract 5.2 Level 2: cultures as relative
OY: Hollywood's better than Thai. I don't think can't really justify what's really better or what good or what's not good and what is (one) English song is better than English music is better than Thai music still the same answer you can't justify that . novels that (tough) because really English and the Thai got different culture and different types of thinking and attitude so you can't really say what is good and what is better
(Baker 2011b: 207)

Extract 5.2 shows Oy (Thai L1, female) in an interview discussing aspects of Thai culture and Anglophone cultures and making comparisons between them. Oy demonstrates a clear awareness of the relative nature of cultural practices and products which is a feature of level two of ICA. She rejects direct comparisons and value judgements between Hollywood and Thai films as well as English music and novels, saying she "can't really justify what's really better or what good or what's not good". Furthermore, she suggests that the meaning and function of these cultural practices is different in each culture, "English and the Thai got different culture and different types of thinking and attitudes". This indicates a more detailed awareness of differences between particular cultures and cultural practices, the possibilities of mismatches and crucially the ability to adopt a relative position in which neither is seen as superior or better. However, there is still a clear maintenance of the intercultural line with Thai and Anglophone cultures seen as distinct and clearly differentiated.

The following extract, 5.3, provides an example of ICA at level two in practice. Ton (Thai L1, male) a university student and Chas (English L1, male) an Australian/Scottish English teacher are discussing places to have a beer in the area of the city in which they both live.

Extract 5.3 Level 2: The ability to compare and mediate between cultures at a specific level, and an awareness of possibilities for mismatch and miscommunication between specific cultures.
1   TON: err the location the location of of the of the shop I think is not suitable for
2   drinking
3   CHAS: why
4   TON: umm it's a junction you know
5   CHAS: [yeah]
6   TON: yes and many car yes
7   CHAS: (?) I don't understand
8   TON: many car
9   CHAS: you mean lots of people can see you or
10   TON: yes
11   CHAS: ah it doesn't bother me ((laughs))

Ton is attempting to explain to Chas why he thinks a particular bar (shop) is not a suitable place to drink. Both participants show a degree of interactional pragmatic competence in Chas's indication of non-understanding (line 3 and 7) and Ton's reformulation (line 4) and repetition (line 6 and 8). However, Chas goes further than just interactional competence and demonstrates an ability to put his understanding of specific cultural differences into practice in this interaction. He recognises in line 9 that Ton is telling him that lots of people can see you drinking in this place and that for Ton students and teachers should not be seen drinking alcohol in public; although, line 11 shows it is not a belief Chas shares.

Extract 5.4 Level 3: adapting liminal cultural practices
NAMI: ... yeah it's not not like a passion that I want to be like American people I want to be like British people it's not like that but it's just the way oh that's interesting that you know that . people . for example people . go drinking people earn their money in a certain age compared with Thai people Thai people we just stick with our family until we get married ... so I feel like ok maybe we should do something something like that something that you should develop your life yeah it's not just the Thai way but also the other way that you think that is good from that
(Baker 2011b: 208)

In Extract 5.4 Nami (Thai L1, female) is talking about her experiences of intercultural communication in an interview. She engages in some cultural comparisons between what she sees as the different levels of independence of American, British and Thai 'people'. Importantly though, from the beginning of this extract Nami makes it clear that being exposed to other cultural values and beliefs does not mean she is adopting American or British culture "it's not not like a passion that I want to be like American people I want to be like British people". She also goes on to indicate that she does not want to act in a "Thai way" either. Rather she seems to be suggesting something that neither conforms to Thai or Anglo cultures but taking what "is good from that" and using it to "develop your life". This extract would indicate ICA at level three since Nami is blurring the intercultural line, rather than maintaining clear cultural distinctions, and adapting and adopting different values and beliefs she has experienced in a liminal manner that suits her. Other examples of ICA have been given in chapters three and four, for example extracts 4.3 to 4.8, which demonstrated individuals adopting mediation roles or identities in which they were 'between' cultures and also the construction of multiple identities which cut across, rather than between, cultures. In chapter three, extracts 3.2 and 3.3, offered examples of ICA in practice with participants negotiating and adapting different communicative practices and characterisations of cultural products and practices.

5.6 Conclusion

The model of ICA presented here is a useful tool for conceptualising the relationship between the different knowledge, skills and attitudes needed for successful intercultural communication through ELF. However, it is important to remember the limitations of models. The model of ICA is obviously an abstraction which serves as a heuristic for exploring intercultural communication through ELF, but like all models it should not be seen as a representation of reality. There are necessary simplifications and distinctions which, while analytically of value, may not be so clearly distinct in an individual's knowledge, skills and attitudes or in their actual communicative practice. As made clear in pervious chapters, intercultural communication involves the confluence or convergence of multiple complex systems not all of which can be represented in a single model. Although I have argued throughout this book that a holistic approach to understanding intercultural communication is needed, and that language, communication and culture cannot easily be separated in practice, for analysis some separation and delineation is necessary. In particular, the role of linguistic and interactional competence, as outlined earlier in the chapter, is only dealt with at a very general level in this model. It is likely that a full account of intercultural competence would need to include the types of competences, or awareness, in relation to flexible use of linguistic forms and interactional strategies already documented in ELF research. But this is not the aim of this model which specifically focuses on the intercultural dimension to ELF communication as this has received less attention to date. The model may also be of limited applicability to settings where there are more clearly defined groups and normative communicative practices than is typically the case in ELF communication. However, proponents of critical approaches to intercultural communication have argued that dynamic understandings of intercultural communication are needed in many different settings (e.g. Holliday 2011; 2013, Piller 2011; Zhu 2014), not only in ELF communication. Furthermore, ICA and similar critical approaches to intercultural communication may also be of relevance outside of L2 uses when L1 users engage in intercultural communication. Native speakers of English are included in conceptions of ELF and they have an equal need to develop ICA.

It is also important to note that the components of ICA are deliberately general in their nature, since the details of what ICA might mean in specific contexts will depend on each individual communicative instance. Like Canagarajah's (2013b) performative competence, details are not specified of what 'forms', 'practices' and 'frames of reference' should be understood, since this is not possible. Although the *types* of knowledge, skills and attitudes needed can be outlined in advance, as the model does, the particular resources needed will be specific to each instance of communication. Indeed, it is important that the model is not viewed as a prescriptive account of 'good' communicative practices in terms of specific language use, discourse structures or knowledge of particular cultural practices. Such approaches have been common place in intercultural communication research and training and have, quite rightly, been criticised as overly prescriptive in imposing the communicative practices of one group over many others in the name of supposedly 'efficient communication' (Cameron 2002; Fairclough 1999; Piller 2011). Research into both ELF and intercultural communication has demonstrated that there is not one way of communicating that is more effective or efficient than others. In particular, ELF communication forces us to recognise the discrimination, ethnocentrism and othering, embedded in viewing intercultural communication through English from an Anglophone native speaker perspective. Again, it also points to the need to understand intercultural competence in a manner that goes both beyond the national and fixed 'target' community. Instead it is crucial that we recognise the pluralism, negotiation and emergent nature of communicative practices associated with ELF and other forms of intercultural communication.

Returning to Kramsch's notion of symbolic competence whereby, "effective communication has increasingly come to mean not only 'getting things done in the real world', but 'redefining the symbolic reality of the real world'" (2010: 5), participants in intercultural communication through ELF can be viewed as drawing on the existing symbolic resources that construct and represent language and culture, but also challenging, reinterpreting and 'redefining' them in ways that are appropriate to the communicative situations in which they find themselves. ICA offers a framework for applying many of the knowledge, skills and attitudes documented in ICC in a more critical and dynamic way that recognises the situated, temporal and negotiable nature of our communicative practices. From this it follows that the symbolic resources and symbolic reality of each interaction will be emergent within the interaction and cannot be fully specified in advanced, hence the importance of an awareness of the processes of intercultural communication in ICA. How this awareness is developed or can be developed is of high importance for second language education that seeks to equip learners for successful intercultural communication. Indeed, as stated at the beginning of this chapter, detailing what the knowledge, skills and attitudes might be that comprise ICA, or other notions of intercultural communicative competence, has been as much a pedagogic endeavour as it has an empirical and theoretical one. The implications of ELF research and ICA for second language teaching will be the subject of the next chapter.

Chapter 6
ELF and intercultural awareness: implications for English language teaching

> Those of us concerned with that branch of applied linguistics that concentrates on language in education are engaged in a long, complex, and infinitely rewarding study. But we shall betray the richness, creativity, and diversity of our subject matter if we imply that definitive solutions to practical problems are easy to arrive at, or that human motivation and behaviour can be reduced to a limited set of predictable dimensions.
>
> – Brumfit (2001: 187)

The previous chapter on ICA (intercultural awareness) represented the start of a move from theoretical issues to more practical concerns, while recognising the interrelationship between theory and practice especially in applied linguistics. ICA outlines the knowledge, skills and attitudes needed for successful intercultural communication with the aim of providing both an empirically grounded, analytically useful description and also a possible model or set of aims for teaching and training. In distinguishing three levels of ICA, moving from basic cultural awareness to intercultural awareness, some suggestions were also provided for possible routes of development; although, with the caveat that an individual does not necessarily progress through the three levels in the linear manner in which they were presented. This chapter will explore the pedagogic implications of ICA in detail particularly in relation to ELF communication. As already suggested in pervious chapters, learning another language is fundamentally an intercultural process that takes the learner beyond their familiar settings and communicative practices, with all the challenges such a process involves. This is likely to be even more so for learners of English where, if the final aim of learning is to communicate through English, the majority of interactions involve English functioning as a lingua franca. In intercultural communication through ELF we can expect the connections between language, culture and identity to be highly diverse and variable and learners of English need to be prepared for this fluidity and complexity. In short, we are now in a position to address the final question posed at the beginning of this monograph, *what are the consequences of ELF and ICA research, if any, for teaching English (ELT)?*

This question will be answered over the next two chapters. In this chapter I will discuss the implications and issues ICA and ELF give rise to for ELT. In the following chapter I will present an empirical study which attempted to put some of the ideas discussed here into practice, together with an evaluation of the processes of implementation and the resultant outcomes. This chapter will begin with a critique of current approaches in ELT to culture and the intercultural, especially in relation to ELF communication. This will involve a consideration of language policy, ELT materials and pedagogic approaches which underscore the continued superficial and essentialist treatment of language and culture. Alternatives approaches to ELT will then be discussed which move intercultural communication and interculturality into a more central role. This begins with intercultural approaches to language education as such approaches have been important in investigating how the intercultural dimension of communication can be successfully integrated into the language learning process. However, the marginalisation of linguistic issues and particularly ELF, and the implications of this, will be highlighted as a weakness in this approach. Following this a discussion of Global Englishes and ELF perspectives on ELT will be offered. Here more attention has been given to linguistic issues and communicative strategies in pedagogy. Nonetheless, although intercultural and cultural aspects of communication have been considered, they have typically not been the main priority. Finally, my own recommendations for incorporating ICA into classroom practice will be presented as an approach which combines insights from both intercultural education and ELF research. However, given the complexity and diversity of language education and the need to eschew definitive solutions, as highlighted in the quote from Brumfit at the beginning of this chapter, I will not be offering a single set of prescriptions for pedagogy which are applicable in all settings. Rather I will be raising issues of concern for pedagogic practice and examples, not definitive solutions, of attempts to address these concerns.

6.1 Culture, the intercultural and ELF in ELT: critiquing current approaches

Although culture has long been part of language education, the previous few decades have seen a rise in the attention paid to intercultural communication and culture in language education theory, policy and research, as many of the sources in chapter five demonstrate (see Risager 2007 for an authoritative overview). However, this engagement with the intercultural has predominantly remained at a superficial level within ELT. The lack of depth can been seen in an examination of language policy, the limited treatment of communicative competence that is still central in many approaches to ELT, the essentialist and uncritical focus on the national level in cultural characterisations in teaching materials and a lack of awareness or willingness to engage with the implications of English used as a global lingua franca as opposed to a native language.

The discourse of interculturality has increasingly worked its way into language policy and, while a full overview of language policy from around the world is obviously not possible, a few examples will illustrate the point. For instance, in Europe the highly influentially CEFR (Common European Framework of Reference for Languages) makes reference to the intercultural and cultural aspects of language learning including drawing on the work of Byram and the notion of ICC (e.g. Council of Europe 2001). Similarly, the 'Standards for foreign language learning in the 21st century' in the US makes extensive references to culture, and the relationship between culture, language and communities (Glisan 2012), as do government reports in other Anglophone settings such as Australia (Scarino and Liddicoat 2009) and New Zealand (Newton et al. 2009). Taking two examples from Asia, the Chinese National English Curriculum contains a section on cultural awareness (Chinese Ministry of Education 2011) and in Thailand culture forms one of the four strands of the national curriculum, the others being communication, connections and communities (Wongsatorn, Hiranburana and Chinnawongs 2003). The inclusion of culture in these policy documents give an indication of how mainstream the notion of culture has become in thinking about language education.

However, despite the inclusion of culture many of the approaches still centre on national, native speaker, target language and culture correlations and it is not clear that the more dynamic intercultural associations between languages, communities and cultures, as envisaged in ELF and ICA, are recognised. Taking an extract from the CEFR for instance, it is stated that an L2 user at B2 level "Can sustain relationships with native speakers without unintentionally amusing or irritating them or requiring them to behave other than they would with a native speaker." (Council of Europe 2001: 122) and this is only one, albeit particularly striking example, among the many examples in the CEFR focused on competence related to native speaker communication. Equally significantly is the frequently noted gap between policy and practice and this increased prominence of culture and the intercultural at research and policy levels has not always been translated in a substantive manner into teaching practice. This is even more so for intercultural communication through ELF where there is still much resistance to incorporating insights from ELF research into ELT pedagogy (e.g. Risager 2007; Sybing 2011; Sowden 2012).

This marginalisation of the findings from intercultural communication and ELF studies can be exemplified in an examination of a central concept within ELT, communicative competence. The limitations of communicative competence were outlined in chapter five, but to briefly summarise in relation to pedagogy, while models of communicative competence such as Canale and Swain's (1980) have been concerned with socio-cultural appropriateness and communication strategies, the emphasis is on linguistics aspects of communication and on native speaker, non-native speaker interaction. The non-native speaker is positioned as the 'deficit' communicator and an idealised native speaker model of communication seen as the goal language learners should aim for. In language teaching this aim or model of competence is frequently restricted further to a focus on a bounded 'code' comprising features of syntax, lexis and phonology associated with this idealised model of a 'native speaker'. Deviations from this code are viewed as errors or evidence of a lack of competence (Widdowson 2012). Furthermore, as Global Englishes research has demonstrated the majority of interactions through English are likely to involve only non-native speakers, with no native speaker present. Thus, learners and teachers are provided with a restricted and unrepresentative model of communication and the knowledge and skills needed to achieve this. ELF studies (e.g. Seidlhofer 2011; Cogo and Dewey 2012; Mauranen 2012) have documented the fluid and flexible way linguistic forms are adapted in response to specific functions, settings and interlocutors often far removed in form from the models of 'standard native English' presented in teaching materials. This would suggest that competent intercultural communicators need to be able to employ linguistic forms in a flexible and reflexive manner rather than adhering to the fixed code presented in the majority of ELT materials and the underlying scaled-down construct of communicative competence.

Most importantly though, this focus on the linguistic dimension of competence with its underlying structuralist view of language as code, at the expense of other aspects of communication, ignores many of the insights of intercultural communication and ELF studies, especially as regards the importance of culture, context, variety, adaptation and change in language and communication. As discussed in detail in the previous chapters, competence, and associated models and goals for teaching need to go beyond structural perspectives and the associated competence in a single linguistic code. This has included a range of communication strategies such as accommodation, code-switching, repetition, explicitness and pre-empting misunderstanding, which facilitate the flexible use of linguistic forms. In ELF research such strategies have been regarded as equally, if not more important, than competence in linguistic forms (e.g. Jenkins, Cogo and Dewey 2011; Seidlhofer and Widdowson 2011). Together with this flexible use of linguistic forms and communicative strategies there needs to be an awareness of the processes of communication and meaning making in intercultural communication. As proposed in ICA (and many of the other notions of competence such as ICC, symbolic competence and performative competence), it is this awareness of plurilithic and changing cultural contexts, communicative practices and their dynamic role in intercultural communication that forms the framework for the effective use of communication strategies and linguistic forms. Nonetheless, there is currently little evidence of the flexible use of linguistic forms, the associated use of communicative strategies and an overarching intercultural awareness being present in ELT materials or pedagogy.

When the non-linguistic aspects of communicative competence are given attention, and social-cultural settings and social rules of communication are considered, this is predominantly presented in an essentialist manner based on an idealised native speaker model derived from the intuitions of teacher trainers, material and exam writers (Leung 2005). Yet, without a fuller understanding of intercultural communicative competence, L2 learners are likely to be poorly equipped for the linguistic and communicative diversity they will face in intercultural communication through ELF. For example, L2 users need knowledge of other communicative practices and to develop favourable attitudes to highly diverse and potentially demanding communication which will frequently involve negotiation and challenge. Finally, and most crucially, as outlined in ICA, a critical and reflexive stance towards such knowledge is needed and the ability to make use of this knowledge in a flexible and context specific manner. Nonetheless, it must be acknowledged that individual ELT teachers are limited by externally imposed constraints from curricula and especially testing. While large scale testing organisations, such as IELTS and TOEFL, continue to utilise a monolingual, 'native speaker' and linguistically dominated view of communicative competence, incorporating a wider view of intercultural competence and ICA in teaching practice may be difficult and even resisted by learners who need to prepare for such exams.

Even when the importance of the cultural and intercultural is recognised in teaching, it often remains low on teachers' lists of priorities and is rarely systematically integrated into teaching (Sercu et al. 2005; Young and Sachdev 2011; Luk 2012; Driscoll, Earl and Cable 2013). Given the increased demands that communicative competence placed on language teachers and classrooms, as well as valid critiques of its relevance in all settings (e.g. Kumaravadivelu 2001), it is not surprising that adding further to the range of knowledge and skills expected of language teachers would meet with resistance, particularly given the time constraints on already busy teachers. This marginalisation is further reinforced by the lack of focus on the intercultural in teacher training, teaching materials, teaching syllabi and language testing. Additionally, with some notable exceptions (particularly the work of Byram and colleagues), compared to other teaching approaches there has been little empirical research on the "uptake and perceived applicability of this [intercultural] approach" (Young and Sachdev 2011: 83). Due to the scarcity of guidance on 'uptake' and 'applicability' it is not always clear to teachers how the intercultural should be integrated into teaching. One of the consequences of this is that even teachers who are interested in the intercultural dimension to L2 teaching and learning often relegate culture to the place of a 'fifth skill' after the other four skills: listening, speaking, reading and writing (see Tomalin (2008) for an example of this). By doing this there is the obvious implication that as the 'fifth' skill culture can be left to last and given the least attention. There is also the problem in viewing culture and intercultural communication as only a skill, when, as has been made clear here, intercultural competence and ICA involves skills, knowledge and attitudes in equal measure. Most importantly though, culture is a central part of intercultural communication, and the associated notions of intercultural competence and ICA, and cannot be dealt with in isolation from other aspects of communication.

In addition to the unsystematic manner in which the intercultural is approached in ELT, culture is frequently presented in an essentialist manner and only at the national level with a focus on cultural 'facts' and products in which these stereotyped portrayals remain unchallenged and un-critiqued. Two studies separated by over ten years revealed very similar findings in relation to the superficial treatments of cultures in ELT text books (Jin and Cortazzi 1999; Vettorel 2010). Gray (2010) also offers a detailed analysis of a number of ELT course books over the last 40 years with regard to their cultural content. However, Gray takes a different perspective on culture to that adopted in this monograph, in that he is not interested in culture per se, but rather adopts a cultural studies approach to analysing text books in which they are viewed as cultural artefacts and "the ways in which culture, in the cultural studies sense, is used in coursebooks to make English mean in specific ways." (2010: 18). Therefore, he does not view textbooks as culturally empty or superficial (as Jin and Cortazzi 1999 or Vetorel 2010 do) since all content, in a cultural studies perspective, is cultural content of one kind or another. However, Gray does question the relevance of the cultural content of the texts he analyses. He identifies a dominant portrayal of language learners as consumers and the aspirational 'celebrity' content of the materials provided (see also Gray 2012). Of particular relevance to the argument in this chapter, Gray notes the restricted range of representations and the native speaker focus. Furthermore, data from teachers in his study reveals frustration at the lack of representation of English as an international language or lingua franca and the absence of locally relevant issues.

Overall then, in ELT materials, and particularly global course books, there appears to be little recognition of the complexity and dynamism of culture and the situated emergent understanding of culture and language as outlined in ICA, ELF and other critical approaches to intercultural communication. In many language learning materials images of other cultures are simplistic and stereotyped focusing solely on national representations of culture. Taking an updated version of one of the texts analysed by Gray (2010), the bestselling New Headway series (Soars and Soars 2011) provides a prime case of such stereotypical representations. The touristic images of Buckingham Palace we find in such materials do not offer much insight into the cultures of the people who live in these communities and in the case of English are even less relevant to the majority of 'non-native' speakers of the language who will not be communicating in these settings. Equally problematic is the adoption of a cross-cultural approach where generalised statements about how people in a particular national culture communicate are compared to generalised statements about communication in another national culture, for example, the directness of Germans versus the indirectness of the British (again see the New Headway series such as 'A World Guide to Good Manners' (Soars and Soars 2003: 34)).

While ICA, along with many other approaches to intercultural education, recognises the place of cultural comparisons and the role they can play in gaining knowledge of other cultural practices and of relativizing one's own cultural practices, cultural comparisons need to be approached carefully. To repeat a number of the arguments presented in pervious chapters, cultural comparisons made at the level of national cultures are not necessarily applicable to individual instances of communication. Such national level descriptions are frequently based on the aggregated communicative practices of a group. However, individuals will vary considerably more in their behaviour than such emergent, and hence irreducible, culturally based descriptions of communication. Furthermore, national cultures are just one level or scale of cultural grouping and other cultural groupings and identifications need to be recognised. Moreover, cross-cultural comparisons assume that people's communicative practices are unchanging; whereas, in intercultural communication interlocutors will typically adapt their behaviour to that of their interlocutor through reciprocal accommodation to enable more effective communication. Finally, cross-cultural comparisons may hide implicit value judgements and power structures that suggest a particular set of communicative practices are more normal and 'preferred' compared to others which are different, deviant and 'inferior'. Such essentialist approaches to culture are more likely to reinforce cultural stereotyping and intercultural divides rather than aid understanding in intercultural communication.

There are some signs of change in mainstream ELT materials with a number of contemporary texts attempting to take a more systematic and less essentialist approach to culture and language. Nonetheless, it is debatable how far this goes beyond surface features and many of the same issues remain, particularly as regards recognition of the use of English as a lingua franca. An examination of two current ELT texts which claim to adopt a more intercultural perspective illustrates this point. 'Global' (Clanfield 2009), as might be expected from the title, recognises the global role of English and emphasises the importance of non-native speakers of English as models in learning the language. It also incorporates some insights from ELF research, in particular the lingua franca core (Jenkins 2000). However, much of the content still reveals an Anglo-centric bias, for example in a selection of literature to be discussed by students the texts chosen are written by Anglophone writers and hence a truly global perspective on the use of English is eschewed with texts or literature produced by non-native writers ignored. Similarly, in the 'function globally' section which offers functional communicative language many of the linguistic structures and dialogue constructions appear to follow the norms of middle class Anglo settings (e.g. ringing up a restaurant in advance to book a table). This mirrors Leung's (2005) earlier criticism of the superficial and restricted representation of pragmatic strategies and sociocultural contexts in ELT materials.

'English Unlimited' (Doff 2011), is another text which also adopts an intercultural perspective and claims in the description to 'focus on intercultural competence as a 'fifth skill'. The inclusion of intercultural competence would appear to represent a move away from the more restrictive focus of communicative competence. However, again, a more detailed analysis brings into question how deeply this is applied. Later in the same description it is stated that the CEFR is at the book's core. However, as discussed above, the focus on 'native speaker' norms, expectations and proficiency in the CEFR suggests a concept of communication more in line with earlier restricted understandings of communicative competence rather than intercultural competence or ICA. In addition, the problem of treating culture or the intercultural as an additional fifth skill has already been noted. Dewey (2015) also explores both 'Global' and 'English Unlimited' in relation to language and comes to a similar conclusion. That is, despite the global orientation in the marketing and outward appearance, the focus is still on British and American English with a traditional ELT syllabus centred on pre-determined linguistic structures.

Of course a brief examination of two texts books cannot make claim to a characterisation of the whole ELT industry. Nonetheless, these texts have been chosen because they represent an attempt on the part of material writers and publishers to engage in and incorporate the growing insights from intercultural communication, Global Englishes and ELF studies. Yet, at the same time the texts highlight how far the ELT industry still has to go to meaningfully engage with non-Anglo-centric perspectives and to move beyond narrow views of what constitutes communication and recognise more complex, critical understandings of language, culture and intercultural communication. As Liddicoat and Scarino argue as regard language education in general, "in spite of claims they may have made about their aims and objectives, many approaches to language education have effectively marginalized culture and the intercultural by focusing solely on the linguistic system and the use of materials that are sanitized of cultural complexity." (2013: 47) and this, I would argue, is particularly true of ELT. This point becomes even more pertinent when we consider intercultural communication through ELF which, although being the most likely use to which English is put, remains largely absent from ELT. A point succinctly summarised by Jenkins, "Despite the phenomenal increase in the use of ELF around the world, the prevailing orientation in English language teaching and testing, and ELT materials remains undoubtedly towards ENL [English as a native language], with correctness and appropriateness still widely driven by NES [native English speakers] use regardless of learners' current or potential communication contexts." (2012: 487).

6.2 Alternative approaches to culture, the intercultural and ELF in ELT

The aim of this section is not to suggest that there is a single alternative approach, and even less an alternative methodology, to those currently offered in ELT. Rather the insights from intercultural research and ELF research are very much commensurable with postmethods perspectives (Kumaravadivelu 2001; 2012) in which no single method is viewed as applicable in all teaching situations. Alternatively, the diversity and dynamism documented in intercultural communication and ELF studies would suggest that in order for ELT to prepare learners for this variety, multiple approaches need to be adopted which are developed and adapted to suit particular contexts and purpose of English language learning. This is, of course, neither an original or particularly controversial position and the importance of locally relevant pedagogy in ELT has been much discussed (e.g. Kramsch 1993; Kramsch and Sullivan 1996; Canagarajah 1999; 2005; 2013b; Brumfit 2001; Kumaravadivelu 2001; 2006; 2012; Bax 2003; Widdowson 2003; Holliday 2005; Jenkins 2007; Pennycook 2007; Phan 2008; Seidlhofer 2011). Nonetheless, the point is worth emphasising to avoid misinterpretations and false accusations that either intercultural communication or ELF scholars are prescribing a particular approach which it is claimed is applicable in all settings. At the same time, though, while a degree of eclecticism is inevitable, it is important that this does not result in unprincipled and unfocused discussions of ELT in which policy makers or practitioners are left with little understanding of how the insights gained from researching intercultural communication through

ELF and are of relevance to them. Therefore, consideration of the aims and purposes of ELT is needed, alongside broad recommendations for principles which can inform practice, as well as specific examples of good practice which other practitioners can draw on. In relation to these principles and practical examples a series of recommendations for incorporating ICA into classroom practice will be offered in the following section together with a detailed empirical study in the next chapter. Before presenting this though, it is necessary to outline the major areas of research and thinking that inform this discussion and the understanding of the purposes and aims of language teaching and specifically ELT.

6.2.1 Intercultural education and ELT

Most obviously intercultural communication research has resulted in a considerable literature on the role of intercultural education as a key part of language education. As Zhu notes (2014: 4) language teaching and learning is often now perceived as an *inevitably* intercultural experience in which language learners learn about other cultures and peoples. This is a view echoed by Liddicoat and Scarino when they write that "language learning is fundamentally engagement in intercultural communication and that the addition of a new language to a person's linguistic repertoire positions that person differently in relation to the world in which they live." (2013: 6). Given this perspective on language learning and the intercultural it is understandable that there is a huge literature on the subject and an overview of all of it is beyond the scope of this chapter (see Risager 2007; Holliday, Hyde and Kullman 2010; Jackson 2014; Zhu 2014), but some of the key principles that underpin the framework presented here need to be sketched out. It should also be noted that many intercultural approaches to language teaching have quite rightly been critiqued for essentialism and uncritically reproducing nationalist characterisations of culture (see above and Holliday 2011; 2013; Piller 2011). Nevertheless, intercultural approaches typically represent an extension of communicative competence beyond a restricted linguistic competence, and incorporate elements of the knowledge, skills and attitudes needed for intercultural communication.

Byram's ICC (1997) and extensions of it (e.g. Guilherme 2002; Risager 2007), which were presented in the previous chapter, are probably the most influential alternatives to communicative competence. Byram's five savoirs (attitudes (savoir être), knowledge (savoirs), skills of interpreting and relating (savoir comprendre), skills of discovery and interaction (savor apprendre/faire), critical cultural awareness/political education (savoir s'engager)) offer a detailed and systematic alternative to communicative competence in which the intercultural aspects of language learning are placed in a central role in education. Combined with Byram's (1997) suggestions for classroom practice, curriculum and testing, in which increasingly complex views of the relationship between cultures and languages are presented to students as they progress through their learning, Byram details an extensive and powerful alternative to current mainstream ELT pedagogy. However, as previously discussed, the focus in Byram's work, and subsequent adaptations, has been on the national view of culture, however complex their presentation may be, and there is little or no consideration of ELF. Moreover, nor is there an extensive treatment of more critical views of culture in which languages are not associated with relatively stable national communities.

Alongside rethinking communicative competence, intercultural education has also looked at alternative models and aims to the ill-defined and typically inappropriate notion of a native speaker as a goal in language teaching. Instead, the intercultural speaker possessing ICC, rather than the native speaker possessing communicative competence, is presented as the model for L2 language learning and teaching (Byram 1997; Kramsch 1998), again as discussed in chapter five. More recently discussions have moved from the model of an intercultural speaker to the notion of an intercultural citizen and citizenship (Guilherme 2002; 2012; Alred, Byram and Fleming 2006; Risager 2007; Byram, 2008; 2012a; Lu and Corbett 2012). Intercultural citizenship is an attempt to bring together language education and citizenship education in a manner that extends citizenship beyond national borders and recognises the global scale of social relations and communications. It also transcends intercultural competence and the intercultural speaker in emphasising the need for more than mediation, by including action with others and an awareness of the global and local responsibilities this brings. As Byram explains intercultural citizenship education involves:

- Causing/facilitating intercultural citizenship experience, and analysis and reflection on it and on the possibility of further social and/or political activity, i.e. activity that involves working with others to achieve an agreed end;
- Creating learning/change in the individual: cognitive, attitudinal, behavioural change; change in self-perception; change in relationships with others (i.e. people of different social groups); change that is based in the particular but is related to the universal. (2008: 187)

Lu and Corbett also agree that L2 education is the most appropriate setting to develop intercultural citizenship arguing that "whatever the concept of citizenship that prevails, 'bounded' or 'global', most educators agree that the language classroom can be a privileged site for the exploration of identity and belonging, key aspects of citizenship." (2012: 336). However, Lu and Corbett here also touch on one of the limitations of citizenship which is the central role it places on nation and 'bounded' concepts of citizenship. While intercultural citizenship may be useful in helping learners explore how global communities and identifications relate to their identities as national citizens, the national still appears to be given a central place in explorations. This may well be important for many learners and it is certainly an approach that many government education ministries are likely to find acceptable. However, ELF research and more critical approaches to intercultural communication have questioned the necessity of always allocating national identities and cultures such central roles. If intercultural citizenship is to be of relevance to the majority of ELT teachers and learners, it is essential that alternatives to national cultural identities are given equal emphasis and learners are able to critically explore dominant cultural characterisations. The discussion around citizenship and intercultural citizenship also extends beyond language learners. This is important since it is not only language learners who engage in intercultural communication. People also use their L1 for intercultural communication, and the types of skills, knowledge and attitudes presented in ICA and ICC are likely to be relevant to L1 use in such cases. A clear example of this is provided in Jenkins' (2014) study of academic English language policies which suggested that in international universities in Anglophone settings it was the native speakers of English that were most in need of developing ICA.

Together with the expansion of communicative competence and the proposal of alternatives to the native speaker model in ELT, intercultural education literature has also frequently shifted the focus of teaching away from final products (e.g. knowledge of linguistic forms and functions) to a focus on the processes of communication and intercultural communication. This is a crucial aspect of intercultural education since learners can never be prepared with knowledge of all the cultural practices and contexts they are likely to encounter in intercultural communication, particularly with a globally used lingua franca such as English. Therefore, learners need to be equipped with an awareness of the processes of intercultural communication which can serve as a starting point for negotiating differences and creating understanding in individual instances of communication. Canagarajah sums up this perspective succinctly in his discussion of performative competence which also makes use of Byram's notion of intercultural citizenship and ICC, "Adopting Byram's (2008) useful distinction, we can say that what translinguals bring is a form of *procedural knowledge*, not the *propositional knowledge* of either grammatical or communicative competence. Their competence isn't constituted of the *what*, but of the *how* of communication." (2013b: 173–174). Following this perspective it is clear that ELT cannot meaningfully be approached from a single methodology since the content of what is taught will inevitably vary given the context in which teaching occurs and the purposes of the class. This was a point underscored earlier in relation to ICA when it was stated that only general features could be identified and delineated since the specifics of what constituted effective and appropriate communication could only be decided in situ. Again Canagarajah makes a similar point arguing that "A form-focused, teacher-led, product-orientated pedagogy will contradict the learning strategies and dispositions students bring for performative competence" (2013b: 184) and he goes on to further state that "teaching these strategies explicitly and formulaically for deductive application is distorting. These strategies are situated and practice-based. They cannot be implemented in a product-orientated and a priori manner." (2013b: 186).

Liddicoat and Scarino (2013) relate such a perspective in intercultural educational, in which process is given precedence over product, to Kumaravadivelu's post-method condition (2001) and its critique of the advocacy of particular teaching methods. Liddicoat and Scarino argue that "it is important to think beyond an understanding of teaching practice as method to consider how the complexity of lived experiences of linguistic and cultural diversity shape both the focus of language teaching and learning and the *processes* through which it happens in classrooms – what we call a perspective." (2013: 2, emphasis mine). This is not to suggest that linguistic 'products' do not have a place in language teaching. Examining examples of language is of course a core port of language teaching and language will still remain central. However, linguistic products should not be treated as the end product in teaching, rather they should be presented as examples of part of the communicative process to be used and adapted as needed together with other aspects of communication such as communication strategies. The same point can be made in relation to learning about other cultures. There is still a place for information about other cultures, but that information is not the end point of learning. Instead it should be viewed as part of the process of engagement with interculturality in which knowledge of 'others' is continually reflected upon, evaluated, adapted and changed.

Another important strand in contemporary perspectives on intercultural communication has drawn extensively on critical pedagogy in exploring and challenging dominant discourses on culture, language and identity and encouraging action on the part of learners. Phipps and Guilherme characterise a critical pedagogy for intercultural education as "a critical use of language(s), a critical approach to one's own and other cultural backgrounds and a critical view of intercultural interaction." (2004: 3). They further propose that such a critical pedagogic approach involves reflection, dissent, difference, dialogue, empowerment, action and hope (2004: 3). Many of these themes have also been addressed by other scholars who likewise have advocated a critical approach to intercultural education and a number of these were discussed in chapter two (Guilherme 2002; 2012; Pennycook 2007; 2010; Kramsch 2009; 2010; Holliday 2011; 2013; Piller 2011;

Canagarajah 2013b; Zhu 2014). Kramsch (2009; 2010), Holliday (2011; 2013) and Piller (2011) have written extensively about the need for teachers and learners to explore the prevailing discourses of culture, particularly national cultures, and to challenge hegemonic perspectives. Reflection is also a central part of critical pedagogy in which learners and teachers are given time to consider and explore their experiences of intercultural communication and this needs to be given adequate space in teaching time (Guilherme 2012: 368). Guilherme also suggests that a critical intercultural approach will necessarily entail an engagement with complex ideas and an acceptance of cultural complexity as opposed to essentialist generalisations. However, this complexity results in a tension with pedagogic principles which require simple and clear explanations; a theme that will be returned to later in this chapter.

Liddicoat and Scarino (2013), among others, emphasise the importance of not just awareness but also of action and change in intercultural education. They make a distinction between a cultural perspective and intercultural perspective which captures this difference between a passive approach to learning about other cultures and active engagement in interculturality. As they explain it,

> A cultural perspective implies the development of knowledge about a culture, which remains external to the learner and is not intended to confront or transform the learner's existing identity, practices, values, attitudes, beliefs, and worldview. An intercultural perspective implies the transformational engagement of the learner in the act of learning. The goal of learning is to decenter learners from their preexisting assumptions and practices and to develop an intercultural identity through engagement with an additional culture. (2013: 28–29)

The significance given to action and transformation also links back to the earlier discussion of intercultural citizenship in which engagement with others, action and responsibility were key features.

6.2.2 Global Englishes, ELF and interculturality in ELT

The approaches to intercultural education outlined so far argue for more complex and multiple understandings of languages and cultures, as well as a critique of static homogeneous representations of national culture. This would suggest a very different view of the relationship between culture, language, identity and communication to that traditionally taken in ELT. A growing number of scholars have gone a step further than critiques of national culture and placed globalisation at the centre of language education (e.g. Pennycook 2007; McKay and Bokhorst-Heng 2008; Kumaravadivelu 2008; Sharifian 2009; Alsagoff et al. 2012;

Matsuda 2012; Canagarajah 2013b). Pennycook (2007), Kumaravadivelu (2008) and Canagarajah (2013b) are discussed in detail here as representative examples of this growing engagement with globalisation and intercultural communication in ELT theory. They have been selected due to the detailed deliberations on this subject presented in each monograph. However, they are not alone in tackling this subject and there are an increasing number of empirical studies and edited collections of teaching approaches related to EIL in particular (e.g. McKay and Bokhorst-Heng 2008; Sharifian 2009; Alsagoff et al. 2012; Matsuda 2012). While these studies and collections offer useful ideas and suggestions, they have not been included here as many of the issues they cover are already addressed elsewhere. They also differ slightly in focus to ELF orientated studies particularly in their focus on World Englishes and the associated nation based varieties of English and cultural contexts (see chapter one). Finally, this chapter does not attempt to provide a comprehensive 'state of the art' review of all current studies but rather highlight key issues of relevance to the present discussion.

Canagarajah underscores the change in focus this global Englishes approach entails in stating that "while joining a new speech community was the objective of traditional pedagogy, now teachers train students to shuttle between communities" (2013b: 191). Canagarajah's (2013b) performative competence of translinguals has already been discussed as a model of intercultural competence with a number of pedagogic implications. To briefly recap, these involve acknowledging the importance of the communicative resources translingual students bring to the classroom; the situated rather than prescriptive nature of any teaching recommendations; and the significance of teaching negotiation strategies and form as negotiable. Pennycook adopts a similar perspective to Canagarajah in his suggestions for "teaching with the flow" (2007: 155) in which he attempts to incorporate the "fluidity, flow and fixity of cultural movement" (2007: 157) into classroom practices for Global Englishes. For Pennycook this means understanding the complexity of cultural encounters in the classroom and recognising cultures and identities that are hybrid and cosmopolitan rather than bounded. Pennycook advocates the use of popular culture, and in particular hip-hop with its global reach and multiple local-global realisations, as a way to explore such themes in teaching.

One of the most detailed approaches is that presented by Kumaravadivelu (2008) in his discussion of cultural realism and pedagogic principles. Kumaravadivelu's (2008) concept of cultural realism was outlined in chapter four and involved an understanding of global, national, social and individual realities and the ability to act on this understanding. Kumaravadivelu argues that such action in relation to language education requires a transition in the teaching of culture and "a teaching programme that is sensitive to the chances and challenges posed by cultural globalisation." (2008: 172). This transition results in five pedagogic priorities and shifts: "(a) from target language community to targeted cultural community, (b) from linguistic articulation to cultural affiliation, (c) from cultural information to cultural transformation, (d) from passive reception to critical reflection, and (e) from interested text to informed context." (2008: 172). Kumaravadivelu's approach brings together many of the elements of critical pedagogy and intercultural education in emphasising reflection and transformation in learning (priorities c, d and e). He also underscores the importance of moving away from particular target communities in language teaching and instead to exploring multiple communities, groupings and identifications along with the formation of new groups and identities opened up by language learning (priorities a and b). Significantly, Kumaravadivelu is also critical of current teaching materials and their presentations of cultures, even when they focus on global issues, as lacking in a deep critical engagement with cultural realism (priority e). As an alternative, rather than single texts, he suggests a range of materials including online resources which offer multiple perspectives on cultural contexts. As Kumaravadivelu argues "[b]y shifting from interested text to informed contexts in which various shades of cultural meanings play out, they [learners] will be able to explore, in detail and from a critical perspective, topics that interest them, and gain a deeper understanding of how they are treated in different cultural contexts" (2008: 189–190).

While there is much of value in the three monographs discussed above, with the exception of Kumaravadivelu (2008), they lack practical guidelines or suggestions for teachers. Yet, it is important to explore how these implications influence classrooms, if teachers are to meaningfully engage with them. There is also a lack of consideration of ELF research, or a misinterpretation in Canagarajah's case, in relation to ELF and culture. This marginalisation of ELF research is significant for the present discussion as for the majority of ELT learners ELF is the most likely communicative scenario in which they will use English. It can also be argued that ELF has been the research field most concerned with decentring English and moving it away from a concentration on Anglophone nationalist links towards more local and global settings. In specific relation to pedagogy many ELF researchers have so far been reluctant to offer prescriptions for classroom teaching (e.g. Jenkins 2007), preferring to allow teachers to decide for themselves what is relevant from ELF findings. Nonetheless, the origins of ELF research were in part the result of pedagogic concerns (Jenkins 2000; 2012; Cook 2012) and recent years have seen an increased interest in detailed engagement with ELT. This has involved both conceptual and empirical research at school and tertiary level, English language teaching as a subject in itself, particularly at school level, English support through EAP instruction, English medium instruction and teacher training (e.g. Seidlhofer 2004; 2011; Jenkins 2006a; 2014; Phan 2008; Llurda 2004; 2006; Smit 2009; 2010; Björkman 2011; 2013; Kirkpatrick 2011; Mimatsu 2011; Sifakis and Fay 2011; Baker 2012b; 2012c; 2012d; Dewey 2012; 2015; Qiufang 2012; Galloway 2013; Galloway and Rose 2013; Vettorel 2013; Xu and Ngoc Dinh 2013; Zheng 2013; Chan 2014; Bayyurt and Akcan 2015). The focus of the majority of these studies has been on the role of linguistic forms and communicative strategies in teaching; however, contexts and cultures have also been considered.

Like the intercultural approaches to language education, ELF discussions have highlighted the importance of local contexts in any consideration of appropriate pedagogy and have typically considered implications and presented general principles or approaches rather than specific methodologies, detailed curricula or materials specifications. Indeed, ELF scholars such as Seidlhofer (2011) and Jenkins (2012) have been clear that there is not an 'ELF pedagogy' as such and that findings from ELF research should be interpreted and translated into meaningful locally relevant pedagogic practice. As Jenkins explains "ELF researchers have always been careful to point out that we do not believe it is our place to tell teachers what to do, but that it is for ELT practitioners to decide whether/to what extent ELF is relevant to their learners in their context." (2012: 492). As with intercultural approaches, ELF researchers have also stressed the importance of process in language learning and teaching rather than product. Seidlhofer writes that "the pedagogic significance of an ELF perspective is that it shifts the focus of attention to the learner and the learning process. It points to the need to reconsider how teaching might provide impetus and support for this process" (2011: 198). This is particularly relevant for ELF since given its inherent variability it is not possible to specify a fixed set of linguistic forms, communicative strategies or cultural norms that would be appropriate in all communicative circumstances. Rather Seidlhofer (2011), following Widdowson (2003), underscores the significance of teaching learners how to learn. This involves exploring how learners can make use of the communicative resources they already have to communicate effectively and also how they can adapt and expand those resources through instances of communication; in other words, a focus on the processes of communication and of learning how to communicate simultaneously.

Such an approach is clearly commensurable with Kumaravadivelu's post-methods condition in its focus on locally relevant pedagogy and adaptable processes. However, Dewey (2012) goes further suggesting it involves not only a post-methods perspective but also a post-normative perspective in which there is no set of fixed language forms or communicative practices which can be considered appropriate in all settings. Clearly current mainstream perspectives in ELT are a long way from either a post-method or post-normative approach, but

Seidlhofer (2011), Dewey (2012) and Jenkins (2012) all believe that through appropriate teacher education an increased awareness of the extensive use of ELF and the implications for pedagogy is possible. In particular, Dewey proposes that part of teacher education should include a greater understanding of the diverse sociocultural contexts of English use and discussions of the influence globalisation has had on language and communication (2012: 163). Nonetheless, to date the only teacher education text book which has engaged extensively with the findings from ELF research is Walker's (2010) text on teaching pronunciation.

There is, however, growing evidence of an increased awareness of intercultural communication and ELF amongst teachers and students. For example, Sifakis and Fay's (2011) survey of teachers in Greek state schools revealed a greater emphasis on intercultural communication and ELF in ELT then in the past; although, the traditional Anglophone dominated EFL approach was still prominent. Like Seidlhofer (2011), Dewey (2012) and Jenkins (2012), Sifakis and Fay emphasize the importance of teacher training in raising critical awareness of the changing roles of English. Similarly, Mimatsu's (2011) ethnographic study of high schools in Japan also highlighted the importance of intercultural communication with non-native speakers through ELF as a goal in ELT for both teachers and in education policy. However, she cautions that this was typically not translated into practice where traditional EFL approaches were followed and that the official education policy was itself ambiguous. Mimatsu concludes that greater consideration needs to be given to the current role of English in language education policies and curriculums. Turning to students, Csizér and Kontra's (2012) survey of Hungarian students showed that the concept of ELF had a strong influence on their aims and beliefs in language learning. Nevertheless, while their study illustrated a move away from the complete domination of Anglophone models of English, such models were still present. Likewise, Kormos, Kiddle, and Csizér's (2011) survey of Chilean school students, university students and young adult learners also showed the importance of ELF, with international communication through ELF emerging as the most important learning goals from the study. Overall, findings from studies such as those reported here are similar to Jenkins' (2007) earlier study, in showing the growing importance of ELF and intercultural communication in teachers and students goals in language learning, but also illustrating the continued influence of traditional native speaker, Anglophone models of ELT.

Two recent studies from Japan go further than just surveying attitudes and have attempted to develop materials and syllabi with a focus on the global role of English. Galloway (2013) developed a programme in Global Englishes for Japanese university students incorporating elements of World Englishes and ELF and highlighting the correspondingly diverse socio-cultural contexts in which

English is used. Crucially she also integrated elements of CA and ICA into the programme. Galloway reports that students generally expressed positive attitudes towards a variety of Englishes and had developed a better understanding of English in intercultural communication. However, for many of the students Anglophone varieties of English remained the most prestigious. Hino and Oda (2015) report on a programme that was developed over a number of years in which students in a Japanese university explored English language news sources from around the world. These included many sources from Asia but also Africa as well as Anglophone settings. Through such a range of news sources students were exposed to many diverse uses of English and also cultural diversity expressed through English. This, Hino and Oda believe, is crucial in developing intercultural awareness among the students and fostering a sense of identity as members of an international community of English users. Perhaps most significantly was the very positive reception the programme has had among all levels of the university where it was undertaken and it has received multiple awards. Both Galloway's (2013) and Hino and Oda's (2015) studies represent important developments in the relationship between ELF research and pedagogy demonstrating the feasibility of ELF aware pedagogy and the generally favourable evaluations of such programmes.

Much ELF research to date has taken place within academic settings (e.g. Smit 2010; Mauranen 2012; Björkman 2013; Jenkins 2014) particularly in university EMI (English medium instruction) settings and this has often been accompanied by suggestions for pedagogy. In specific relation to intercultural communication, Jenkins (2014) mentions the need for lecturers and students to develop intercultural communication skills, intercultural competence and intercultural awareness. Importantly, she is clear that in EMI environments where there is a significant international body of students, including within Anglophone settings, it is crucial that all participants, whether local or international, staff or students, take equal responsibility for successful communication. Indeed, based on the results of her study Jenkins suggest that it is the native English speaking staff and students who typically have the lowest levels of intercultural awareness and need the most help (2014: 203). Mauranen makes similar recommendations in regards to English language teaching and testing outside of Anglophone academic environments, proposing that "Intercultural sensitivity and adaptation skills are crucial in successful communication in a globalised world, and more often than not they bear no reference to Anglo-American cultural presuppositions." (2012: 239).

In the related area of CLIL (content and language integrated learning) at school level, Dalton-Puffer suggests that CLIL classrooms can provide a site for the development of intercultural competence through ELF. Dalton-Puffer (2009:

211) recognises that CLIL settings are not prototypical ELF settings, since it may be that all of the participants share an L1 and English forms the shared L2. This may also be the case in some EMI settings where students and instructors share the same L1. However, given that the most likely use of English in these settings is in ELF communication they are clearly relevant to ELF studies. It would also seem unhelpful to include some EMI settings which contain varying numbers of other L1 speakers and exclude others from consideration. This points to the necessity of accepting the fuzziness of definitions and boundaries so as to not close down productive avenues of research. Based on her research Dalton-Puffer believes that students are not being enculturated into the norms of native English classrooms but instead "some kind of 'transcultural flow' takes place where teachers with a multicultural educational experience or a multicultural identity are involved" (2009: 211). However, she adds that for this to be pedagogically productive explicit recognition and teaching strategies are needed, it cannot be taken for granted. While the majority of this research and the pedagogic recommendations are related to spoken academic English, some tentative proposals are also beginning to emerge as regards the cultural content of writing as well (Solin 2010; Baker 2013; Canagarajah 2013a).

In BELF (English as a business lingua franca) studies there seems to be a greater awareness on the part of research participants of the multilingual and multicultural nature of ELF communication and less attachment to native speaker norms and Anglophone cultures with subsequent implications for pedagogy. At the same time BELF studies have also reported less focus on the national cultural background of interlocutors in favour of other groupings. For example, Louhiala-Salminen and Kankaanranta's (2011) survey of business professionals reported the perceived importance of recognising the cultural background of interlocutors but more significant was their role in their organisation. They suggest that for BELF the model of communicative competence should be replaced by one of Global Communicative Competence emphasising the importance of 'multicultural competence', alongside 'competence in BELF' and 'business know-how'. (2011: 258). In terms of pedagogy Louhiala-Salminen and Kankaanranta recommend more focus on communication strategies and flexibility towards the variety of communicative practices business professionals are likely to encounter. Bjørge (2012) analysed the presentation of expressions of disagreement in business English text books and compared this with the actual expressions of disagreement used by business students in BELF communication. Her research findings highlighted a mismatch between the language of the text books and actual communicative practices in BELF negotiation, although the use of mitigation was a common element. Crucially, Bjørge (2012: 423) is critical of the simplistic correlations between communicative practices and national cultures often presented in text books. Her findings reveal no correspondence between the communicative practices of her speakers and their regional or national culture. Drawing on Ehrenreich (2009, see chapter three) she proposes that the concept of community of practice is more appropriate than national culture for BELF communication. Galloway and Rose (2013) report on a bilingual business degree programme at a Japanese university which incorporated aspects of Global Englishes, including World Englishes and ELF, and provided opportunities for ELF communication. As with the more general English teaching programmes discussed above there were mostly very positive attitudes towards the programme from the students. However, unlike the general English programmes, and in contrast to the teachers' perceptions, there appeared to less attachment to a native English speaker norms and cultures as the most prestigious models and an increased awareness of the global role of English and the importance of communication strategies and negotiation.

6.3 Intercultural awareness in the classroom

To restate the position outlined so far, intercultural communication research has given rise to extensive considerations of the pedagogic implications of a greater understanding of intercultural communication, primarily through the field of intercultural education. However, while the cultural and identity aspects of intercultural communication have typically been dealt with comprehensively, language issues have often been marginalised and this has been especially the case for intercultural communication through ELF. On the other hand, discussions among ELF scholars have frequently focused on linguistic issues for pedagogy, emphasising the need for flexible, post-normative approaches to language and communication which gives equal importance to linguistic form and communication strategies. While intercultural issues have not been ignored in ELF considerations of teaching, they have received less attention than in intercultural communication and education research. Suggestions for pedagogic practice from ELF scholars have been tentative so far but are beginning to emerge in more detail. Recommendations for pedagogy have also tended to be at a general level rather than specific suggestions for practice or materials; although, again, this is changing.

In my own research I have attempted to bridge the supposed divide between theory and practice and produce empirically grounded suggestions for teaching as well as materials which incorporate insights from intercultural communication and ELF research (Baker 2012a; 2012b; 2012c). Nonetheless, it should be repeated that such suggestions are not presented as an 'ELF' or 'ICA' pedagogy. I am in agreement with the majority of ELF researchers in eschewing prescriptions for classroom practices and so it is still crucial that teachers interpret the suggestions here in a way that is relevant to their own teaching contexts. Nonetheless, it is hoped that there will be elements and aspects of the ideas presented here that will resonate in a variety of teaching settings.

My suggestions for translating ICA and ELF research into classroom practice can be divided into five strands: 1. exploring the complexity of local cultures; 2. exploring cultural representations in language learning materials; 3. exploring cultural representations in the media and arts both online and in more 'traditional' mediums; 4. making use of cultural informants; 5. engaging in intercultural communication both face to face and electronically. While these suggestions go further than general teaching principles in offering guidance for teaching, they are still quite broad since the particular details of applying these strands will depend on local contexts (a more detailed example will be presented in the following chapter). Of course, not all of these ideas will be relevant in all contexts and there may be other opportunities for developing ICA in classrooms which have not been included here. The five strands can be explicated as follows:

1. **Exploring the complexity of local cultures** – This strand is presented first as it is an approach that is available in all settings. Through exploring their own culture learners can be introduced to the diversity and complexity of local and national cultural groupings. Discussion between the students and teachers within any class, even in supposedly monolingual and monocultural settings, often reveals a surprising diversity of linguistic and cultural identifications and groupings, such as different heritage languages, religions and family backgrounds. Such explorations should lead to an awareness of the multi-voiced nature of cultural characterisations and the complexity of the relationship between languages and cultures. Learners should also become aware of cultural characterisations and identifications other than at the national level. This should result in a greater understanding of cultural groupings at different scales both within and across national boundaries. It should also highlight the manner in which local communities can connect with global communities, whether it is religious or ethnic groups, identifying with other learners and users of English or groups such as music or sports fans. Finally, learners should begin to gain an understanding of how individuals relate in different ways to a variety of cultural groupings and that cultural characterisations, at whatever scale, are not synonymous with individuals' practices or beliefs. In considering the complexity of their own cultural context and background learners should begin to become aware of the complexity of other cultures and also of others cultural identifications

and practices. Approaches to implementing this in the classroom might include class discussions and project work including small or larger scale ethnographic projects (e.g. Roberts et al. 2001).

2. **Exploring cultural representations in language learning materials** – Given the primacy of materials and particularly text books in ELT, these are likely to provide a major source of cultural content in the classroom. However, as already noted the representation of other cultures in ELT materials has typically been limited and essentialist. Nonetheless, such materials, even stereotyped ones, can still be put to productive use in developing ICA. Students can be asked to critically evaluate images and descriptions of cultures in their materials. This can include depictions of their own culture and of other cultures. It can also include locally produced materials and text books as well as imported materials and text books. Learners can compare the images presented with their own interpretations and experiences of their own and other cultures. They can also consider what has been chosen to be represented, what is missing and why. They may explore the types of cultural groupings represented i.e. are there only national groupings. They may also compare different cultural representations in different sets of materials. In this way learners should begin to develop the abilities needed to make critical comparisons between cultures as well as learning to critically evaluate any characterisation of culture; their own or 'other'.

3. **Exploring cultural representations in the media and arts both online and in more 'traditional' mediums** – Alongside text books, the arts, and particularly literature, has often been used as a source of cultural content in language teaching (e.g. Brumfit and Carter 1986; Kramsch 1993). However, this can include a wide variety of sources that present images or examples of culture that can be brought into the classroom such as film, television, radio, newspapers, novels, and magazines from the 'traditional media' and websites, blogs and podcasts from online sources. This can contain both representations of local cultures and other cultures through English. Importantly, cultural representations of non-Anglophone cultures through English should be made use of and this will introduce learners to the global role of English, particularly on the internet (e.g. Hino and Oda 2015). Online resources also provide good examples of hybrid and global cultural forms and practices which may not easily be associated with any particular national group. These materials should be explored in a similar manner to the text books and materials discussed in strand two with comparisons and critical interpretations encouraged (see for example Kramsch 2009).

4. **Making use of cultural informants** – In keeping with the ethnographic approach suggested in strand one, cultural informants can provide a source of knowledge and interpretations of other cultures and the learners' own culture. Non-local English teachers and local English teachers with experience of intercultural communication and other cultures can be asked to share their experiences with classes. Students are often curious about non-local teachers' cultural backgrounds and this can be exploited in a systematic way to provide cultural content in the classroom through, for example, discussion topics or reading texts. Non-local teachers can also provide 'outsiders' perspectives on the students' own cultures where the students are in their local setting (i.e. many school ELT classrooms). Informants can not only share their experience of other cultures but also of intercultural communication and of both the similarities and differences between cultures they are familiar with. They may also be able to introduce students to the notions of hybridity and of groupings and identifications that are transcultural and multiple. An obvious example of a transcultural, global grouping would be that of local English teachers identifying with other English teachers around the world. Of course, these experiences and interpretations will necessarily be subjective and partial, as are all characterisations of cultures, but as long as this is recognised they provide a valuable source of cultural content and an effective way of developing ICA.

5. **Engaging in intercultural communication both face to face and electronically** – Experience is a key part of developing intercultural competence and ICA and, if possible, experiences of intercultural communication should be integrated into language teaching. If the language teacher is a non-local teacher then the learners may already be viewed as engaged in intercultural communication. There may also be opportunities in the local environment to engage in intercultural communication, for example with tourists. Within Europe student exchanges have been a traditional element of language education and these provide a rich source of intercultural communication experience. From the perspective of ELT these exchanges do not necessarily have to be to Anglophone settings. Outer circle countries where English is widely spoken such as Hong Kong or Singapore are likely to prove equally relevant; perhaps even more so given the multilingual nature of such settings. Furthermore, regional settings where English functions as the lingua franca, even when it is not an official language of the country, for example in ASEAN (Association of South East Asian Nations), will also provide valuable opportunities for intercultural communication through English. Again given the multilingual character of these settings they may be more relevant to many

learners than Anglophone settings. This may be equally true in other settings where English is not an official lingua franca but still the most commonly used language for intercultural communication (see for example Kalocsai's (2014) study of European exchange students).

Physical and geographic exchanges of this type are expensive and difficult to organise and are clearly not suitable in all settings. However, exchanges can be organised with learners remaining in their own classrooms but engaging in intercultural communication through projects shared with language learners in other cultures (see Jones (1995) and Morgan and Cain (2000) for examples of this). Perhaps of more relevance, the last few decades have seen a huge rise in online exchanges in teletandem or telecollaboration learning where learners experience intercultural communication through communicating virtually with language learners in other countries (e.g. Belz and Thorne 2006; Telles and Vassallo 2006; O'Dowd 2011). This can be simple asynchronous email exchanges but has increasingly involved synchronous communication through instant chat messaging, Voice over Internet Protocol (VoIP) and now video through software such as Skype. Teletandem, while still requiring organisation and effort on the part of teachers and learners, offers a very accessible manner of bringing actual instance of intercultural communication into many language classrooms (see for example www.intent-project.eu and http://www.teletandembrasil.org). Experiences of intercultural communication, face to face or virtual, are valuable in themselves as offering opportunities to develop and put ICA into practice. However, equally crucial is that they provide materials and experience to reflect on and discuss in class. As already outlined developing ICA requires time and reflection, so it is important that space is given in class to consider the students experiences of intercultural communication, for example considering what was successful or not successful or how they felt about the experiences. Even when immediate opportunities for intercultural communication do not exist students and teachers can bring their pervious experiences to the class for discussion and reflection.

The five strands outlined here try to make use of all the resources available in the language classroom which can highlight the cultural and intercultural dimensions to language learning. These include materials and text books, teachers, other students, the surrounding environment, the internet and also outside experiences which can be brought into the classroom for discussion and reflection. With each of these strands approaching cultural content and intercultural experience critically is fundamental. This does not involve dismissing subjective interpretations and experiences as unimportant but rather recognising that any characterisation of culture will be partial and subjective and that it needs to be understood critically with alternative interpretations always possible. Similarly, the critical focus should also be applied to the relationship between language and culture, with learners becoming aware of the multitude of settings in which English is used and the range of cultural and communicative practices performed through English. This will necessarily involve a de-centring of the Anglophone settings and cultures which currently dominate ELT materials. However, this does not mean they are ignored, in settings where they are of relevance to the learners they should be critically explored. Furthermore, given their extensive presence in many existing ELT materials, critical consideration of them is likely to remain part of the intercultural dimension of ELT in the near future at least. Through engaging in the types of activities proposed here learners should be able develop the necessary critical and reflective skills, knowledge and attitudes outlined in the model of ICA presented in chapter five.

Such an approach to incorporating ICA into the classroom may seem demanding for both teachers and students given the complexity of cultural characterisations presented. However, the tension between simplicity and complexity is a common one in language teaching and applies to all aspects of the process from linguistic forms, to discourse structures and cultural content. Selection and simplification of content to make it manageable for teaching and learning are important aspects of pedagogy. As Brumfit explains, "Processes of making general statements, of fixing and formalising, and ultimately of stressing particular features for particular effects are inherent in the simplification process, but they also have inherent risks. Thus simplification results in a reliance on generalisations; generalisations can easily degenerate into stereotyping, and insensitive stereotyping rapidly becomes caricature" (2001: 35). Crucially though Brumfit's answer is not to avoid simplification, as without it Brumfit believes there will only be confusion. Instead he recommends that any simplifications are contextually justified and continually evaluated in relation to changing contexts to avoid stereotyping and caricature.

In relation to the cultural and intercultural dimensions of ELT this means focusing on those elements which are locally relevant in terms of learning goals and English use. Given that most learners experiences of and uses of English are likely to be as a lingua franca in intercultural communication, exploring the relationship between language, culture and communication in ELF would seem an appropriate starting point, including the attendant notions of complexity and diversity. This would, as noted by Brumfit, have to be presented in a manageable and simplified manner, but nonetheless, it represents an alternative to most current ELT practices with their uncritical and stereotypical focus on native speakers and Anglophone cultures and essentialist language, nation, culture correlations.

Of course, as already suggested, where Anglophone settings are of most relevance they will be the initial focus, but there should no longer be an a priori assumption that this is the case. In many ways this offers greater flexibility and choice for teachers, suggesting that they should be free to focus on teaching the aspects of language, culture and communication that are most relevant to their local context and their own (and learners) experiences. As such this can be seen as a more liberating alternative to the imposition of externally decided cultural content and notions of successful communication. This approach also connects with much contemporary discussion of intercultural communication, ELF and English language teaching in which there is a growing consensus around the role of education to be critical and challenge the status quo, making teachers and learners aware of other ways to conceive of the culture, communication and language relationship (e.g. Pennycook 2007; Byram 2008; Kumaravadivelu 2008; Kramsch 2009; Piller 2011; Seidlhofer 2011; Dewey 2012; Canagarajah 2013b; Jenkins 2014).

6.4 Conclusion

The discussion in this chapter has highlighted the limitations of current mainstream approaches in ELT and the need for changes which incorporate a recognition of English as a global lingua franca for intercultural communication. At present the predominant focus in ELT is on the teaching of a fixed linguistic code based on a narrow interpretation of the already limited notion of communicative competence. Yet, knowledge of a bounded set of features of lexis, syntax and phonology is unlikely to equip English language learners and users for the variable demands of intercultural communication. Where ELT does attempt to integrate other aspects of communication into teaching, such as communication strategies and cultural content, this has frequently been done in an ad hoc and equally limited manner. Socio-cultural norms are typically based on the intuitions of material writers which results in a bias towards an idealised set of practices based on the experiences of a particular social grouping in Anglophone settings (often white, middle class, English L1 speakers). Furthermore, cultural representations and images in materials, while perhaps more international in outlook, still retain superficial touristic portrayals of other cultures restricted to the national level. This results in overly simplified and essentialist portrayals of culture and intercultural communication in ELT and a failure to represent the experiences of the majority of learners.

Alternative approaches in intercultural education argue for a shift in teaching practice which brings the intercultural and cultural into a more central position. Linguistic forms and structure are still relevant to language teaching but equally important are communication strategies and a familiarity with the processes of intercultural communication. This also involves an awareness of the influences cultural backgrounds, settings and identifications have on communication. A fundamental aspect of intercultural approaches to language teaching is a move to a process orientated conception of learning where learners are taught about learning and communication rather than particular ways of communicating. Given the variety of communicative practices learners are likely to encounter using a global lingua franca such as English, learners can never be equipped with a comprehensive knowledge of all of this. Therefore, learning how to adapt and negotiate existing communicative resources as well as appropriate new resources in situ is crucial. Alongside a focus on the processes of intercultural communication has been an appreciation of the importance of local contexts in determining the needs and gaols of ELT. This has led to the post-methods condition (Kumaravadivelu 2001) whereby no single approach or methodology is viewed as applicable in all settings. Rather it is recognised that ELT pedagogy needs to be made locally relevant for and by local practitioners, while also recognising the global scope of ELT and English use. ELF research has added another dimension to the move away from prescriptive recommendations in ELT through advocating a post-normative perspective (Dewey 2012) alongside a post-methods perspective. The post-normative perspective in which the highly variable and diverse ways in which English, including linguistic forms, is used, as highlighted in ELF research, has, thus, added further support to the argument that learners need to be able to adapt and negotiation their communicative practices for intercultural communication through ELF. This means that no single set of linguistic and other communicative norms can be put forward as the most suitable for all ELT contexts. Again the implication is that instead of norms, learners need to be taught about adaptation and negotiation. This involves all aspects of communication including the cultural and intercultural.

Finally, I offered an exploration of how the model of ICA presented in chapter six can be translated into teaching practice in a manner that integrates findings from ELF and intercultural communication and education research. In the previous chapter I suggested that ICA could serve as a model for the development of the intercultural aspects of intercultural competence required for successful ELF communication. In this chapter I have attempted to outline the opportunities for the development of ICA in the classroom. These have included: 1. Exploring the complexity of local cultures; 2. exploring cultural representations in language learning materials; 3. exploring cultural representations in the media and arts both online and in more 'traditional' mediums; 4. making use of cultural informants; 5. engaging in intercultural communication both face to face and electronically. While going further than the general principles for pedagogy often presented in previous discussion concerning the implications of ELF research, the five strands are still quite general since the details of how they can be implemented and the relevant content will be dependent on local settings, opportunities and needs. Nonetheless, it may be valuable to look in more detail at how ICA translates into practice in particular settings and the demands this places on teachers and learners. It is also important to take the discussion beyond theory and principle and move it into the realm of empirical investigation and just such an empirical investigation forms the content of the next chapter.

Chapter 7
Putting it into practice: A study of a course in ELF and ICA for language learners in Thailand

> "it's like I have travelled the world @ in er you know in an hour"
> – Pai (research participant)

This chapter attempts to draw together many of the strands developed throughout this monograph concerning, ELF, intercultural communication, intercultural education and ICA (intercultural awareness). In the previous two chapters the type of competences and awareness needed for successful intercultural communication through ELF have been laid out, together with the reconceptualisation of models and paths of English language learning these entail. The implications for ELT have also been considered alongside a critique of current mainstream approaches which often ignore, marginalise or essentialise the intercultural aspects of second language learning and use. A range of principles for pedagogy have been presented which share a common emphasis on the need for locally relevant and adaptable approaches. This was combined with suggestions from ELF scholars that an equally adaptable approach needed to be taken not just to pedagogic techniques and priorities, but also to the content of ELT itself. In other words, the English language and the manner it is used in communication needed to be approached in locally relevant and variables ways. This represents a major challenge to current orthodoxy in ELT which is typically focused on teaching English as a fixed set of linguistic structures. These insights into interculturality, variability and adaptability were brought together in a series of recommendations for bringing the intercultural dimension into the ELT classroom and developing ICA. In particular, exploring ICA in the classroom underscored that English needed to be approached as a global language which in the majority of scenarios functions as a lingua franca. This means a more diverse cultural content in ELT. It also means a focus on preparing learners for variability and strategies for dealing with this variability.

The increased diversity and widening of the scope of ELT may seem to be unrealistically challenging or idealistic given the many demands already placed on teachers. However, as was suggested in the previous chapter, teachers already have to make choices in regard to making complex phenomena manageable for effective pedagogy. As such, selecting appropriate content based on, or adapted from, ELF and intercultural communication research findings or teaching recommendations is not a new process for teachers, even if the subject matter is. Furthermore, an increasing number of surveys of the attitudes of both teachers and students are revealing a growing awareness of the global role of English and a move away from the traditional Anglo-centric focus. Crucially, identification with an international community of English users (as opposed to native speaker communities) and a desire to join that community has begun to emerge as a central motivation for English learners. These are changes in attitudes and motivations that need to be taken up in pedagogy.

In this chapter I present a case study of a course that attempted to take up these challenges through the development and delivery of a course in intercultural communication, intercultural awareness and Global Englishes to English language learners at a Thai university[7]. The study involved the participation 31 undergraduate English majors and six teachers of English. In presenting this study I am trying to link many of the themes developed so far in a practical manner that is of direct relevance to teachers. This is, of course, not to suggest that the approach presented here should be replicated in its exact from in other settings. Rather it is offered as an example of how these seemingly complex themes and ideas can be translated into meaningful and effective pedagogy. In so doing the hope is that there are elements that will resonate in other contexts and lead to reflection on alternative means of presenting the intercultural and cultural in ELT classrooms. The main aims of the study were thus: to explore the feasibility of developing content for ELT materials which took a Global Englishes perspective as their baseline and that incorporated aspects of ICA into the approach; to investigate how such a course could be delivered; to consider the types of learning that took place; and to document teachers' and students' evaluations of such a course. These are formulated into three research questions (adapted from Baker 2012d: 6[8]):

---

7 The research reported here is an output from the ELT Research Award scheme (2010–2011) funded by the British Council to promote innovation in English language teaching research. The views expressed are not necessarily those of the British Council.

8 These research questions are adapted from an earlier stage of the study. At the preliminary stage the research had two aims, firstly to explore an application of an intercultural and Global Englishes perspective to language teaching and secondly to investigate the effectiveness of online learning as a medium for delivery of such a course. In the data reported here this second aim will not be the focus; although, a brief account of why this approach was chosen is given (see Baker 2012d for a more thorough discussion of this). Instead more detailed consideration is given to the first of the two aims, intercultural communication and Global Englishes, and new data related to these themes is presented. The focus in this chapter is therefore more on the selection and presentation of content than on pedagogic approaches; although, there is of course overlap between the two areas.

1. Is it possible to translate the conceptions of successful intercultural communication envisaged in intercultural awareness (ICA) and Global Englishes/ ELF research into teaching materials?
2. To what extent are ICA and an understanding of English as global language developed through this course?
3. What are participants' attitudes towards and evaluations of such a course?

It should be noted that the term Global Englishes is used alongside ELF here as the course also dealt with subjects related to World Englishes as well as ELF. Before answering these questions in detail I will give a brief contextualisation of the study related to English use and teaching in ASEAN and Thailand, as to some extent the issues that arise in this context provide a rationale for the aims of this study. Then I will engage in a more detailed discussion of the main study and its key findings as related to ELT content, Global Englishes, ICA and specifically the three questions above. Some of the central findings that emerged from this research were the practicality and relevance of more globally and intercultural orientated ELT materials and the positive attitudes of both students and teachers towards them. This raises questions as to why concerns with Global Englishes and interculturality are currently such a minor part of ELT and suggests that they should move to a more central role.

7.1 Background and rationale: English in ASEAN and Thailand

It is important to provide a brief outline of English language use and teaching in ASEAN and Thailand, where the study took place, in order to contextualise the research and also to establish the relevance of this pedagogic approach to such a setting. English has a long history in Asia and a substantial presence in South, East and South East Asia. Indeed, both McArthur (2003) and Kachru (2005) regard English as an Asian language. Furthermore, Bolton (2008) believes there may be as many as 812 million users of English in the region. World Englishes research has documented many varieties of Asian Englishes, such as Indian English, Singaporean English and Filipino English (e.g. Kachru and Nelson 2006; Kirkpatrick 2010a), and English functions as an official lingua franca in ASEAN (Association of South East Asian Nations) and ASEAN +3 (which includes China, Japan and South Korea). Research into the forms and uses of ELF in Asia more generally and ASEAN in particular is also beginning to gather pace, for example through the ACE (Asian Corpus of English) project (Kirkpatrick 2010b) and other studies in ASEAN countries (e.g. Deterding and Kirkpatrick 2006; Deterding 2013; Phan 2009; Kirkpatrick 2010a; Baker 2011a; 2012a). As might be expected such research has document a large variety of forms and functions of English in intercultural, as well as intracultural, communication that are very different to idealised native speaker models and Anglophone standard Englishes.

Clearly such widespread use of English as an Asian language has implications for education policy and practice. In all but one (Indonesia) of the ASEAN countries English is a core subject from primary school and in a number of countries some schooling such as maths and science is delivered through the medium of English (Kirkpatrick 2010a; 2011). However, as Kirkpatrick reports (2011), there have been mixed responses to such extensive use of English in schooling. Malaysia, for example, reversed its decision to teach maths and science through English due to a lack of suitably qualified teachers and the disadvantages experienced by students from poorer and more rural backgrounds. Nonetheless, other countries, such as Brunei, have continued to increase the role of English in education and the opening up of economic borders between ASEAN countries in 2015 has further raised the profile of English in education policy. For instance Thailand's speak English year project in 2012 was initiated as a response to the need for greater English proficiency with this closer integration in ASEAN. In terms of teaching practices and the models of English used it is questionable how far models other than that of standard English associated with Anglophone native speakers have had an influence. The continuing large scale recruitment of native English teachers in many ASEAN countries and the prestige attached to them demonstrates the pervasive influence this model still has. Yet, as discussed in the previous chapter the most appropriate model for learners of English is not the monolingual native speaker (and of course not all native speakers of English are monolingual) but rather the multilingual intercultural speaker. Kirkpatrick (2010a) in specific reference to ASEAN proposes the notion of the multilingual model and the multilingual English teacher as a replacement to the native speaker. This, Kirkpatrick argues, provides a more appropriate linguistic model, since English is predominantly used as a lingua franca in multilingual scenarios in ASEAN and the majority of its users are thus likely to be multilingual. This also entails drawing on pragmatic norms and cultural content from ASEAN countries rather than the Anglophone world, as again this is more relevant to English learners in ASEAN (Kirkpatrick 2010a: 2011).

Turning specifically to Thailand many of the issues brought up as regards English in ASEAN are repeated in Thailand. However, unlike many ASEAN countries such as Malaysia and Singapore, Thailand has never been colonised and so English has never had an official role within Thailand. Although, as Draper

(2012b) notes, plans to make English an official second language have not been successful, English is often regarded as the principal or 'de-facto' second language in Thailand. This is represented by the many roles in which it functions including, as a compulsory subject in school and in higher education, as a medium of instruction in international education programmes, as the language of international organisations and conferences (including ASEAN and ASEAN +3), for international business transactions, tourism, the internet, global advertising, scientific and technology transfer, media (including imported films and music), international safety and international law (Wongsatorn et al. 1996; 2003; Foley 2005; Baker 2012a). Given English's status as an 'unofficial' second language there has been no concerted effort to promote a standardised version of 'Thai English' and so it is frequently characterised as a lingua franca used to connect economically, culturally and politically with the rest of the region and world (Foley 2007; Baker 2009; 2012a; Kirkpatrick 2010a). This is further reinforced by the majority use of English with other non-native speakers, for example in ASEAN or in the tourism industry where the majority of visitors are from East Asia and ASEAN (Tourism Authority of Thailand 2013). Within the urban middle classes English also increasingly functions as a language of intracultural communication alongside Thai, including through the growth of bilingual and EMI programmes in education, in electronic communication, the media and even in urban linguistic landscapes through signs and advertisement (Huebner 2006; Baker 2009; 2012a; Glass 2009; Keyuravong 2010; Seargeant, Tagg and Ngampramuan 2012).

However, the role of English is more complex than as a second language with Thai as the sole first language. Although government reports and research often portray Thailand as a monolingual country (National Identity Board 2000; Keyuravong 2010) in reality the situation is considerably more complex. For the majority of Thais the official dialect of Thai used in education and government is different from their regional dialect and in additional there are estimated to be over 70 minority languages and related varieties such as, Chinese, Lao, Malay, Khmer and Mon (Foley 2005; Simpson and Thammasathien 2007; Darasawang and Watson Todd 2012; Premsrirat 2014). There is also debate as to whether all the dialects of Thai are actually dialects or rather separate languages (Darasawang and Watson Todd 2012); although, of course, this is more an ideological/ political question than a matter of linguistic description. For speakers of minority languages, and even perhaps some 'dialects', Thai functions as an L2 and English is likely to be an additional language to this. Furthermore, the spread of English within Thailand, as with many other countries in ASEAN, has been uneven. Although it is a daily feature of the lives of many of the urban middle classes, especially in Bangkok, its spread has been much less extensive in rural communities away from business or tourism centres (Kosonen 2008; Hayes 2010; Draper 2012a; 2012b). In addition, while the forms of English used by the middle classes, often validated through international testing organisations such as IELTS and TEOFL, are considered an important part of their cultural capital, other forms of English used by poorer workers in areas such as tourism are usually not considered as prestigious and do not confer the same status.

Given the importance accorded English in many sections of Thai society it features as a prominent strand in education. English is introduced into the curriculum at primary level being a compulsory subject all the way through to tertiary education where it is often a requirement to complete a number of credits in English language courses before passing a degree (see Ministry of Education Thailand http://www.en.moe.go.th). However, despite the extensive resources and time given to English the level of proficiency of English in Thailand is still perceived as low and this is supported by Thai students' poor performance in international tests (ETS 2011; English First 2012). This would seem to contradict the above characterisation of extensive English use in certain sections of society. However, tests such as TOEFL, which are based on 'standard' native speaker English and a narrow range of structural features of communication, are of questionable validity in ELF settings such as those present in Thailand (Jenkins 2006b; Baker 2012a). Nonetheless, there is still a perception within Thailand that English proficiency is very low (The Nation 2013) and that native English is still the most prestigious model. This has a pervasive influence on ELT in Thailand with native speaker teachers seen as language authorities, despite often having fewer qualifications and less experience than local teachers (Watson-Todd 2006; Baker 2012a). Many job advertisements specifically ask for native speakers, including in government schools (http://www.obec.go.th) despite prominent organisations involved in teaching explicitly rejecting native speakerism as a teaching criterion (e.g. http://www.tesol.org/docs/pdf/5889.pdf?sfvrsn=2).

It would thus appear that ELF and multilingual models of ELT and teachers have yet to have a noticeable influence on ELT in Thailand. In addition, many of these same divides between the middle classes and the poor and urban and rural areas are reflected in English language education as well. Access to English language education and qualified teachers is typically concentrated in urban areas with private tutoring and language schools frequently used to supplement school teaching, for those that can afford it (Kosonen 2008; Hayes 2010; Draper 2012a; 2012b). Furthermore, for many of the speakers of minority languages English is a third language introduced at school alongside Thai as a second language, further increasing the learning burden (Draper 2012a; 2012b). These differences have led to large discrepancies in education achievements between urban Bangkok and poorer rural areas leading to questions regarding the value of investing so much time and resources into ineffective English teaching at the expense of other subjects and locally relevant languages (Hayes 2010; Draper 2012a; 2012b). This is particularly acute in areas where English is likely to be of little relevance to the daily life of many of the students. However, it is an issue of concern that communities may be restricted in their access to English which is a resource that carries such a high level of cultural capital in Thai society. Furthermore, this lack of access to adequate ELT further exacerbates the already wide gaps between the affluent urban middle classes and rural poor.

In sum, English has taken on an increasingly prominent role in Thai society and education. It is perceived as an important language of intercultural communication for regional contacts, particularly in ASEAN, and also globally. English is typically viewed as a lingua franca in Thailand since it is predominantly used for intercultural communication and with other non-native speakers. However, English is also taking on a larger role in urban areas in some domains of intracultural communication; although, this is much less prominent than its role as a lingua franca in intercultural communication. Given the significant place English currently occupies in Thai society it is the most extensively taught 'foreign' language in education and is a compulsory subject from primary through to tertiary levels. Although, there are concerns about the proficiency levels achieved by Thai learners of English, much of this can be viewed as a result of the continuing prestige given to 'standard' and native speaker varieties of English and a lack of awareness, in education at least, of multilingual and locally relevant English teaching models. Alongside these concerns about the effectiveness and appropriateness of current ELT policies and practices, there are issues related to the uneven spread of English in rural and poorer communities and this has also been transferred to concerns about access to adequate English education, as well as the relevance of the English language education received. This is particularly acute for speakers of minority languages who receive less recognition in language education policies and practices. In short, the local linguistic landscape of Thailand is more complex than generally recognised in official education policies and practices both in relation to a greater diversity of local languages and dialects and also the use of English, especially ELF. Many of these issues are of course not unique to Thailand but are repeated throughout ASEAN (see Kirkpatrick 2010a) and in other Asian settings too (e.g. Nunan 2003). It is against this backdrop that the current study takes place. It is these issues that also provide part of the rationale for exploring the complexity of language (both local languages and English), communication and culture in local, regional and global settings with a group of Thai students.

7.2 Research methodology

7.2.1 Participants and setting

The study took place in a prestigious government university in central Thailand. The relevance of Thailand as a setting in which English predominantly features as a lingua franca has already been established. Additionally, as noted in chapter six, English also functions as the main lingua franca of global academic connections and universities have proved productive sites for ELF research (e.g. Mauranen 2012; Björkman 2013; Jenkins 2014). This study was undertaken at the main university campus where the majority of students and staff are Thai nationals. The research participants were volunteers drawn from the English major undergraduate students at the university's department of English. These students were considered the most suitable participants since given their higher level of English, compared to the general student population, and experiences of using English for intercultural communication they were most likely to see the relevance of, be receptive to and engage with a course in intercultural communication and Global Englishes. As such the approach to selecting participants can be viewed as purposive sampling (Cohen, Manion and Morrison 2011; Silverman 2011: 388).

In total 31 student participants took part in the study. Six of the participants were male and 25 female, which reflects the gender balance of their classes. They were aged between 20 and 23. They all spoke Thai as their L1. The average length of time for which they had studied English was 14 years. The majority of participants reported using English outside of their class and using English online. The majority also reported using English with both non-native speakers of English (including other Thais) and with native speakers. In addition, six teachers from the department of English also took part in the study. Four of the teachers were Thai L1 speakers and two were English L1 speakers. Four were female and two male. Their teaching experience ranged for two years to over ten. All the participants took part in the research voluntarily and ethical protocols for the researcher's university in the UK and the Thai university were followed.

I was the principal researcher and although at the time of the research I was based in the UK, I had previously worked and conducted research at this university over an extensive period of time. This made access to the setting and gaining an insider perspective easier; although, with the obvious risk of over-familiarity with the research site and missing potentially revealing aspects of the environment that may have been easier to identify as an outsider. I was supported by two research partners from the Thai university who also provided further insider perspectives as English teachers there. All of the researchers were participant observers on the course as we both collected data and took part in the teaching activities, particularly the discussion forums (see below).

7.2.2 Research approach and instruments

The research approach adopted was mixed methods making use of quantitative and qualitative data and triangulation of different data sources (Dörnyei 2007). This enabled the researcher to gather a larger data set of quantitative data from all of the research participants' questionnaire responses, together with a more in depth data set from interviews with a smaller number of the participants, as well as detailed analysis of a number of critical incidents from the students' course participation. By employing mixed-methods research it was hoped that the limitations of one particular research instrument would be balanced by the strengths of another. Furthermore, through multiple data sources a range of perspectives on the participants' experiences, attitudes and evaluations of the course could be gained. However, by adopting a mixed methods, triangulated approached no claim is made to have established a definitive interpretation of the participants involvement with the course (Denzin and Lincoln 2011: 5; Silverman 2011: 369), but rather in keeping with the foundations of ethnographically influenced qualitative research a richer description from multiple perspectives and layers is produced. In conjunction with a mixed-methods approach the study can also be interpreted as a case study following Dörnyei's definition of a case as constituting "a single entity with clearly defined boundaries" (2007: 151). In this instance the single entity being the course that all the participants are involved in. Through building up data on the construction of the course, delivery of the course and participants experiences and evaluations of the course, it was hoped that a detailed picture would emerge of the researched phenomena. In keeping with both qualitative and case study methodologies the research was longitudinal and took place over a 16 week period. The main focus here is on the qualitative data since this is most appropriate to providing in-depth answers to the three research questions posed at the beginning of the chapter and is closest to the overall aims of this book. Further details of the quantitative data can be found in Baker (2012d) and in appendix four.

Research question one was addressed through development of the course materials and delivery of the course and is discussed below in the section on the course. It should be noted that the main concern was on evaluation of the content of the course materials rather than on the pedagogic approach to delivery of the course (see Baker 2012d for further details on the use of online interactive learning activities as a pedagogic approach). As regards research questions two and three, questionnaires and interviews were employed. The initial data collection instrument was a paper based questionnaire. Questionnaires are an efficient means of collecting factual information as well as attitudinal and behavioural information (Dörnyei 2007). This data included background information about the student participants including their experiences of and attitudes to learning and using English and importantly their attitudes to intercultural communication through English and their awareness of English as a global language. At the end of the course another questionnaire was given to the participants regarding their experiences of and evaluation of the course. The participants also completed a questionnaire containing the same questions as the initial questionnaire in relation to intercultural communication and Global Englishes to investigate if any changes in their attitudes had occurred. Both these final questionnaires were offered either online or in paper-based form dependent on the participants' preferences. The participants completed the final questionnaires anonymously so that they would not feel pressured to report overly positive responses. Although this meant it was not possible to compare the initial and final intercultural communication questionnaire on an individual level, it was still possible to do so at the group level. This was a compromise that was necessary to ensure anonymity. The six teachers were also given access to the course and asked to complete a questionnaire similar to the students' final evaluation questionnaire but also asked to reflect on the relevance of the course to their teaching[9]. Data analysis of the questionnaires involved descriptive statistics including tabulations of responses, averages, percentages and mean scores. Inferential statistics were not considered appropriate given the small number of participants (see Cohen, Manion and Morrison 2011). The data from the questionnaires was used to provide initial general group level answers to research question three concerning participants' evaluations of and attitudes towards the course.

At the end of the course interviews were conducted with 17 of the student participants. The interviews typically lasted around 20–30 minutes and were designed to provide more in-depth data than the more widely distributed questionnaires concerning their experiences of the course, intercultural communication and Global Englishes. The selection of participants for the interviews was based on their participation in the programme. This involved purposive sampling (Cohen, Manion and Morrison 2011; Silverman 2011: 388) in which those that participated extensively as well those that participated very little were asked to take part. A number of other student participants volunteered as well. Four of the

---

9 As the questionnaires are not the primary focus of the research reported here further details of the questionnaire design are not given but can be found in Baker (2012d).

teachers (all Thai L1 speakers) were also asked to take part in an interview to discuss their impressions of the course. Semi-structured interviews (Richards 2003) were used in which all interviewees received questions about the same topics but the wording and order of the questions was adapted in response to each interview. I was also able to ask follow-up questions depending on and in response to the participants' answers. Semi-structured interviews provided a good balance between following the research aims, particularly in regard to research questions two and three, allowing the participants to comment on and expand on areas that were of interest to them and enabling themes or issues that I had not previously considered to emerge from the responses. Thus, following Kvale and Brinkmann (2009: 49), the interviews can be viewed as joint knowledge construction between the interviewer and interviewee rather than 'mining' for already existing information. The interview data was analysed through content based coding (Dörnyei 2007: 245–246; Silverman 2013: 64) in which transcripts were coded for both emergent themes (Miles, Huberman and Saldaña 2014) and those that related to the research questions. This involved a degree of quantitative analysis in identifying the most frequently arising themes. However, the main approaches were qualitative and made use of latent content analysis (Dörnyei 2007: 245–246) or critical content analysis in which the researchers' interpretations, rather than just surface meanings, were drawn on in categorising data into codes. Critical incidents were also used, in which particularly representative, articulate or interesting examples drawn from the participants own responses were used to support or offer counter examples to the researcher's identification of prevailing themes. The coding was carried out using QSR NVivo 10 software for qualitative data analysis.

Finally, data was collected from the participants as they took part in the course. This came from data tracking each student's online activities including reading materials, completion of tasks and postings in discussion forums and chat sessions (see explanation below). This data was analysed quantitatively to provide an overview of overall participation as well as individual student's participation. Transcriptions of data from the discussion tasks and chat sessions were also analysed qualitatively in a similar manner to the interviews. This included both emergent and a priori coding with a focus on answering question two. A number of critical incidents were also identified for more detailed analysis from the discussion forum and chat sessions. In many ways this approach can be seen as similar to unstructured classroom observation (Dörnyei 2007: 179) in which I as the researcher and the teacher took on the role of a participant observer identifying salient issues as they emerged from students posting. However, in this setting I was a virtual observer whose presence could only be seen by students when I posted in the discussion forum or chat session. In addition, all interaction was written rather than spoken.

7.2.3 Reliability and validity

Reliability and validity are far from straightforward in qualitative research and there is much debate as to what the most appropriate criteria for establishing either might be (e.g. Lincoln and Guba 1985; Richards 2003; Hammersley and Atkinson 2007; Silverman 2011). However, it is crucial that research is established as credible to other researchers, practitioners who have an interest in the research (in this case policy makers, administrators, teachers and students of English) and the research participants themselves. In this study Lincoln and Guba's (1985) notion of trustworthiness was followed related to the four criteria of credibility, transferability, dependability and confirmability. Lincoln and Guba (1985) reject the terms reliability and validity as too closely associated with quantitative research and an underlying positivist and realist research philosophy. Trustworthiness is proposed as an alternative, not an equivalent, more suited to qualitative research. Nonetheless, the term trustworthiness is used under the heading reliability and validity here since these terms are more easily recognised. However, the approach followed is closely related to Lincoln and Guba in that a rich description of the case study is offered rather than a definitive 'truth'. In relation to credibility my own familiarity with the research setting, as well as that of the other researchers from the university and also the longitudinal nature of the study represented prolonged engagement in the setting. Credibility was further enhanced through the use of triangulation of different data sources, not to establish a more 'accurate' description, but "as a strategy that adds rigour, breadth, complexity, richness and depth to any inquiry" (Denzin and Lincoln 2005: 5). Transferability was met through offering a rich description with features that may resonate (Richards 2003) in other settings. Dependability and confirmability were addressed through a clear audit trail or documentation of the research. This included records of the course material and students participation in the course; recordings of the interviews and field notes; transcriptions of participants' contributions to chat sessions and discussion forums; and records of all participants' questionnaire responses. In case studies there are issues as to the extent a single instance can be generalised from; however, while each setting is particular and so is unlikely to be replicated in either another place or time there are many advantages to conducting a detailed case study. As Silverman (2011: 387) points out, case studies offer a valuable means of testing hypotheses and theories since, following Popper's falsification criterion, it only takes one case to refute or challenge established theory. Furthermore, the level of depth and complexity offered by a case study can result in more opportunities to rigorously test ideas and allow new theories to emerge.

7.3 A course in Global Englishes, intercultural communication and intercultural awareness

As stated earlier in order to answer the first research question concerning the relevance and feasibility of using ICA and Global Englishes (especially ELF) research in teaching material, it is necessary to examine the course itself. The course aims were for learners to develop knowledge and understanding of the relationship between language and culture in intercultural communication, the role of English as a global lingua franca of intercultural communication and an understanding of the knowledge, skills and attitudes associated with ICA and ICA's role in intercultural communication through English (see Baker 2012d: 9). The course was delivered online through the Moodle VLE (Virtual learning environment)[10]. Online learning has been used extensively in intercultural education and has proved an effective approach to bringing intercultural aspects of language learning into classrooms (Lewis and Walker 2003; Belz and Thorne 2006; Guth and Helm 2010; O'Dowd 2011). The course comprised ten topics presented through interactive online learning task or objects (LOs). These online learning objects (LO) are characterised as "activity-driven LO in which a pedagogic task or tasks forms the basis for the learning. A single asset or combination of assets support the task(s), and might include video, audio, graphic or textual assets' (Watson, 2010: 42). In this course the LOs consisted of graphics and texts based on key aspects of intercultural communication, ICA and Global Englishes and particularly the five strands for pedagogy outlined in chapter six. There were also seven asynchronous discussion tasks related to these topics and three synchronous chat sessions. The ten topics which formed the course syllabus are listed below (more details can be found in appendix two).

1. Defining culture
2. Intercultural communication
3. Cultural stereotypes and generalisations in communication
4. The individual and culture
5. English as a global language
6. Exploring my own culture
7. Intercultural communication and the internet
8. Comparing cultures: politeness

---

10 The online programme was developed and delivered in collaboration with eLanguages, an e-learning research and development group in Modern Languages at the University of Southampton http://www.elanguages.ac.uk/.

9. Globalisation and transcultural global flows
10. Intercultural Awareness

The topics were designed to offer an introduction to Global Englishes and intercultural communication from a perspective that was relevant to Thai university students. This included fundamental topics such as characterisations of culture, the relationships between culture and language and how this relates to intercultural communication. The notions of hybrid, multiple and fluid cultural forms and practices was also introduced. The role of generalisations in intercultural communication was explored, particularly through comparisons and cultural differences, together with the potential for negative stereotyping and essentialism. This involved a consideration of the relationship between individuals and cultures with an emphasis on avoiding essentialist correlations in which individuals were reduced to cultural stereotypes. Students were asked to explore this in relation to their own language use and cultural context to gain a greater awareness of the complexities of culture and language in a setting familiar to them. The role of English as a global language, going beyond Anglophone settings, was dealt with including varieties of World Englishes such as Indian English, Nigerian English and Hong Kong English as well as English as a lingua franca. Other issues that were covered on the course included the growing role of online intercultural communication, the use of English to create and transmit hybrid cultural artefacts and practices in 'transcultural flows', with a focus on local examples of this, and the relationship between Englishes and globalisation, including issues of linguistic imperialism and language rights. Finally, the concept of ICA was introduced through the types of skills, knowledge and attitudes envisaged in the model and students asked to reflect on the relevance of this for their experiences of intercultural communication through ELF. Throughout each of these topics students were asked to consider these issues in relation to their own experiences and to reflect on their personal relationship to the cultures they identified with and the languages they used, together with the role this had in the way they constructed their identities in both intracultural and intercultural communication. In this way the students were encouraged to engage critically with the topics through considering the complexity and diversity of their own experiences. As underscored in the discussion in chapter six, taking a critical approach to images and presentations of culture is a crucial part of developing ICA.

The pedagogic approach was primarily designed for independent study but supplemented with tutorial support and a number of peer activities. The core to each topic was the learning object (LO) which the students completed by themselves. These LOs included reading tasks, podcasts, reflective activities, note taking and comprehension checks which were scaffolded through contextualisation, interactive activities and extensive feedback (see appendix three for examples). Additional scaffolding was provided through an online glossary of key terminology. Closely related to the LOs were the asynchronous discussion forum tasks which provided an opportunity for the students to discuss their ideas related to each topic with other students and the course tutors. Three optional synchronous one hour chat sessions were offered to students. The first two sessions involved discussions with other students and the tutors and in the final session three students studying applied linguistics and intercultural communication from the principal researcher's university took part. Both the discussion forum and the chat sessions provided more interactive opportunities for the students to engage in the course and in the case of the chat sessions also offered experiences of intercultural communication to reflect on. The tutorial support was offered through an online tutor (the principal researcher) who could be contacted through the online course forum or by email. The two co-researchers at the Thai university also provided support and could be contacted through the course or face to face. Furthermore, technical support was given by a member of the eLanguages team at the researcher's university.

The course was offered as an optional independent study programme. Participation in the course was voluntary and no grades were given but students who completed the course received a certificate. The students were given 15 weeks to complete the ten topics with the total time needed estimated at around 15 hours. They did not have to complete tasks each week as some flexibility was needed to allow students time for exams, course work deadlines and holidays. However, it was recommended that they followed the order of the syllabus. They were also asked to contribute to at least five of the seven discussion forums at the same time as other students were contributing. The synchronous chat sessions obviously had fixed times and participation was optional because of this. Of the 31 students who undertook the course the participation rates varied quite considerably with six of the students contributing to all the topics and ten of the students contributing to three or less of the topics. The average participation rate was six topics, or 60%, which compares well to the expected participation rate of 80% for compulsory courses at the university. Many of the students participated in both the LOs and discussion forums although some preferred to just use the discussion forums and others only the LOs. Only nine students took part in the chat sessions but this is not surprising given the fixed time and that they were not compulsory. Furthermore, larger numbers than this would have made the chats unmanageable.

7.3.1 Course evaluation

The participants and teachers were asked to rate the course at the end of the 15 weeks. The majority of the evaluation questionnaire was related to the elearning approach adopted for the course and so will not be examined in detail (see Baker 2012d). However, both groups, and especially the teachers, rated the course positively (1 being the lowest score and 5 the highest), as can be seen in Figures 7.1 and 7.2 below, and this included ratings for the course content.

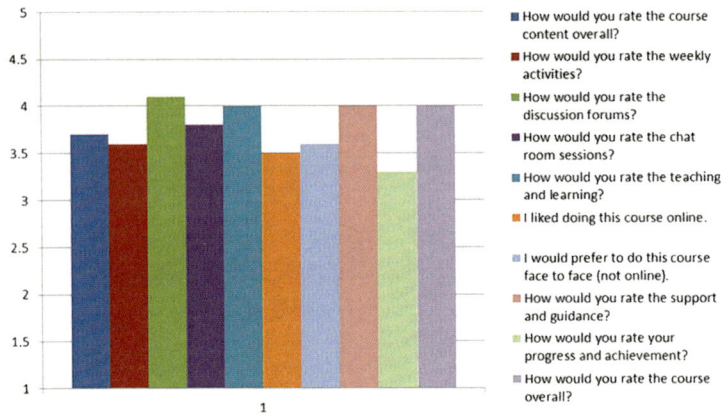

Fig. 7.1: Students' course evaluation

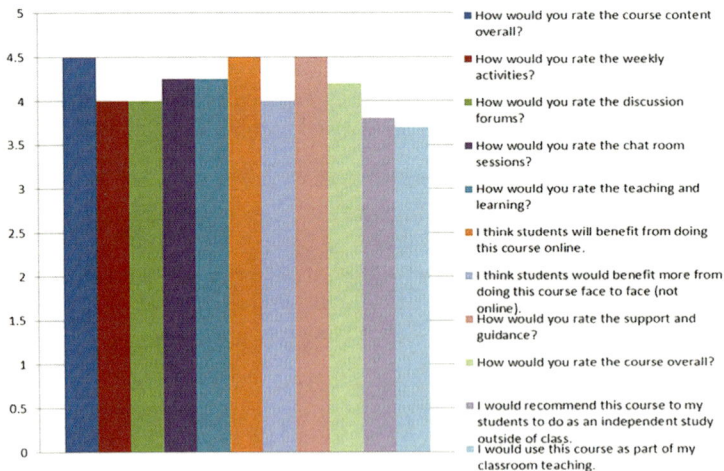

Fig. 7.2: Teachers' course evaluation

In the follow up interviews many of the students expressed positive evaluations of the course content overall. The three examples below illustrate some of the main themes that emerged from the interviews including appreciating the range of English uses, the relationship between language and culture through English and interest in intercultural communication.

Extract 7.1
Pai: good er it's like I have travelled the world @ in er you know in an hour
Or: l like the chat se- session better because um we can er have a real intercultural communication . and I feel like we can share the opinions face to face
Anya: I think it's useful ... to do this course makes me to be aware of er the relation of culture and language especially er . the people who use English to communicate with other people

However, not all the students were so positive about the course content and a small number were uncomfortable with the shift in content away from Anglophone settings.

Extract 7.2
Yam: I do think that err it will be better if we learn if we learn like about the British English or the American English I don't really think that we we should learn something different than that

As already noted the teachers were particularly positive about the course and this was reinforced in their interviews. Like the students they valued the range of Englishes presented and also added that this was useful for future employment or study.

Extract 7.3
Nun: learning about this is very useful especially when they go to study abroad or have a job in the future
Niti: I think we need to be more aware of the variety of English these days it's there's no such standard as you know it has to be Oxford accent British or American or Australia ... so um I think there there is um an awareness it's an awareness that we need to have
No: I think we should cover all kinds of English because we we cannot predict what English the student will face in the future so we have to prepare for all kinds of English

Although, again like the students, not all the teachers were positive and in particular the two native English speakers rated the course somewhat lower and felt it was detached from what they were familiar with, as the comment from the questionnaire in extract 7.4 shows.

Extract 7.4

James: It is always a good thing for the students to have access to knowledge in any form, but this is so far removed from my teaching methodology that I cannot see that it would become part of my teaching.

In summary, and in answer to research question three, the participants' evaluations of this course were positive overall with a small number of exceptions and caveats. This is in keeping with the few earlier studies, reported in Chapter 6, of global Englishes approaches to ELT (e.g. Galloway 2013) and surveys of students and teachers' attitudes (e.g. Jenkins 2007; Csizér and Kontra 2012). These reported generally favourable responses to more pluralistic perspectives on Englishes but with some remaining attachment to the prestige of Anglophone, 'native speaker' English.

7.3.2 Development of ICA and an understanding of Global Englishes

Participants were asked to complete an intercultural communication questionnaire at the beginning and end of the course. The questionnaire was the same in both instances with the aim being to record any changes in participants attitudes or knowledge over the course. There were a number of different sections to the questionnaires related to reasons for studying English, factors that help in intercultural communication through English, attitudes towards different types of Englishes, attitudes towards intercultural communication and attitudes towards their own and other cultures. The quantitative findings are discussed in detail in Baker (2012d) and so will not be presented in detail here but are given in appendix four for reference. Overall, there was little change in the participants' responses over the course with similar scores given in the initial and final questionnaire. There are a number of reasons for this, most importantly that the participants already had very positive attitudes towards intercultural communication in the initial survey and also seem to have had some understanding and knowledge of Global Englishes before beginning the course. This is perhaps not surprising as the participants have all been studying English for a number of years and many of them regularly use English outside of the classroom and so will have had experiences of intercultural communication and exposure to different Englishes. Nonetheless, the positive responses by the students towards the course material that dealt with intercultural communication and intercultural awareness adds further support to the already positive attitudes displayed by students in the overall course evaluation and adds to the favourable evaluation in response to research question three. Overall, participants indicated that the cultural dimension to language learning and use were important and formed a significant part of their language learning experiences. Although, it should also be noted that despite their positive attitudes to intercultural communication and knowledge of Global Englishes, native speaker English associated with Anglophone settings (the UK and US) was still regarded as most prestigious. Furthermore, the quantitative data was less salient to answering research question two relating to learning and development over the course. This may indicate that little learning or change occurred, which would not be an unexpected result given the shortness of the course and the already well-informed starting point. However, the qualitative data presents a more nuanced account of changes and development in participants over the course and this will form the main focus of the rest of this section.

The interview data demonstrates that the participants are aware of the global role of English and its use outside of Anglophone contexts. The majority of participants also expressed positive attitudes to this and to the inclusion of a variety of Englishes in the course.

Extract 7.5
Pan: because like peo- everybody use English now so it's not just the British and the American's anymore um and that will open up like a window for us for er business doing business in the future
Aim: Nowadays English becomes like the official language in many countries not only in the UK or the US and . each country have their own culture so even though they are using English they have some things that something that are different from in the US or in the UK so if if we got to learn all of them I think we will. I think we it can make us like open up our mind like better
Tip: Nowadays English is truly global language and people in many nationalities in the world use English to communicate and I think it's interesting . to to learn about English much more than in English in the UK or in the United States
No: I think it's ok . because English has plural now I mean World EnglishES is not-English has a plural

However, these positive attitudes where not universal and a number of participants felt that Anglophone English was still the most appropriate for study as exemplified in the extract below.

Extract 7.6
Yam: English is from basically from the UK right and then to the US so are they are like the what to say the origins of English so if we basically talk about English in Asian countries then it might give a weird feeling to me

Data from the discussion forum responses provided further insights into the reasons for these different opinions.

Extract 7.7

Ann: We don't have to speak like the Native speaker because we are not them. We are born in our country so it is ok for us to have Thai accent in English

Jan: I agree with (Ann). They can choose any accent they like or remain their own.

Pat: In my opinion, I think it's good to sound like native speaker. However, it's the issue of prestige, we mostly think that if we have the native accent, we look more honourable.

Nit: Standard English isn't an important thing to be considered as a factor of speaking. Even in native speaker country, there are different accent, grammar and words as well. However, for academic writing or public speaking, it's needed to consider about grammatical correct.

The first two posts from Ann and Jan both agree that there is no need to have a native accent in English. But the following post from Pat suggests that a native accent will be more prestigious. Nit, a teacher and tutor on the course, goes on to add that while variety is acceptable in some circumstances in more formal settings 'standard' English is still needed. Both of the final posts appear to be reinforcements of standard language ideologies and even in the two posts accepting variety this is only for speaking. These ambiguous responses reveal the mixed attitudes towards variety and standard language and native and non-native English that has been extensively documented in ELF research (e.g. Jenkins 2007). Given the dominance of the native/non-native distinction in ELT and the prestige attached to an idealised model of 'standard' native English, the prevalence of such attitudes, and the ambiguity that arises when pluralistic perspectives are introduced, should hardly be surprising (see Chapter 6.1). It is also not clear from this data to what extent the participants' attitudes towards Global Englishes changed during the course. There was little evidence of an understanding of the hybrid and fluid forms of English in ELF communication but instead more discussion of Englishes from a World Englishes perspective involving many varieties of English. As such it is not clear to what extent the learners were operating within level 2 of ICA, advanced cultural awareness, which concerns complex understandings of culture within defined cultural groups (often at national levels), rather than level 3 of ICA, *intercultural* awareness, which transcends fixed boundaries and language-culture-nation correlations (see chapter 5.5).

In relation to intercultural communication and intercultural awareness again many participants expressed positive attitudes towards learning about this in the interviews. Here there were also reports of having developed a greater understanding of these concepts during the course.

Extract 7.8

Chit: I think I can know the different perceptions of culture include in Thailand culture so you can see that there are many different things about peoples thoughts towards their cultures of our culture or foreign culture ... your course made us to clarify about our culture first ... about the language and about the culture that is something that concerned together ... and we can compare our culture with others

More: I have never heard of er intercultural awareness ... lead me to think about the stereotype of Thailand and the generalisation of cultures in the world and about the . about . um about our my country our Thai culture

Gai: I learn that people should be open minded when they communicate to each other because we will raise from um different background and it's not like people from certain country will be the same because um family background are not the same they don't go to the same school so um we must be really open when we communicate with people even people in my own er country er we use the Thai language but everybody's different

An area that was particularly prominent in the students' responses, as shown in extract 7.8, was a greater understanding of the complexity of the relationship between language, culture and identity in their own experiences and settings and a realisation that such complexity applied to all cultures and people. As demonstrated in these extracts, this was something that students felt they had gained more awareness of from doing the course. This would reinforce the interpretation taken in the previous paragraph that students developed ICA at level 2; within cultures.

As well as the students own self-reports in the questionnaires and interviews the course provided opportunities to discuss and experience intercultural communication through the discussion forum and chat sessions. The data analysis revealed a number of critical incidents which documented the emergence of increasing intercultural awareness and a deeper understanding of the relationship between language, culture and identity in communication. Two particularly salient examples will be discussed here. In the first example, extract 7.9, the students were given an extract from a popular Thai hip-hop song which contained code-switching between English and Thai and asked to discuss the use of language in the song.

Extract 7.9 Sud kob fah

This example is taken from a popular Thai hip-hop song.

Sud kob fah สุดขอบฟ้า Thaitanium feat. Add Carabow

ขัน คาดเข็มขัด ติดเครื่องยนต์ แล้วเตรียมตัวพร้อมทะยาน GPS จุดมุ่งหมาย นั่นคือสุดจักรวาล ส่งจูบ
good bye...my mama and Say Good bye to Earth แล้วปาดน้ำตา ออกจากแก้ม no matter how
much its hurts มา take a trip กับพวกเรา this one is for your soul รางวัลที่จะได้รับ นั่นคือความ
pure ที่จะ cure the whole world เตรียมพร้อมเดินทาง if you are with me อีกแค่ไม่กี่อึดใจ จุด
ระเบิดเครื่องมันติดแล้ว ถ้าคุณณะพร้อม เราก็พร้อมจะ ไป

(From: http://www.thaitanium.biz/biography/sud-kob-fah.php)

The following extract (7.10) shows the postings of one of the students who did not like the use of code-switching. She refers to the specific example of poetry, rather than the song, but suggests that code switching 'makes the poem worse'. However, her attitudes are somewhat ambiguous as she admits to code-switching herself and also suggests that there are areas such as technology where it is appropriate.

Extract 7.10
Pat: I'm used to using English into Thai words, some Thai people use Thai language by switching Thai and [E]nglish words to make themselves superior to other people. Moreover, I found the example of using English words in Thai poems and that makes the poem worse. However, I think using English word in Thai language is important for the things that Thai people can't make up the better Thai word, this is the list about the words that I think Thai people should call it by English, Computer (Thai used to try to call it "Sa-Mong-kon" and it didn't work.), Software (Thai used to try to make up the word "La-Mon-pun", but it sounds too funny ...

She is then asked to explain herself in more detail (extract 7.11) and she focuses on the power and ideology of English arguing that code-switching is done in order to indicate a higher level of education and hence status. She also suggests that in certain areas, poetry, code-switching should be avoided as in her opinion it would make something less 'authentically' Thai and presumably alter the cultural practice in a negative manner.

Extract 7.11
Pat: The reason why some people think using English words when they speak Thai make themselves be superior to other people because nowadays common Thai people who have strong English has a few number, therefore they think people who know English have

higher education. About poem, I think Thai poem is antique and valuable, it's appropriate for Thai luxury words, I think using English word in Thai poem doesn't match. Sound of Thai and English words are completely different, so I think we should know which situation we choose use what registers.

However, another student responds to her claim about the relationship between languages and poetry in Thai and offers an alternative perspective.

Extract 7.12

Ton: I'd like to say something more on traditional Thai literature as Pat mentioned about it above. I have recently studied one great literature of Thailand and I disagree with Pat because I do not see any problems if the poets or literature composers use some English words in his or her literature. As English is one of the foreign language in Thai, and we Thais have many foreign languages used nowadays. In most of Thai literature, a poet uses Sanskrit or Pali or Khmer in his or her writing, nearly very single sentence reader will find words that are not Thai. Thais considers Sanskrit as the highest and we normally use it for something that is not normal, something that we want it to look superior, therefore it has been used mostly in literature. So is Pali and Khmer. You will find that most of Thai language that is used with the Royal Family is from those three languages.

In extract 7.12 Ton claims that code-switching has always been a feature of Thai poetry and literature in general. He argues that in the past this was Sanskrit, Pail or Khmer and that these languages are still used with the very high register of the Royal language. He also suggests that code-switching into English is simply a continuation of this process; although, he is in agreement with Pat that this is done to indicate 'superiority' or status.

The example of the hip-hop song and the students' discussion forum posts in response to it provide an effective illustration of the complexity of the relationships between language, culture and communication and the different scales at which the connections come into being. In the first instance we have a cultural practice, hip-hop, that is very much part of globalisation and which is linked to global cultural and linguistic flows (Pennycook 2007). The form of the music itself through rapping and hip-hop is a global phenomenon and the use of code-switching is also common in much hip-hop (Pennycook 2007). However, in extract 7.9 this is also locally contextualised, most obviously through the use of Thai, but also with the inclusion of a Thai folk/rock singer 'Add Carabow' well-known for addressing local working class and rural issues. The use of code-switching and the mix of hip-hop and local forms of folk and rock also adds elements of hybridity to the song. The students' responses to the song and code-switching in general contribute another level of complexity to the interpretation. Firstly, we have the power dimension which is brought up by both of the students who believe that being able to code-switch between Thai and another prestigious language is a sign of being well-educated and hence a prestigious communicative practice, at least in art forms. Perhaps most interestingly we have Ton's reinterpretation of code-switching as a traditional Thai cultural practice in literature. In claiming that previous writers switched between Thai, Khmer, Pali and Sanskrit, Ton is locating the current practice of code-switching between English and Thai in hip-hop as part of a long tradition in the arts in Thailand. Furthermore, the contemporary form carries similar cultural capital to earlier forms of code-switching in indexing education and prestige. Importantly, this interpretation adds an essential diachronic level to the analysis and enables an interpretation that views code-switching and hip-hop as a contemporary manifestation or development of an already established local cultural practice.

In sum, this example provides an instantiation of the flow of global linguistic and cultural practices and the manner in which they are locally contextualised, but also crucially the way in which locally embedded cultural practices are as influential and relevant to understanding language use as global scales of analysis. In addition, it also highlights the importance of power and ideology in our interpretations. Finally, the need to locate cultural practices diachronically in their socio-historical setting is underscored. As such this example can be seen as illustrating many of the key themes addressed so far in this book in relation to the complex links between communicative practices, language and culture. In particular, this includes the notions of convergent and divergent flows (Risager 2006; Pennycook 2007); the importance of locality which places these flows in a diachronic, socio-historical context (Blommaert 2010; Pennycook 2010); the complexity and multi-scalar level of connections between communicative practices, language and culture (Blommaert 2010; 2013); and the criticality envisaged by Kramsch (2009) on the part of participants in positioning their communicative practices within a range of social structures and power relationships but also in turn re-evaluating and repositioning those relationships.

The second example is taken from the chat sessions and provides an illustration of the relevance of interculturality (Zhu 2014a; 2015) to understanding the way in which cultural identifications are negotiated in intercultural communication. In this extract (7.13) a group of students from a UK university and the Thai university of this study are taking part in a synchronous chat sessions. The participants are Sarah (female, English L1), Ying (female, Chinese L1), Som (female, Thai L1), Wasana (female, Thai L1) and Ana (female, Portuguese L1). They are discussing both their use of English and where each of them comes from.

Extract 7.13

1   Sarah: I originally come from Canada, but grew up in Germany. So I consider myself to be inbetween a native and a non-native speaker.

2   Ying: Actually, when I am with my friends who are from the same country as me, I always speak my mother tongue. But when I am alone, I speak English to myself.

3   Som: wow that's really good.

4   Wasana: Are you Chinese, Ying?

5   Ying: Yes!

6   Som: Ni Haw Ma?

7   Wasana: Ni hao!

8   Ying: Ni hao!

9   [...]¹¹

10 Ana: this is a real intercultural communication, uh? People from different backgrounds.

11 Som: sorry i tried to say hi in chinese.

12 [...]

13 Som: what about you Ana?

14 Som: where are you from?

15 Ana: I am originally from Brazil

16 [...]

17 Wasana: My ancestors are Chinese.

18 [...]

19 Sarah: Wasana. Do you consider yourself multilingual then?

20 Ying: Oh, nice to meet you! Perhaps that's why you say you are not talktive?

21 Ying: For Chinese are sometimes overmodest.....

22 [...]

23 Wasana: I don't consider that because I don't talk chinese when I was a child.

24 Wasana: I just have taken some chinese courses and I don't speak it in my daily life.

25 [...]

26 Sarah: Wasana. Did you spend some time in China as well?

27 Ana: Ying is a great teacher! She taught our class some mandarin the other day

28 [...]

29 Wasana: I never been in China, too.

In lines 1 and 2 both Sarah and Ying reject a simple language and identity correlation. Sarah, although she has Canadian nationality, does not consider herself a native English speaker but rather an 'inbetween' (line 1) as she grew up in Germany. Ying who identifies as Chinese (line 5) and reports Chinese as her 'mother tongue' says she uses English to talk to herself. When discovering that Ying is Chinese both Som and Wasana code-switch into Chinese and this is responded to in Chinese by Ying (lines 6–8). Following this in line 17 Wasana

---

11 Multiple conversations were taking place simultaneously in the chat session but for ease of reading they have not all been transcribed. '[...]' represents an untranscribed section.

appears to identify herself with Chinese culture when she says her ancestors are Chinese. Ying seems to interpret this as a Chinese cultural identification when she suggests that being Chinese is the reason for Wasana's quietness in the chat session (lines 20–21). However, Wasana goes on to reject this identification and provides a number of reasons why she does not identify herself as Chinese including, not speaking it as a child, not using Chinese every day and never having been to China (lines 23–29).

This extract demonstrates how for these participants identities are negotiated in intercultural communication and the importance of language in this process. At the same time though, the example also underscores the need to avoid simplistic one-to-one correlations. As with the example presented in chapter four (extract 4.2) from Zhu's (2015) research, identities cannot be delineated before the interaction but rather are constructed through the interaction. Both Sarah and Ying resist an association between their national identities, cultural heritage identities and the languages they speak. Similarly, we can see the important role language plays in the online negotiation of cultural identities for Wasana with her resistance to Ying's suggestion she is Chinese, with the role of, or rather lack of, the Chinese language in her communicative repertoire provided as one of the justifications.

While there is no evidence here of whether these participants developed their intercultural awareness through this exchange, it offers a good example of the type of interactions that can be offered in classroom teaching. Importantly, such interactions provide opportunities for students to reconsider essentialist approaches to language, culture, identity and communication (see also Kramsch 2009; Holliday, Hyde and Kullman 2010; Liddicoat and Scarino 2013). Examples like this also provide ideal material for subsequent classroom discussion and reflection. In sum, and in answer to research question two, the qualitative data provides some self-reported evidence for the development of intercultural awareness during the course. The discussions of intercultural communication and the chat sessions provide further evidence of aspects of intercultural awareness in practice, particularly an awareness of the complexity of the relationships between language, cultural, identity and communication. However, it must be acknowledged that it is not clear how conscious the participants are of this and it was not demonstrated by all the participants.

7.4 Conclusion

Before summarising the findings from the study and considering some of the implications the limitations of the study need to be noted. Firstly, this is only a single case study and as such no attempt at generalisations can be made. While there may be aspects of the study and course that are transferable and resonate in other settings, it is not suggested that the course should be replicated in this exact from in other contexts or that participants' responses would be the same. However, the purpose of the study was not to provide a teaching methodology for replication but rather to demonstrate that the theories and research discussed so far could be adapted and made applicable to ELT classrooms. Secondly, the focus in this chapter has been on the content of the materials developed rather than on the pedagogic approach adopted; in other words, on *what* is taught rather than *how* it is taught. More consideration needs to be given to approaches to pedagogic practice as well as content (see Baker 2012d). Thirdly, my role as a participant-observer needs to be accounted for. While familiarity with the setting and active participation in the teaching and development allowed for an insider perspective, this is inevitably at the expense of some objectivity. Furthermore, my research focus and interest in intercultural communication and Global Englishes are likely to have influenced my interpretations as well as participants' responses to the research and me. Lastly, the limitations of the data collected should be recognised. The majority of the data comes from the questionnaires and interviews and these provide second hand reports or meta-data on participants' actual experiences of intercultural communication and of learning. As such they are a step removed from participants' experiences of intercultural communication and their reports are likely to differ somewhat from the actual experience. Nonetheless, this was countered to an extent by the inclusion of discussion forum posts which providing examples of learning and the chat sessions which offered instances of intercultural communication.

Alongside the limitations in the research approach the limitations of the course itself should be documented. No course can be expected to cover all aspects of communication, particularly a course as short as this; nevertheless some consideration should be given to what was not included. Most importantly language, and specifically linguistic forms were not addressed in detail and this has traditionally formed the core of most ELT approaches. The perspective taken in the course, and throughout the monograph, has been one in which communication is viewed from a much wider perspective than linguistic form alone; however, this is not to suggest that language itself is not important. Discussions of the English language were presented in the course materials and an emphasis was placed on the variability of ELF and global uses of English as well as the importance of negotiation and flexibility in language use. However, it is likely that more attention would need to be given to language forms if this programme was extended. Other studies and discussions reported in chapter six have already explored these issues in greater depth (e.g. Seidlhofer 2011; Dewey 2012;

Canagarajah 2013b). They have recommended that the ability to negotiate forms and take a flexible rather than normative approach to language is most relevant. Associated with this has been a shift in emphasis in teaching from product to processes of learning and language use. Secondly, the format of the course is another limitation. The course was offered as optional, non-assessed, extra study. This is likely to have influenced the students' participation in the course and a compulsory course may have produced different responses and evaluations. A related point is that the comparative shortness of the course and the study needs to be considered. Although the study was reasonably longitudinal taking place over 16 weeks, the themes being investigated, the development of ICA and understanding of Global Englishes in language learning, are likely to occur over a much longer time scale than the study. This makes any attempt to document learning and development tentative and partial.

Despite these limitations this study offers detailed responses to the three research questions posed at the beginning of this chapter. The successful development of the course and the materials within it, alongside the opportunities for discussions and engagement in intercultural communication demonstrates that the concept of ICA and the five pedagogic strands outlined in chapter six can be usefully translated into classroom practice. The positive evaluations of the students and particularly the teachers show that such a course and approach to English and communication is perceived as valuable and relevant in this setting. Indeed, the already positive attitudes to Global Englishes and intercultural communication demonstrate that participants were aware of many of the issues covered in this course. However, the continued prestige given to 'standard' native English associated with Anglophone settings, particularly the UK and US, also needs to be recognised. It was also not clear if students had understood the hybridity and fluidity of language and other communicative practices in ELF or interpreted ELF from a World Englishes framework in which it is viewed as one of many distinct varieties. In terms of development of ICA and an understanding of Global Englishes through the course the findings are less clear. The questionnaire data suggests little change over the course, although it also demonstrated an already high degree of awareness among these students and generally positive attitudes, particularly towards intercultural communication. The interview data provides some evidence for reported change among the participants especially as regards an awareness of the complexity of their own cultural setting and identities. The discussion forum and chat sessions provided further evidence of aspects of ICA in practice among the participants. Although, these comprised a small number of critical incidents involving only a few of the participants and so cannot be generalised to all of the participants. Given the difficulty of documenting change and learning and the long time scale on which it is likely to occur it is not surprising that the findings in relation to development are more ambiguous.

Overall, this case study demonstrates the feasibility of developing a programme within ELT that incorporates insights from intercultural communication and ELF/Global Englishes research and crucially that such a course is positively received by both teachers and students. As such it offers further answers to the question posed at the beginning of this monograph, and addressed over the last few chapters, concerning the implications of current research on intercultural communication and ELF for pedagogy. Most significantly this study offers a challenge to the current orthodoxy in ELT with its focus on normative applications of a narrow range of linguistic structures, Anglo centric perspectives on communication and culture and the associated restricted approach to communicative competence. Instead, given the relevance of alternative more locally focused approaches, especially concerning cultural content and intercultural competence, as well as the positive evaluation of key stakeholders to more diverse approaches to communication through English, the question arises as to why such approaches still remain on the fringes of ELT.

This study joins a growing number of studies, as summarised in chapter six (e.g. Pennycook 2007; Byram 2008; Kumaravadivelu 2008; Seidlhofer 2011; Dewey 2012; Jenkins 2012; Liddicoat and Scarino 2013; Galloway and Rose 2015), that challenge current approaches in ELT and call for a more diverse and less restricted conceptualisation of the content of the ELT classrooms as well as greater variety in the approaches taken to teaching and learning. Furthermore, and significantly, this study and many others (e.g. Csizér and Kontra 2012; Galloway 2013; Hino and Oda 2015) highlight the positive reception more diverse approaches to language, communication and culture receive in the classroom from both teachers and students. As such there is now a growing body of evidence that would suggest materials writers, curriculum designers, teacher trainers, test writers and programme administrators, among others, need to address the changing realities of English use and the implications for ELT. While intercultural communication and ELF studies have, somewhat tentatively, advocated such changes for some time, it is significant that more pedagogically orientated research that takes account of learners and teachers needs and motivations as well as sound pedagogic practice has now also joined the call for change. These changes will hopefully lead to an approach to ELT that is better suited to the needs of majority of learners of English who use it as a lingua franca for intercultural communication.

Chapter 8
Conclusion

> The experience of understanding the other is "more like grasping a proverb, catching an allusion, seeing a joke – or as I have suggested, reading a poem – than it is like achieving communion."
>
> – Geertz (1980: 70)

> There is no way we can fully understand one another, even though we have no other recourse than to try again and again to translate the untranslatable, and thereby gain sympathy for and acceptance of one another.
>
> – Kramsch and Uryu (2012: 218)

This book began with a question from Salman Rushdie's character Max Ophuls about the possibility of ever understanding the other. The quote from Clifford Geertz and the following interpretation from Kramsch and Uryu would suggest that the answer is a negative one. However, this is not necessarily a cause for pessimism or a reason to dismiss intercultural communication as a field of study. The impossibility of fully understanding another person is of course in no way unique to intercultural communication and ELF communication and applies equally to all social relations and interactions. Reminding us of this serves to underline the need to avoid neat, simplistic answers in understanding culture and identity in intercultural communication through ELF. Our understandings will always be interpretations rather than rules and laws, partial and provisional, not fixed and complete. An interest in communication, culture and identity is an interest in social phenomena, not in laws of nature or physics. Complexity, fluidity, dynamism, contradictions and fracture are integral parts of such phenomena. As researchers we need to abstract, delineate, categorise and set boundaries to be able to effectively engage in analysis but this has to be undertaken with an awareness of the limitations of such practices. We therefore need research approaches that recognise the limitations that result from attempts to produce coherent accounts of complex phenomena. In this book I have suggested that complexity theory offers one such lens or metaphor through which to approach theories of culture, identity, communication and language that incorporates both the needs of researchers to produce coherent accounts of phenomena and an awareness that this coherence is temporary and partial.

Furthermore, as educators we face a similar dilemma. In teaching culture or raising awareness of identity issues in the language classroom we are presented with more complexity than can be dealt with in a single lesson, course or syllabus. This applies equally to local cultures or the vast range of cultures represented and constructed in intercultural communication through ELF. Selection and simplification are a necessary part of teaching but these do not entail eschewing complexity. What we select needs justification, critical evaluation and constant revision. From the beginning we can, and should, select to make language learners aware of the diversity and complexity of the relationships between language, communication, identity and culture, even if we then need to choose aspects of that relationship which can be manageably presented in the class. Finally, as Kramsch and Uryu write, to understand others "we have no other recourse than to try again and again" (2012: 218). This is an area where language education can offer a key part of a general education in equipping learners with an awareness of difference and diversity as well as the ability to actively engage with others. Indeed, intercultural awareness is an issue that is important for all in education, not only language students. As Jenkins (2014) emphasises in her examination of academic English language policies, it is often those communicating in their L1 in multilingual environments (i.e. native speakers of English in international settings) that are most in need of increased intercultural awareness; even though they may not be conscious of this. As suggested in this book these issues lead into notions of social responsibility and concepts of citizenship at the national level and intercultural citizenship at the global level. The critical dimension is crucial here in raising an awareness of the complexity of cultures and identities and the need to question and challenge dominant discourses, as well as in the ability to act and engage with others based on this increased awareness. Although we may not be able to produce definitive and comfortable answers to understanding culture and identity in intercultural communication, it is, to quote Max Ophuls again, "one hell of a question", and a question intercultural communication researchers, ELF researchers and language educators should be fully engaged with.

Given what is written above, no neat answers can be provided here to understanding culture and identity through ELF. It may, nonetheless, be helpful to provide a summary of the theories, research and positions outlined in this monograph through explicitly addressing the four questions set out in chapter one. To recap the four questions are repeated below and each will be addressed in turn.

1. What are points of convergence and divergence between ELF and intercultural communication research?

2. What influence (if anything) do studies of intercultural communication through ELF have on our understanding of the relationship between culture, identity and language?
3. What are the implications of ELF research for conceptualising intercultural communicative competence?
4. What are the consequences (if any) of ELF and intercultural awareness (ICA) research for teaching English (ELT)?

8.1 What are points of convergence and divergence between ELF and intercultural communication research?

Firstly, it has been noted that intercultural communication is a large and diverse field of study and the discussion in this book has predominantly dealt with intercultural communication as related to applied linguistics and language education. Likewise any claims about ELF research cannot be seen as representing the whole field but rather the current consensus, where a consensus exists. With these caveats borne in mind, it can be argued that ELF research shares much with contemporary, critical and poststructuralist perspectives in intercultural communication. Most obviously, ELF is a form of intercultural communication by its very definition since it involves interlocutors who have different linguistic and culture backgrounds and ELF researchers have been clear about identifying ELF communication as intercultural communication. There has been some debate as to the extent ELF might be approached as unique in some way as a form of intercultural communication, but the position adopted here, and by many ELF scholars, is that ELF is not *sui generis*. In other words aspects or features of ELF communication are likely to be part of other kinds of multilingual or plurilingual intercultural communication. Nonetheless, given the huge scale on with ELF is used as a medium of intercultural communication, and the large amount of data currently being collected documenting such communication, it is likely to be of central importance in understanding the processes of intercultural communication.

ELF research should be distinguished from earlier forms of cross-cultural research in which cultural and linguistic difference were assumed a priori. In cross-cultural research languages, identities and cultures were often treated in an essentialist manner in which only the national scale was recognised and a correlation was assumed between the language spoken and the identity and culture represented. Given the diversity in uses and users of ELF, ELF research clearly does not fit well into such a simplistic framework. Instead, ELF research, as noted, typically takes a critical and poststructuralist perspective on language, identity and culture in intercultural communication. This involves approaching such categories as fluid and situated. Thus, for example, particular cultural identities associated with national cultures or terms such as native and non-native speakers are not assumed a priori to be relevant to the communication studied. Such a perspective aligns well with the critical framework for intercultural communication research outlined by Scollon and Scollon (2001) who highlight the need for researchers to ask who introduces the concepts of culture, or the intercultural, with what purposes and with what consequences. Researchers of ELF and intercultural communication need to justify and demonstrate the relevance of intercultural categorisations related to cultural and linguistic differences, to both the participants in the interaction and the analyst while at the same time not conflating the two. Equally importantly the ideological dimensions of both participants' and researchers' use of particular categories need to be recognised together with a concern with power relationships and status, especially as regards language choice and form in ELF.

Key concepts made use of in intercultural communication research, and increasingly in ELF research too, are third places and the related concepts of hybridity and liminality, transcultural flows linked to notions of local and global, and interculturality. ELF research offers important contributions to these ideas in presenting examples of communication which do not easily fit into national categories of language use, cultural identifications or cultural settings. We regularly see hybrid forms of language use and related hybrid communicative and cultural practices. These can be viewed as 'third place' practices in not being related to any particular culture. At the same time though, it is important to also be aware that ELF communication does not necessarily take place 'between' anything. Participants in ELF communication, and other forms of intercultural communication, may be constructing new communicative and cultural references, practices and identities in situ. Equally they may be representing multiple identifications and references at once, moving across different communities simultaneously. In such instances the metaphors of flows and the transcultural may be more salient.

The notion of interculturality highlights the negotiated nature of such dynamic communicative practices and an interest in negotiation is another shared concern of ELF and intercultural communication research. However, as Zhu (2015) points out, in intercultural communication studies this has frequently been approached from a perspective of negotiating difference, whereas, in ELF it has related to negotiating what is shared. Most obviously in ELF communication what is shared is some understanding of the English language but it has also involved shared identities such as multilingual communicators, professionals, students and even as ELF users. Nonetheless, both intercultural communication and ELF studies have focused on the aspects of communication that contribute to effective intercultural interaction and this typically goes beyond linguistic features and positions issues of pragmatics, power, and identity as equally important.

Despite the extensive range of shared interests, it is of concern that within the field of intercultural communication ELF studies are still frequently ignored, marginalised or misunderstood. This is partly explained by the marginalisation of language in much intercultural communication research but even in applied linguistics, where language is clearly of importance, English is often treated simplistically. It may be unremarked on, or associated with an idealised native speaker 'standard' variety, either as an inappropriate 'baseline' measure of competence, or as evidence of linguistic imperialism through native speaker dominance. Yet ELF research has demonstrated considerably more complexity in uses of English, underscoring the inappropriateness of any one model of communication and language (native speaker or otherwise) in conceptualising intercultural communication, as well as the interplay of many scales and flows of linguistic and cultural practices which, while not denying the role of linguistic imperialism, show it is just one of many influences on the way in which English is used in intercultural communication. This would suggest that intercultural communication researchers need to take greater account of the findings emerging from ELF research. Likewise, ELF researchers should engage with other intercultural communication scholars as well as addressing issues of concern to the wider applied linguistics community. Given the shared interests, particularly around investigations of successful intercultural communicative practices and the themes of culture and identity, there are many potentially fruitful points of convergence between the two fields.

8.2 What influence (if anything) do studies of intercultural communication through ELF have on our understanding of the relationship between culture, identity and language?

Following on from the answer to the first question, ELF studies offer a powerful and growing body of theoretical and empirical research which contributes to poststructuralist understandings of the relationships between culture, identity and language. ELF research, in documenting the diversity of English uses and the range of cultural practices and settings English is used to represent and construct, provides strong support for a move away from structuralist language, culture, nation and identity correlations. Therefore, cultural practices and references expressed through ELF are not inextricably tied to Anglophone cultures (a problematic term in itself since there is no homogeneous Anglophone culture). At the same time participants in ELF communication are not restricted to representing and constructing cultural practices and references associated with their L1. This can result in hybrid culture practices and ELF communication taking place in a third space between more stable cultural communities. However, as noted above, we need to be careful not to reify the notions of hybridity or third spaces. ELF communication and the cultural practices expressed and created through it may not be 'between' anything and can be multiple rather than hybrid, associated with different cultural groupings simultaneously.

We also need to recognise that this does not entail the end of nation as a frame of reference for cultural groupings. The ideology which posits the link between nation, culture and language is a powerful one, often embedded within political and educational establishments, and for many participants in intercultural communication through ELF it may still be meaningful. Nonetheless, researchers, while acknowledging the influence of national cultures, also need to approach this as just one level or scale of cultural grouping and identification among many.

Lastly, we also need to be clear that ELF communication is not culture and identity neutral (or any other kind of neutral). There is no such thing as neutral communication, intercultural, lingua franca, or otherwise. All communication involves participants, settings, purposes, relationships, discourse and language choices none of which are neutral. It may be that identity and/or culture are not particularly salient to understanding interaction in some instances, but it would be a mistake to assume they have somehow been 'erased' from the communication. ELF studies to date have demonstrated the richness and diversity of cultural references, practices and identities represented and created in intercultural communication in which multiple scales from the local, national and global are present, with individuals moving between and across these different scales and with a high degree of negotiation occurring, often resulting in new cultural practices and references emerging from the interaction.

Such a complex, dynamic and fluid characterisation of culture, identity and communication has significant implications for how we conceive of culture and identity and their relationships to language and communication. Firstly, as already discussed, critical poststructuralist conceptions of culture and identity in which they are approached as a process, something that we do, or a social practice are most appropriate. We can view culture as shared knowledge, discourse, practices and ideologies. However, given the degree of diversity and fluidity documented in any characterisation of culture, especially in intercultural communication and ELF, from a critical poststructuralist perspective it is reasonable to question whether culture has any validity as a category outside of everyday 'folk' beliefs. Yet, given the extensive and productive use culture has in both everyday life and in academic research it would seem unwarranted to abandon it. This suggests that we need another level of analysis or lens to complement the multiplicity of characterisations envisaged in poststructuralist theories. I have argued in this book that complexity theory provides just such a lens or meta-theory. Complexity theory allows us to examine culture as a whole but as a constantly changing and evolving whole. Crucially cultural characterisations and systems are approached as emergent. They are not reducible to individuals or individual social interactions. Rather they emerge from the aggregation of many individuals and interactions; in other words, culture is continuously emerging with no fixed end point. As researchers this allows us to examine shared behaviour, beliefs and practices within cultural groupings but at the same time recognising that they only offer partial explanations of individual interactions.

This view of culture is also significant for how we conceive of the relationship between language and culture. As already highlighted, particular characterisations of cultures and languages, such as the English language and British culture, are not inextricably linked. It is important here to be aware of the different levels at which language and culture can be approached. At the level of linguistic and cultural systems, the macro-perspective, we can see language and culture as two linked but not synonymous complex adaptive systems. At this macro level the English language has thus been influenced by and can be linked to national conceptions of English culture or US culture (however, we might characterise them) but equally it can be, and indeed must be if it is to be of use as a lingua franca, influenced by other conceptions of cultures. However, at a more general level, i.e. theories of language and culture (rather than specific languages and cultures), they are always linked. That is language in general is a cultural tool or process. Also at the more micro perspective cultures and languages are linked for the individual. Individuals learn languages through processes of socialisation into cultural groups; although, for languages such as English used as lingua franca this can involve multiple groups. Thus, for the individual, languages will have particular linguacultural associations based on past experiences. Nonetheless, these associations will of course change with new experiences. For researchers investigating communicative interactions this means that pre-established links between languages and cultures cannot be assumed. Instead, the connections between the language or languages used in the interactions and culture or cultures represented and constructed are made in each instance of communication. This involves the convergence of various linguistic, linguacultural, discourse and other cultural flows in a communicative event to create the particular cultural practices and references in situ.

As outlined throughout this book identity has received considerable attention in ELF research and applied linguistics and hence there is already quite a substantial body of work in this area. As with culture it has been approached from a poststructuralist perspective in which identity is seen as a social practice and a process; in other words, identity is performed. However, it should be stressed that culture and identity are not synonymous and we need to be wary of essentialist correlations between self, identity and cultures. Cultural identities are viewed as emerging from a complex network of interacting group identifications including ethnic, racial, regional, national and global groupings. Nonetheless, cultural groupings are an important group which we identify with or are identified with by others. ELF studies have shown the significance of identity issues in intercultural communication through ELF and again underscored that this is not a 'neutral' form of communication. Findings have revealed English being used to create and index multiple identities including cultural identities. These cultural identities have been associated with hybrid cultural identities with speakers embracing being 'in-between' cultures and adopting the role of mediators between different cultural groupings. However, participants have also reported the use of ELF as a medium through which they can construct identities that are not between any particular cultures or cultural identifications but something more fluid and liminal. In such cases participants may identify with others as proficient multilingual and multicultural communicators. At the same time national cultural identities are still relevant in relation to the participants' own L1 and national culture as well as the influence of Anglophone cultures and native English speaker ideologies. Thus, ELF research has often revealed tensions and contradictions between local cultural identifications, national cultural identifications and more liminal intercultural identifications.

This links ELF research to other research into identity, intercultural communication and globalisation. Globalisation has resulted in an opening up of new spaces and resources for identity construction and negotiation. Yet, we need to be cautious of assuming that individuals are free to choose or construct any identity they wish. Identity construction takes places within existing social structures and these provide constraints on the choices available to individuals as well as the identities others may impose. Identification with national cultures is perhaps the most obvious form of this as both a self-selected and other ascribed identity. It is thus important to remain alert to issues of power and dominance in identity construction in intercultural communication. This is especially salient to intercultural communication through ELF due to the continued dominance and prestige of native speaker varieties of English and the associated cultural practices, often in idealised or simplified forms presented in ELT materials and tests. I have argued that the work on interculturality provides a productive framework for investigating identity construction and negotiation in a manner that avoids pre-determined assumptions about participants' cultural identities. Indeed, it is crucial that a priori assumptions about cultural identities are avoided since this has been the source of much misunderstanding, stereotyping and othering in intercultural communication studies.

8.3 What are the implications of ELF research for conceptualising intercultural communicative competence?

How participants successfully manage the diversity and variety of communicative practices in intercultural communication through ELF has been an issue of much concern and this is a concern shared with intercultural communication and applied linguistics research more generally. Central to all these fields has been conceptualising the knowledge, skills and attitudes necessary for successful communication. In applied linguistics, and particularly language teaching, the notion of communicative competence has been foundational to discussions of this. Similarly in intercultural communication research the concept of intercultural competence has been equally salient. Although communicative competence has served language teaching well in focusing methodology and teaching on developing learners' ability to communicate in the language, there are some serious limitations in relation to intercultural communication and ELF. Communicative competence has typically been conceived as either related to native speaker communication (Hymes 1972) or native to non-native speaker communication (Canale and Swain 1980). Neither of these two scenarios are especially relevant to ELF communication in which there are usually no native speakers of English present. Furthermore, communicative competence is often interpreted from a deficit position in which non-native speakers are expected to adapt and adjust their communication to a fixed set of native speaker norms. This is very different to the mutual accommodation and negotiation that have been shown to be crucial in ELF studies and other intercultural communication research.

Linked to this native speaker bias, communicative competence has frequently been associated with the notion of particular speech communities and settings which language learners need to assimilate or acculturate to, but again in intercultural communication through ELF there are often no fixed or stable communities. Perhaps most significantly communicative competence has predominantly focused on linguistic competence (although other competences are contained within the characterisation). This is problematic for ELF communication as given the diverse range of linguistic forms used in ELF it is difficult to specify in advance what particular linguistic forms are needed, although clearly some shared knowledge of linguistic forms is necessary. Instead of a competence in particular linguistic forms, more appropriate is an ability to make use of and adapt existing linguistic repertoires and to continuously learn and develop new linguistic repertoires. Additionally, as much intercultural communication and ELF research has underscored, successful communication is about much more than linguistic structure. ELF research has shown a high degree of pragmatic and interactional competence demonstrated by successful intercultural communicators. This includes communication skills and strategies such as pre-empting misunderstanding, repetition and paraphrasing, signalling non-understanding when appropriate, it has also involved code-switching, willingness to accommodate and negotiate, and linguistic and intercultural awareness.

Within intercultural communication studies work on the notion of intercultural competence has taken a much wider and more holistic approach to communication than communicative competence. This has involved examining a range of skills, knowledge, attitudes, motivations and outcomes related to successful communication across cultures. This broader approach to intercultural communication is important in moving away from a narrow focus on grammar and linguistic form. However, this has often been at the expense of language which has been ignored or treated simplistically in intercultural communication. While this book has emphasised that language is only one part of successful intercultural communication, it is still a crucial part. Furthermore, many discussions of intercultural competence have taken a cross-cultural perspective in which languages, cultures and nations are correlated and rather simplistic and static views of intercultural communication are adopted. This is obviously problematic for much intercultural communication research and especially ELF where national cultures are of less relevance and only one scale of interpretation among many. A more powerful and influential concept, at least in applied linguistics and language education, has been intercultural communicative competence (ICC) (particularly Byram (1997)). ICC combines features of communicative competence and intercultural competence. It recognises the importance of language in intercultural communication but also the need for a wider range of knowledge, skills and attitudes. In particular ICC recognises L2 use as different from L1 use and shifts the attention from native speaker communication and norms to intercultural communication and the intercultural speaker. Within this model critical cultural awareness is central. This involves the intercultural communicator being aware of their own and others cultural backgrounds and communicative practices. Crucially the successful intercultural communicator should have the ability to interact, mediate and negotiate between different communicative practices in intercultural exchanges.

ICC research is commensurable with ELF research in the way it emphasises the importance of negotiation and mediation in interaction. It also extends the notion of competence to include language attitudes and communication skills which have been a major concern in ELF research. ICC also 'decentres' the native speaker from conceptions of competence and recognises the intercultural and multilingual nature of intercultural communication. Furthermore, given the extensive discussions and research projects investigating the pedagogic applications of the model, many alternative approaches to ELT are offered. However, there are also a number of significant points of difference between ICC and the manner in which successful communication has been conceived in ELF research. Most significantly ICC is still focused on the national level of culture (although it is a complex and multi-voiced national culture) and the associated model of communication between speakers of nationally based varieties of language and communicative practices based on nationally grounded cultures. Thus, as with other models of intercultural competence, this limits the applicability of ICC to ELF communication. Indeed, in discussions of ICC and English, ELF is explicitly rejected as being meaningful in understanding ICC or as having implications for pedagogy, with native English speaker communities still given a central place. This is obviously at odds with ELF studies and means that any discussion of ICC in relation to ELF will need to either reject ICC as a model of the elements of successful communication or work with an adapted version of ICC.

Intercultural awareness (ICA) was outlined as just such an adapted version of ICC that specifically engaged with the more fluid notions of culture and communication underlying much ELF research. ICA is defined as "a conscious understanding of the role culturally based forms, practices and frames of reference can have in intercultural communication, and an ability to put these conceptions into practice in a flexible and context specific manner in communication" (adapted from Baker 2011b: 202). This was further expanded to include 12 elements which moved from a basic understanding of the influence of and relationships between culture and communication, to more detailed cultural awareness which involved an understanding of the complexity of cultures and communicative practices, as well as an awareness of differences in cultures and communicative practices, and finally intercultural awareness which concerned an awareness of the relationships between cultures and communicative practices in intercultural communication and emphasised the complexity of this relationship as well as the emergent nature of the relationship in much intercultural communication, and the ability to negotiate, mediate, and adapt to this complexity and fluidity in intercultural communication. ICA was in part based on the types of cultural references, practices and identities documented so far in ELF research and so is directly relevant to ELF communication. Furthermore, the elements of ICA are deliberately general in nature since the specifics of what linguistic and cultural knowledge is needed and which particular communicative strategies are necessary will depend on each instance of communication. As such there is an emphasis on the processes of intercultural communication and developing awareness. Linked to this, ICA also contains a high degree of reflexivity and criticality since participants in intercultural communication through ELF often need or desire to challenge and reinterpret communicative practices and related cultural practices in ways that are appropriate to the communicative situations in which they find themselves.

8.4 What are the consequences (if any) of ELF and intercultural awareness (ICA) research for teaching English (ELT)?

The answer to question three clearly has implications for question four as well. If we are to reconsider the types of knowledge, skills and attitudes needed for successful communication and to re-evaluate our conceptions of communicative or intercultural communicative competence, then these will have consequences for both what and how we teach English. However, I have argued that currently the predominant focus in ELT is on the teaching of a fixed linguistic code based on a narrow interpretation of the already limited notion of communicative competence. Furthermore, within mainstream approaches to ELT there has been little recognition of the role of English as a global lingua franca. In ELT English is still principally associated both linguistically and culturally with the Anglophone world and within this a very narrow section of that world (typically white, middle class, male and monolingual). Yet, such knowledge and skills are unlikely to equip learners of English for the variable demands of intercultural communication through ELF. Even when ELT does attempt to integrate other aspects of communication into teaching, such as communication strategies and cultural content, this is often conducted in an ad hoc and limited manner. Over-simplified and essentialist portrayals of culture and intercultural communication in ELT are common and as such they fail to represent the current and future experiences of the majority of English learners.

A number of contemporary approaches to language teaching offer viable alternatives that incorporate a more rounded perspective on the aims and purposes of ELT and recognise the variable global roles English plays. These involved post-methods, post-normative and intercultural perspectives on language teaching. Following such a perspective entails a move away from prescriptive approaches to teaching and towards a recognition of L2 learning and use as an intercultural process as well as a process orientated conception of learning in which learners are taught *about* learning and communication rather than fixed linguistic forms and communicative practices. This is crucial as due to the diversity of communicative practices users of English are likely to encounter, given its role as a global lingua franca, they could never be equipped with comprehensive knowledge of all of the different scenarios in which they are likely to encounter English. ELF studies have documented the highly variable ways in which English is used, including diverse linguistic forms, communication strategies, pragmatic strategies and cultural references. Learners and users, therefore, need to be able to adapt and negotiate their communicative practices for successful intercultural communication through ELF. No one set of linguistic or other communicative norms can be proposed as most appropriate for all ELT settings. This further highlights the importance of local contexts, informed by an awareness of the global role of English, in determining the content and goals of ELT.

I suggested that the model of ICA was commensurable with such approaches, particularly in relation to intercultural education, and provided a framework that integrated findings from ELF, intercultural communication and education research. ICA offers a model and set of pedagogic goals for the knowledge, skills and attitudes needed for intercultural communication through ELF as well as how these can be put into practice in intercultural communication. ICA also provided suggestions for routes of development; although, with the caveats that the different levels should not be viewed as necessarily the routes learners will take and that further empirical study is needed. I also outlined five themes detailing the opportunities for the development of ICA in the classroom. These were: 1. exploring the complexity of local cultures; 2. exploring cultural representations in language learning materials; 3. exploring cultural representations in the media and arts both online and in more 'traditional' mediums; 4. making use of cultural informants; 5. engaging in intercultural communication both face to face and electronically. The strands were deliberately general in nature since it is important to acknowledge that how they are implemented and the relevant content will be dependent on local settings, opportunities and needs. It should also be recognised that not all these strands would be relevant in all settings and classrooms. Nonetheless, even in the most supposedly monolingual and monocultural classrooms exploration of themes, such as exploring local cultures and exploring language learning materials, often reveals a surprising degree of cultural and linguistic diversity. These five strands for developing ICA in the classroom aim to better equip ELT learners for intercultural communication through ELF.

Alongside these five general strands for developing ICA in the classroom a more detailed exploration of how they can be implemented in practice was given through a case study of a course in intercultural communication, intercultural awareness and Global Englishes. This was presented, not as a model to be copied in other settings, but rather as an example of how the implications of intercultural communication and ELF research can be translated in a practical manner into pedagogic practice. In terms of findings, the successful development of the course and materials demonstrates that the concept of ICA and the five pedagogic strands outlined in chapter six can be usefully translated into classroom practice, at least in the setting of this study (a university in Thailand). Particularly important were the positive evaluations of the students and the teachers showing that such a course and the associated approach to English and intercultural communication were perceived as valuable and relevant. Additionally, the findings revealed an already existing awareness and set of positive attitudes towards Global Englishes and intercultural communication among many of the participants. However, this needs to be balanced with a recognition of the continued prestige given to native English associated with Anglophone settings, particularly the UK and US, among some of the participants. These findings suggest an evolving or changing situation as regards the role and perception of ELT in this setting.

In demonstrating the relevance of an approach in ELT which is both locally and globally focused, especially concerning cultural content and intercultural competence, as well as the positive evaluation of key stakeholders to diverse approaches to communication through English, this study offers a challenge to the current orthodoxy in ELT. This alternative approach represents a move away from the focus on normative applications of a narrow range of linguistic structures, Anglo-centric perspectives on communication and culture and a restricted notion of communicative competence. As such this study joins the increasing number of studies discussed in this book that have highlighted the need for a more diverse approach to the content and processes of the ELT classroom and have demonstrated the positive reception these alternative perspectives to language, culture and communication receive from both teachers and students. There is now a growing body of evidence that indicates ELT stakeholders including materials writers, curriculum designers, teacher trainers, test writers and programme administrators, need to recognise and act on the changing realities of English use (see Bayyurt and Akcan 2015; Galloway and Rose 2015 and Jenkins 2015 for recent overviews).

In sum, the answer to these four questions underscores the implications ELF research has for an understanding of culture and identity in intercultural communication. Given the growing body of research emerging from the field of ELF studies, intercultural communication and applied linguistics scholars need to take note of the findings. In particular ELF research has further reinforced and expanded poststructuralist perspectives on culture and identity which view both concepts as fluid and dynamic. Linked to this, ELF research has been especially valuable in demonstrating the diversity of cultures and identities expressed through English and the emergent nature of this process. As such this offers both theoretical and empirical challenges to essentialist accounts of language, communication, identity and culture that posit simplistic and deterministic connections between them. This is something that needs to be recognised in intercultural communication research, training and education where national stereotypes and unproblematic accounts of language are still common. These implications are equally relevant for ELT, where such simplified and stereotyped characterisations of languages and cultures still form the core of the current orthodoxy.

Given the present stage of ELF research, in which it is now firmly established as a field in its own right (although not without controversy), it is time for ELF researchers to engage more fully with the implications of their research for other areas of applied linguistics. This is, I think, particularly true in respect to ELT. More empirical studies are needed exploring how alternative notions of language, communication, culture and identity can inform pedagogy and also how the needs of teachers and learners can influence future research in ELF. This will necessarily entail more interdisciplinary research and the collaboration of practitioners as more than just research participants. Through such research, both in relation to intercultural communication and ELT, it is hoped a fuller understanding of English as it used and learnt globally will be possible. This is not just important for English but for how we understand languages, cultures and identities in intercultural communication and education more generally.

Appendices

Appendix 1: Transcription conventions

Spelling: British English spelling is used.
Punctuation: New utterances begin on a new line with no capital letter. Capital letters are used for pronoun I and proper names. Apostrophes are used for abbreviations, e.g., don't, haven't.

(?)	inaudible
(xxx)	uncertain that word is correctly transcribed
((laughs))	Nonlinguistic features of the transcription
.	pause (untimed)
...	indicates a section of dialogue not transcribed
[ ]	overlapping or interrupted speech
=	The utterance on one line continues without a pause where the next = picks it up
CAPS	strong emphasis

Appendix 2: Intercultural communication and intercultural awareness: Course overview and outline

Course aims

This course aims to provide an introduction to intercultural communication through English and the knowledge, skills and attitudes needed to successfully do this.
- By the end of the course you have an understanding of the relationship between language and culture in intercultural communication.
- The role of English as the global lingua franca of intercultural communication.
- An understanding of the knowledge, skills and attitudes associated with intercultural awareness and its role in intercultural communication through English.

Please remember that this course is not a test of your English, so do not worry about making mistakes. The most important thing is to communicate and take part in the course.

Course structure and timetable

Learning in this course will take place online through Language House which is the name given to the University of Southampton's virtual learning environment.

– You have **10 weekly topics** to cover which contain interactive activities for you to complete with feedback. The weekly topics should take between 30 minutes to 1 hour to complete.

– You also have a **discussion forum** where you can share your ideas about the topics you have completed with other students on this course and with your tutor. There will also be special guest appearances from students at the University of Southampton. The discussion forum should take about 30–45 minutes to complete. You are expected to contribute to 5 of the discussion forums. This mean you do not have to post every week; although, you can if you would like to.

– There will be a number of live **chat sessions** as well where you can also discuss ideas with your tutor and other students. This will last around 1 hour.

– You have also been asked to keep a **learning journal** where you record your experiences of studying this course. Your journal entries should take around 20–30 minutes a week.

It is probably easiest if you follow the order that the topics are presented in here. However, you can try some of the topics in a different order if you wish and you do not have to do just one a week. You can do more if you prefer, or miss a week if you are busy and catch up later. The discussion tasks will need to be started in the weeks suggested so that everyone can contribute, but they never close so you can add more thoughts later if you wish. In total the course should take around 15 hours and will finish just before the end of term in February next year.

When you have successfully finished the course, including contributions to the discussion forum, you will receive a **certificate from the University of Southampton** indicating that you have undertaken a course in intercultural communication and intercultural awareness.

Topics and discussion tasks

1. Defining culture

Culture is generally something we all feel we know something about, whether it is our own culture or another culture we are familiar with. However, arriving at a definition of culture is difficult. In these activities you will be introduced to some of the different elements of culture and a range of definitions.

Week 1 discussion task – Based on the definitions of culture given in the activities try to write your own definition of culture.

2. Intercultural communication

What is the relationship between culture and language? What does this mean in intercultural communication? That is, what is the relationship between languages and cultures when people from different cultural backgrounds are communicating using the same language? In these activities you will consider the relationship between language and culture, with a focus on the English language, and what we mean by intercultural communication.

3. Cultural stereotypes and generalizations in communication

What do we mean by stereotypes and generalisations? How do they affect intercultural communication? We all have ideas and impressions of our own and other cultures, are they stereotypes or generalisations? Do they help intercultural communication are cause problems? In these activities you will distinguish features of generalisations and stereotypes and consider some stereotypes about the UK and Thailand.

Week 3 discussion task – Have you ever heard or experienced any stereotypes about Thailand? Are there any stereotypes that you may have had about other cultures?

4. The individual and culture

When you communicate in intercultural communication you are communicating with another individual. It is individual people who communicate not cultures (Thai culture does not speak to French culture!). What is the relationship between an individual and their culture? In these activities you will compare your own behaviour to some common generalisations about Thai culture and explore all the different groups that you belong alongside being Thai.

5. English as a global language

English is not just the language of the UK and USA. English is the official first language of 75 territories throughout the world. Furthermore, English is the most commonly spoken lingua franca on a global scale. In these activities you will be introduced to the wide range of English speaking countries, you will also consider some of the ways of categorising the different types of English and you will explore some of the features of the many varieties of English around the globe.

Week 5 discussion task – Are there any examples of other varieties of English you know? Do you think other forms of English (e.g. Hong Kong English) from the traditional native speaker Englishes are 'standard' English? What type of English do you think students of English should learn? Why?

6. Exploring my own culture

To be able to communicate effectively in intercultural communication it is important to understand different ways of communicating. To do this you must first be aware of your own culture and also the complexity of this. In these activities you will consider the reasons for different types of communicative behaviour in Thailand and also explore the variety and complexity of different dialects and languages in Thailand.

Week 6 discussion task – Think about the languages and dialects you are familiar with. What languages or dialects do you speak at home and at the university? Do you speak any other languages? If yes, when and where? Does anyone in your family or any of your close friends speak a different language or dialect?

7. Intercultural communication and the Internet

The Internet provides an important source of opportunities for intercultural communication and contact through English. Many cultures and countries are represented through English on the Internet. However, how much can we really learn about another culture from the Internet? In the first activity you will consider the different ways you can interact with people and information from other cultures through the Internet and in the second activity you will examine some representations of culture on the Internet.

Week 7 discussion task – Find your own representation of another culture on the Internet. What aspects of this other culture are represented on the website (think of the areas you looked at in this week's activities)?

8. Comparing cultures: Politeness

To be able to communicate successfully in intercultural communication it is necessary to be able to make comparisons between cultures. In these activities you will consider why comparisons between cultures are important for intercultural communication and you will make comparisons between Thailand and the UK in relation to politeness.

9. Globalisation and transcultural global flows

The benefits of having one language, English, that is so dominant in the world has been controversial. Is English inevitably linked to Western culture and dominance or is it, as we have seen, changed and adapted to many different cultures and uses? In these activities you will consider the benefits and disadvantages of English as a global language. You will then analyse some examples of local (Thai) uses of English and how they relate to globalisation and the idea of transcultural global flows.

Week 9 discussion task – Can you think of any other examples that mix global and local cultures in a similar way to the instances you explored in this weeks activities e.g. language, music, video, films or personal experiences?

10. Intercultural Awareness

Successful intercultural communication in English involves more than native speaker like grammar, vocabulary and pronunciation. One way of describing the skills, knowledge and attitudes needed for intercultural communication is intercultural awareness. In these activities you will be introduced to some of the competencies needed for intercultural communication and consider the importance of different elements of intercultural awareness.

Week 10 discussion task – Based on what you have learnt about intercultural communication on this course and in particular the skills, knowledge and attitudes of intercultural awareness (ICA), what do you think are the most important things to learn about when studying English? For example, native speaker like English grammar or pronunciation, experience of other cultures, bilingual communication, knowledge of your own cultures and languages, comparing cultures, globalisation. Do you think ICA should be part of English teaching and learning?

Appendix 3: Screen shots from the learning objects (LO) in the course

Topic outline

Intercultural communication and intercultural awareness

- Introductory podcast
- Course overview and outline
- Course forum
- News forum
- Chat room
- Glossary

ยินดีต้อนรับ
Van harte welkom
Welcome
Bienvenue à tous
欢迎

1 Week 1: Defining culture

Culture is generally something we all feel we know something about, whether it is our own culture or another culture we are familiar with. However, arriving at a definition of culture is difficult. In these activities you will be introduced to some of the different elements of culture and a range of definitions.

- Activity: Defining culture
- Discussion: Defining culture

2 Week 2: Intercultural communication

What is the relationship between culture and language? What does this mean in intercultural communication? That is, what is the relationship between languages and cultures when people from different cultural backgrounds are communicating using the same language? In these activities you will consider the relationship between language and culture, with a focus on the English language, and what we mean by intercultural communication.

- Activity: Intercultural communication

3 Week 3: Cultural stereotypes and generalisations in communication

What do we mean by stereotypes and generalisations? How do they affect intercultural communication? We all have ideas and impressions of our own and other cultures, are they stereotypes or generalisations? Do they help intercultural communication or cause problems? In these activities you will distinguish features of generalisations and stereotypes and consider some stereotypes about the UK and Thailand.

Intercultural communication

You have already seen how our cultural background influences our beliefs and behaviour including the way we communicate. In particular you have seen the importance of language in both creating and representing a culture. Therefore, it is important to understand the relationship between culture and language in more detail, especially for the English language. We also need to think about what this means in intercultural communication. That is, what is the relationship between languages and cultures when people from different cultural backgrounds are communicating using the same language?

In these activities you will consider the relationship between language and culture, with a focus on the English language, and what we mean by intercultural communication.

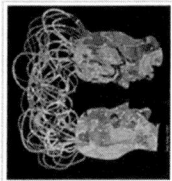

Intercultural communication

Activity 1: Culture and language

To communicate effectively in different cultural settings it is important to have an understanding of the relationship between culture and language in communication.

Instruction

Select the tick ✓ for the statements below that you agree with and the cross ✗ for those you disagree with. Then read the feedback.

1. Culture and language are closely linked.

2. Language is culture.

3. A language represents a specific culture with its world views, values and beliefs.

4. The English language is linked to English culture only.

5. Cultures and specific languages can be separated (for example the English language can be separated from British culture).

6. English is used in global settings to enable speakers to share their different cultures.

7. In order to communicate effectively it is necessary to understand the influence of culture on communication.

8. In order to communicate effectively it is necessary to understand the culture of the person you are communicating with.

Show feedback

English as a global language

Signs in Hong Kong

English is not just the language of the UK and USA. English is the official first language of 75 territories throughout the world. Furthermore, English is the most commonly spoken lingua franca on a global scale. It has been estimated that there are over 2 billion users of English as a non-native language. This means there are 4 times as many non-native speakers as there are native speakers of English.

In these activities you will be introduced to the wide range of English speaking countries, you will also consider some of the ways of categorising the different types of English and you will explore some of the features of the many varieties of English around the globe.

Activity 1: English speaking territories

There are presently around 75 territories which are considered English speaking, where English is spoken as a first language (L1) or an institutionalised second language (L2), for example in law, education or government.

Instruction

Below is a list of 25 territories. Tick the ones which are considered English speaking countries (as either an L1 or L2). Then read the feedback.

☐ Algeria
☐ Bangladesh
☐ Bhutan
☐ Brazil
☐ China
☐ Dominica
☐ Fiji
☐ Gibraltar
☐ Greenland
☐ Hong Kong
☐ India
☐ Ireland
☐ Indonesia
☐ Kenya

Exploring my own culture

To be able to communicate effectively in intercultural communication it is important to understand different ways of communicating. To do this you must first be aware of your own culture and also the complexity of this. This will enable you to make comparisons with other cultures and also to realise that other cultures will be just as rich and complicated as your own.

In these activities you will consider the reasons for different types of communicative behaviour in Thailand and also explore the variety and complexity of different dialects and languages in Thailand.

4 Thai greeting

Activity 1: Communicating in Thailand

In this activity you are going to think about some common communicative behaviour in Thailand and consider what their meanings are or the reasons for them.

Instruction

Look at the examples of communicative behaviour. Make notes on what you think the meaning is or the reason for this behaviour. Then read the feedback. An example answer is given in the help.

Show help

1. You 'wai' your parents or teachers when you meet them.

Meaning/Reason:

Show feedback

2. Pointing to someone with your foot is considered rude.

Meaning/Reason:

Intercultural Awareness

Successful intercultural communication in English involves more than native speaker like grammar, vocabulary and pronunciation. Instead a range of other skills, attitudes and knowledge associated with multilingual and multicultural communication are needed as well. These skills, attitudes and knowledge have been called Intercultural Awareness.

In these activities you will explore what intercultural awareness involves through examining some of the competences needed for intercultural communication and considering the importance of different elements of intercultural awareness.

Intercultural Awareness

Activity 1: Intercultural communication competencies

A range of skills, attitudes and areas of knowledge (sometimes known as competencies) have been proposed as part of English language learning for successful intercultural communication. These include, accommodation, code switching, cooperation, let-it-pass principle, repair, language awareness and cultural/intercultural awareness. In this activity you are going to focus on the meaning of these terms for intercultural communication in English.

Instruction

Select the skill or competency which best matches the description. Then read the feedback. An example is given in the help.

Show help

1. Select your answer ▸ The ability to switch between different languages or varieties of the same language in response to the person we are communicating with to help communication (e.g. begin able to switch between English and Japanese when talking with a Japanese English speaker).

2. Select your answer ▸ The ability to negotiate and resolve misunderstanding in communication, through for example the use of different words to explain a previously misunderstood word or phrase.

Appendix 4: Intercultural communication questionnaire additional responses

Reasons for studying English

- ■ I'll need it for my future career.
- ■ it will allow me to meet and converse with more and varied people from many different cultures
- ■ it will allow me to meet and converse with native speakers of English.
- ■ it will allow me to travel to many different countries and to learn about different cultures.
- ■ it will allow me to have a fun and enjoyable experience.
- ■ it will make me a more knowledgeable person.
- ■ it will allow me to get good grades at university.
- ■ other people will respect me more if I have knowledge of the English language.

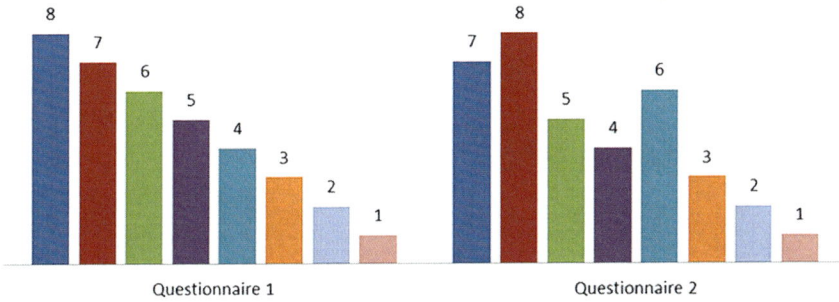

Ranking factors that help in intercultural communication through English

- Knowing about the way other non-native English speakers use English
- Knowing about the culture of the non-native English speaker you are communicating with
- Knowing about intercultural communication
- Having a native-like pronunciation.
- Using correct native-like grammar
- Knowing about the relationship between language and culture
- Knowing about the culture of native English-speaking countries

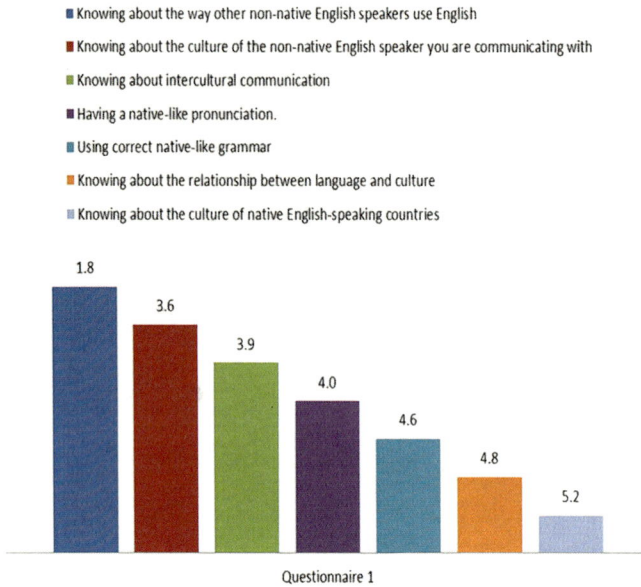

Questionnaire 1

- Knowing about the way other non-native English speakers use English
- Having a native-like pronunciation.
- Using correct native-like grammar
- Knowing about intercultural communication
- Knowing about the culture of the non-native English speaker you are communicating with
- Knowing about the relationship between language and culture
- Knowing about the culture of native English-speaking countries

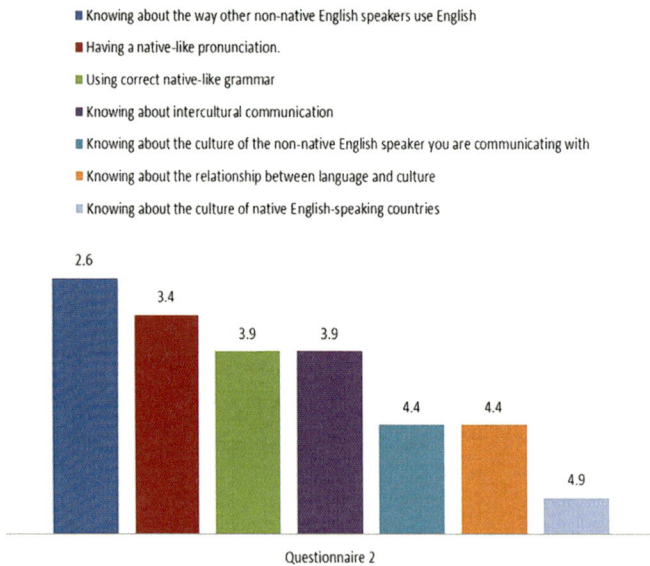

Questionnaire 2

Attitudes towards different types of English

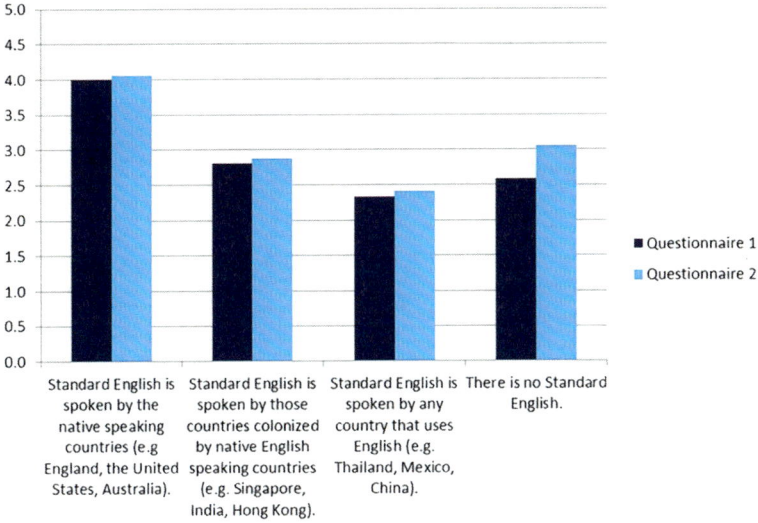

Standard English is spoken by the native speaking countries (e.g England, the United States, Australia).

Standard English is spoken by those countries colonized by native English speaking countries (e.g. Singapore, India, Hong Kong).

Standard English is spoken by any country that uses English (e.g. Thailand, Mexico, China).

There is no Standard English.

■ Questionnaire 1
■ Questionnaire 2

Attitudes towards intercultural communication

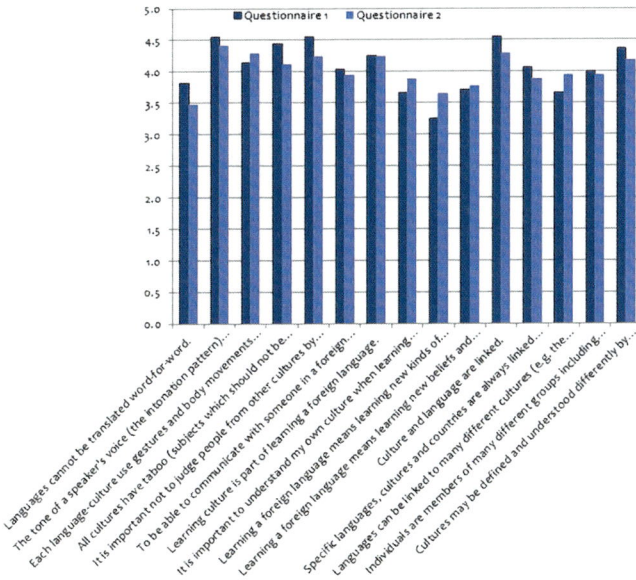

References

Alred, Geof, Byram, Michael, and Fleming, Mike. 2006. *Education for intercultural citizenship: concepts and comparisons*. Clevedon: Multilingual Matters.

Alsagoff, Lubna, McKay, Sandra Lee, Hu, Guangwei, and Renandya, Willy A. (eds.). 2012. *Principles and Practices for Teaching English as an International Language*. Abingdon: Routledge.

Anderson, Benedict. 2006. *Imagined communities: reflections on the origin and spread of nationalism* (Rev. ed.). London: Verso.

Appadurai, Arjun. 1996. *Modernity at large: cultural dimensions of globalization*. Minneapolis; London: University of Minnesota Press.

Archibald, Alasdair, Cogo, Alessia, and Jenkins, Jennifer (eds.). 2011. *Latest Trends in ELF Research*. Newcastle: Cambridge Scholars Press.

Arnold, Matthew. 1869. *Culture and anarchy: an essay in political and social criticism*. London: Smith, Elder and co.

Bachman, Lyle F. 1990. *Fundamental considerations in language testing*. Oxford: Oxford University Press.

Baird, Robert, Baker, Will, and Kitazawa, Mariko. 2014. The Complexity of English as a Lingua Franca. *Journal of English as a Lingua Franca, 3*(1), 171–196.

Baker, Will. 2008. A critical examination of ELT in Thailand: the role of cultural awareness. *RELC, 39*(1), 131–146.

Baker, Will. 2009. The cultures of English as a lingua franca. *TESOL Quarterly, 43*(4), 567–592.

Baker, Will. 2011a. Culture and identity through ELF in Asia: Fact of Fiction? In Archibald, Alasdair, Cogo, Alessia, and Jenkins, Jennifer (eds.), *Latest Trends in ELF Research* (pp. 35–52). Newcastle: Cambridge Scholars.

Baker, Will. 2011b. Intercultural awareness: modelling an understanding of cultures in intercultural communication through English as a lingua franca. *Language and Intercultural Communication, 11*(3), 197–214.

Baker, Will. 2012a. English as a Lingua Franca in Thailand: Characterisations and Implications. *English in Practice: Working Papers of the Centre for Global Englishes, 1*(1), 18–27.

Baker, Will. 2012b. From cultural awareness to intercultural awareness: culture in ELT. *ELT Journal, 66*(1), 62–70.

Baker, Will. 2012c. Global cultures and identities: refocusing the aims of ELT in Asia through intercultural awareness. In Theron Muller, Steven Herder, John Adamson and Philip Shigeo Brown (eds.), *Innovating EFL Education in Asia* (pp. 23–34). Basingstoke: Palgrave Macmillan.

Baker, Will. 2012d. Using online learning objects to develop intercultural awareness in ELT: a critical examination in a Thai higher education setting. *British Council Teacher Development Research Papers*. Retrieved from http://www.teachingenglish.org.uk/publications

Baker, Will. 2013. Interpreting the culture in intercultural rhetoric: a critical perspective from English as a lingua franca studies. In Diane Belcher and Gayle Nelson (eds.), *Critical and Corpus-Based Approaches to Intercultural Rhetoric* (pp. 22–45). Ann Arbor: University of Michigan Press.

Baker, Will. 2015. Culture and complexity through English as a lingua franca: rethinking competences and pedagogy in ELT. *Journal of English as a Lingua Franca, 4* (1). 9–30

Baker, Will., & Jenkins, Jennifer. 2015. Topic and Comment: Criticising ELF. *Journal of English as a Lingua Franca, 4*(1). 191–198

Bauman, Zygmunt. 2000. *Liquid Modernity*. Cambridge: Polity.

Bauman, Zygmunt. 2004. *Identity*. Cambridge: Polity.

Bauman, Zygmunt. 2011. *Culture in a liquid modern world*. Cambridge: Polity.

Bax, Stephen. 2003. The end of CLT: a context approach to language teaching. *ELT Journal, 57*(3), 278–287.

Bayyurt, Yasemin, and Akcan, Sumru (eds.). 2015. *Current Perspectives on Pedagogy for ELF*. Berlin: De Gruyter Mouton.

Belz, Julie, and Thorne, Steven. 2006. Internet-mediated Intercultural Foreign Language Education and the Intercultural Speaker. In Julie Belz and Steven Thorne (eds.), *Internet-mediated intercultural foreign language education*. Boton: Thomson Heinle.

Bennett, Milton J. 1986. A developmental approach to training for intercultural sensitivity. *International Journal of Intercultural Relations, 10*, 179–186.

Bhabha, Homi. 1994. *The Location of Culture*. Abingdon: Routledge.

Billing, Michael. 1995. *Banal Nationalism*. London: Sage.

Bjørge, Anne K. 2012. Expressing Disagreement in ELF Business Negotiations: Theory and Practice. *Applied Linguistics, 33*(4), 406–427.

Björkman, Beyza. 2011. Pragmatic strategies in English as an academic lingua franca: Ways of achieving communicative effectiveness? *Journal of Pragmatics, 43*(4), 950–964.

Björkman, Beyza. 2013. *English as an Academic Lingua Franca*. Berlin: De Gruyter Mouton.

Block, David. 2006. Identity in applied linguistics. In Tope Omoniyi and Goodith White (eds.), *The Sociolinguistics of Identity* (pp. 34–49). London: Continuum.

Block, David. 2012. Economising globalisation and identity in applied linguistics in neoliberal times. In David Block, John Gray and Marnie Holborow (eds.), *Neoliberalism and Applied Linguistics* (pp. 56–85). Abingdon: Routledge.

Blommaert, Jan. 2010. *The sociolinguistics of globalization*. Cambridge: Cambridge University Press.

Blommaert, Jan. 2013. *Ethnography, superdiversity and linguistic landscapes: chronicles of complexity*. Bristol: Multilingual Matters.

Blum-Kulka, Shoshana and Olshtain, Elite. 1984. Requests and apologies: a cross-cultural study of speech act realisation patterns (CCSARP). *Applied Linguistics, 5*(3), 196–213.

Boas, Franz. 1911. Language and thought. In Joyce Merrukk Valdes (ed.), *Culture bound* (pp. 5–7). Cambridge: Cambridge University Press.

Bolton, Kingsley. 2008. English in Asia, Asian Englishes, and the issue of proficiency. *English Today, 24*(2), 3–12.

Bourdieu, Pierre. 1991. *Language and Symbolic Power*. Cambridge: Polity Press.

Brown, Penelope, and Levinson, Stephen C. 1987. *Politeness: some universals in language usage*. Cambridge: Cambridge University Press.

Brubaker, Rogers and Cooper, Frederick. 2000. Beyond "identity". *Theory and Society, 29*(1), 1–47.

Brumfit, Christopher. 1995. Teacher professionalism and research. In Guy Cook and Barbara Seidlhofer (eds.), *Principle and practice in applied linguistics*. Oxford: Oxford University Press.

Brumfit, Christopher. 2001. *Individual freedom in language teaching: helping learners to develop a dialect of their own*. Oxford: Oxford University Press.

Brumfit, Christopher. 2006. A European perspective on language as liminality. In Clare Mar-Molinero and Patrick Stevenson (eds.), *Language Ideologies, Policies and Practices: Language and the Future of Europe* (pp. 28–43). Basingstoke: Palgrave Macmillan.

Brumfit, Christopher, and Carter, Ronald. 1986. *Literature and Language Teaching*. Oxford: Oxford University Press.

Butler, Judith. 1990. *Gender trouble*. London: Routledge.

Bybee, Joan. 2006. From usage to grammar: the mind's response to repetition. *Language, 82*(2), 711–733.

Byram, Michael. 1991. Teaching culture and language: towards an integrated model. In M. Byram and D. Buttjes (Eds.), *Mediating Languages and Cultures* (pp. 17–32). Clevedon: Multilingual Matters.

Byram, Michael. 1997. *Teaching and assessing intercultural communicative competence*. Clevedon: Multilingual Matters.

Byram, Michael. 2008. *From foreign language education to education for intercultural citizenship: essays and reflections*. Clevedon: Multilingual Matters Ltd.

Byram, Michael. 2010. Linguistics and cultural education for *bildung* and citizenship. *The Modern Language Journal, 94*(ii), 317–321.

Byram, Michael. 2012a. Conceptualizing intercultural (communicative) competence and intercultural citizenship. In Jane Jackson (ed.), *The Routledge handbook of language and intercultural communication* (pp. 85–97). London: Routledge.

Byram, Michael. 2012b. Language awareness and (critical) cultural awareness – relationships, comparisons and contrasts. *Language Awareness: Special Issue: Awareness Matters: Language, Culture, Literacy. Selected Papers from the 10th International Conference of the Association for Language Awareness, University of Kassel, July 2010, 21*(1), 5–13.

Byram, Michael, and Buttjes, Dieter (eds.). 1991. *Mediating Languages and Cultures*. Clevedon: Multilingual Matters.

Byram, Michael, and Fleming, Michael (eds.). 1998. *Language Learning in Intercultural Perspective*. Cambridge: Cambridge University Press.

Byram, Michael, and Grundy, Peter (eds.). 2003. *Context and culture in language teaching and learning*. Clevedon: Multilingual Matters.

Byram, Michael, Nichols, Adam, and Stevens, David (eds.). 2001. *Developing intercultural competence in practice*. Clevedon: Multilingual Matters.

Cameron, Deborah. 2002. Globalization and the teaching of 'communication skills'. In David Block and Deborah Cameron (Eds.), *Globalization and language teaching* (pp. 67–82). London: Routledge.

Canagarajah, Suresh. 1999. *Resisting linguistic imperialism in English teaching*. Oxford: Oxford University Press.

Canagarajah, Suresh. 2007. Lingua Franca English, Multilingual Communities, and Language Acquisition. *The Modern Language Journal, 91*(5), 923–939.

Canagarajah, Suresh. 2013a. *Literacy as Translingual Practice: Between Communities and Classrooms*. London: Routledge.

Canagarajah, Suresh. 2013b. *Translingual Practice: Global Englishes and Cosmopolitan Relations*. London: Routledge.

Canagarajah, Suresh (ed.). 2005. *Reclaiming the local in language policy and practice.* Mahwah, N.J.; London: L. Erlbaum Associates.

Canale, Michael. 1983. From communicative competence to communicative language pedagogy. In J. Richards and R. Schmidt (Eds.), *Language and communication* (pp. 2–27). Harlow: Longman.

Canale, Michael, and Swain, Merrill. 1980. Theoretical bases of communicative approaches to second language teaching and testing. *Applied Linguistics 1*(1), 1–47.

Celce-Murcia, Marianne, Dörnyei, Zolta, and Thurrell, Sarah. 1995. Communicative Competence: A Pedagogically Motivated Model with Content Specifications. *Issues in Applied Linguistics, 6*(2), 5–35.

Chan, Jim. 2014. An evaluation of the pronunciation target in Hong Kong's ELT curriculum and materials: influences from WE and ELF? *Journal of English as a Lingua Franca, 3*(1), 145–170.

Chomsky, Noam. 1965. *Aspects of the theory of syntax.* Cambridge, Mass.: MIT Press.

Chomsky, Noam. 1986. *Knowledge of language: its nature, origin, and use.* London: Praeger.

Cilliers, Paul. 1998. *Complexity and postmodernism.* London: Routledge.

Clanfield, Lindsay. 2009. *Global.* Basingstoke: Macmillan.

Cogo, Alessia. 2009. Accommodating difference in ELF conversation. In Anna Mauranen and Elina Ranta (eds.), *English as a lingua franca: studies and findings* (pp. 254–273). Newcastle: Cambridge Scholars Press.

Cogo, Alessia. 2010. Strategic use and perceptions of English as a Lingua Franca. *Poznań Studies in Contemporary Linguistics, 46*(3), 295–312.

Cogo, Alessia. 2012. ELF and super-diversity: a case study of ELF multilingual practices from a business context. *Journal of English as a Lingua Franca, 1*(2), 287–313.

Cogo, Alessia, and Dewey, Martin. 2006. Efficiency in ELF communication: From pragmatic motives to lexico-grammatical innovation. *NJES, 5*(2).

Cogo, Alessia, and Dewey, Martin. 2012. *Analysing English as a Lingua Franca: A corpus-based investigation.* London: Continuum.

Cohen, Louise, Manion, Lawrence, and Morrison, Keith. 2011. *Research Methods in Education* (7th ed.). London: Routledge/Falmer.

Cook, Guy. 2012. ELF and translation and interpreting: common ground, common interest, common cause. *Journal of English as a Lingua Franca, 1*(2), 241–262.

Cook, Vivian. 1991. The poverty-of-the-stimulus argument and multi-competence'. *Second Language Research, 7*(2), 103–117.

Cook, Vivian. 1999. Going beyond the native speaker in language teaching. *TESOL Quarterly, 33*(2), 185–209.

Cook, Vivian. 2005. Multi-competence: Black Hole or Wormhole? Retrieved 13 July 2014, from http://homepage.ntlworld.com/vivian.c/Writings/Papers/SLRF05.htm

Cook, Vivian. 2007. The goals of ELT: reproducing native-speakers or promoting multi-competence among second language users? In Jim Cummins and Chris Davison (eds.), *Handbook on English Language Teaching* (pp. 237–248): Kluwer.

Cook, Vivian. 2012. Multi-competence. Retrieved 18 July, 2013, from http://homepage.ntlworld.com/vivian.c/Writings/Papers/MCentry.htm

Cook, Vivian (ed.). 2002. *Portraits of the L2 User.* Clevedon: Multilingual Matters.

Council of Europe. 2001. *Common European Framework of Reference for Languages: learning, teaching, assessment.* Cambridge: Cambridge University Press.

Csizér, Kata, and Kontra, Edit H. 2012. ELF, ESP, ENL and their effect on students' aims and beliefs: A structural equation model. *System, 40*(1), 1–10.

Dalton-Puffer, Christine. 2009. Communicative Competence and the CLIL lesson. In Y. Ruiz de Zarobe and R. M. J. Catalán (Eds.), *Content and Language Integrated Learning: Evidence from Research in* (pp. 197–214). Clevedon: Multilingual Matters.

Darasawang, Pornapit, and Watson Todd, Richard. 2012. The Effect of Policy on English Language Teaching at Secondary Schools in Thailand. In E.-L. Louw and A. Hashim (Eds.), *English in Southeast Asia: Features, Policy and Language in Use* (pp. 207–220). Amsterdam: John Benjamins.

Davis, Alan. 2003. *The native speaker: myth and reality*. Clevedon: Multilingual Matters.

Deardorff, Darla (ed.). 2009. *The Sage Handbook of Intercultural Competence*. Thousand Oaks: Sage.

Denzin, Norman K., and Lincoln, Yvonna S. 2005. *The SAGE handbook of qualitative research* (3rd ed.). Thousand Oaks; London: Sage Publications.

Dervin, Fred. 2012. Cultural identity, representation and othering. In Jane Jackson (ed.), *The Routledge handbook of language and intercultural communication* (pp. 181–194). London: Routledge.

Dervin, Fred, Gajardo, Anahy, and Lavanchy, Anne (eds.). 2011. *Politics of Interculturality*. Newcastle: Cambridge Scholars.

Deterding, David. 2013. *Misunderstandings in English as a Lingua Franca*. Berlin: De Gruyter Mouton.

Deterding, David, and Kirkpatrick, Andy. 2006. Emerging South-East Asian Englishes and intelligibility. *World Englishes, 25*(3), 391–409.

Deutscher, Guy. 2010. *Through the language glass: how words colour your world*. London: William Heinemann.

Dewey, Martin. 2007. English as a lingua franca and globalization: an interconnected perspective. *International Journal of Applied Linguistics, 17*(3), 332–354.

Dewey, Martin. 2012. Towards a post-normative approach: learning the pedagogy of ELF. *Journal of English as a Lingua Franca, 1*(1), 141–170.

Dewey, Martin. 2015. Time to wake up some dogs! Shifting the culture of language in ELT. In Yasemin Bayyurt and Samru Akcan (eds.), *Current Perspectives on Pedagogy for ELF* (pp. 121–143). Berlin: De Gruyter Mouton.

Doff, Adrian. 2011. *English Unlimited*. Cambridge: Cambridge University Press.

Dörnyei, Zoltan. 2007. *Research methods in applied linguistics*. Oxford: Oxford University Press.

Draper, John. 2012a. Reconsidering Compulsory English in Developing Countries in Asia: English in a Community of Northeast Thailand. *TESOL Quarterly, 46*(4), 777–811.

Draper, John. 2012b. Revisiting English in Thailand. *Asian EFL Journal, 14*(4), 9–38.

Driscoll, Patricia, Earl, Justine, and Cable, Carrie. 2013. The role and nature of the cultural dimension in primary modern languages. *Language, Culture and Curriculum, 26*(2), 146–160.

Duff, Patricia. 2002. The discursive co-construction of knowledge, identity, and difference: an ethnography of communication in the high school mainstream. *Applied Linguistics, 23*(3), 289–322.

Durkheim, Émile. 1964. *The division of labor in society*. New York: Free Press.

Eagleton, Terry. 2000. *The idea of culture*. Oxford: Blackwell.

Edge, Julian (ed.). 2006. *(Re)locating TESOL in the age of empire*. Basingstoke: Palgrave Macmillan.

Edwards, John Dec. 2011. *Challenges in the social life of language*. Basingstoke: Palgrave Macmillan.

Ehrenreich, Susanne. 2009. English as a lingua franca in multinational corporations: exploring business communities of practice. In Anna Mauranen and Elina Ranta (eds.), *English as a lingua franca: studies and findings* (pp. 126–151). Newcastle: Cambridge Scholars.

Ehrenreich, Susanne. 2011. The Dynamics of English as a Lingua Franca in International Business: A Language Contact Perspective. In Alasdair Archibald, Alessia Cogo, and Jenkins, Jennifer (eds.), *Latest Trends in ELF Research* (pp. 11–34). Newcastle: Cambridge Scholars.

Ehrenreich, Susanne. 2010. English as a business lingua franca in a German multinational corporation. *Journal of Business Communication, 47*(4), 408–431.

Ellis, Nick, and Larsen-Freeman, Diane. 2006. Language Emergence: Implications for Applied Linguistics – Introduction to the Special Issue. *Applied Linguistics, 27*(4), 558–589.

Ellis, Nick, and Larsen-Freeman, Diane. 2009. Constructing a Second Language: Analyses and Computational Simulations of the Emergence of Linguistic Constructions From Usage. *Language learning, 59* (Supplement 1), 90–125.

English-First. 2012. EF English Proficiency Index. Retrieved from www.ef.com/epi

ETS. 2011. Test and Score Data Summary for TOEFL Computer-Based Tests and Paper-Based Tests January 2010–December 2010 Test Data. Retrieved April, 2011, from http://www.ets.org/research/policy_research_reports/toefl-sum-10

Everett, Daniel Leonard. 2012. *Language: the cultural tool*. London: Profile.

Fairclough, Norman. 1999. Global capitalism and critical awareness of language. *Language Awareness, 8*(2), 71–83.

Fantini, Alvino E. 2007. *Exploring and Assessing Intercultural Competence*. St. Louis, MO: Center for Social Development Washington University in St. Louis.

Fantini, Alvino E. 2012. Multiple strategies for assessing intercultural communicative competence. In Jane Jackson (ed.), *The Routledge handbook of language and intercultural communication* (pp. 390–406). London: Routledge.

Feng, Anwei, Byram, Michael, and Fleming, Michael (eds.). 2009. *Becoming interculturally competent through education and training*. Bristol Multilingual Matters.

Firth, Alan. 1996. The discursive accomplishment of normality: on "lingua franca" English and conversational analysis. *Journal of Pragmatics* (26), 237–259.

Firth, Alan. 2009. The lingua franca factor. *Intercultural pragmatics, 6*(2), 147–170.

Foley, Joseph. 2005. English in Thailand. *RELC Journal, 36*(2), 223–234.

Foley, Joseph. 2007. English as a global language: my two Satangs' worth. *RELC, 38*(1), 7–17.

Galloway, Nicola. 2013. Global Englishes and English Language Teaching (ELT) – Bridging the gap between theory and practice in a Japanese context. *System, 41*(3), 786–803.

Galloway, Nicola, and Rose, Heath. 2013. "They envision going to New York, not Jakarta": the differing attitudes toward ELF of students, teaching assistants, and instructors in an English-medium business program in Japan. *Journal of English as a Lingua Franca, 2*(2), 229–253.

Galloway, Nicola, and Rose, Heath. 2015. *Introducing Global Englishes*. Abingdon: Routledge.

Gee, James Paul. 2008. *Social Linguistics and Literacies: Ideology in Discourses*. Abingdon: Routledge.

Geertz, Clifford. 1973. *The Interpretation of Cultures*. New York: Basic Books.

Geertz, Clifford. 1980. *Local knowledge: further essays in interpretive anthropology*. New York: Basic Books.

Gell-Mann, Murray. 1994. *The quark and the jaguar: adventures in the simple and the complex*. London: Little Brown.

Giles, Howard. 2009. The process of communication accommodation. In Nikolas Coupland and Adam Jaworski (eds.), *The new sociolinguistics reader* (pp. 276–286). Basingstoke: Palgrave Macmillan.

Giles, Howard, Bonilla, Douglas and Speer, Rebecca. 2012. Acculturating intergroup vitalities, accommodation and contact. In Jane Jackson (ed.), *The Routledge handbook of language and intercultural communication* (pp. 244–259). London: Routledge.

Glass, Tom. 2009. Why Thais write to other Thais in English. *World Englishes, 28*(4), 532–543.

Gleick, James. 1998. *Chaos: Making a New Science.* London: Vintage.

Glisan, Eileen. 2012. National Standards: Research into practice. *Language Teaching, 45*(4), 515–526.

Goodenough, Ward. 1964. Cultural anthropology and linguistics. In D. Hymes (Ed.), *Language in culture and society* (pp. 36–39). New York Harper and Row.

Gray, John. 2010. *The Construction of English: Culture, Consumerism and Promotion in the ELT Global Coursebook.* Basingstoke: Palgrave Macmillan.

Gray, John. 2012. Neoliberalism, celebrity and 'aspirational content' in English language teaching textbooks for the global market. In David Block, John Gray and Marnie Holborow (eds.), *Neoliberalism and Applied Linguistics* (pp. 86–113). Abingdon: Routledge.

Gu, Qing. 2009. Editorial. *Language and Intercultural Communication, 9*(3), 139–143.

Gudykunst, William B. 2004. *Bridging Differences: Effective Intergroup Communication* (Fourth ed.). London: Sage.

Guido, Maria Grazia. 2012. ELF authentication and accommodation strategies in crosscultural immigration encounters. *Journal of English as a Lingua Franca, 1*(2), 219–240.

Guilherme, Manuela. 2002. *Critical Citizens for an Intercultural World.* Clevedon: Multilingual Matters.

Guilherme, Manuela. 2012. Critical language and intercultural communication pedagogy. In Jane Jackson (ed.), *The Routledge handbook of language and intercultural communication* (pp. 357–371). London: Routledge.

Guillot, Marie-Noëlle. 2012. Cross-cultural communication at a theoretical and methodological crossroads: cultural and media interfaces. *Language and Intercultural Communication, 12*(4), 277–283.

Gumperz, John. 1982. *Discourse strategies.* Cambridge: Cambridge University Press.

Gumperz, John. 1992. Contextualization and understanding. In Alessandro Duranti, and Charles Goodwin (eds.), *Rethinking context* (pp. 229–254). Cambridge: Cambridge University Press.

Gumperz, John. 2001. Interactional sociolinguistics: A personal perspective. In Deborah Schriffin, Deborah Tannen and Heidi Hamilton (eds.), *The handbook of discourse analysis* (pp. 215–228). Oxford: Blackwell.

Gumperz, John J. and Hymes, Dell. 1986. *Directions in sociolinguistics: the ethnography of communication.* Oxford: Basil Blackwell.

Gumperz, John, and Levinson, Stephen (eds.). 1996. *Rethinking Linguistic Relativity.* Cambridge: Cambridge University Press.

Günthner, Susanne. 2000. Argumentation and Resulting Problems in the Negotiation of Rapport in a German-Chinese Conversation. In Helen Spencer-Oatey (ed.). *Culturally Speaking* (pp. 217–239). London: Continuum.

Guth, Sarah, and Helm, Francesca (eds.). 2010. *Telecollaboration 2.0: Language, Literacies and Intercultural Learning in the 21st Century.* Bern: Peter Lang.

Hall, Christopher. 2013. Cognitive Contributions to Plurilithic Views of English and Other Languages. *Applied Linguistics, 34*(2), 211–231.

Hall, Edward T. 1959. *The Silent Language*. New York: Doubleday Anchor.

Hall, Edward T. 1966. *The Hidden Dimension*. New York: Doubleday Anchor.

Hall, Edward T. 1976. *Beyond Culture*. New York: Doubleday Anchor.

Hall, Stuart. 1995. Who needs identity. In Stuart Hall (ed.), *Questions of cultural identity* (pp. 1–17). London: Sage.

Hall, Stuart. 1997. The local and the global: globalisation and ethnicity. In Anne McClintock (ed.), *Dangerous Liaisons: Gender, Nation and Postcolonial Perspectives* (pp. 173–187). Minneapolis: University of Minnesota Press.

Halliday, Michael A. K. 1975. *Learning how to mean*. London: Edward Arnold.

Halliday, Michael A. K. 1979. *Language as social semiotic*. Victoria: Edward Arnold.

Halliday, Michael A. K. 1985. *An introduction to functional grammar*. London: Arnold.

Hammersley, Martyn, and Atkinson, Paul. 2007. *Ethnography: principles in practice* (3rd ed.). London: Routledge.

Hannerz, Ulf. 1996. *Transnational connections: culture, people, places*. London: Routledge.

Harris, Roy. 1981. *The Language Myth*. London: Duckworth.

Harris, Roy. 1998. Making sense of communicative competence. In Roy Harris and George Wolf (eds.), *Integrational linguistics* (pp. 27–45). Oxford: Elsevier.

Harris, Roy, and Wolf, George (eds.). 1998. *Integrational linguistics*. Oxford: Elsevier.

Hayes, David. 2010. Language learning, teaching and educational reform in rural Thailand: an English teacher's perspective. *Asia Pacific Journal of Education, 30*(3), 305–319.

Higgins, Christina. 2007. Constructing membership in the in-group: affiliation and resistance among urban Tanzanians. *Pragmatics, 17*(1), 49–70.

Hino, Nobuyuki, and Oda, Setsuko. 2015. Integrated practice in teaching English as an international language (IPTEIL): A classroom ELF pedagogy in Japan. In Yasemin Bayyurt and Samru Akcan (eds.), *Current Perspectives on Pedagogy for ELF* (pp. 35–50). Berlin: De Gruyter Mouton.

Hofstede, Geert H. 1984. *Culture's Consequences: International Differences in Work-Related Values* (2nd ed.). Beverly Hills: Sage.

Hofstede, Geert H. 1991. *Cultures and organizations: software of the mind*. London: McGraw-Hill.

Hofstede, Geert H., Hofstede, Gert Jan, and Minkov, Michael. 2010. *Cultures and organizations: software of the mind: intercultural cooperation and its importance for survival* (3rd ed.). New York; London: McGraw-Hill.

Holland, Dorothy, and Quinn, Naomi (eds.). 1987. *Cultural Models in Language and Thought*. Cambridge: Cambridge University Press.

Holland, John Henry. 1998. *Emergence: From Chaos to Order*. Redwood City, California: Addison-Wesley.

Holliday, Adrian. 2005. *The struggle to teach English as an international language*. Oxford: Oxford University Press.

Holliday, Adrian. 2009. The role of culture in English language education: key challenges. *Language and Intercultural Communication, 9*(3), 144–155.

Holliday, Adrian. 2010. Cultural descriptions as political cultural acts: an exploration. *Language and Intercultural Communication, 10*(3), 259–272.

Holliday, Adrian. 2011. *Intercultural Communication and Ideology*. London: Sage.

Holliday, Adrian. 2013. *Understanding intercultural communication: Negotiating a grammar of culture*. Abingdon: Routledge.

Holliday, Adrian, Hyde, Martin, and Kullman, John. 2010. *Intercultural Communication* (2nd ed.). London: Routledge.

Hopper, Paul. 1987. Emergent grammar. *Proceedings of the thirteenth annual meeting of the Berkeley Linguistics Society, 13*, 139–157.

Hopper, Paul. 1998. Emergent Grammar. In Michael Tomasello (ed.), *The New Psychology of Language* (pp. 155–175). London: Lawrence Erlbaum.

House, Juliane. 1999. Misunderstanding in intercultural communication: Interactions in English as a lingua franca and the myth of mutual intelligibility. In Claus Gnutzmann (ed.), *Teaching and Learning English as a Global Language* (pp. 73–89.). Tübingen: Stauffenburg.

House, Juliane. 2002. Developing pragmatic competence in English as a lingua franca. In Karlfried Knapp and Christiane Meierkord (eds.), *Lingua franca communication* (pp. 245–267). Frankfurt am Main: P. Lang.

House, Juliane. 2003. English as a lingua franca: A threat to multilingualism. *Journal of Sociolinguistics, 7*(4), 556–578.

House, Juliane. 2009. Introduction: The pragmatics of English as a Lingua Franca. *Intercultural pragmatics, 6*(2), 141–145.

House, Juliane. 2014. English as a global lingua franca: A threat to multilingual communication and translation? *Language Teaching, 47*(3), 363–376.

Huebner, Thom. 2006. Bangkok's Linguistic Landscapes: Environmental Print, Codemixing and Language Change. *International Journal of Multilingualism, 3*(1), 31–51.

Hülmbauer, Cornelia. 2009. "We don't take the right way. We just take the way that we think you will understand" – The shifting relationship between correctness and effectiveness in ELF. In Anna Mauranen and Elina Ranta (eds.), *English as a lingua franca: studies and findings* (pp. 323–347). Newcastle: Cambridge Scholars.

Hülmbauer, Cornelia. 2013. From within and without: the virtual and the plurilingual in ELF. *Journal of English as a Lingua Franca, 2*(1), 47–74.

Hurn, Brian, and Tomalin, Brian. 2013. *Cross-cultural communication: theory and practice.* Basingstoke: Palgrave Macmillan.

Hymes, Dell. 1972. On communicative competence. In J. B. Pride and Janet Holmes (eds.), *Sociolinguistics* (pp. 269–293). Harmondsworth: Penguin.

Jackson, Jane. 2012a. Introduction and overview. In Jane Jackson (ed.), *The Routledge handbook of language and intercultural communication* (pp. 1–13). London: Routledge.

Jackson, Jane. 2014. *Introducing Language and Intercultural Communication.* Abingdon: Routledge.

Jackson, Jane. (ed.). 2012b. *The Routledge handbook of language and intercultural communication.* London: Routledge.

Jandt, Fred E. 2010. *Intercultural communication: an introduction* (Sixth Edition). Thousand Oaks: Sage.

Javier, Eljee. 2010. The foreign-ness of native speaking teachers of colour. In David Nunan and Julie Choi (eds.), *Language and culture: reflective narratives and the emergence of identity* (pp. 97–102). London: Routledge.

Jenkins, Jennifer. 2000. *The phonology of English as an international language: new models, new norms, new goals.* Oxford: OUP.

Jenkins, Jennifer. 2006a. Current perspectives on teaching world Englishes and English as a lingua franca. *TESOL Quarterly, 40*(1), 157–181.

Jenkins, Jennifer. 2006b. The spread of EIL: a testing time for testers. *ELT Journal, 60*(1), 42–50.

Jenkins, Jennifer. 2007. *English as a Lingua Franca: attitude and identity*. Oxford: Oxford University Press.

Jenkins, Jennifer. 2012. English as a Lingua Franca from the classroom to the classroom. *ELT Journal, 66*(4), 486–494.

Jenkins, Jennifer. 2014. *English as a Lingua Franca in the International University. The politics of academic English language policy*. London: Routledge.

Jenkins, Jennifer. 2015. *Global Englishes: a resource book for students* (Third ed.). London: Routledge.

Jenkins, Jennifer, Cogo, Alessia, and Dewey, Martin. 2011. Review of developments in research into English as a Lingua Franca. *Language Teaching, 44*(3), 281–315.

Jenks, Chris. 2005. *Culture* (2nd ed.). London; New York: Routledge.

Jenks, Christopher. 2012. Doing Being Reprehensive: Some Interactional Features of English as a Lingua Franca in a Chat Room. *Applied Linguistics, 33*(4), 386–405.

Jenks, Christopher. 2013. Are you an ELF? The relevance of ELF as an equitable social category in online intercultural communication. *Language and intercultural communication: Special Issue: The discourse of ethics and equity, 13*(1), 95–108.

Jin, Lixian, and Cortazzi, Martin. 1998. The culture the learner brings: a bridge or a barrier. In Michael Byram and Michael Fleming (eds.), *Language learning in intercultural perspective* (pp. 98–118). Cambridge: Cambridge University Press.

Jones, Brian. 1995. *Exploring otherness – An approach to cultural awareness*. London: CILT.

Joseph, John. 2004. *Language and Identity*. Basingstoke: Palgrave Macmillan.

Kachru, Braj. 1990. *The alchemy of English*. Illinois: University of Illinois.

Kachru, Braj. 2005. *Asian Englishes: beyond the canon*. New Delhi: Oxford University Press.

Kachru, Braj, and Nelson, Cecile. 2006. World Englishes. In Sandra McKay and Nancy H. Hornberger (eds.), *Sociolinguistics and Language Teaching*. Cambridge: Cambridge University Press.

Kalocsai, Karolina. 2009. Erasmus exchange students: A behind-the-scenes view into an ELF community of practice. *Apples – Journal of Applied Language Studies, 3*(1), 25–49.

Kalocsai, Karolina. 2014. *Communities of practice and English as a lingua franca: A study of Erasmus students in a Central-European context*. Berlin: DeGruyter Mouton.

Kaur, Jagdish. 2009. Pre-empting problems of understanding in English as a lingua franca. In Anna Mauranen and Elina Ranta (eds.), *English as a lingua franca: studies and findings* (pp. 107–123). Newcastle: Cambridge Scholars Press.

Kaur, Jagdish. 2011. "Doing being a Language Expert": The Case of the ELF Speaker. In Archibald, Alasdair, Alessia Cogo, and Jenkins, Jennifer (eds.), *Latest Trends in ELF Research* (pp. 53–76). Newcastle: Cambridge Scholars.

Kecskes, Istvan. 2012. Interculturality and intercultural pragmatics. In Jane Jackson (ed.), *The Routledge handbook of language and intercultural communication* (pp. 67–84). London: Routledge.

Keyuravong, Sonthida. 2010. Insights from Thailand. In Richard Johnstone (ed.), *Learning through English: Policies, challenges and prospects* (pp. 69–95). Malaysia: British Council East Asia.

Kirkpatrick, Andy. 2003. English as an ASEAN lingua franca: Implications for research and language teaching. *Asian Englishes, 6*(2), 82–91.

Kirkpatrick, Andy. 2007. *World Englishes: implications for international communication and English language teaching*. Cambridge: Cambridge University Press.

Kirkpatrick, Andy. 2010a. *English as a lingua franca in ASEAN*. Hong Kong: Hong Kong University Press.

Kirkpatrick, Andy. 2010b. Researching English as a lingua franca in Asia: the Asian Corpus of English (ACE) project. *Asian Englishes, 13*(1).

Kirkpatrick, Andy. 2011. English as an Asian lingua franca and the multilingual model of ELT. *Language Teaching, 44*(2), 212–224.

Kirkpatrick, Andy. (ed.). 2012. *The Routledge Handbook of World Englishes*. Abingdon: Routledge.

Kitazawa, Mariko. 2013. *Approaching Conceptualisations of English in East Asian Contexts: Ideas, Ideology, and Identification*. Unpublished Thesis, University of Southampton, Southampton.

Klimpfinger, Theresa. 2009. "She's mixing the two languages together" – Forms and functions of code switching in English as a lingua franca In Mauranen, Anna and Elina Ranta (eds.), *English as a lingua franca: studies and findings* (pp. 348–371). Newcastle: Cambridge Scholars Press.

Kormos, Judit, Kiddle, Thom, and Csizér, Kata. 2011. Systems of Goals, Attitudes, and Self-related Beliefs in Second-Language-Learning Motivation. *Applied Linguistics 32*(5), 495–516.

Kosonen, K. 2008. Literacy in Local Languages in Thailand: Language Maintenance in a Globalised World. *International Journal of Bilingual Education and Bilingualism, 11*(2), 170–188.

Kramsch, Claire. 1993. *Context and culture in language teaching*. Oxford: Oxford University Press.

Kramsch, Claire. 1998. *Language and culture*. Oxford: Oxford University Press.

Kramsch, Claire. 2009. *The multilingual subject*. Oxford: Oxford University Press.

Kramsch, Claire. 2010. The symbolic dimensions of the intercultural. *Language Teaching*, 1–14.

Kramsch, Claire, and Sullivan, Patricia. 1996. Appropriate pedagogy. *ELT Journal, 50*(3), 199–212.

Kramsch, Claire, and Uryu, Michiko. 2012. Intercultural contact, hybridity and third space. In Jane Jackson (ed.), *The Routledge handbook of language and intercultural communication* (pp. 211–225). London: Routledge.

Kumar, Krishan. 2003. *The Making of English National Identity*. Cambridge: Cambridge University Press.

Kumaravadivelu, B. 2001. Towards a Postmodern Pedagogy. *TESOL Quarterly, 35*(4), 537–560.

Kumaravadivelu, B. 2003. *Beyond methods: macrostrategies for language teaching*. New Haven: Yale University Press.

Kumaravadivelu, B. 2006. TESOL Methods: Changing Tracks, Challenging Trends. *TESOL Quarterly, 40*(1), 59–81.

Kumaravadivelu, B. 2008. *Cultural globalization and language education*. New Haven, Conn.; London: Yale University Press.

Kumaravadivelu, B. 2012. *Language teacher education for a global society: a modular model for knowing, analyzing, recognizing, doing, and seeing*. Abingdon, Oxon: Routledge.

Kvale, Steinar, and Brinkmann, Svend. 2009. *InterViews: Learning the Craft of Qualitative Research Interviewing*. London: Sage.

Larsen-Freeman, Diane. 2002. Language acquisition and language use from a chaos/complexity theory perspective. In C. Kramsch (ed.), *Language acquisition and language socialization: Ecological perspectives* (pp. 33–46). London: Continuum.

Larsen-Freeman, Diane. 2006. The Emergence of Complexity, Fluency, and Accuracy in the Oral and Written Production of Five Chinese Learners of English. *Applied Linguistics, 27*(4), 590–619.

Larsen-Freeman, Diane. 2011. A complexity theory approach to second language development/acquisition. In D. Atkinson (ed.), *Alternative approaches to second language acquisition* (pp. 48–72). Abingdon: Routledge.

Larsen-Freeman, Diane. 2013. *A Successful Union: Linking ELF with CAS.* Paper presented at the 6th International Conference of English as a Lingua Franca.

Larsen-Freeman, Diane, and Cameron, Lynne. 2008. *Complex systems and applied linguistics.* Oxford: Oxford University Press.

Lavanchy, Anne, Gajardo, Anahy, and Dervin, Fred. 2011. Interculturality at Stake. In Fred Dervin, Anahy Gajardo and Anne Lavanchy (eds.), *Politics of Interculturality* (pp. 1–24). Newcastle: Cambridge Scholars.

Leech, Geoffrey. 1983. *Principles of Pragmatics.* London: Longman.

Leech, Geoffrey. 2005. Politeness: Is there an East-West Divide? *Journal of Foreign Languages, 6.* Retrieved from http://www.lancaster.ac.uk/fass/doc_library/linguistics/leechg/leech_2007_politeness.pdf

Leung, Constant. 2005. Convivial communication: recontextualizing communicative competence. *International Journal of Applied Linguistics, 15*(2), 121–144.

Leung, Constant. 2013. The "social" in English Language Teaching: abstracted norms versus situated enactments. *Journal of English as a Lingua Franca, 2*(2), 283–313.

Lévi-Strauss, Claude. 1966. *The savage mind (La penseé sauvage).* London: Weidenfeld and Nicolson.

Lewis, Tim, and Walker, Lesley (eds.). 2003. *Autonomous Language Learning in Tandem.* Sheffield: Academy Electronic Publications Limited.

Liddicoat, Antony, and Scarino, Angela. 2013. *Intercultural Language Teaching and Learning.* London: Wiley-Blackwell.

Lincoln, Yvonna S., and Guba, Egon G. 1985. *Naturalistic inquiry.* Beverly Hills, Calif.: Sage Publications.

Llurda, Enric. 2004. Non-native-speaker teachers and English as an International Language. *International Journal of Applied Linguistics, 14*(3), 314–323.

Llurda, Enric. 2006. *Non-native language teachers: Perceptions, challenges and contributions to the profession.* New York: Springer.

Louhiala-Salminen, Leena, and Kankaanranta, Anna. 2011. Professional Communication in a Global Business Context: The Notion of Global Communicative Competence. *IEEE Transactions on Professional Communication, 54*(3), 244–262.

Lu, Peih-ying, and Corbett, John. 2012. An intercultural approach to second language education and citizenship. In Jane Jackson (ed.), *The Routledge handbook of language and intercultural communication* (pp. 325–329). London: Routledge.

Lucy, John A. 1992. *Language diversity and thought: a reformulation of the linguistic relativity hypothesis.* Cambridge: Cambridge University Press.

Luk, Jasmine. 2012. Teachers' ambivalence in integrating culture with EFL teaching in Hong Kong. *Language Culture and Curriculum, 25*(3), 249–264.

Mar-Molinero, Clare. 2004. Spanish as a world language: language and identity in a global era. *Spanish in context, 1*(1), 3–20.

Martin, Judith, Nakayama, Thomas, and Carbaugh, Donal. 2012. The history and development of the study of intercultural communication and applied linguistics. In Jane Jackson (ed.),

The Routledge handbook of language and intercultural communication (pp. 17–36). London: Routledge.

Matsuda, Amy (ed.). 2012. *Principles and Practices of Teaching English as an International Language*. Clevedon: Multilingual Matters.

Matsuda, Amy, and Friedrich, Paul. 2012. Selecting an instructional variety for an EIL curriculum In Amy Matsuda (ed.), *Principles and Practices of Teaching English as an International Language* (pp. 17–29). Clevedon: Multilingual Matters.

Matsumoto, Yoshiko. 1988. Reexamination of the universality of face: politeness phenomena in Japanese. *Journal of Pragmatics, 12*, 403–426.

Mauranen, Anna. 2006. A rich domain of ELF – the ELFA corpus of academic discourse. *The Nordic Journal of English Studies, 5*(2), 145–159.

Mauranen, Anna. 2012. *Exploring ELF: academic English shaped by non-native speakers*. Cambridge: Cambridge University Press.

Mauranen, Anna, and Ranta, Elena (eds.). 2009. *English as a lingua franca: studies and findings*. Newcastle: Cambridge Scholars Press.

McArthur, Tom. 2003. English as an Asian language. *English Today, 19*(2), 19–22.

McKay, Sandra, and Bokhorst-Heng, Wendy D. 2008. *International English in its sociolinguistic contexts: towards a socially sensitive EIL pedagogy*. London: Routledge.

McNamara, Tim. 1995. Modelling Performance: Opening Pandora's Box. *Applied Linguistics, 16*(2), 159–179.

Meierkord, Christiane. 2002. 'Language stripped bare' or 'linguistic masala'? Culture in lingua franca communication. In Karlfried Knapp and Christiane Meierkord (eds.), *Lingua franca communication* (pp. 109–134). Frankfurt am Main: P. Lang.

Miles, Matthew, Huberman, Michael and Saldaña, Johnny. 2014. *Qualitative data analysis: A methods sourcebook* (Third ed.). London: Sage.

Miller, John H., and Page, Scott E. 2007. *Complex adaptive systems: an introduction to computational models of social life*. Princeton, N.J.; Oxford: Princeton University Press.

Milroy, James, and Milroy, Lesley. 2012. *Authority in language: investigating standard English* (4th ed.). Abingdon, Oxon; New York: Routledge.

Mimatsu, Toshie. 2011. ELF versus EFL: Teaching English for International Understanding in Japan. In Alasdair Archibald, Alessia Cogo, and Jenkins, Jennifer (eds.), *Latest Trends in ELF Research* (pp. 251–268). Newcastle: Cambridge Scholars Press.

Ministry of Education China. 2011. *Revision: [National English Curriculum Standard for Compulsory]*. Beijing: Beijing Normal University Press.

Ministry of Education Thailand. 2006. *Key Facts on Thai Education, 2005*. Retrieved from http://www.moe.go.th/English/nu/stat.htm.

Morgan, Carol, and Cain, Albane. 2000. *Foreign Language and Culture Learning from a Dialogic Perspective*. Clevedon: Multilingual Matters.

Mori, Junko. 2003. The construction of interculturality: A study of initial encounters between Japanese and American students. *Research on Language and Social Interaction, 36*(2), 143–184.

Mortensen, Janus. 2013. Notes on English used as a lingua franca as an object of study. *Journal of English as a Lingua Franca, 2*(1), 25–46.

Mühlhäusler, Peter. 1996. *Linguistic ecology: Language change and linguistic imperialism in the Pacific region*. London: Routledge.

Murata, Kumiko. 2012. Introduction: reconsidering research paradigms from an ELF perspective. *Waseda Working Papers in ELF, 1*, 1–8.

Murata, Kumiko, and Jenkins, Jennifer (eds.). 2009. *Global Englishes in Asian contexts: current and future debates*. Basingstoke: Palgrave Macmillan.

National Identity Borad. 2000. *Thailand into the 2000s*. Bangkok: Office of the Prime Minister.

Nation. 2013, Feb 28 2013. Thai's score lowest in TOEFL. *The Nation*. Retrieved from http://www.nationmultimedia.com/national/Thais-score-lowest-in-TOEFL-30200874.html

Newton, Jonathan, Yates, Eric, Shearn, Sandra, and Nowitzki, Werner. 2009. *Intercultural Communicative Language Teaching: Implications for Effective Teaching and Learning*. Wellington: Ministry of Education.

Nishizaka, Aug. 1995. The interactive constitution of interculturality: How to be a Japanese with words. *Human Studies 18*(2), 301–326.

Norton, Bonny. 2000. *Identity and Language Learning*. Harlow, Essex: Pearson Education.

Norton, Bonny. 2010. Language and identity. In Nancy. H. Hornberger and Sandra. McKay (eds.), *Sociolinguistics and language education* (pp. 349–369). Bristol: Multilingual Matters.

Nunan, David. 1991. *Language teaching methodology: a textbook for teachers*. New York; London: Prentice-Hall.

Nunan, David. 2003. The impact of English as a global language on educational policies and practices in the Asia-Pacific region. *TESOL Quarterly, 37*(4), 589–613.

Nunan, David, and Choi, Julie. 2010. *Language and culture: reflective narratives and the emergence of identity*. London: Routledge.

O'Dowd, Robert. 2011. Online foreign language interaction: Moving from the periphery to the core of foreign language education? *Language Teaching, 44*(3), 368–380.

O'Regan, John. 2014. English as a lingua franca: an immanent critique. *Applied Linguistics, 35*(5), 533–552.

O'Sullivan, Kerry, and Tajaroensuk, Songphorn. 1997. *Thailand: A handbook in intercultural communication*. Sydney: NCELTR Macquarie University.

Ochs, Eleanor. 1996. Linguistic resources for socializing humanity. In John Gumperz and Stephen Levinson (eds.), *Rethinking Linguistic relativity*. Cambridge: Cambridge University Press.

Ochs, Eleanor. 2002. Becoming a speaker of culture. In Claire Kramsch (ed.), *Language acquisition and language socialization: Ecological perspectives* (pp. 99–120). London: Continuum.

Tope Omoniyi, and Goodith White (eds.). 2006. *The Sociolinguistics of Identity*. London: Bloomsbury Academic.

Paul, Gee James. 2008. *Social Linguistics and Literacies: Ideology in Discourses*. Abingdon: Routledge.

Pavlenko, Aneta, and Blackledge, Adrian. 2004. *Negotiation of identities in multilingual contexts*. Clevedon: Multilingual Matters.

Pennycook, Alastair. 2003. Global Englishes, Rip Slyme and performativity. *Journal of Sociolinguistics, 7*(4), 513–533.

Pennycook, Alastair. 2007. *Global Englishes and transcultural flows*. London: Routledge.

Pennycook, Alastair. 2010. *Language as a local practice*. London: Routledge.

Pennycook, Alastair. 2012. *Language and Mobility: Unexpected Places*. Bristol: Multilingual Matters.

Phan, Le Ha. 2008. *Teaching English as an international language: identity, resistance and negotiation*. Clevedon: Multilingual Matters.

Phan, Le Ha. 2009. English as an international language: international student and identity formation. *Language and Intercultural Communication, 9*(3), 201–214.

Phillipson, Robert. 1992. *Linguistic imperialism*. Oxford: Oxford University Press.

Phipps, Alison M., and Guilherme, Manuela. 2004a. *Critical pedagogy: political approaches to language and intercultural communication*. Clevedon: Multilingual Matters.

Phipps, Alison M., and Guilherme, Manuela. 2004b. Introduction: Why languages and intercultural communication are never just neutral. In Alison M. Phipps and Manuela Guilherme (eds.), *Critical pedagogy: political approaches to language and intercultural communication* (pp. 1–6). Clevedon: Multilingual Matters.

Piller, Ingrid. 2011. *Intercultural communication: a critical introduction*. Edinburgh: Edinburgh University Press.

Pitzl, Marie-Luise. 2005. Non-understanding in English as a lingua franca: Examples from a business context. *Vienna English Working Papers, 15*(2), 50–71.

Pitzl, Marie-Luise. 2009. "We should not wake up any dogs" Idiom and Metaphor in ELF. In Anna Mauranen and Elina Ranta (eds.), *English as a lingua franca: studies and findings* (pp. 298–322). Newcastle: Cambridge Scholars.

Pitzl, Marie-Luise. 2012. Creativity meets convention: idiom variation and re-metaphorization in ELF. *Journal of English as a Lingua Franca, 1*(1), 27–55.

Pölzl, Ulrike. 2003. Signalling cultural identity: the use of L1/Ln in ELF. *Vienna English Working Papers, 12*(2), 2–23. Retrieved from http://www.univie.ac.at/Anglistik/views/03_2/POEL_SGL.PDF

Pölzl, Ulrike, and Seidlhofer, Barbara. 2006. In and on their own terms: the "habitat factor" in English as a lingua franca interactions. *International Journal of the Sociology of Language* (177), 151–176.

Popper, Karl Raimund. 1992. *All life is problem-solving*. London: Routledge.

Premsrirat, Suwilai. 2014. *Endangered Languages in Thailand and SEA*. Paper presented at the Collaboration for language preservation and revitalisation in Asia, Mahidol University, Thailand (July, 2014).

Pullin Stark, Patricia. 2009. 'No joke – this is serious!' Power, solidarity and humour in business English as a Lingua Franca (BELF). In Anna Mauranen and Elina Ranta (eds.), *English as a lingua franca: studies and findings* (pp. 152–177). Newcastle: Cambridge Scholars Press.

Qiufang, Wen. 2012. English as a lingua franca: a pedagogical perspective. *Journal of English as a Lingua Franca, 1*(2), 371–376.

Quinn, Naomi. 1987. Convergent evidence for a cultural model of American marriage. In Dorothy Holland and Naomi Quinn (eds.), *Cultural Models in Language and Thought* (pp. 173–192). Cambridge: Cambridge University Press.

Rampton, Ben. 1995. *Crossing: Language and ethnicity among adolescents*. London: Longman.

Rampton, Ben. 1990. Displacing the 'native speaker': expertise, affiliation and inheritance. *ELT Journal, 44*(2), 97–101.

Rathje, Stefanie. 2007. Intercultural competence: the status and future of a controversial concept. *Language and Intercultural Communication, 7*(4), 254–266.

Richards, Keith. 2003. *Qualitative Inquiry in TESOL*. Basingstoke: Palgrave Macmillan.

Riley, Philip. 2007. *Language, culture and identity: an ethnolinguistic perspective*. London: Continuum.

Risager, Karen. 2004. Cultural Awareness. In M. Byram (ed.), *Routledge Encyclopaedia of language teaching and learning* (pp. 159–162). London: Routledge.

Risager, Karen. 2006. *Language and culture: global flows and local complexity*. Clevedon: Multilingual Matters.

Risager, Karen. 2007. *Language and culture pedagogy*. Clevedon Multilingual Matters.

Risager, Karen. 2012. Linguaculture and transnationality: the cultural dimensions of language. In Jane Jackson (ed.), *The Routledge handbook of language and intercultural communication* (pp. 101–115). London: Routledge.

Roberts, Celia, Byram, Michael, Barro, Ana, Jordan, Shirley, and Street, Brian. 2001. *Language Learners as ethnographers*. Clevedon: Multilingual Matters.

Roberts, Celia, and Campbell, Sarah. 2006. *Talk on Trial: Job interviews, language and ethnicity*. Retrieved from http://webarchive.nationalarchives.gov.uk/20130314010347/http://research.dwp.gov.uk/asd/asd5/rports2005-2006/rrep344.pdf.

Rogerson-Revell, Pamela. 2003. Developing a cultural syllabus for business language e-learning materials. *ReCALL, 15*(2), 155–169.

Rogerson-Revell, Pamela. 2007. Using English for international business: A European case study. *English for Specific Purposes, 26*, 103–120.

Rushdie, Salman. 1981. *Midnight's Children*. London: Johnathan Cape.

Rushdie, Salman. 2006. *Shalimar the clown: a novel*. London: Vintage.

Said, Edward. 1985. *Orientalism*. Middlesex: Peregrine.

Sarangi, Srikant. 1994. Intercultural or not? Beyond celebration of cultural differences in miscommunication analysis. *Pragmatics, 4*, 409–427.

Saville-Troike, Muriel. 2003. *The Ethnography of Communication* (3rd ed.). Oxford: Blackwell.

Scarino, Angela. 2009. Assessing intercultural capability in learning languages: Some issues and considerations. *Language Teaching, 42*(1), 67–80.

Schneider, Edgar. 2007. *Postcolonial English*. Cambridge: Cambridge University Press.

Scholte, Jan Aart. 2008. Defining Globalisation. *The World Economy, 31*(11), 1471–1502.

Scollon, Ron, and Scollon, Suzanne Wong. 2001. Discourse and intercultural communication. In Deborah Schiffrin, Deborah Tannen and Heidi Hamilton (eds.), *The handbook of discourse analysis* (pp. 538–547). Oxford: Blackwell.

Scollon, Ronald, Scollon, Suzanne B. K., and Jones, Rodney H. 2012. *Intercultural communication: a discourse approach* (3rd ed.). Chichester: Wiley-Blackwell.

Sealey, Alison, and Carter, Bob. 2004. *Applied linguistics as social science*. New York; London: Continuum.

Seargeant, Philip. 2009. Language ideology, language theory, and the regulation of linguistic behaviour. *Language Sciences, 31*, 345–359.

Seargeant, Philip. 2010. The historical ontology of language. *Language Sciences, 32*, 1–13.

Seargeant, Philip, Tagg, Caroline, and Ngampramuan, Wipapan. 2012. Language choice and addressivity strategies in Thai-English social network interactions. *Journal of Sociolinguistics, 16*(4), 510–531.

Seidlhofer, Barbara. 2004. Research perspectives on teaching English as a lingua franca. *Annual Review of Applied Linguistics, 24*, 209–239.

Seidlhofer, Barbara. 2006. English as a lingua franca in the expanding circle: what it isn't. In R. Rubdy and M. Saraceni (eds.), *English in the world: Global rules, global roles*. London: Continuum.

Seidlhofer, Barbara. 2007. English as a lingua franca and communities of practice. In Sabine Volk-Birke and Julia Lippert (eds.), *Anglistentag 2006 Halle Proceedings* (pp. 307–318). Trier: Wissenschaftlicher Verlag.

Seidlhofer, Barbara, and Widdowson, Henry G. 2009. Accommodation and the idiom principle in English as a lingua franca. In Kumiko Murata and Jennifer Jenkins (eds.), *Global Englishes in Asian contexts: current and future debates* (pp. 26–39). Basingstoke: Palgrave Macmillan.

Seidlhofer, Barbara. 2011. *Understanding English as a Lingua Franca*. Oxford: Oxford University Press.

Sharifian, Farzad. 2011. *Cultural conceptualisations and language: theoretical framework and applications*. Amsterdam: John Benjamins.

Sharifian, Farzad. 2012. World Englishes, intercultural communication, and requisite competencies. In Jane Jackson (ed.), *The Routledge handbook of language and intercultural communication* (pp. 85–97). London: Routledge.

Sharifian, Farzad (ed.). 2009. *English as an International Language: Perspectives and Pedagogical Issues*. Clevedon: Multilingual Matters.

Sifakis, Nicos, and Fay, Richard. 2011. Integrating an ELF pedagogy in a changing world: the case of Greek state schooling. In Alasdair Archibald, Alessia Cogo and Jennifer Jenkins (eds.), *Latest Trends in ELF Research* (pp. 285–297). Newcastle: Cambridge Scholars.

Silverman, David. 2011. *Interpreting qualitative data: a guide to the principles of qualitative research* (4th ed.). London: SAGE.

Simpson, Andrew, and Thammasathien, Noi. 2007. Thailand and Laos. In Andrew Simpson (ed.), *Language and national identity in Asia* (pp. 391–414). Oxford: Oxford University Press.

Slobin, Dan. 1996. From "thought and language" to "thinking for speech". In John Gumperz and Stephen Levinson (eds.), *Rethinking Linguistic relativity*. Cambridge: Cambridge University Press.

Smit, Ute. 2009. Emic evaluations and interactive processes in a classroom community of practice. In A. Mauranen and E. Ranta (eds.), *English as a lingua franca: studies and findings* (pp. 200–223). Newcastle: Cambridge Scholars.

Smit, Ute. 2010. *English as a lingua franca in higher education: a longitudinal study of classroom discourse*. Berlin: De Gruyter Mouton.

Soars, Liz, and Soars, John. 2003. *New Headway: Intermediate Third Edition: Student's Book*. Oxford: Oxford University Press.

Soars, Liz, and Soars, John. 2011. *New Headway: Elementary Fourth Edition: Student's Book*. Oxford: Oxford University Press.

Solin, Anna. 2010. New genre resources in academia: self-evaluation in academic portfolios. *Helsinki English Studies 6*, 102–117.

Sowden, Colin. 2012. ELF on a mushroom: the overnight growth in English as a Lingua Franca. *ELT Journal, 66*(1), 88–96.

Spencer-Oatey, Helen. 2008. *Culturally speaking: managing rapport through talk across cultures* (Second ed.). London: Continuum.

Spencer-Oatey, Helen, and Franklin, Peter. 2009. *Intercultural interaction: a multidisciplinary approach to intercultural communication*. Basingstoke: Palgrave Macmillan.

Spitzberg, Brian H., and Changnon, Gabrielle. 2009. *Conceptualizing Intercultural Competence*. London: Sage.

Strauss, Claudia, and Quinn, Naomi. 1997. *A Cognitive Theory of Cultural Meaning*. Cambridge: Cambridge University Press.

Street, Brian. 1993. Culture is a verb. In David Graddol, Linda Thompson and Michael. Byram (eds.), *Culture and language* (pp. 23–43). Clevedon: Multilingual Matters/British Association of Applied Linguistics.

Sweeny, Emma, and Hua, Zhu. 2010. Accommodating Toward Your Audience: Do Native Speakers of English Know How to Accommodate Their Communication Strategies Toward Nonnative Speakers of English? *International Journal of Business Communication 47*(4), 477–504.

Sybing, Roehl. 2011. Assessing perspectives on culture in EFL education. *ELT Journal, 65*(4), 467–469.

Tajfel, Henri. 1981. *Human groups and social categories: studies in social psychology.* Cambridge: Cambridge University Press.

Taylor, Mark C. 2001. *The moment of complexity: emerging network culture.* Chicago; London: University of Chicago Press.

Telles, João A., and Vassallo, Maria Luisa. 2006. Foreign language learning in-tandem: Teletandem as an alternative proposal in CALLT. *The Especialist* (27), 189–212.

Tomalin, Barry. 2008. Culture – the fifth language skill *Teaching English.* Retrieved from http://www.teachingenglish.org.uk/articles/culture-fifth-language-skill

Tomalin, Barry, and Nicks, Mike. 2010. *The world's business cultures, and how to unlock them* (2nd ed.). London: Thorogood.

Tomasello, Michael. 2003. *Constructing a language: a usage-based theory of language acquisition.* Cambridge, Mass.; London: Harvard University Press.

Tomasello, Michael. 2008. *Origins of human communication.* Cambridge, Mass: MIT.

Tourism Authority of Thailand. 2013. TAT News 2013. Retrieved 23 July, 2014, from http://www.tatnews.org/images/press_kit/TTM%202013%20%20FINAL.pdf

Tsui, Amy B. M., and Tollefson, James W. 2007. *Language policy, culture, and identity in Asian contexts.* London: Lawrence Erlbaum Associates.

Tylor, Edward Burnett. 1871. *Primitive Culture.* London: John Murray.

Valdes, Joyce Merrill. 1986. *Culture bound: bridging the cultural gap in language teaching.* Cambridge [Cambridgeshire]; New York: Cambridge University Press.

van Ek, Jan A. 1986. *Objectives for Modern Language Learning.* Strasbourg: Council of Europe.

Vettorel, Paola. 2010. EIL/ELF and representation of culture in textbooks: only food, fairs, folklore and facts? In Cesare Gagliardi and Alan Maley (eds.), *EIL, ELF, Global English: Teaching and Learning Issues.* Bern: Peter Lang.

Vettorel, Paola. 2014. *ELF in wider networking: Blogging practices.* Berlin: De Gruyter Mouton.

VOICE. 2011. VOICE the Vienna-Oxford International Corpus of English. Retrieved 18/11, 2011, from http://www.univie.ac.at/voice/

Walker, Robin. 2010. *Teaching the pronunciation of English as a Lingua Franca.* Oxford: Oxford University Press.

Wang, Ying. 2013. Non-conformity to ENL norms: a perspective from Chinese English users. *Journal of English as a Lingua Franca, 2*(2), 255–282.

Watson, Julie. 2010. A Case Study: Developing Learning Objects with an Explicit Learning Design. *Journal of e-Learning 8*(1), 41–50. Retrieved from www.ejel.org

Welsch, Wolfgang. 1999. Transculturality – the puzzling form of cultures today. In M. Featherstone and S. Lash (eds.), *Spaces of culture: city, nation, world* (pp. 194–213). London: Sage.

Wenger, Etienne. 1998. *Communities of practice: learning, meaning, and identity.* Cambridge: Cambridge University Press.

Whorf, Benjamin. 1939. The relation of habitual thought and behavior to language. In John Carroll (ed.), *Language, Thought and Reality – Selected writings of Benjamin Lee Whorf.* Cambridge Massachusetts: MIT Press.

Widdowson, Henry G. 1980. Models and fictions. *Applied Linguistics, 1*(2), 165–170.

Widdowson, Henry G. 1994. The ownership of English. *TESOL Quarterly, 28*(2), 377–389.

Widdowson, Henry G. 2000. On the limitations of linguistics applied. *Applied Linguistics, 21*(1), 3–25.

Widdowson, Henry G. 2003. *Defining issues in English language teaching*. Oxford; New York: Oxford University Press.

Widdowson, Henry G. 2012. ELF and the inconvenience of established concepts. *Journal of English as a Lingua Franca, 1*(1), 5–26.

Wierzbicka, Anna. 1985. Different cultures, different languages, different speech acts. *Journal of Pragmatics, 9*, 145–178.

Wierzbicka, Anna. 1997. *Understanding cultures through their key words: English, Russian, Polish, German, and Japanese*. Oxford: Oxford University Press.

Wierzbicka, Anna. 2006. *English: Meaning and Culture*. Oxford: Oxford University Press.

Williams, Raymond. 2014. *Keywords: A Vocabulary of Culture and Society*. London: Fourth Estate.

Wolfartsberger, Anita. 2011. ELF Business/Business ELF: Form and Function in Simultaneous Speech. In Alasdair Archibald, Alessia Cogo and Jennifer Jenkins (eds.), *Latest Trends in ELF Research* (pp. 163–184). Newcastle: Cambridge Scholars.

Wongsothorn, A., Hiranburana, K., and Chinnawongs, S. 2003. English language teaching. In Thailand today. In H. Wah Kam and R. L. Wong (eds.), *English language teaching in East Asia today: changing policies and practices* (pp. 441–453). Singapore: Eastern Universities Press.

Wongsothorn, A., Sukamolsun, S., Chinthammit, P., Ratanothayanonth, P., and Noparumpa, P. 1996. National profiles of language education: Thailand. *PASAA, 26*(1), 89–103.

Xu, Zhichang, and Dinh, Thuy Ngoc. 2013. How do "WE" (World Englishes) make sense in ELF communication? Words and their meanings across cultures. *Journal of English as a Lingua Franca, 3*(2), 365–388.

Yashima, Tomoko. 2009. International posture and the ideal L2 self in the Japanese EFL context. In Zoltan Dörnyei and Ema Ushioda (eds.), *Motivation, language identity and the L2 self* (pp. 144–163). Bristol: Multilingual Matters.

Ylanne-McEwen, Virpi, and Coupland, Nikolas. 2000. Accommodation theory: a conceptual resource for intercultural sociolinguistics. In Helen Spencer-Oatey (ed.), *Culturally speaking: managing rapport through talk across cultures* (pp. 191–215). London: Continuum.

Young, Richard. 2011. Interactional Competence in Language Learning, Teaching, and Testing. In Eli Hinkel (ed.), *Handbook of research in second language teaching and learning* (pp. 426–443). London: Routledge.

Young, Tony J., and Sachdev, Itesh. 2011. Intercultural communicative competence: exploring English language teachers' beliefs and practices. *Language Awareness, 20*(2), 81–98.

Young, Tony J., and Sercombe, Peter. 2010. Communication, discourses and interculturality. *Language and Intercultural Communication, 10*(3), 181–188.

Zheng, Yongyan. 2013. An inquiry into Chinese learners' English-learning motivational self-images: ENL learner or ELF user? *Journal of English as a Lingua Franca, 2*(2), 341–364.

Zhu Hua. 2010. Language socialization and interculturality: address terms in intergenerational talk in Chinese diasporic families. *Language and Intercultural Communication, 10*(3), 189–205.

Zhu Hua. 2014. *Exploring intercultural communication: language in action*. Abingdon: Routledge.

Zhu Hua. 2015. Negotiation as the way of engagement in intercultural and lingua franca communication: frames of reference and Interculturality. *Journal of English as a Lingua Franca*, 4(1), 63–90.

Zhu Hua (ed.). 2011. *The language and intercultural communication reader*. Abingdon: Routledge.

Index